THE NUCLEAR RENAISSANCE
AND INTERNATIONAL SECURITY

THE NUCLEAR RENAISSANCE AND INTERNATIONAL SECURITY

Edited by Adam N. Stulberg and Matthew Fuhrmann

Stanford Security Studies
An Imprint of Stanford University Press
Stanford, California

Stanford University Press
Stanford, California

Special discounts for bulk quantities of Stanford Security Studies are available to
corporations, professional associations, and other organizations. For details and
discount information, contact the special sales department of Stanford University
Press. Tel: (650) 736-1782, Fax: (650) 736-1784.

Printed in the United States of America on acid-free, archival-quality paper.

Library of Congress Cataloging-in-Publication Data

   The nuclear renaissance and international security / edited by Adam N. Stulberg
and Matthew Fuhrmann.
      pages cm
   Includes bibliographical references and index.
   ISBN 978-0-8047-8417-7 (cloth)
      1. Nuclear nonproliferation.   2. Nuclear energy.   I. Stulberg, Adam N., 1963–
editor of compilation.   II. Fuhrmann, Matthew, 1980– editor of compilation.
   JZ5675.N83865 2013
   355'.033—dc23

                                                                    2012037023

Typeset by Newgen in 10/14 Minion.

Contents

Acknowledgments

THIS PROJECT BENEFITED FROM THE SUPPORT OF NUMEROUS individuals and institutions. The chapters contained in this volume are the product of the workshop "The Nuclear Renaissance and International Security" held at Georgia Tech in January 2010. Special thanks are due to Scott Sagan for attending the workshop and providing valuable feedback on the chapters and the overall framing of the project. We are also indebted to the John D. and Catherine T. MacArthur Foundation for a generous grant that made our workshop and this edited volume possible. Geoffrey Burn and his colleagues at Stanford University Press provided helpful guidance and encouragement in preparing the manuscript, for which we are grateful. Bernard Gourley deserves particular thanks for his deft administrative support throughout the project.

Additionally, Stulberg expresses gratitude to numerous scholars, students, and policy insiders for sharing their insights and support for the project. Liz Thompson Dallas, in particular, made many constructive suggestions for improving the manuscript, as well as provided invaluable research assistance and copyediting during the final stages. Special thanks also go to the faculty, technical experts, and students who commented on the project and select chapters during dedicated presentations at the University of Wisconsin, North Carolina State University, Oak Ridge National Laboratory, and the Baker Center at the University of Tennessee. In addition, former Senator Sam Nunn, as well as members of the working group on internationalization of the fuel cycle that accompanied the 2008 Sam Nunn–Bank of America Policy Forum, offered unique insights into many of the practical problems that informed the intellectual origins of the project. He is also grateful to William C. Potter and Elena Sokova for providing sage advice and access to the wealth of materials on the spread of sensitive stages of the nuclear fuel cycle housed at the James Martin Center for Nonproliferation Studies.

Fuhrmann thanks the Stanton Foundation for providing funding for a Stanton Nuclear Security Fellowship at the Council on Foreign Relations during the 2010–2011 academic year that helped make this project happen. He expresses his appreciation to Victoria Alekhine, Janine Hill, Michael Levi, James Lindsay, Paul Stares, and Micah Zenko for the opportunity to spend the year at the Council. The impetus for this project began while he was at the University of Georgia and Harvard University. He wishes to thank his advisors, colleagues, and friends at these institutions for their excellent feedback and support, especially Emma Belcher, Gary Bertsch, Matthew Bunn, Jonathan Caverley, Erica Chenoweth, Alexander Downes, Bryan Early, John Holdren, Sean Lynn-Jones, Sarah Kreps, Matthew Kroenig, Susan Lynch, Martin Malin, Steven Miller, Jonathan Monten, Vipin Narang, Wendy Pearlman, Negeen Pegahi, Philip Potter, Todd Sechser, Paul Staniland, Jaroslav Tir, and Stephen Walt. Colleagues at the University of South Carolina, where he was an assistant professor from 2009 to 2011, and Texas A&M University also provided encouragement and support throughout the course of this project. In addition, he would like to thank participants in seminars at Duke University, Georgia Tech, George Washington University, Harvard University, North Carolina State University, the Savannah River National Laboratory, and the University of South Carolina for feedback that ultimately helped improve this book.

Finally, for their enduring love, patience, and understanding, we extend our deepest gratitude to Cara M. Gilbert and Lauren and Kate Fuhrmann— our real "nuclear" families. This book is dedicated to them.

Adam N. Stulberg
Atlanta, GA

Matthew Fuhrmann
College Station, TX

Contributors

Victor Asal is Director of the Center for Policy Research and an Associate Professor in the Department of Political Science at the University at Albany–SUNY. He has been involved in research projects funded by the Defense Advanced Research Projects Agency, Defense Threat Reduction Agency, the Department of Homeland Security, the National Science Foundation, and the Office of Naval Research.

Kyle Beardsley is an Associate Professor of Political Science at Emory University. Beardsley received his Ph.D. from the University of California, San Diego in 2006. In addition to his work on nuclear proliferation, Beardsley maintains an active research agenda on topics related to conflict management and resolution. His book, *The Mediation Dilemma*, was published in 2011.

Joshua William Busby is an Assistant Professor at the LBJ School of Public Affairs at the University of Texas at Austin. His book *Moral Movements and Foreign Policy* was published in 2010. Dr. Busby has written extensively on climate change, energy issues, and security for such outlets as the Brookings Institution, the Center for a New American Security, the Council on Foreign Relations, the German Marshall Fund, Resources for the Future, and the Woodrow Wilson International Center for Scholars.

Matthew Fuhrmann is an Assistant Professor of Political Science at Texas A&M University. He is the author of *Atomic Assistance: How "Atoms for Peace" Programs Cause Nuclear Insecurity* (2012). His research on international security, international institutions, and nuclear proliferation has also been published in *International Security, Journal of Conflict Resolution*, and *Journal of Peace Research*, among other journals.

Erik Gartzke has held faculty positions at Pennsylvania State University, Columbia University, and the University of California, San Diego (currently). He received his Ph.D. in Political Science from the University of Iowa in 1997. His work focuses on peace, war, and international institutions. He has published widely on these and related issues.

Bernard Gourley is the Program Manager of the Sam Nunn Security Program of Georgia Tech's Center for International Strategy, Technology, and Policy. He holds Master's degrees in International Relations and Economics from Georgia Tech and Georgia State University, respectively.

Justin V. Hastings is a Lecturer in International Relations and Comparative Politics at the University of Sydney in Australia. He is the author of *No Man's Land: Globalization, Territory, and Clandestine Groups in Southeast Asia*.

Michael C. Horowitz is an Associate Professor of Political Science at the University of Pennsylvania and the author of *The Diffusion of Military Power: Causes and Consequences for International Politics*. His work has been published in *International Organization, International Security, International Studies Quarterly*, the *Journal of Conflict Resolution*, and elsewhere. He received his Ph.D. from the Department of Government at Harvard University.

Matthew Kroenig is an Assistant Professor of Government at Georgetown University. He is the author of *Exporting the Bomb: Technology Transfer and the Spread of Nuclear Weapons*.

Allison Macfarlane is an Associate Professor of Environmental Science and Policy at George Mason University. She was a member of the White House's Blue Ribbon Commission on America's Nuclear Future from 2010 to 2012 and chairs the Bulletin of the Atomic Scientist's Science and Security Board. She is co-editor of *Uncertainty Underground: Yucca Mountain and the Nation's High-Level Nuclear Waste* (2006).

Alexander H. Montgomery is an Associate Professor at Reed College. He has a B.A. in Physics from the University of Chicago, an M.A. in Energy and Resources from the University of California, Berkeley, and an M.A. in Sociology and a Ph.D. in Political Science from Stanford University. He has been a joint

International Security Program/Managing the Atom Project Research Fellow at the Belfer Center for Science and International Affairs, Kennedy School of Government, Harvard University; a postdoctoral fellow at the Center for International Security and Cooperation, Stanford University; and is currently a Council on Foreign Relations International Affairs Fellow in Nuclear Security. He has published articles on nuclear proliferation and on the effects of social networks of international organizations on interstate conflict, and is engaged in research on political organizations, social networks, weapons of mass disruption and destruction, social studies of technology, and interstate social relations.

Dan Reiter is Chair of the Department of Political Science at Emory University. He is the author of dozens of scholarly articles as well as *Crucible of Beliefs: Learning, Alliances and World Wars, Democracies at War* (with Allan C. Stam), and *How Wars End.*

Adam N. Stulberg is an Associate Professor and Co-Director of the Center for International Strategy, Technology, and Policy at the Sam Nunn School of International Affairs, Georgia Institute of Technology. His current research focuses on energy security dilemmas and statecraft, new approaches to strategic stability and denuclearization of military arsenals, internationalization of the nuclear fuel cycle, counter-network warfare, and the implications of nanotechnology and other emerging technologies for international security.

Christopher Way is an Associate Professor of Government at Cornell University. His research on the politics of macroeconomic policy has covered central bank independence, partisan theories of the macroeconomy, labor organization, and inequality in the Organisation for Economic Co-operation and Development (OECD) countries. His recent research focuses on the proliferation of weapons of mass destruction and on the nonproliferation regime.

Introduction

Understanding the Nuclear Renaissance

Adam N. Stulberg and Matthew Fuhrmann

INTEREST IN NUCLEAR ENERGY HAS SURGED IN RECENT YEARS, prompting some to tout a "global nuclear renaissance." Iran became the first new member of the nuclear energy club since 1996, and it may be followed by the United Arab Emirates, Turkey, and Vietnam—states with profoundly different profiles. More than fifty other countries, including Chile, Jordan, Nigeria, and Saudi Arabia, are seriously considering nuclear power for the first time in decades. Other states, such as China, Russia, India, and South Korea, have recently announced plans to expand existing nuclear power programs, while Brazil is enlarging its fuel cycle activities, both independently and jointly with Argentina. Still other nuclear power states, such as the United States, stand on the precipice of ending a prolonged hiatus of new reactor construction. Meanwhile, some governments are rethinking their commitments to nuclear power in the aftermath of the March 2011 accident at Japan's Fukushima Daiichi nuclear power plant. There, an earthquake and tsunami resulted in mechanical failures that caused some of the fuel rods to melt down, causing radioactive materials to spread into the surrounding environment. This disaster helped persuade Germany to shut down its oldest reactors and to implement plans to phase out the sector altogether. Other European states, such as Spain and Switzerland, may follow suit.

There are a number of explanations for the renewed interest in nuclear power. Concerns about global climate change, spiraling electricity demand, and excessive import dependency on fossil fuels are among the reasons cited most frequently by pundits and policy analysts. Growing confidence in international nuclear fuel cycle markets and enhanced safety and efficiency of the sector are also winning over longtime critics. This confluence of factors seems to augur well for real growth of commercial nuclear energy worldwide.

Even before the dreadful Japanese nuclear accident, it was unclear whether the nuclear renaissance would blossom or fizzle. Nuclear plant construction is highly capital intensive and requires significant start-up costs that must be aligned with human capital and baseload power generation infrastructure. These requirements, combined with the industry's propensity for monumental cost overruns, limit the commercial appeal of nuclear power for some countries. Moreover, as evidenced by the global public debate precipitated by Japan's crisis, the consequences associated with even a single nuclear accident and the lack of long-term solutions for nuclear waste disposal continue to stoke public uneasiness and sap political will for jump-starting nuclear power programs across the globe. Some of these factors have derailed nuclear power ambitions in the past in countries that lacked active power programs, such as Egypt and Turkey; and as suggested by the freeze on new construction and attendant political fallout from the accident in Japan, it is possible that these factors will stymie the current nuclear renaissance even among nuclear states that currently rely on nuclear power generation.

At the same time, there is mounting anxiety that the diffusion of peaceful nuclear programs could undermine international security. Nuclear technology, materials, and know-how are dual-use in nature, meaning that they can be used for the production of electricity or nuclear weapons. India, for example, used nuclear materials supplied by the United States and a reactor provided by Canada to produce plutonium for a nuclear explosive that was tested in 1974; this early civilian nuclear assistance was the foundation upon which New Delhi built its nuclear program in the 1990s. Scientists who later produced the South African bomb in the 1970s—including the head of the nuclear weapons program—were trained by the United States as a result of government-backed programs. And a research reactor exported by the United States to Iran in the 1960s helped provide training to scientists that later became relevant for Tehran's nuclear weapons program. These stories are, unfortunately, not uncommon. There is an ongoing debate about the connection between proliferation and peaceful nuclear assistance, which is highlighted in the book, but such anecdotes underscore why some worry that the global diffusion of nuclear technology could lead to the spread of nuclear weapons (see Fuhrmann 2009b, 2012b).

Nuclear proliferation may not be the only strategic consequence associated with the nuclear energy renaissance. Some scholars argue, for instance, that the global expansion of nuclear infrastructure could raise the risk of nuclear or radiological (NR) terrorism by facilitating terrorists' efforts to acquire NR materials, increasing targets of opportunity, and magnifying the economic and psychological costs of an attack (Early et al. n.d.; see also Miller and Sagan 2009). We now know, for example, that al Qaeda considered flying airplanes into nuclear facilities in the United States as part of the 9/11 attacks (Holt and Andrews 2007). Terrorists may attempt to target nuclear plants in other countries, potentially triggering a Fukushima-like disaster.

Peaceful nuclear programs also could be a source of international conflict. Because nuclear technology can be used for both civilian and military purposes, uncertainty about a country's intentions could raise the risk of preventive military action. This danger is best illustrated by Israel's 1981 "bolt from the blue" bombing of an Iraqi nuclear reactor known as Osiraq. Iraq procured this civilian facility from France and placed it under International Atomic Energy Agency (IAEA) safeguards designed to detect diversions of key materials to a military program. The Israelis, however, feared that Saddam Hussein intended to use this plant to produce plutonium for nuclear weapons, and it chose to take military action to limit Iraq's capacity to build the bomb. Israel took similar action in September 2007 when it destroyed a nuclear reactor under construction in Syria, although this facility was not under IAEA safeguards and it is unclear whether its purpose was military or civilian.

Such concerns are accentuated by debate over the desirability and feasibility of nuclear weapons that has gathered unprecedented momentum across the globe, most significantly among security communities within the nuclear weapons states. This has been accompanied by mounting anxiety that the resuscitation of interest in commercial nuclear power and fuel production portends the spread of sensitive technologies and know-how beyond the few countries that dominate the field. The result, if not managed appropriately, could be a leveling of nuclear capacities that effectively lowers the threshold for dangerous arms racing, crisis instability, and international insecurity (Glaser 2009).

This book examines the causes, processes, and broad international security consequences of the spread of nuclear power development, in light of the shifting terrain and growing concerns. Recent books seek to explain nuclear proliferation or nuclear weapons strategy (e.g., Hymans 2006; Solingen 2007; Rublee 2009; Sagan 2009; Potter and Mukhatzhanova 2010; Fuhrmann 2012b). This volume, however, takes another tack by addressing the motivations for acquiring commercial and dual-use technology, material, and expertise short of the development of weapons systems, as well as by exploring the strategic implications associated with this diffusion that go beyond traditional weapons proliferation or energy security concerns. It extends recent scholarship on nuclear power and international security both to redress important empirical puzzles and intellectual questions derived from past commercial and strategic behavior, and to get out in front of future policy challenges and opportunities.

The authors of this book understand that they face a tall order, especially amid ill-defined and moving targets. Yet we believe that scholars and policymakers possess the tools to refine their analyses and decisions, premised on rigorous and systematic examination of critical issues and patterns of behavior. Accordingly, the chapters together address a series of interrelated questions surrounding the sources and strategic consequences of the spread of nuclear energy. What will come of the nuclear renaissance? Will the benefits of nuclear power trump the costs, leading to the massive expansion in nuclear power that some have forecasted? Or will the risks and strategic consequences of nuclear energy development, brought vividly into focus by the 2011 Fukushima nuclear accident, discourage countries from developing or expanding civilian nuclear programs? These questions must be answered if we are to understand the contours and significance of the tensions between growing interest in and anxiety about nuclear power for international security.

The remainder of this introduction will proceed in three parts. First, we discuss the alternative futures for nuclear energy that inform respective chapter analyses. Second, we comment on the distance between efforts by academics and policymakers to grapple with the international security puzzles posed by nuclear energy and outline our approach to "bridging" this gap. We conclude with a succinct overview of the book.

A Nuclear Renaissance or Back to the Future?

While it is nearly conventional wisdom that the twenty-first century will witness a global expansion of nuclear energy, even in the wake of the 2011 Japanese crisis, neither the trajectory nor the dimensions of growth of the nuclear expansion are well specified or commonly accepted (Economist Intelligence Unit 2011; Ferguson 2011). Industry, policy, and scholarly articles are replete with projections of a nuclear energy renaissance. But what does that mean? Explication of the puzzles linked to the sources and strategic consequences of nuclear energy require sound baselines for thinking about growth.

There are three possible alternative futures for nuclear energy. The first scenario, *stagnation*, is defined by straight-line projections of past performance of the nuclear sector. This presumes the continuation of negligible rates of reactor construction and growth in fuel cycle services that, in practice, have failed to keep pace with stated intentions or official targets. Such projections accord with both case-specific and macro-level evidence. In the United States, for example, almost half of all reactors ordered from 1953 to 2003 were canceled before the beginning of commercial operation (Bodansky 2004). There have been notable examples, most recently in the United States and Philippines, of reactors that were constructed but never made operational, as well as reactors in Germany and Spain that were not replaced upon retirement.

The share of total global electricity generation from nuclear plants leveled off in the late 1980s and began to decline by 2010. Extrapolations from this pattern hardly provide grounds for optimism concerning a nuclear energy renaissance (Squassoni 2009). The IAEA projects that the nuclear energy sector must grow significantly just to maintain present global and national shares in the face of accelerating worldwide demand for electricity through 2030. Low estimates, based on current trends augmented by assumed changes underway, reveal that the portion of total power plant capacity from nuclear reactors is likely to decline from 8.0 percent in 2008 to 7.1 percent in 2030, with total generation projected to decline from 14.0 percent in 2008 to 12.6 percent in 2030 (IAEA 2009a).

A second scenario reflects a *resurgence* of nuclear energy, marked by deepening reliance on the sector by states that currently possess nuclear fuel cycle capabilities. This too finds empirical support from contemporary trends. According to IAEA statistics, over two-thirds of the sixty plants under construction as of March 2012 (WNA 2012) are being built in just four countries that currently embrace nuclear power—China, India, South Korea, and Russia (IAEA 2010b). Notwithstanding temporary moratoria on construction and delays owing to safety checks precipitated by the Fukushima accident, China is projected to be home to more than one-third of the world's new reactors,

doubling power generation from the sector by 2020. Russia plans to build between two to three new reactors per year and for the sector to meet 25 percent
of domestic demand for electricity by 2050; and India intends to triple nuclear
power production by 2020. The United States is poised to regain its global stature in the industry, with twenty-one new construction and operating license
applications on file as of March 2012 (Blake 2012). Similarly, the growth in
power production is projected to be met primarily by the expansion of natural
uranium mining and nuclear fuel production among existing suppliers. These
states are expected to cover the global demand that exceeds the capacity of
secondary supply sources (e.g., stockpiles, fuel blended down from destroyed
weapons), leveraging respective national fuel cycle capabilities to compete intensely for greater market shares.

The trends toward concentration of growth would jibe with historical patterns, as over 58 percent of the 435 reactors currently in use are located in the
United States (104), France (58), Japan (51), Russia (33), and Germany (9), and
uranium enrichment is dominated by only five international suppliers (WNA
2012).[1] Similarly, rates for bringing new plants on line have come in waves for
large nuclear states, with peak years of new construction corresponding with
growth in only a few countries. Underpinning these projections are presump-
tions that start-up costs, economies of scale, tacit knowledge accumulation,
export and market constraints, and the political clout of current stakehold-
ers in commercial nuclear energy will favor growth among existing nuclear
power generation and fuel cycle states, while raising barriers for aspirant
states.

A third future to contemplate entails a nuclear energy *renaissance*, defined
in terms of both the global deepening and broadening of nuclear fuel cycle
and power generation activities. This scenario would constitute more than
a simple rebirth of the sector among the existing "haves" but would be distinguished most notably by the success of a large share of the more than fifty
current aspirant states at realizing ambitious plans for nuclear expansion.
As suggested by one study, for this to transpire we would expect to witness
the continued growth of nuclear power construction and generation (MIT
2003). States in East Asia, the United States, and Europe would have to fully
meet respective new reactor construction targets to transcend the inertia of
the lost decades since the late 1970s, and there would have to be widespread
adoption of nuclear energy among emerging market and developing states.
As proponents are quick point out, such projections should not be dismissed

as far-fetched, even in the aftermath of the scarring tragedy in Japan, as over 80 percent and 66 percent of total nuclear energy produced since the dawning of the nuclear era was generated following the accidents at Three Mile Island and Chernobyl, respectively (Glaser 2011). Such resilience in the face of few viable alternatives provides the basis for a protracted and muddled but stable expansion of the sector across both nuclear stalwarts and newcomers around the globe (Economist Intelligence Unit 2011).

Such a renaissance also would be characterized by reinvigorated technological innovation across both the front and back ends of the nuclear fuel cycle, as well as by new forms of public and private management and shared infrastructure arrangements. Here, the public outcry for enhanced safety to mitigate concerns about catastrophic accidents would redirect R&D toward fundamentally new reactors designs and dispositions that would avert vulnerability to experiencing meltdowns or costliness of large-scale, idiosyncratic units (Glaser 2011). In addition, there would be new entrants into global nuclear fuel supply markets, as states such as Brazil and South Africa would succeed in leveraging indigenous capacity to compete for growing shares in global and regional markets. The game changers for an over threefold increase in global nuclear power production by 2050 are associated with concerted political will, government intervention, and international institutional innovation aimed at reducing carbon emission targets and mitigating climate change, producing industrial-scale clean water, attracting an expert trade and technical workforce to the field worldwide, and reassuring safe and secure expansion of global nuclear fuel cycle and energy markets.

This book examines the drivers and strategic effects of nuclear power development in light of the global nuclear expansion. Applying diverse qualitative and quantitative research methods, the contributors strive to uncover historical patterns in nuclear energy development, pinpoint the connection between commercial nuclear programs and latent military activities, and forecast the implications of a global nuclear energy expansion for international security. The chapters address a number of specific questions that lie at the crux of understanding the sources and strategic consequences associated with these alternative nuclear scenarios. Why do countries rely on nuclear power? Will the Fukushima Daiichi accident be a game changer for the trajectory of global nuclear energy development? How do buyers and sellers of nuclear technology talk about nuclear power, and what does this reveal about their intentions? Why do countries provide peaceful nuclear assistance to other states? Under what conditions do countries embrace multinational nuclear approaches, such as the establishment of international fuel banks? To what extent is global climate change a driver of the nuclear renaissance, and would nuclear power development make a meaningful dent in global greenhouse gas emissions? Do peaceful nuclear programs contribute to nuclear weapons proliferation? Will the diffusion of nuclear technologies lead to an increase in the trafficking of nuclear and radiological materials? Does the diffusion of sensitive enrichment and reprocessing technologies and latent nuclear weapons capabilities influence crisis stability and international conflict? If so, how?

Bridging the Policy-Scholarly Gap

The questions outlined above are critical for understanding the significance of the growing interest in nuclear power for international security for scholars and policy makers alike. Yet we know surprisingly little about the answers. There are several classic case studies of national nuclear energy programs (e.g., Poneman 1982), as well as burgeoning inquiries into the dynamics of illicit nuclear trafficking (e.g., Braun and Chyba 2004; Montgomery 2005) and the supply side of nuclear proliferation (e.g., Fuhrmann 2009a,b; Kroenig 2009a,b). A small but growing body of work is beginning to analyze what drives the spread of nuclear energy and the potential strategic effects of the nuclear energy renaissance (e.g., Fitzpatrick 2009; Malley and Ogilvie-White 2009; Miller and Sagan 2009; Tertrais 2009; Findlay 2011; Fuhrmann 2012a), but our knowledge about the empirical puzzles or policy challenges presented by a global nuclear energy expansion remains incomplete. Indeed, relative to the research on nuclear weapons proliferation and strategy, there is a paucity of systematic analysis of the drivers of the spread of nuclear energy or the implications of nuclear power development for international cooperation and conflict. Consequently, the extant scholarly literature offers only a limited insight into the empirical puzzles or policy challenges presented by a global nuclear energy expansion.

At the same time, policy makers, businesspeople, and other professionals must prepare for future commercial and strategic realities, contending with the uncertainties surrounding a prospective global expansion of nuclear energy. This strategic forecasting, however, must be based on more than ad hoc case analyses, selective empirical evidence, untested assumptions, and gut instincts. Rather, forecasting requires the development of sound analytical frameworks and rigorous examination of historical motivations, patterns of behavior, and strategic interaction that form the foundation of scholarly inquiry (Bueno de Mesquita 2009).

As the demand for systematic analysis of nuclear behavior has increased, the distance between scholars and government officials has widened. This is due in part to divergent research priorities within the two communities. On one hand, in the social sciences a premium is placed on employing sophisticated methodologies to discern epochal patterns of behavior and to advance the frontier of knowledge within respective disciplines. For scholars in the subfield of nuclear security, many of the interesting questions relate to why so few states are attracted to nuclear weapons, rather than to the causes or effects of civilian nuclear programs. Government officials and corporate executives, on the other hand, must contend with specific, concrete issues, and lack the time or resources to divine the policy relevance of methodological or theoretical debates. It is also taken almost as a given that both commercial and sensitive nuclear technologies and know-how will diffuse to state and non-state actors, presenting practical opportunities and challenges that necessitate taking action. The tension between these professional communities and respective orientations limits our collective capacity to understand and manage complex issues related to the sources and international consequences of an expansion of nuclear energy.

This volume aims to help bridge this gap. The respective chapters strive to extend scholarly research on the spread of nuclear energy in a manner that is policy relevant. The book contributes to the existing literature and narrows the distance between the scholarly and policy communities in four main respects. First, each chapter explicates an empirical puzzle associated with either the sources or international security consequences of the diffusion of nuclear energy and/or sensitive fuel cycle capabilities, identifying important patterns and practical issues for consideration. Second, the authors extend previous research, present alternative analytical frameworks, and employ cutting-edge qualitative and statistical methods to test respective arguments. Each author also teases out the practical implications or insights into forecasting developments under alternative nuclear futures as derived from systematic analysis. Third, to broaden accessibility and to reinforce the significance of seemingly arcane academic research, we invited three senior scholars to offer commentaries that succinctly compare and contrast the findings of a subset of chapters, and to distill the relevant policy implications. In addition to generating substantive insight and highlighting themes that emerge from the different parts of the book, these commentaries serve as a critique of respective arguments and research methods posited by the authors within each part of the book. As a novel twist and complement to the substantive chapters, these commentaries purposefully expose analytical blind spots and reframe supplementary issues in need of deeper reflection by scholars and policy makers alike. Finally, recognizing that the chapters offer only an initial foray into this dynamic field of study, both the authors and commentators illuminate new directions for theoretical development, identifying critical case studies for future qualitative research and key-issues areas for future statistical analysis and closer policy attention.

Organization of the Book

The book is divided into three parts. Part I addresses the drivers of the nuclear energy renaissance. In Chapter 1, Bernard Gourley and Adam N. Stulberg analyze the correlates of nuclear power development from 1950 to 2001. They find that high levels of economic development and energy insecurity have historically motivated countries to rely on nuclear power. Conversely, they do not find support for the popular argument that countries pursue peaceful nuclear programs when they have an interest in building nuclear weapons (i.e., nuclear hedging). Their analysis has important implications for the future of the nuclear renaissance. It suggests, for instance, that stagnation or decline in developed countries such as France, South Korea, and the United States could prevent the realization of a true renaissance.

In Chapter 2, Allison Macfarlane examines multiple discourses surrounding the acquisition of nuclear energy technology to shed light on the motivations and intentions of actors who will shape the future of the nuclear renaissance. She finds that suppliers and buyers often tout the ambiguities of nuclear power in their rhetoric. In particular, discourses tend to emphasize the connection between nuclear power and nuclear weapons. Macfarlane does not suggest that countries pursue nuclear technologies because they have an interest in developing the bomb. Rather, buyer countries can enhance their power and prestige by maintaining ambiguity about their intentions. At the same time, suppliers have incentives to emphasize the ambiguity of nuclear technology because it helps them sell their product.

Matthew Fuhrmann addresses the supply side of the nuclear renaissance in Chapter 3. He analyzes why nuclear supplier countries assist other states in developing nuclear energy programs. We cannot fully understand the renaissance in nuclear power without grasping the incentives of nuclear suppliers, because most states depend on external sources for nuclear technology and materials. Fuhrmann shows that supplier states enter the marketplace to enhance their political influence. Normative concerns and a desire to sustain the domestic nuclear industry are less decisive for explaining civilian nuclear assistance than is commonly assumed. He concludes that the supply side will influence the renaissance mostly by affecting where—not if—countries are able to obtain nuclear assistance.

In Chapter 4, Adam N. Stulberg tackles the puzzle of international fuel supply cooperation. He explains why the historical record of multilateral nuclear approaches (MNAs) is mixed even though internationalizing the nuclear fuel cycle could make markets function more efficiently and reduce the risk of proliferation by eliminating the need for indigenous enrichment or reprocessing facilities. Framing this issue as an international credible commitment problem, Stulberg argues that the efficacy of MNAs hinges on the degree of power asymmetry and vulnerability among the bargaining parties. He demonstrates that countries are most likely to support MNAs when suppliers do not wield sufficient market power to blackmail other states and when customers do not expect to be overly reliant on nuclear energy.

Joshua William Busby analyzes the relationship between global climate change and nuclear power development in Chapter 5. Nuclear power is a possible solution to the problem of climate change because it is one of the few relatively carbon-free energy sources. Busby argues, however, that it is unlikely to play a major role in reducing global greenhouse gas emissions. Lingering concerns about cost, safety, and security are likely to prevent the requisite expansion in nuclear power development. He concludes that concerns about global warming will not singlehandedly drive a renaissance in nuclear power.

In Chapter 6, Christopher Way concludes Part I of the book by summarizing the key findings from the first five chapters and highlighting the underlying implications for the nuclear renaissance. Ostensibly, these chapters are a diverse lot, but as Way indicates, they all highlight the important role of politics in driving or limiting nuclear power development. Given the number of states seeking to provide nuclear assistance to enhance their international influence and the primacy of politics in the nuclear marketplace more generally, access to the requisite technology and know-how is unlikely to stymie the renaissance. Taken together, the chapters in Part I are not necessarily optimistic about the prospects for a massive global expansion in nuclear energy. As Way discusses, the domestic politics of the renaissance are not promising in many countries. In the end, the renaissance may be more likely to fizzle than to thrive. At the same time, we cannot know for certain what form the renaissance will take. Whatever happens, it is likely that at least a few new nuclear power states will emerge. Even this modest resurgence could have consequences for international security.

Part II of the book addresses the effects of the nuclear renaissance on nuclear weapons proliferation. In Chapter 7, Alexander H. Montgomery explores whether nuclear assistance increases the likelihood that countries will explore, pursue, or acquire nuclear weapons. He finds that nuclear assistance appears to decrease the probability that countries pursuing nuclear weapons will successfully develop the bomb. This result emerges, Montgomery argues, because certain countries are unable to utilize technologies provided from foreign sources. In particular, neopatrimonial regimes, which are characterized by personalized rule and little or no accountability to domestic actors, take shortcuts by importing dual-use nuclear technology without having the capacity to absorb it properly. The result is that these countries end up taking longer to build nuclear weapons than they otherwise would have if they had not received foreign assistance.

In Chapter 8, Matthew Kroenig argues that the nuclear renaissance is unlikely to cause widespread nuclear weapons proliferation because it is difficult for states to obtain sensitive nuclear assistance in the international marketplace. States seeking to build domestic fuel cycle facilities will struggle to obtain foreign assistance, except under relatively rare strategic conditions. Without this assistance, Kroenig posits, countries will be unable to build nuclear weapons.

Justin V. Hastings analyzes the consequences of the nuclear renaissance for nonstate nuclear trafficking in Chapter 9. Trafficking in radioactive materials such as plutonium and highly enriched uranium constitutes one of the major nonstate proliferation threats. Hastings argues that the nuclear renaissance will diversify the locations from which nuclear materials can be obtained, which is potentially problematic given that many of the nuclear power aspirants have limited organizational and bureaucratic capacity. Yet the practical effects of the renaissance for nuclear trafficking are likely to be limited, because the strategies adopted by nuclear traffickers to transport materials will not change as more countries build nuclear power plants. Current strategies are vulnerable to state crackdowns given that they utilize commercial transportation infrastructure that is controlled in part by governments.

Erik Gartzke's commentary, Chapter 10, concludes Part II of the volume. As Gartzke discusses, one unifying theme that emerges from the chapters by Montgomery, Kroenig, and Hastings is that the nuclear renaissance is likely to be relatively innocuous from a proliferation standpoint. He cautions that the proliferation risks of the nuclear renaissance could magnify as the number of states with the capacity to provide nuclear assistance or with the basic infrastructure to build the bomb increases. Gartzke uses the chapters in Part II of the book as a springboard to address an important puzzle: Why have countries refrained from transferring complete nuclear weapons to non-nuclear weapons states? While civilian nuclear assistance could lead to proliferation in the long term, a quicker way to strengthen an ally or constrain an adversary would be to export an intact nuclear bomb. That we have not yet observed this implies that a complex combination of factors—including international norms, economics, and politics—explains the export practices of nuclear weapons states.

Part III of the book deals with the effects of the nuclear renaissance on international conflict. In Chapter 11, Kyle Beardsley and Victor Asal analyze the relationship between nuclear weapons programs and international crisis behavior. This issue is related to the central theme of Part III of the book because the nuclear renaissance could lead to further nuclear weapons proliferation.[2] Beardsley and Asal argue that the pursuit of nuclear weapons is threatening to other states because possessing the bomb yields important bargaining leverage. Consistent with their core argument, they find that countries facing potential opponents with nuclear weapons programs are much more likely to experience a crisis. States attempting to proliferate are themselves more likely to perceive a crisis as well. Yet Beardsley and Asal find that the mere possession of sensitive nuclear technology does not affect international crisis behavior. This suggests that the spread of civilian nuclear programs will be destabilizing only to the extent that such programs increase the likelihood of nuclear weapons pursuit.

Michael C. Horowitz examines in Chapter 12 how the pursuit of nuclear weapons and the possession of nuclear energy programs influence states' propensities to initiate militarized conflict against other countries. He finds that states with active nuclear weapons programs are more likely to initiate interstate disputes, but countries with commercial nuclear power programs are much less likely to act aggressively toward their neighbors. Further analysis indicates that the amount of time that countries have had active nuclear weapons programs does not significantly change how they behave or how they are perceived by others.

In Chapter 13, Dan Reiter wraps up Part III of the book by discussing Chapters 11–12 and offering directions for future research. Reiter notes that, while the authors in Part III of the book present a series of nuanced empirical findings, the central theme is that nuclear power has historically had rather modest consequences for international conflict. Based on historical patterns, civilian nuclear energy programs may be more problematic for terrorism than international conflict. From a policy standpoint, Reiter suggests that the possible costs discussed in this part of the book are alone insufficient to derail the nuclear renaissance. At the same time, like Gartzke, he warns that the future may not necessarily resemble the past, and he encourages policy makers to remain vigilant in guarding against the strategic risks stemming from nuclear programs.

In the concluding chapter, we integrate the book's insights and distill the central conclusions. We argue that the future of nuclear power is most likely to resemble a nuclear resurgence rather than a renaissance or stagnation. In light of this projected nuclear future, we comment on the possible strategic effects of peaceful nuclear programs in the coming years and decades. We also discuss the main contributions of the book and flesh out its implications for international relations theory. The chapter ends by articulating policy recommendations for states that are considering building nuclear power plants and for countries that are interested in limiting the strategic effects of civilian nuclear development.

Notes

1. These numbers change monthly, with global reactors going on and off line for various reasons. However, the number of reactors in operation may change significantly for Japan and Germany in the near to midterm future.

2. Some have argued that the renaissance will lead to proliferation (e.g., Fuhrmann 2009b, 2012b), but the chapters in Part II of the book expose an important debate on this issue.

References

Blake, E. M. 2012. "The Year Ahead: This Time for Sure?" *Nuclear News* 55 (1): 44–49.

Bodansky, David. 2004. *Nuclear Energy Principles, Practices, and Prospects.* New York: Springer.

Braun, Chaim, and Christopher F. Chyba. 2004. "Proliferation Rings: New Challenges to the Nuclear Nonproliferation Regime." *International Security* 29 (2): 5–49.

Bueno de Mesquita, Bruce. 2009. *The Predictioneer's Game: Using the Logic of Brazen Self-Interest to See and Shape the Future.* New York: Random House.

Early, Bryan R., Matthew Fuhrmann, and Quan Li. n.d. "Atoms for Terror? Nuclear Programs and Non-Catastrophic Nuclear and Radiological Terrorism." *British Journal of Political Science*, forthcoming.

Economist Intelligence Unit. 2011. "The Future of Nuclear Energy: One Step Back, Two Steps Forward." *A Special Report of the Economist Intelligence Unit*, June.

Ferguson, Charles. 2011. *Nuclear Energy: What Everyone Needs to Know.* New York: Oxford University Press.

Findlay, Trevor. 2011. *Nuclear Energy and Global Governance: Ensuring Safety, Security, and Non-Proliferation.* London: Routledge.

Fitzpatrick, Mark. Ed. 2009. *Preventing Nuclear Dangers in Southeast Asia and Australasia.* London: International Institute for Strategic Studies.

Fuhrmann, Matthew. 2009a. "Taking a Walk on the Supply Side: The Determinants of Civilian Nuclear Cooperation." *Journal of Conflict Resolution* 53 (2): 181–208.

———. 2009b. "Spreading Temptation: Proliferation and Peaceful Nuclear Cooperation Agreements." *International Security* 34 (1): 7–41.

———. 2012a. "Splitting Atoms: Why Do Countries Build Nuclear Power Plants?" *International Interactions* 38 (1): 29–57.

———. 2012b. *Atomic Assistance: How "Atoms for Peace" Programs Cause Nuclear Insecurity.* Ithaca, NY: Cornell University Press.

Glaser, Alexander. 2009. "Internationalization of the Nuclear Fuel Cycle." International Commission on Nuclear Non-proliferation and Disarmament, *ICNND Research Paper*, No. 9. February.

———. 2011. "After the Nuclear Renaissance: The Age of Discovery." *Bulletin of the Atomic Scientists.* March 17. Available at: http://www.the bulletin.org/print/web-edition/op-eds/after-the-nuclear-renaissance.

Holt, Mark, and Anthony Andrews. 2007. *Nuclear Power Plants: Vulnerability to Terrorist Attack.* Washington, DC: Congressional Research Service.

Hymans, Jacques E. C. 2006. *The Psychology of Nuclear Proliferation: Identity, Emotions, and Foreign Policy.* New York: Cambridge University Press.

IAEA (International Atomic Energy Agency). 2009a. *Energy, Electricity and Nuclear Power Estimates for the Period up to 2030.* Vienna: IAEA.

———. 2010b. *International Status and Prospects for Nuclear Power.* Vienna: IAEA.

Kroenig, Matthew. 2009a. "Exporting the Bomb: Why States Provide Sensitive Nuclear Assistance." *American Political Science Review* 103 (1): 113–133.

————. 2009b. "Importing the Bomb: Sensitive Nuclear Assistance and Nuclear Proliferation." *Journal of Conflict Resolution* 53 (2): 161–180.

Malley, Michael S., and Tanya Ogilvie-White. 2009. "Nuclear Capabilities in Southeast Asia." *The Nonproliferation Review* 16 (1): 25–45.

MIT (Massachusetts Institute of Technology). 2003. *The Future of Nuclear Power: An Interdisciplinary Study.* Cambridge, MA: MIT.

Miller, Steven E., and Scott D. Sagan. 2009. "Nuclear Power Without Nuclear Proliferation?" *Daedalus* 138 (4): 7–18.

Montgomery, Alexander H. 2005. "Ringing in Proliferation: How to Dismantle an Atomic Bomb Network." *International Security* 30 (2): 153–187.

Poneman, Daniel. 1982. *Nuclear Power in the Developing World.* London: George Allen & Unwin.

Potter, William, and Gaukhar Mukhatzhanova. Eds. 2010. *Forecasting Nuclear Proliferation in the 21st Century.* Palo Alto, CA: Stanford University Press.

Rublee, Maria Rost. 2009. *Nonproliferation Norms: Why States Choose Nuclear Restraint.* Athens: University of Georgia Press.

Sagan, Scott. Ed. 2009. *Inside Nuclear South Asia.* Stanford, CA: Stanford University Press.

Solingen, Etel. 2007. *Nuclear Logics: Contrasting Paths in East Asia and the Middle East.* Princeton, NJ: Princeton University Press.

Squassoni, Sharon. 2009. *Nuclear Energy: Rebirth or Resuscitation?* Washington, DC: Carnegie Endowment for International Peace.

Tertrais, Bruno. 2009. "The Middle East's Next Nuclear State." *Strategic Insights* 8 (1).

WNA. 2012. *World Nuclear Power Reactors & Uranium Requirements.* Available at: http://www.world-nuclear.org/info/reactors.html.

I DRIVERS AND PATTERNS OF THE NUCLEAR RENAISSANCE

1 Correlates of Nuclear Energy

Back to the Future or Back to Basics?

Bernard Gourley and Adam N. Stulberg

O N MARCH 11, 2011, WAVES AS HIGH AS 14 METERS HIT the nuclear power plants (NPPs) of Fukushima Daiichi in Japan, knocking out backup power and resulting in a loss-of-coolant accident when pumps went off line and temperatures rose high enough to damage fuel elements. The aftermath of the crisis left the utility operator of the ill-fated NPPs, Tokyo Electric Power Company or TEPCo, contemplating bankruptcy after suffering the largest loss ever for a Japanese firm outside the financial sector. Japan's Prime Minister, then Naoto Kan, subsequently called for upgrading safety and security inspections and announced that the country would not build new nuclear plants—a strict volte-face from pre-tsunami plans of a 30 percent growth in nuclear capacity over the coming decade (Economist Intelligence Unit 2011). The shutdown of almost two-thirds of the country's reactors (in response to both the accident and accelerated schedules of inspections) saddled utilities across the country with short- and long-term electricity shortages. Coupled with the formal scathing indictment of "human error" and poor safety planning, this stirred national debate over the costs and risks associated with future expansion of nuclear energy (FNAIIC 2012). Similarly, global public reflection on the costs and possible consequences of nuclear energy led many states to reexamine their nuclear industries, with divergent conclusions. For example, while the Germans committed to phasing out nuclear power and Italy scrapped plans to reconstitute nuclear capacity, other nuclear energy states (e.g., Russia and China), as well as aspirants (e.g., Vietnam and the United Arab Emirates [UAE]), elected to press ahead with existing plans for nuclear power development. As discussed below, Tokyo faces a confluence of factors that render nuclear a particularly appealing power source, and which resulted in the Japanese building nuclear plants when almost no other country was doing so. If Japan—given the powerful drivers motivating its pursuit of nuclear that include geographic isolation, resource scarcity, and status as a proponent of climate change mitigation—follows suit with Germany in abandoning this energy source, what can be expected of states with far less pressing motivations?

The issue takes on added significance in light of the mixed bag of nuclear energy states. As of 2012, thirty-one countries possess an operational commercial-scale nuclear energy infrastructure; and they are a diverse set of states, including Armenia, Belgium, China, Finland, Pakistan, the United Kingdom, Mexico, and Argentina. These states, as well as more than fifty others that have expressed interest in joining them, run the gamut in terms of standard of living, governance, location, population size, security environments, resource allocation, and levels of industrial development.

This raises the following questions: Are there characteristics shared by nuclear power–generating states that distinguish them from non-nuclear energy states? Do historical commonalities hold for contemporary nuclear energy aspirants? What are the implications for projecting the scope and scale of alternative nuclear energy futures? In short, how much do we know (or not know) about the correlates of nuclear power generation?

Answers to these questions are important for illuminating the contours of a prospective global expansion of nuclear energy. First, identification of common attributes can assist with distinguishing rhetoric from reality surrounding a much-heralded nuclear energy renaissance. Notwithstanding both the widespread resuscitation of interest in nuclear power before the Fukushima Daiichi disaster and the public shock waves that ensued, the lion's share of new reactor construction has occurred, to date, in states already in possession of a nuclear energy infrastructure, especially China, India, and Russia. There are notable cases of states that have articulated a strong commitment to nuclear power for decades but have achieved, at best, modest success, such as Indonesia and Turkey. Do these trends represent a new era or a temporary waypoint in the development of nuclear energy? Exploration of shared traits among existing and aspirant nuclear energy states can shed light on

similarities and distinctions between historical and contemporary trajectories of nuclear energy stagnation, resurgence, or renaissance.

Second, systematic inquiry into shared characteristics of nuclear energy
states can advance the nascent scholarly debate over the drivers of nuclear
energy acquisition. Little is known about what motivates states to acquire nuclear power generation capacity beyond disparate statements by national leaders and governing bodies. Indeed, scholars are only beginning to probe the
drivers of nuclear energy development using quantitative empirical analysis
(Nelson and Sprecher 2008; Jewel 2011; Fuhrmann 2012). The extant literature
typically focuses on explanations for either weapons capabilities or access to
weapons-related technologies, or whether there is a link between acquisition
of nuclear energy and weapons programs (latent or otherwise) (e.g., Meyer
1984; Sagan 1996/97, 2010; Singh and Way 2004; Jo and Gartzke 2007; Barnaby
2009; Fuhrmann 2009a,b; Kroenig 2009a,b; Findlay 2011). Most studies that
address the acquisition of nuclear energy programs tend to give priority to
idiosyncratic political motivations and decision-making processes, or analyze
the political interests, national aspirations, or strategic consequences associated with the empowerment of domestic nuclear energy lobbies, rather than
offering systematic analyses of general patterns and trends of commercial
energy acquisitions across time, states, or regions (e.g., Hymans 2006; Solingen 2007; Fitzpatrick 2009; Malley and Ogilvie-White 2009; Rublee 2009).
Although correlation cannot be equated with causation, by filling methodological gaps and refining metrics to test rival claims, a large-N study of common attributes among states with civilian nuclear power industries can build
on recent scholarly insight by exposing important and systematic inflection
points for alternative nuclear scenarios, as well as by identifying critical case
studies for the future and rich analysis of drivers and processes associated
with the diffusion of nuclear energy (Jewell 2011).

Finally, the character of the expansion of nuclear power has implications
for policy. Will nuclear energy optimists or pessimists carry the day (see
Busby, Chapter 5 in this volume)? Some people have noted that the aspiring
nuclear energy states, considered in the aggregate, are decidedly weaker in
governance and political stability than existing nuclear energy states, which
accentuates concerns about accidents, terrorism, and weapons proliferation of
a global nuclear energy revival. Given the historical correlation of political instability with states that possess nuclear weapons, this observation also draws

attention to additional levels of national commitment required by newcomers to realize their nuclear energy ambitions (Miller and Sagan 2009; Jewell 2011). Yet without a systematic assessment of the range of potential drivers or an understanding of how current possessor states compare both over time and to non-nuclear energy states, it is difficult to comprehend the ramifications of these observations for managing future nuclear safety and security. A refined appreciation of distinguishing traits can provide purchase on whether the future nuclear energy club will be characterized by pariahs, such as Iran, or by engagers, such as the UAE—the former being the newest nascent state and the latter expected to be the next—with attendant implications for balancing international commercial and security policy responses.[1]

This chapter synthesizes what we know and do not know about common characteristics of nuclear energy states. The first section reviews the diversity of the nuclear energy club and the challenges posed by extant explanations for nuclear power generation. The next section discusses the results of a statistical model that tests rival hypotheses concerning shared attributes among nuclear power–generating states from 1950 to 2001. Our findings confirm that nuclear energy states typically have large national incomes. There also is empirical evidence that energy insecurity, defined as reliance on foreign sources of energy, is positively correlated with construction of nuclear energy capacity. Our results also tentatively support the notion of a conspicuous drop-off in the pursuit of nuclear energy in the wake of major nuclear safety accidents, most notably following the Chernobyl disaster. In contrast, many popular explanations such as those rooted in economic growth, regime type, and strategic considerations do not appear to influence nuclear power development in a systematic manner. While it is clear that some nuclear energy programs grew from weapons programs and that some nuclear energy aspirants have been primarily interested in nuclear weapons, given that other states pursued nuclear energy wholeheartedly without working toward the bomb, the question of whether there is a systematic connection remains relevant.[2] The third part discusses the implications of these historical patterns for projecting the emerging nuclear energy landscape, highlighting both limitations of quantitative models and prospective inflection points for discerning alternative scenarios. The final section explores implications that will help determine whether contemporary nuclear energy aspirants are either doomed to stasis or poised to propel a global deepening and broadening of nuclear energy.

The Nuclear Energy Club: A Mixed Bag

What is the profile of a nuclear power–generating state? This question does not lend itself to straightforward answers, given the checkered nuclear landscape. A cursory review of the thirty-one states that operate commercial NPPs, as well as those that have shut-down NPPs (i.e., Kazakhstan, Lithuania, and Italy), reveals tremendous variation along basic parameters. For example, while wealthy states are prevalent in the realm of nuclear energy, there are possessor states with low per capita national incomes (often considered a defining indicator of economic development). Historical inertia also resonates among the majority of the nuclear energy states. Most of the early entrants into the nuclear power domain were either North Atlantic high-income democratic countries with market economies or former Warsaw Pact members. States that meet one of these criteria still comprise nearly two-thirds of the countries that operate NPPs.[3] The history of nuclear energy development is marked by countries that pursued nuclear energy after launching a bomb-related program (e.g., the United States and China), as well as by countries that embarked on extensive civilian nuclear energy programs without undertaking significant efforts to develop nuclear weapons (e.g., Japan and the Netherlands). There also are states—such as India, Brazil, Sweden, South Korea, Taiwan, Pakistan, Yugoslavia, and Iraq—that at one time or another displayed ambiguous motivations by pursuing parallel development of civilian and military nuclear programs (Bose 2005; Ollapally 2001). As well, NPP states have exhibited varying propensities to maintain a dedication to nuclear energy in the face of changing conditions, such as those concerning safety. As noted above, in the wake of the Fukushima Daiichi incident, Germany opted to scrap its plans to extend the life of its nuclear plants to 2036 in favor of phasing out domestic nuclear by 2022, while Italy and Switzerland canceled plans for new NPPs (Monitor's Editorial Board 2011). However, a recent report forecasted that of thirteen major nuclear energy states, only two (Japan and Germany) were not projected to increase nuclear installed capacity by 2020 (Economist Intelligence Unit 2011).[4]

At the same time, a heterogeneous group of more than fifty countries shows varying degrees of interest in developing national nuclear infrastructures—mostly power plants, but for a few this includes fuel cycle facilities downstream of existing mining or milling activities (WNA 2009; IAEA 2010b). Some of these aspirants have vacillated on the issue with changes in political administrations, economic conditions, or world events. Australia's varying policy stances offer prime examples of the effect of political change on nuclear power development (Coorey 2009). Egypt pursued nuclear power but changed course—allegedly in response to the Chernobyl accident—only to renew a favorable disposition toward nuclear energy (MIIS 2009). After protracted periods of disinterest, countries with large natural uranium reserves, such as Australia, Brazil, and Kazakhstan, now trumpet the advantages of moving up the value chain by constructing reactors and producing nuclear fuel (Falk, Green, and Mudd 2006; IAEA 2006; SCIR 2007).[5] Some states, located in the Baltic, Persian Gulf, and Balkan regions, have been satisfied with arrangements that enable them to consume electricity from NPPs situated in other countries, such as the Slovenian/Croatian Krško power plant (WNA 2009). Nuclear power aspirants have ranged from Italy, a wealthy state that formerly generated nuclear power, to countries such as Ghana, Namibia, and Bangladesh that face acute limitations of resources and infrastructures. There have been a number of attempts in recent years to gauge which aspirant states are most likely to succeed. However, basing projections on the past may be problematic given that, until Iran's Bushehr NPP came on line, there had been no new entrants in decades (Jewell 2011).

There are conspicuous differences between aspirants and existing nuclear energy states. Although many developing states are interested in nuclear energy, including several in Africa and the Middle East, these types of states are not well represented among those with nuclear power. Most aspirants considered credible contenders are either large emerging-market countries (e.g., Indonesia or Turkey) or small but fast-growing nations (e.g., Vietnam).

On the surface, it seems obvious why many aspirants would covet nuclear power. Some (e.g., Bangladesh, the Philippines, and Indonesia) stand out as having low rates of access to electricity and negligible consumption per capita.[6] Vietnam must build considerable capacity to sustain its rapid economic growth, and a fifth of the population has no access to electricity (UNDP 2007). Adding capacity on a large scale to meet rising demand while sustaining economic growth appears to be especially attractive for nations with similar profiles.

Notwithstanding generic motivations, the variation across existing and aspiring nuclear energy states presents challenges for systematic analysis. Part of the problem stems from ambiguity about basic requirements for building a nuclear power plant. Although some infrastructural and financial elements are straightforward—such as adequate water for cooling, an electrical grid of sufficient installed capacity to absorb the addition of a large-wattage nuclear plant, a highly specialized workforce (or the resources to attract such a workforce from abroad), and the ability to raise or borrow billions of U.S. dollars—there are less tangible requirements, including the political will, public support, and institutional capacity to shoulder the risks necessary to promote and sustain nuclear power development (Busby, Chapter 5 in this volume; Zhou 2010; Jewell 2011). Some aspirants more consistently display these requirements than others; and some of the requirements (such as grid limitations or public anxiety about nuclear energy) may only preclude aspirants that are otherwise long shots for NPP acquisition.

The diverse nuclear energy landscape poses particular challenges to individual case analysis. Although comparative studies generate critical insight into historical motivations and processes of nuclear energy acquisition for select states, they reveal little about patterns that can be generalized across cases (Poneman 1982; Jasper 1990; Zhou 2010). Similarly, the general attributes of nuclear energy states can be obscured by the idiosyncrasies of decision makers that may be crucial to historical cases but less readily transferable to contemporary aspirants.

Despite the challenges, and consistent with the global revival of interest in nuclear power, there has been a spate of research on the general patterns of nuclear energy acquisition that embrace alternative substantive and methodological approaches. Some studies identify how much nuclear energy production must expand to meet a specific goal—most notably climate change mitigation. One study, in particular, suggests that the sector must experience an almost threefold global increase by 2050 to serve as a wedge of a carbon-constraining strategy (Busby, Chapter 5 in this volume; MIT 2003, 2009). Even if attainable, this reveals little about historical trends, as only a few nations have imposed costs on carbon emissions, and they did so only recently.[7]

Other analyses are rooted in direct extrapolations from historic trends. These studies start from assumptions that issues that have traditionally plagued the sector will persist (Feiveson 2009; Squassoni 2009; Findlay 2010). Chief among these are financial costs (rising capital costs, cost overruns, and construction delays) and technological barriers (lack of market for small and medium-sized reactors or progress in more cost-effective designs). However, qualitative analyses of historic trends are problematic, because they neither systematically test the significance of specified drivers or impediments nor evaluate the idiosyncratic choices, characteristics, or technological advances associated with states that overcome inertia (Adamantiades and Kessides 2009).

Other studies examine prospective correlates of nuclear energy among states that possess a nuclear infrastructure. One study—which statistically tests, via a stepwise regression model, fourteen attributes across eighty-six states that either possess nuclear power or are considered to be candidates— concludes that factors such as size of coal reserves and fuel cycle capacity are negatively correlated with nuclear reliance; whereas international openness, democratic institutions, and energy insecurity are positively correlated (Nelson and Sprecher 2008; Nelson 2010). Although the study advances comparative analysis and offers insight into prospective common attributes across a range of states with nuclear intent, the methodological problems posed by the absence of a normally distributed dependent variable, a narrow data set that excludes states without nuclear capabilities or intentions, and neglect of large-scale temporal variation, give pause to its preliminary conclusions. Another paper makes benchmark comparisons between aspirant states and nuclear energy states at the time of adoption across a range of technical, economic, political, and energy security variables. As mentioned earlier, one problem with this approach (as the author readily admits) is that it is not clear that historical benchmarks are good indicators, given changes with respect to financing conditions, nuclear safety accidents, and developing technologies. This paper also did not consider strategic or security motivations; rather, it assumed the drivers to be in the realm of economics and energy security (i.e., driven by energy demand and diversification) for all aspirants (Jewell 2011). That said, both studies represent important advances at systematic analysis and suggest the promise and new directions for large-N statistical studies of the correlates of nuclear energy.

Model, Myths, and Findings

The dataset for our analysis, which is designed to capture variation in nuclear power development across time and between countries, includes 150 states for which consistent data was available for the period 1950 to 2001. Because this period exhibited distinct phases of NPP construction, we also analyze two time periods within it: 1950–1980 and 1981–2001.[8] Figure 1.1 depicts the breakdown of NPP starts, defined as construction beginning on an individual

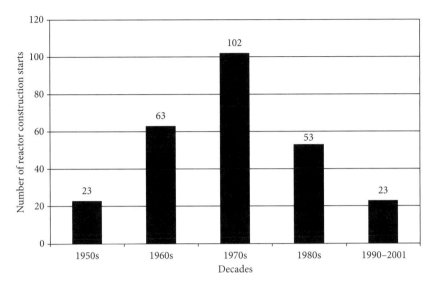

FIGURE 1.1 Worldwide NPP starts by decade
SOURCE: IAEA 2010a.

plant, by decade. Roughly 94 percent of the NPP builders entered the field from 1950 to 1980, and nearly 75 percent of NPP starts occurred during that period. In contrast, the 1980s and 1990s were marked by a dearth of nuclear plant construction in all but a few countries. This is generally ascribed to a combination of long-wave construction cycles, reaction to nuclear accidents, and an escalation of capital costs (Farber 1991). Accordingly, two runs of the model were conducted with dummy variables capturing the before and after periods of Three Mile Island (TMI) and Chernobyl.

Following a standard scholarly practice, we used logistic regression analysis to estimate the relationships between independent variables and nuclear power development. Logistic regression is especially appropriate, given the structure of the dependent variable (discussed below) and the expected non-linear relationship between the independent variables and NPP starts.

The dependent variable, referred to as NPP starts, consists of a dummy that is coded 1 if, in the country-year in question, the state initiated construction of one or more NPPs, and 0 otherwise. A dichotomous dependent variable is employed to discern common characteristics among states that decide to construct NPPs, as opposed to determining the intensity of reliance on nuclear power. The 1950–2001 period captures the earliest commercial NPP starts. The values are determined from data in the International Atomic Energy Agency's (IAEA's) Power Reactor Information System (PRIS), with the exception of a few NPPs that never came on line but are included in the analysis (Diaz-Balart 1990; IAEA 2010a; Nuclear Engineering International 2010). Data on research reactors or those used for purposes other than electricity generation for public consumption are not included, because the purpose here is to understand commercial nuclear energy development. To control for temporal dependence in construction start years, four control variables are employed that capture the time without a construction event and three cubic splines (Beck, Katz, and Tucker 1998).

The independent variables account for strategic, economic, and political factors that are believed to influence states' pursuit of nuclear energy. Below, we discuss the covariates in greater detail and review the empirical findings, which are displayed in Table 1.1.

TABLE 1.1 Nuclear power plant construction model

Variable	Overall model	Golden age of nuclear power (1950–1980)	Dark ages of nuclear power (1981–2001)	Model with Three Mile Island variable	Model with Chernobyl variable
LATENCY					
MIDs five-year moving average	−0.1254 (0.0905)	0.0036 (0.1424)	−0.2806 (0.2269)	−0.1207 (0.1061)	−0.1010 (0.0989)
Enduring rivalries	0.1410 (0.2416)	−0.0856 (0.4523)	1.1662* (0.5640)	0.2332 (0.3248)	0.2285 (0.2920)
ENERGY SECURITY					
Energy security (ln)	−0.7659* (0.3830)	−3.1914* (1.4773)	−2.2635** (0.9521)	−0.7672 (0.3929)	−0.9723** (0.4040)
ECONOMICS					
GDP (ln)	0.7687*** (0.0878)	1.6255*** (0.2779)	1.1572*** (0.2224)	1.3116*** (0.1705)	1.1336*** (0.1417)
Economic growth	0.0360 (0.0202)	−0.0071 (0.3235)	0.0012 (0.0442)	−0.0114 (0.0243)	0.0173 (0.0236)
Economic openness	−0.0040 (0.0033)	0.0066 (0.0043)	0.0006 (0.0056)	0.0019 (0.0039)	0.0006 (0.0036)
POLITICS					
Polity	−0.0066 (0.0143)	−0.0009 (0.0270)	−0.0650 (0.0413)	−0.0235 (0.0211)	−0.0042 (0.0187)
Regime durability	0.0026 (0.0031)	0.0039 (0.0065)	−0.0055 (0.0073)	0.0029 (0.0047)	0.0007 (0.0041)

TABLE 1.1 (*Continued*)

Variable	Overall model	Golden age of nuclear power (1950–1980)	Dark ages of nuclear power (1981–2001)	Model with Three Mile Island variable	Model with Chernobyl variable
NUCLEAR SAFETY					
Three Mile Island				−1.9531*** (0.2700)	
Chernobyl					−1.9917*** (0.3033)
CONTROLS					
Nonstart years	−0.446*** (0.059)	−0.332** (0.127)	−0.439** (0.192)	−0.3060*** (0.0614)	−0.3505*** (0.0609)
Spline 1	−0.002* (0.001)	−0.008 (0.006)	0.001 (0.019)	−0.0013 (0.0010)	−0.0023* (0.0011)
Spline 2	0.000 (0.001)	0.003 (0.004)	−0.042 (0.071)	−0.0002 (0.0010)	0.0005 (0.0011)
Spline 3	0.001 (0.001)	0.000 (0.002)	0.068 (0.103)	0.0007 (0.0006	0.0006 (0.0008)
Constant	−5.787* (2.712)	−2.783 (10.435)	−3.485 (6.247)	−12.493*** (3.3524)	−9.2554*** (3.1731)
Number of countries	150	150	150	150	150
Number of observations	5,690	2,800	2,890	5,690	5,690

NOTE: $*p < .1$, $**p < .05$, $***p < .01$; MIDs = Militarized Interstate Disputes; GDP = gross domestic product; ln = the natural logarithm, which is used to reduce the influence of high skewedness in data.

Security and Nuclear Weapons Hedging

The first set of independent variables relates to nuclear weapons hedging. The hypothesis is that states in high-conflict environments will be more likely to build NPPs as a means to a nuclear weapons breakout option. Although few states have developed nuclear weapons compared to those that have pursued nuclear energy, states nonetheless can be expected to develop capabilities that would allow them to balance against threats or adverse power alignments in short order.[9] To build a nuclear weapon, a state must either secure foreign fissile material or produce it in indigenous fuel cycle facilities. Development of fuel cycle facilities sans a domestic power plant fleet can betray a state's offensive rather than peaceful motivations, thus accentuating perceived security dilemmas (Beardsley and Asal, Chapter 11 in this volume).[10]

Following the example of Singh and Way (2004), two variables capture the degree of conflict and rivalry exhibited by a country during the period. A five-year moving average of militarized interstate disputes captures the number of conflicts in which a country was engaged without inflating the significance of episodic bouts. The data comes from Version 3.0 of the Correlates of War project's Militarized Interstate Dispute (MID) dataset (Ghosen, Palmer, and Bremer 2004). We include only those conflicts rated two or higher on the hostility index to capture actual militarized disputes.[11] A second variable captures the effect of long-term rivalries that may escalate into "hot" conflicts (Klein, Goertz, and Diehl 2006).

The model indicates that there is no significant relationship between international conflict or rivalry and the construction of nuclear reactors. Neither our hypothesis nor the counterhypothesis that a conflict-prone country is not conducive to the economic development or stability required to construct a commercial nuclear power infrastructure was supported. Accordingly, states that build a nuclear energy program in response to a high-threat environment should be considered the exception not the rule. Notwithstanding apparent security concerns and the unfavorable economies of scale associated with its nuclear program, any strategic hedging motive behind Iran's pursuit of commercial nuclear energy, therefore, seems especially anomalous (Sciolino 2006; Cole 2009). Indeed, the behavior of other countries is inconsistent with the hedging motive. The UAE, which contracted with a South Korean consortium in December 2009 to construct NPPs, vowed not to develop sensitive fuel cycle facilities, as discussed by Macfarlane and Stulberg (Chapters 2 and 4 in this volume).

As illustrated in Table 1.1, however, enduring rivalries appeared significant at a 90 percent confidence interval during 1981–2001, the "dark ages" of nuclear power generation. This might signal that hedging was an important driver for those few states that continued building during the lull, but this conclusion should be treated with caution given the high national concentration of NPP starts. Of the five countries that accounted for 70 percent of the NPP starts during the period (Japan, South Korea, China, France, and Russia), only France was free of enduring rivalries. States that were both engaged in NPP starts and experienced enduring rivalries constituted only 6.3 percent of the enduring rivalry country-years from 1981 to 2001.

Energy Security

The second key independent variable we test is energy security. Although the concept has many definitions and dimensions, the primary focus in the literature is on a state's self-sufficiency or dependence on foreign supply (So-vacool and Brown 2009). We measure this variable in terms of the difference between total primary domestic energy production and total primary energy consumption per capita (Banks 2010; EIA 2010a). Although this captures the overall degree to which a state is import dependent, it does not differentiate deficits in the electricity sector that can be attenuated by nuclear production from those in the transportation sector that currently cannot be efficiently redressed by greater reliance on nuclear energy. However, while many states today (after numerous oil shocks) cannot substitute nuclear energy to reduce oil import dependency, that was not the case over much of the study period (Toth and Rogner 2006; Lee and Chiu 2011). Also, defining energy security strictly in terms of electricity generation overlooks the fact that some states can cheaply import power to balance domestic deficits, while others lack this capacity (due to strategic and geographical challenges). Analyzing only electricity rates, therefore, obfuscates the degrees to which states can substitute different forms or sources of energy (Jewell 2011).

Nuclear energy is expected to be most popular among states that depend on foreign energy supply. The rationale for this hypothesis derives from the characteristics of nuclear fuel that render its supply chain less vulnerable than in the hydrocarbon sector. First, most nuclear plants do not frequently refuel. A typical light water reactor trades out one-third of its fuel every eighteen months. Second, the high density of nuclear fuel makes it feasible to store multiple loads on site (Hore-Lacy 2006).[12] Whereas brief delays in fossil fuel deliveries can wreak economic havoc via the price of electricity as well as inflating strategic insecurities, nuclear fuel supply is significantly less vulnerable to short-term disruptions; and, because fuel costs are a small portion of nuclear-generated power costs, electricity prices are less affected by uranium price volatility than by fossil fuel price volatility.

Evidence from the model supports the hypothesis that states that are more dependent on foreign sources of energy are more likely to build NPPs. This is consistent for the overall model, as well across the 1950–1980 and 1981–2001 subsets. The energy security motive is exemplified by Japan and South Korea, two countries with limited indigenous energy supplies and intense energy demand that have relied on nuclear energy to redress deficits between national production and consumption. Tokyo's white paper on nuclear energy policy, written before the Fukushima Daiichi accident, states that: "The first priority in Japanese energy supply policy is securing the steady supply of energy necessary to support the lives of the people" (Atomic Energy Commission of Japan 2000). However, some states, such as the United States, experienced rising import dependency during a period when they ceased building new reactors. This may reflect a more complex dynamic associated with energy surpluses or deficits, such as the proximity to or availability of alternative supply infrastructures.

The model reveals that the energy security variable is significant only at a 90 percent confidence interval during the first period, while significant at a 95 percent interval during the second period. This is not surprising, for two reasons. First, especially during the early period, there were prominent cases of large-scale energy surplus states (e.g., the USSR, Canada, and Iran[13]) that pursued nuclear energy. Second, during the later period, Japan and South Korea were building at a substantial rate while most others, including the highly import-dependent United States, had slowed down or stopped constructing NPPs. This supports the notion that energy dependence is not merely determined by the national aggregate energy deficit or surplus, and that physical constraints on pipeline and transmission line construction may indeed compound the significance of the national energy security equation.

Economic Motives

There are reasons to believe that economics may drive the pursuit of nuclear energy. Most important, economic factors can directly shape the national demand for energy. Almost all nuclear energy states were among the largest economies in the world at the time they adopted nuclear power (e.g., although Armenia is a small economy, its nuclear program was initiated while it was part of the Soviet Union). Curiously, there is no similar conspicuous relationship tied to per capita gross domestic product (GDP). Even a cursory observation reveals that some of the highest per capita GDP states are small and do not display the magnitude of demand conducive to building nuclear plants, whereas a number of large emerging-market countries (with relatively small per capita GDPs) are increasingly major players in nuclear power development. This suggests that the scale of economic activity is more important than the standard of living in decisions to build NPPs. Because commercially available NPPs are large-scale plants (on the order of 1 gigawatt), there can be technical and economic barriers to small economies seeking to embrace nuclear energy. While there is a clustering of nuclear energy states among the highest GDP states, there are countries that developed nuclear energy which had relatively low GDPs at the time of adoption (Pakistan, Bulgaria, Finland,

Hungary, and Romania), as well as aspirants that failed to develop nuclear power despite having GDPs of a similar magnitude to the nuclear energy states as a whole (Turkey, Poland, and Indonesia). However, even the poorest nuclear energy states were among the richest forty-five national economies when they adopted nuclear energy. In light of this situation, we include GDP as a measure of overall scale of economic activity within a country to capture the demand for energy, and expect that high GDP should correlate positively with NPP starts.

Economic growth is another common indicator of energy demand. While the specific causal connection remains contested, the correlation between energy consumption and growth remains inviolable (Ockwell 2008). It is expected that fast-growing economies should be more likely to construct NPPs in order to keep pace with rapidly rising demand. The East Asia nuclear energy states (Japan, South Korea, China, and Taiwan) are particularly emblematic of this argument. However, there are numerous examples of nuclear energy states with low growth rates, particularly in East-Central and Western Europe. There also are potential countervailing macroeconomic effects, in that wealthy states tend to experience slow growth rates relative to developing states.

We also include economic openness to test the assumption that a state that is more fully integrated into the global economy will have a higher probability of successfully constructing nuclear plants than will isolated states (Comin and Hobijin 2003). The historical record lends tentative credence to this logic, as only about a quarter of nuclear energy states developed their first plant indigenously (WNA 2010a). Almost none of the leading nuclear energy aspirants are capable of building plants without foreign assistance.

We use several variables to test the relationship between economic factors and NPP starts. The base GDP figure is a constant year dollar presented in purchasing power parity terms (i.e., Geary–Khamis international dollars) to avoid depressing the financial strength of emerging-market countries (Maddison 2009). The use of constant year dollars minimizes the confounding effects of countries with high rates of inflation or deflation. The raw GDP figure is transformed by taking the natural logarithm to mitigate the extreme skew of the variable. The economic growth rate is derived from the Geary–Khamis dollar GDP figures to measure national income. The standard measure of economic openness ([exports + imports]/GDP) is used in constant year dollar form (Heston, Summers, and Aten 2009; Banks 2010). However, we appreciate that the scale of some domestic economies, such as the United States and Japan, could make them appear to be closed when, in fact, those states are active traders.

The model demonstrates that the national income variable is significant and of the anticipated sign for both the entire 1950–2001 period and the two subset periods at a p value less than 0.001. This supports the hypothesis that the size of a country's economy is positively correlated to the likelihood of building nuclear power. However, neither economic growth nor openness is significant. It turns out that the average growth rate for builders of nuclear plants is 3.98 percent—almost identical to the overall average growth rate of 3.76 percent, given a standard deviation on the order of 6.00 percent. As mentioned, there are problems with using total trade over GDP as a measure of openness, because the very largest economies tend to look closed despite conducting sizable trade in absolute terms. Similarly, major transshipment points, such as Singapore, and small developing nations, such as Ghana, appear as open, suggesting that more research may be required to fully assess the significance of international openness.

Political Variables
Historically, nuclear energy states reflect varying governance types. One study noted a positive correlation between democracy and nuclear power reliance (Nelson and Sprecher 2008). Another study found that democracies are more likely to be responsive to nuclear accidents and, thus, less likely to build nuclear capacity in the wake of such events (Fuhrmann 2012). The relationship between regime type and preferences for nuclear energy, however, may vary over time. After all, the United States dominated the field in its early decades, but China is home to over one-third of the NPPs under construction. Still other studies disaggregate relevant governance issues beyond a straightforward autocratic-democratic index. Regime duration, for example, may capture the stability needed to promote nuclear energy. Similarly, one qualitative study compared the influence of U.S. and French regulatory systems on the development of nuclear power industries and found that the combination of a concentrated executive authority, a weak judiciary, and heavy reliance on bureaucratic expertise rendered France significantly more conducive to the development of a national nuclear sector (Delmas and Heiman 2001). Still another study defined institutional capacity in terms of stability and reliability of regulatory procedures that bear directly on the confidence in government policies to attract private investment (Jewell 2011).

We use data on both regime type and duration from the Polity IV dataset of Marshall and Jaggers (2009). The polity measure, consisting of a twenty-one-point scale that ranges from +10 for highly democratic states to −10 for highly autocratic states, forms the basis of the governance variable. This scale is derived from five subcomponent scores dealing with executive recruitment competitiveness, executive recruitment openness, constraints on the executive, regulation of political participation, and competitiveness of political participation. Regime duration begins with 0 during a transition year and increases by 1 for each year thereafter.

Neither regime type nor stability of governance is significant in either the overall model or the temporal subsets. This time-series–cross-section approach offers no support for a hypothesized link between democratic regimes and NPP development. Also, while most nuclear energy states appeared to be stable over the period they were building NPPs, there were several examples of nuclear energy states that built plants during periods of intense political transition, including Argentina, Brazil, Mexico, Pakistan, and South Korea. This also is generally consistent with other large-N studies that identified a diversity of regime types associated with past and present nuclear energy states (Jewell 2011).

Nuclear Safety Variables

In order to control for the effects of major nuclear disasters, two runs were conducted with an additional variable each. These crude analyses consist of a dummy coded 0 for every country-year before the event (TMI in the first run and Chernobyl in the second) and 1 for country-years thereafter. Three Mile Island (1979) and Chernobyl (1986) were the most notable accidents during the study period, and there has been much discussion of the impact of each of these events on the nuclear industry. In both runs, this variable was significant. However, the limited information content of the variable, contending alternative explanations (e.g., rising costs that may not be linked to these disasters), and the fact that construction start has a varying and sometimes substantial lag from the decision to build an NPP are suggestive of caveats to these conclusions.

From Knowns to Unknowns

Although the statistical model reveals the historical significance of economic size, energy insecurity, and the effect of accidents as correlates of nuclear power development, as well as suggesting a lack of support for other hypothesized correlates, it provides only limited insight into the causal logic of nuclear energy decision making. The basic challenges of this large-N study are compounded by the high concentration of NPP construction starts (almost 25 percent of countries included in the study have NPP starts during the study years, but over 70 percent of events are observed in just ten states) and the infrequency of events (NPP starts occurred in less than 5 percent of country-year observations).

More conspicuous, the model obfuscates the divergent patterns of NPP construction (depicted in Figure 1.2) that affected historical waves of acquisition among archetypal nuclear energy states—the United States, France, and Japan—and the implications these hold for aspirants. The United States, for example, engaged in a massive buildup of nuclear plants in the 1960s and 1970s, and then entered a period of protracted dormancy. France displayed a similar pattern during the period but with different long-run implications. France receives 75 percent of its electricity from the nuclear sector, which cannot meet all electricity needs owing to technological constraints; and, therefore, having reached its maximum nuclear capacity, France experienced a lull in new construction (WNA 2010b). Accordingly, while France's pattern of growth and stagnation in NPP construction is seemingly tied to the life cycle of nuclear plants, the similar pattern exhibited by the United States can more readily be attributed to the nuclear economics of increasing capital costs influenced by accidents, poor returns on investments, market uncertainties, and escalating delays and cost overruns (Ellis and Zimmerman 1983; Sommers 1980).[14] In contrast to both of these cases, Japan displays a steady pattern of long-term NPP construction that has only recently wavered in the wake of the 2011 earthquake and tsunami.

The model offers only partial insight into several possible inflection points for a nuclear energy revival. First, while it supports the findings of other studies about the significance of energy insecurity as a motivation for nuclear power generation (Jewell 2011; Fuhrmann 2012), it suggests the need for delving deeper into understanding how states make trade-offs among options for reducing energy deficits, such as by imports via regional pipelines or transmission infrastructures. It is plausible that the unique technical and geographic vulnerabilities of Japan and South Korea shaped their respective patterns of NPP construction when virtually all other states had stopped new development.

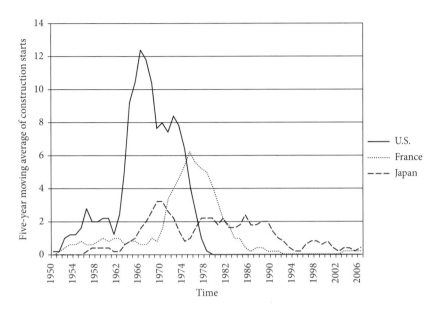

FIGURE 1.2 U.S., French, and Japanese construction patterns, five-year moving averages of construction starts, 1950–2010
SOURCE: IAEA 2010a.

Second, the model highlights the limitations for understanding NPP starts associated with traditional measures of autocratic and democratic regime types (see Montgomery, Chapter 7 in this volume; Hymans 2008). Study of the data reveals cases in which similarly rated states produce significantly divergent outcomes. For example, the United States and Japan, both highly rated democracies, have embraced different trajectories for nuclear energy growth from the 1980s until the 2010s. This suggests either the relative insignificance of the variable or that governance is not completely captured by the model. The latter may be the case, as we know that relevant decision-making and regulatory systems pertaining to nuclear power vary greatly across democratic regimes. In some cases, the state is the sole relevant decision maker, while in others private firms or public-private corporations are major players. Contrasting French (majority publicly-owned utility) and German (private utility market) approaches to nuclear power suggests that this may be a promising line of inquiry. Yet while distinction between public and private ownership may be a necessary component of understanding the role of governance, it alone is not likely to be sufficient to account for variation, since both the

United States and Japan have maintained primarily private utilities. As some scholars suggest, China's centralized government and state-driven economy may be well-positioned to transcend otherwise paralyzing political interests and public ambivalence to spearhead a massive national buildup of nuclear energy (Zhou 2010).

Rather, what may be left out of the model and other conventional political indicators is how specific governance factors relate to risk-taking propensities, especially with respect to overcoming public anxiety and financing nuclear plant construction. Financing NPPs involves more capital than most private utilities hold as cash or can collateralize, or for which a single bank can diversify against a default. As one study indicates, the elimination of the excess risk premium for nuclear energy over coal or natural gas alone would make the sector economically competitive (MIT 2009). This suggests that different national risk perceptions and related mitigation strategies for nuclear energy are potentially important inflection points. Although the United States has undertaken initiatives to redress financial risks via loan guarantees and liability caps, these measures have not spurred significant growth in the nuclear sector. However, China has used loan guarantees, financial aid to the state-owned enterprises involved in the nuclear sector, and an insurance pool to successfully spur a buildup of nuclear energy at a rate not seen since the early 1970s (Zhou 2010). The majority of nuclear energy states have financed NPP construction directly with public funds so as to broadly distribute financial risks. Few states, such as South Korea, rely primarily on private equity or debt to initiate and sustain commercial nuclear power development, though the United States and Germany employed this method when they were building (IAEA 2008).[15] Accordingly, part of the difficulty of capturing risk in the model is that both the definition and policy responses are subjectively determined. As reviewed by Macfarlane (Chapter 2 in this volume), the risk perception of policy makers, experts, the general public, and subnational actors can be radically different with direct implications for policy. Identifying how and why specific national institutional factors may accentuate or mitigate such risk perceptions, therefore, may provide crucial addenda to the literature on governance types and nuclear energy correlates (Hamalainen 1991; Sjoberg and Drottz-Sjoberg 2008).

The model also does not capture several emerging variables. Excluded from the analysis is the impact of climate change, owing to the relatively new focus on the issue as a tipping point for nuclear energy (Busby, Chapter 5 in this volume). China, for example, has set a goal to have carbon dioxide emissions 40–45 percent below 2005 levels by 2020, and plans to do this without curbing its impressive growth (Zhou 2010). There are other pollutants that raised concerns over part of the study period, including sulfur dioxide and nitrogen oxide, and regulation or taxation of them may have strengthened the relative appeal of nuclear power. One study, for example, showed support for the hypothesis that the Clean Air Act increased the attractiveness of nuclear power for the United States during the 1970s (Ellis and Zimmerman 1983). However, the lack of consistent international time-series–cross-section data for these pollutants makes it difficult to include them in a statistical model.

Similarly, the model does not capture the prestige value of nuclear energy, to the extent it exists. This variable is particularly difficult to include in a quantitative model because of its qualitative nature and the lack of a readily apparent proxy. The use of alliance portfolios as a surrogate measure, under the assumption that prestige-deficient powers likely would be dissatisfied with the status quo and would choose their alliances accordingly, provided mixed results for discerning the correlates of nuclear weapons pursuit and acquisition (Singh and Way 2004). Another study noted that there were statements by members of the leadership of six countries (the United States, the United Kingdom, France, the USSR, Germany, and Canada) that hyped the prestige associated with a national nuclear energy research and development program. This study also acknowledged that the elusiveness of the subject made it difficult to discern the relative impact of prestige on development of such programs (DeLeon 1980). Thus, without deeper qualitative and case analysis of the national prominence of prestige, it will be difficult to uncover its relative importance via statistical study of the correlates of nuclear power generation.

As one can see in Figure 1.1 and, less broadly, in Figure 1.2, nuclear energy experienced a clear tipping point in the 1980s. The nuclear accidents at Three Mile Island and Chernobyl are often cited as key causal factors in the collapse of the global nuclear energy industry. Although this conclusion may seem reasonable—based on the timing of the collapse, the literature on the economic effects of these events (e.g., Kalra, Henderson, and Raines 1993), and apparent sea changes in countries such as Egypt—the fortunate rarity of large-scale nuclear accidents and the evidence that nuclear energy was losing appeal before these events should encourage caution about simplistically concluding that the accidents were the dominant cause of the collapse.[16] There is more to learn about the effects of nuclear accidents, and undoubtedly future studies addressing the Fukushima Daiichi disaster will provide further illumination of the significance of this relationship.

Looking to the Future

Forecasting nuclear energy scenarios is challenging under the best of circumstances, owing to the complexity of the landscape. It is especially problematic in the absence of sound deductive reasoning about decision making and critical testing of alternative scenarios, which are premature given the state of knowledge about the drivers of nuclear energy (Bueno de Mesquita 1984). However, both the statistical model and respective caveats together identify important conditions and safe bets for discerning characteristics of alternative trajectories for global nuclear energy growth.

First, with projections of rapidly increasing electricity consumption rates, the nuclear energy sector must grow significantly if only to maintain aggregate shares in global and national energy portfolios. Before the tsunami in Japan, the Energy Information Administration projected a 70 percent increase in worldwide use of nuclear between 2012 and 2035 to meet an approximately 50 percent increase in global energy consumption over the period (EIA 2010b). Our analysis suggests that signs of stagnation versus an expansion of nuclear power should be explored primarily in the behavior of the current nuclear energy states. Those with large economies and mounting gaps between domestic energy production and consumption—particularly those with few geographic or infrastructural alternatives for cheap imports—will be most capable of driving an expansion. For this reason, any evidence of stagnation or decline in key states, such as China, the United States, South Korea, and France, would likely be ominous for the future of a nuclear energy expansion. Japan will prove to be a key test, given its recent talk of discontinuing nuclear power and the temporary shutdown of almost all of its NPPs. China is engaged in a major nuclear power building boom, with over 25 gigawatts-electric (GWe) worth of NPP construction in the works, that looks similar to the U.S. position in the 1960s. Until the accident at Fukushima Daiichi, Japan and South Korea seemed poised to keep building nuclear power plants until they reach the technically feasible limits of nuclear capacity, to replace aging plants, and to make nuclear part of their strategy for meeting growing energy needs. Given France's enthusiasm for nuclear energy, it, too, is likely to maintain as much nuclear capacity as is technically feasible. However, the

United States, which alone currently comprises over 25 percent of global installed nuclear capacity, presents a more ambiguous picture. Because the average operational U.S. NPP is over thirty years old, the United States will have
to engage in substantial NPP starts just to replace plants that are nearing the
end of their life cycles. To date, progress has been slow.[17]

The model leads us to believe that states with substantial and rising energy
demands and energy security concerns will provide indicators of the extent to
which states will be able to deepen their reliance on nuclear power. Accordingly, the first place to look for a nuclear resurgence will be in the decisions
taken by states such as China, India, Russia, South Korea, and the United
States. The important role of the large emerging-market countries in the expansion of nuclear power seems to be playing out. The BRIC (Brazil, Russia,
India, and China) countries account for over 68 percent of the nuclear plants
under construction, and adding South Korea raises that figure to almost
75 percent. However, some of these countries appear to more intensely participate in a deepening than others. India, for example, with 4.8 GWe of nuclear
installed capacity in the pipeline, has had to add almost 7.0 GWe per year over
the past few years to meet its energy needs (Busby, Chapter 5 in this volume;
EIA 2010a). Russia provides an interesting case as a major net exporter of energy that is actively engaged in developing nuclear energy. With over 8 GWe
in the works, Russia is the second largest NPP-building state behind China;
though, unlike China, it has a reactor fleet almost as old, on average, as that
of the United States.

The model also illuminates prospective attributes associated with a potential broadening of the nuclear energy field. Italy, for example, would have been
considered the most likely to join (once again) the nuclear energy club before
a June 2011 referendum that succeeded in blocking development of nuclear
power. Italy is an advanced industrialized country with a history of operating
nuclear power plants, thus avoiding the first-of-kind challenges that hound
nuclear energy aspirants. Italy's decision not to pursue nuclear energy in the
wake of the Japanese accident could be said to yield important insight into
national risk assessment for nuclear power development. Other aspirants with
an economic mass on par with nuclear energy states include Turkey, Indonesia, and Saudi Arabia. These states warrant close examination to discern the
prospects for a broadening nuclear energy expansion.[18]

While the model predicts that states with an energy surplus are less likely
to develop nuclear energy, several energy-producer states should not be

overlooked. From the group noted above, only Turkey is not a significant net energy producer. Historically, a number of large-scale energy producers have built NPPs, including the Soviet Union/Russia, Canada, Mexico, and most recently Iran. Furthermore, Qatar, Kuwait, Saudi Arabia, and the UAE are among the countries with the highest per capita petroleum consumption in the world (significantly above the United States and Canada), and they are all Kyoto Protocol members. These countries still rely on petroleum-based power generation for which they can substitute nuclear energy in order both to facilitate meeting respective emission reduction targets and to free up hydrocarbons for global export. This factor could account for the UAE's progress toward nuclear power and would suggest that Kuwait and Saudi Arabia may not be far behind.

The specific contours of a global expansion undoubtedly will be influenced by factors that are uncertain and idiosyncratic and will not necessarily reflect historical trends. While there are problems of both collective action and scale inherent in reducing greenhouse gas emissions (Busby, Chapter 5 in this volume), this may likely be a motivator for some states. However, reducing these emissions will require some form of cost on carbon output. Furthermore and notwithstanding successive and recent events in Japan, nuclear power has had an impressive safety record, and the IAEA points to safety as the single most important factor for improving the viability of NPP financing worldwide (IAEA 2009). This speaks to the possibility of technical solutions, such as smaller reactors that may be more cost-effective (especially for smaller aspirants) and inspire greater confidence. Irrespective of how these unknowns unfold, it is clear that before we can forecast the precise trajectory of commercial nuclear energy, we need a more systematic and richer understanding of both past attributes and drivers of the sector.

Notes

1. We can see in the historical record countries that moved from "engager" to "pariah," such as when India transitioned from valued customer for nuclear energy technology of both the United States and Canada to being shunned after its 1974 nuclear device test (Gopalakrishnan 2002).

2. Besides the well-discussed case of Iran as a nuclear energy aspirant in search of the bomb, there is reason to believe that the discontinued Australian program of the 1970s was the result of Prime Minister Gorton's interest in nuclear weapons (Falk, Green, and Judd 2006)

3. The list below shows countries fitting the aforementioned criteria in bold, with Soviet/Warsaw Pact countries marked with one asterisk and North Atlantic market democracies marked with two asterisks: *Armenia, **Belgium, Brazil, *Bulgaria, **Canada, China, *Czech Republic, **Finland, **France, **Germany, *Hungary, India, Iran, Japan, South Korea, Mexico, **Netherlands, Pakistan, *Romania, *Russia, *Slovakia, Slovenia, South Africa, **Spain, **Sweden, **Switzerland, Taiwan, *Ukraine, **United Kingdom, and **United States. Additionally, three countries once operated commercial NPPs and have subsequently shut their plant (s) down: *Lithuania, **Italy, and *Kazakhstan.

4. The countries in this report were the United States, France, Japan, Russia, Germany, South Korea, Ukraine, Canada, the United Kingdom, China, Brazil, India, and Pakistan.

5. Falk, Green, and Mudd (2006) describe a Prime Minister comparing Australia's uranium ore sales to the days when they sent wool to England to be made into expensive garments.

6. Among the nuclear energy states, only India and Pakistan have electrification rates and per capita consumption at comparably low levels to these aspirants.

7. As of 2011, Japan, Russia, and Canada indicated their intentions not to extend commitments under the Kyoto Protocol upon its lapsing at the end of 2012.

8. The dividing line, 1980, was at approximately the global height of NPP construction. The actual pinnacle of NPP construction was in 1979, with a steady climb in the number of plants up to that year and an equally steady decline thereafter, whereas 1980 was the height in terms of maximum design net capacity. A graph showing this based on IAEA data can be seen in Schneider et al. (2009).

9. A correlation between security concerns and nuclear energy also is suggested by the fact that over 50 percent of established nuclear power states either considered or pursued nuclear weapons, with the majority of those states using access to international civilian nuclear technology as a source or justification for acquiring fissile material and tacit knowledge for their military programs. By contrast, the United States, the Soviet Union, the United Kingdom, and China launched dedicated military programs well before initiating commercial programs.

10. It should be noted that even building or operating a power plant or two could make indigenous development of fuel cycle facilities suspect, as seen in the case of Iran. The economies of scale for nuclear fuel are such that it would be impossible for a state to cost-effectively produce its own fuel for a very small reactor fleet. For example, a typical NPP of 1 GWe requires about 140,000 separative work units (SWUs) per year (WNA 2012); but, according to an estimate produced by Rothwell (2009), increasing returns to scale are seen up to approximately 2.5–2.9 million SWU/year. This means the unit price on SWUs for Iran might be twice or more what the big producers can make it for, because Iran is on the portion of the average cost curve at which increased production would radically drop costs per mass of fuel.

11. Level 1 hostilities are not included, as they do not involve military activity.

12. For example, to produce eight megawatt-hours of electricity requires 230 grams of uranium oxide concentrate (from 30–70 kilograms of uranium ore). This contrasts with three tons of black coal or nine tons of brown coal. While nuclear fuel costs are a minor portion of total generating costs, fuel costs for coal and liquefied natural gas plants typically comprise 40 percent and 60 percent of overall generation costs, respectively.

13. Bushehr NPP's initial construction start was in 1975, though it experienced many intervening fits and starts.

14. While there are not many studies that look internationally at the rise and fall of nuclear energy, there are several that look within given nations, particularly the United States. Ellis and Zimmerman (1983) show that cost escalation was more rapid for nuclear than coal, and evidence supported the belief that longer construction times were unfavorable for nuclear. Sommers (1980) showed that uncertainty about construction times seemed to be a factor in the growing disfavor of nuclear in the United States.

15. South Korea only shifted to private financing after publicly financing its first few NPPs. This makes it an interesting and unique case.

16. Farber (1991) shows that, for a limited case in the United States, the cost of adopting nuclear energy (i.e., the risk premium on borrowing) was rising significantly well in advance of the Three Mile Island event; and although TMI exacerbated this effect, the die was already cast. While it cannot be assumed this applies universally, it is reasonable to hypothesize that it would apply where private-sector financing dominated (e.g., Japan and Germany), since cost overruns and delays were not uniquely American problems. Furthermore, plant cancellations were being seen before these events (Kalra, Henderson, and Raines 1993).

17. Subtracting those on hold or withdrawn, the U.S. Nuclear Regulatory Commission (NRC) has Combined Operating License applications for 30 GWe nuclear installed capacity (twenty-three units). In 2012, the NRC issued the first U.S. construction permit (Combined Operating License) in thirty-five years for two new units at the Vogtle complex in Georgia.

18. These are the countries with a GDP above the median for nuclear power states, but all were well below the mean.

References

Adamantiades, A., and I. Kessides. 2009. "Nuclear Power for Sustainable Development: Current Status and Future Prospects." *Energy Policy* 37 (2): 5149–5166.

Atomic Energy Commission of Japan. 2000. *Long-Term Program for Research, Development and Utilization of Nuclear Power.* Tokyo: AEC, Japan.

Banks, Arthur S. 2010. *Cross-National Time-Series Data Archive.* Jerusalem: Databanks International.

Barnaby, Frank. 2009. "The Nuclear Renaissance: Nuclear Weapons Proliferation and Terrorism." Institute for Public Policy Research (March). Available at: http://

www.ippr.org/publication/55/1679/the-nuclear-renaissance-nuclear-weapons-proliferation-and-terrorism.

Beck, Nathaniel, Jonathan Katz, and Richard Tucker. 1998. "Taking Time Seriously: Time-Series–Cross-Section Analysis with a Binary Dependent Variable." *American Journal of Political Science* 42 (4): 1260–1288.

Bose, Arshiya Urveeja. 2005. "Nuclear Energy in India: Development, Performance & Public Opinion." *Energy, Resources & Environmental Policies*, March 2.

Bueno de Mesquita, Bruce. 1984. "Forecasting Policy Decisions: An Expected Utility Approach to Post-Khomeini Iran." *PS* 17 (2): 226–236.

Cole, Juan. 2009. "Does Iran Really Want the Bomb?" *Salon.com*, October 7. Available at: http://www.salon.com/news/opinion/feature/2009/10/07/iran_nuclear/index.html.

Comin, Diego, and Bart Hobijin. 2003. "Cross-Country Technology Adoption: Making the Theories Face the Facts." *Federal Reserve Bank of New York Staff Report, No. 169*, June.

Coorey, Phillip. 2009. "Rudd's Hostility Forces Nuclear Group to Bail Out." *The Sydney Morning Herald*, August 25. Available at: http://www.smh.com.au/environment/rudds-hostility-forces-nuclear-group-to-bale-out-20090824-ewla.html.

DeLeon, Peter. 1980. "Comparative Technology and Public Policy: The Development of the Nuclear Power Reactor in Six Nations." *Policy Sciences* 11 (3): 285–307.

Delmas, Magali, and Bruce Heiman. 2001. "Government Credible Commitment to the French and American Nuclear Power Industries." *Journal of Policy Analysis and Management* 20 (3): 433–456.

Diaz-Balart, Fidel C. 1990. "Nuclear Energy in Cuba: An Indispensable Link toward Development." *IAEA Bulletin* 32: 49–52.

Economist Intelligence Unit. 2011. "The Future of Nuclear Energy: One Step Back, Two Steps Forward." *A Special Report of the Economist Intelligence Unit*, June.

EIA (Energy Information Administration). 2010a. *International Energy Database.* Available at: http://tonto.eia.doe.gov/cfapps/ipdbproject/IEDIndex3.cfm.

———. 2010b. *International Energy Outlook.* Available at: http://www.eia.doe.gov/oiaf/ieo/graphic_data_world.html.

Ellis, Randall, and Martin Zimmerman. 1983. "What Happened to Nuclear Power: A Discrete Choice Model of Technology Adoption." *The Review of Economics and Statistics* 65 (2): 234–242.

Falk, Jim, Jim Green, and Gavin Mudd. 2006. "Australia, Uranium, and Nuclear Power." *International Journal of Environmental Studies* 63 (6): 845–857.

Farber, Stephen. 1991. "Nuclear Power, Systemic Risk, and the Cost of Capital." *Contemporary Policy Issues* 9 (1): 73–82.

Feiveson, Harold. 2009. "A Skeptic's View of Nuclear Energy." *Daedalus* 138: 60–70.

Findlay, Trevor. 2010. *The Future of Nuclear Energy to 2030 and Its Implications for Safety, Security and Nonproliferation: Overview.* Waterloo, Canada: Center for International Governance Innovation: Nuclear Energy Futures Project.

———. 2011. *Nuclear Energy and Global Governance: Ensuring Safety, Security, and Non-Proliferation.* London: Routledge.

Fitzpatrick, Mark. Ed. 2009. *Preventing Nuclear Dangers in Southeast Asia and Australasia*. London: International Institute for Strategic Studies.Fuhrmann, Matthew. 2009a. "Taking a Walk on the Supply Side: The Determinants of Civilian Nuclear Cooperation." *Journal of Conflict Resolution* 53 (2): 181–208.

———. 2009b. "Spreading Temptation: Proliferation and Peaceful Nuclear Cooperation Agreements." *International Security* 34 (1): 7–41.

———. 2012. "Splitting Atoms: Why Do Countries Build Nuclear Power Plants?" *International Interactions* 38 (1): 29–57.

Fukushima Nuclear Accident Independent Investigation Commission (FNAIIC). 2012. *The Official Report of the Fukushima Nuclear Accident Independent Investigation Commission*. July. Tokyo: The National Diet of Japan.

Ghosn, Faten, Glenn Palmer, and Stuart Bremer. 2004. "The MID3 Data Set, 1993–2001: Procedures, Coding Rules, and Description." *Conflict Management and Peace Science* 21: 133–154.

Gopalakrishnan, A. 2002. "Evolution of the Indian Nuclear Power Program." *Annual Review of Environment and Resources* 27: 369–395.

Hamalainen, Raimo. 1991. "Facts or Values—How Do Parliamentarians and Experts See Nuclear Power?" *Energy Policy* 19 (5): 464–472.

Heston, Alan, Robert Summers, and Bettina Aten. 2009. *Penn World Table, Version 6.3*, Philadelphia: University of Pennsylvania, Center for International Comparisons of Production, Income and Prices.

Hore-Lacy, Ian. 2006. *Nuclear Energy in the 21st Century*. London: World Nuclear University Press.

Hymans, Jacques E. C. 2006. *The Psychology of Nuclear Proliferation: Identity, Emotions, and Foreign Policy*. New York: Cambridge University Press.

———. 2008. "Assessing North Korean Nuclear Intentions and Capacities: A New Approach." *Journal of East Asian Studies* 8 (2):259–292.

IAEA (International Atomic Energy Agency). 2006. "Country Nuclear Fuel Cycle Profiles." *IAEA Technical Reports*, 2nd ed., Technical Reports Series, No. 425. Vienna: IAEA.

———. 2008. "Financing of New Nuclear Power Plants." *IAEA Nuclear Energy Series*, No. NG-T-4.2. Vienna: IAEA.

———. 2009. "Issues to Improve the Prospects of Financing Nuclear Power Plants." *IAEA Nuclear Energy Series*, No. NG-T-4.1. Vienna: IAEA.

———. 2010a. *Power Reactor Information System*. Vienna: IAEA.

———. 2010b. *International Status and Prospects for Nuclear Power*. Vienna: IAEA.

Jasper, James M. 1990. *Nuclear Politics: Energy and the State in the United States, Sweden, and France*. Princeton, NJ: Princeton University Press.

Jewell, Jessica. 2011. "Ready for Nuclear Energy? An Assessment of Capacities and Motivation for Launching New National Nuclear Programs." *Energy Policy* 39 (3): 1041–1055.

Jo, Dong-Joon, and Erik Gartzke. 2007. "Determinants of Nuclear Weapons Proliferation." *Journal of Conflict Resolution* 51 (1): 1–28.

Kalra, Rajiv, Glenn Henderson, and Gary Raines. 1993. "Effects of the Chernobyl Nuclear Accident on Utility Share Prices." *Quarterly Journal of Business and Economics* 32 (2): 52–77.

Klein, James, Gary Goertz, and Paul Diehl. 2006. "The New Rivalry Dataset: Procedures and Patterns." *Journal of Peace Research* 43 (3): 331–348.

Kroenig, Matthew. 2009a. "Exporting the Bomb: Why States Provide Sensitive Nuclear Assistance." *American Political Science Review* 103 (1): 113–133.

———. 2009b. "Importing the Bomb: Sensitive Nuclear Assistance and Nuclear Proliferation." *Journal of Conflict Resolution* 53 (2): 161–180.

Lee, Chien-Chiang, and Yi-Bin Chiu. 2011. "Oil Prices, Nuclear Energy Consumption, and Economic Growth: New Evidence Using Heterogeneous Panel Analysis." *Energy Policy* 39 (4): 2111–2120.

Maddison, Angus. 2009. *Historical Statistics of the World Economy: 1–2006 AD*; Table 2: GDP Levels, 1 AD—2006 AD. Available at: http://www.ggdc.net/MADDISON/oriindex.htm, under "Historical Statistics."

Malley, Michael S., and Tanya Ogilvie-White. 2009. "Nuclear Capabilities in Southeast Asia." *The Nonproliferation Review* 16 (1): 25–45.

Marshall, Monty, and Keith Jaggers. 2009. "Polity IV Project: Political Regime Characteristics and Transitions, 1800–2007." Severn, MD: Center for Systematic Peace.

Meyer, Stephen M. 1984. *The Dynamics of Nuclear Proliferation*. Chicago: University of Chicago Press.

MIIS (Monterey Institute of International Studies). 2009. "Egypt Profile." *NTI Research Library*. Available at: http://www.nti.org/country-profiles/egypt/nuclear/.

Miller, Steven E., and Scott D. Sagan. 2009. "Nuclear Power Without Nuclear Proliferation?" *Daedalus* 138 (4): 7–18.

MIT (Massachusetts Institute of Technology). 2003. *The Future of Nuclear Power: An Interdisciplinary Study*. Cambridge, MA: MIT.

———. 2009. *Update of the MIT 2003 Future of Nuclear Power*. Cambridge, MA: MIT.

Monitor's Editorial Board. 2011. "Germany's Costly Decision to Give up Nuclear Power." *Christian Science Monitor*, June 2.

Nelson, Paul. 2010. "Reassessing the Nuclear Renaissance." *Bulletin of the Atomic Scientists* 66: 11–22.

Nelson, Paul, and Christopher Sprecher. 2008. "What Determines the Extent of National Reliance on Civil Nuclear Power?" NSSPI-08-014. College Station, TX: Nuclear Security Science & Policy Institute, Texas A&M.

Nuclear Engineering International. 2010. "Turning Back to Bataan?" *Neimagazine.com*, June 1. Available at: http://www.neimagazine.com/story.asp?sc=2056536.

Ockwell, David. 2008. "Energy and Economic Growth: Grounding Our Understanding in Physical Reality." *Energy Policy* 36 (12): 4600–4604.

Ollapally, Deepa. 2001. "Mixed Motives in India's Search for Nuclear Status." *Asian Survey* 41 (6): 925–942.

Poneman, Daniel. 1982. *Nuclear Power in the Developing World*. London: George Allen & Unwin.

Rothwell, Geoffrey. 2009. "Market Power in Uranium Enrichment." *Science and Global Security* 17: 132–154.

Rublee, Maria Rost. 2009. *Nonproliferation Norms: Why States Choose Nuclear Restraint.* Athens: University of Georgia Press.

Sagan, Scott D. 1996/97. "Why Do States Build Nuclear Weapons? Three Models in Search of a Bomb." *International Security* 21 (3): 54–86.

———. 2010. "Rethinking Nuclear Latency." In *Forecasting Nuclear Proliferation in the 21st Century: Volume 1, The Role of Theory,* ed. William Potter. Stanford, CA: Stanford University Press, pp. 80–101.

Schneider, Mycle, Steve Thomas, Antony Froggatt, and Doug Koplow. 2009. *The World Nuclear Industry Status Report: With Particular Emphasis on Economic Issues.* Paper commissioned by the German Federal Ministry of Environment, Nature Conservation and Reactor Safety.

Sciolino, Elaine, and William Broad. 2006. "Iran's Civilian Nuclear Program May Link to Military, UN Says." *New York Times,* February 1. Available at: http://www.nytimes.com/2006/02/01/international/middleeast/31cndiran .html?pagewanted=all.

SCIR (Standing Committee on Industry and Resources), House of Representatives, Australian Parliament. 2007. "Value Adding—Fuel Cycle Services, Industries, Nuclear Power, Skills and Training in Australia." *Australia's Uranium: Greenhouse Friendly Fuel for an Energy Hungry World.* Parliament of Australia: House of Representatives.

Singh, Sonali, and Christopher Way. 2004. "The Correlates of Nuclear Proliferation: A Quantitative Test." *Journal of Conflict Resolution* 48 (6): 859–885.

Sjoberg, Lennart, and Britt-Marie Drottz-Sjoberg. 2008. "Risk Perception by Politicians and the Public." *Energy & Environment* 19: 455–483.

Solingen, Etel. 2007. *Nuclear Logics: Contrasting Paths in East Asia and the Middle East.* Princeton, NJ: Princeton University Press.

Sommers, Paul. 1980. "The Adoption of Nuclear Power." *The Bell Journal of Economics* 11 (1): 283–291.

Sovacool, Benjamin, and Marilyn Brown. 2009. "Competing Dimensions of Energy Security: An International Perspective." *Georgia Tech School of Public Policy Working Paper,* #45. January 13.

Squassoni, Sharon. 2009. *Nuclear Energy: Rebirth or Resuscitation?* Washington, DC: Carnegie Endowment for International Peace.

Toth, Ferenc, and Hans-Holger Rogner. 2006. "Oil and Nuclear Power: Past, Present, and Future." *Energy Economics* 28 (1): 1–25.

UNDP (United Nations Development Programme). 2007. *Human Development Report: Fighting Climate Change, Human Solidarity in a Divided World.* New York: Palgrave/Macmillan.

WNA (World Nuclear Association). 2009. *Emerging Nuclear Energy Countries.* London: World Nuclear Association.

———. 2010a. *Country Reports.* Available at:. http://www.world-nuclear.org/info/.

————. 2010b. *Nuclear Power in France.* August 30. Available at: http://www.world-nuclear.org/info/inf40.html.

————.2012. *Uranium Enrichment.* June. Available at: http://www.world-nuclear.org/info/inf28.html.

Zhou, Yun. 2010. "Why is China Going Nuclear?" *Energy Policy* 38 (7): 3755–3762.

2 Where, How, and Why Will Nuclear Happen?

Nuclear "Renaissance" Discourses from Buyers and Suppliers

Allison Macfarlane

S TARTING IN THE EARLY 2000s, THE AMERICAN NUCLEAR industry began discussing the coming "nuclear renaissance," jumping on the bandwagon of conventional wisdom that climate change would force the move toward energy technologies that are free of carbon dioxide emissions. At first, the expectation of this renaissance was confined to Western countries and particularly the United States. Within five or six years, though, the focus became global, prompted in part by studies showing that nuclear power could only make inroads into carbon emissions by expanding to countries that currently do not possess it (MIT 2003).

By 2011, more than fifty developing countries expressed interest in acquiring nuclear power reactor and associated fuel cycle technology, according to the International Atomic Energy Agency (IAEA).[1] Although none of these countries presently possesses nuclear power reactors, a few have attempted to acquire this technology but failed for a number of reasons. Others are moving more seriously down the road to acquisition. As discussed in Chapter 1, these countries represent a wide variety of technological, economic, demographic, cultural, and political backgrounds.

Envisioning a global expansion has given some in the business[2] pause: Many of the countries that do not have nuclear power but appear to want it are developing nations, many in parts of the world that are considered unstable by a number of Western nations. Can these countries handle nuclear power safely and securely? Can they be trusted to do so?

This line of inquiry raises fundamental subjective and normative questions about nuclear power expansion, in general: Why does nuclear power receive such attention? Why is it so attractive to countries, and why does its acquisition appear to pose a threat to others? Which countries could or should acquire nuclear power? Should there be limits? Who decides? After all, the Treaty on the Non-Proliferation of Nuclear Weapons (the Non-Proliferation Treaty) guarantees all signatories the right to peaceful nuclear technology associated with the nuclear fuel cycle under Article IV.

Historically, distinct normative claims have been associated with nuclear energy. It can be categorized as positive—through the electrification and therefore economic advancement of countries—as experienced by South Korea and Japan, for instance. Nuclear energy also can confer prestige and status upon its possessors. Alternatively, it can be cast in a negative light—via diversion of enrichment processes or spent nuclear fuel for the creation of nuclear weapons, as was the case with India, North Korea, and South Africa. More often, nuclear energy occupies a murky middle ground, positively associated with providing baseload carbon-free electricity, while at the same time posing safety (think Chernobyl, Three Mile Island, Fukushima Daiichi), environmental (absence of high-level nuclear waste repositories in any country), and proliferation risks.

This chapter argues that divergent subjective interpretations render nuclear energy as a fundamentally ambiguous technology. *Ambiguous* technologies have been defined by Brian Rappert, in discussing nonlethal weapons: "Their definition, function and effects are multiply conceived and contested. Key issues hinge on the claims made about the capacities of this arguably ambivalent class of technology" (Rappert 2001). As Wynne (1988) further remarks:

> It is not particularly interesting merely to point out that there are multiple, and apparently contradictory, discourses "describing" technology. The important point is to analyze how these discourses work in relation to one another and to the wider politics of technology.

In the wake of the nuclear crisis at the Fukushima Daiichi power plant in Japan in March 2011, the ambiguous nature of nuclear power is more evident than ever. Schmid (2011) points out that the "facts" of the accident, such as the amount of radiation released into water and air, the sequence of events in the reactors and spent fuel pools, and the environmental impact of the accident were not known or understood—not only by the public, but also by the Tokyo Electric Power Company (the plant owner), the Japanese government, and the IAEA. In fact, months after the accident these "facts" are still contested. The point is that nuclear power, a complex and potentially unpredictable technology, is both comprised of and produces multiple interpretations from the variety of disciplines and viewpoints of the experts and analysts who observe it. As such, it is a fundamentally ambiguous technology.

This chapter will examine the multiple discourses surrounding the acquisition of nuclear energy technology by countries that currently do not have it in an attempt to deconstruct the tangled threads of the debate over who might acquire it and how. Views of this technology reflect different perspectives on the motivations and self-conceptions of nations and significant actors within those nations at the center of this debate. Some people have pointed out that science and technology (S&T) studies have largely overlooked the reciprocal question: how do national S&T projects encode and reinforce particular conceptions of what a nation stands for (Jasanoff and Kim 2009)? Only by confronting such questions can we begin to understand why S&T policies take the form they take, why they often diverge radically across nation states, and how S&T policy making could better serve democratic interests in an era of globalization (Jasanoff and Kim 2009).

In an article examining Western views of nuclear weapons, Gusterson (2007) demonstrated how experts' claims of a complete distinction between the acquisition and management of nuclear weapons in Western and non-Western countries embody the fears and ambivalences about their own nuclear weapons, recast as problems presented by the developing world. In the same vein, this chapter examines the discourse on emerging nuclear energy countries to expose the self-conceptions of all actors involved. Thus, the larger purpose of this chapter is to illuminate the motivations and self-conceptions of key actors who have influence over the debate in order to complement formal analyses of the emerging nuclear landscape and to inform future policies towards the safe and secure diffusion of related technology.

Background on Case Countries

Five countries—the United Arab Emirates (UAE), Jordan, Turkey, Vietnam, and Indonesia—form the basis for the discourse analysis in this chapter. Of these countries, the UAE has the most advanced nuclear program. It has established a nuclear utility, Emirates Nuclear Energy Corporation; a regulator, headed by a former U.S. Nuclear Regulatory Commission member; and an international advisory board, with Hans Blix, the former IAEA director general at the helm. The UAE also completed a deal with the South Korean company KEPCo to purchase four APR-1400 reactors for US$20 billion. It also agreed to pay an additional US$20 billion for KEPCo to operate the plants for sixty years and provide a training program for Emiratis (Daya and Kang 2009). The first reactor is slated to come on line in 2017. Furthermore, the UAE completed a 123 Agreement[3] with the United States that, as discussed in other chapters of this volume, has been deemed a "gold standard" by which to judge other nuclear agreements. In it, Abu Dhabi pledged to forgo both enrichment and reprocessing capabilities (USGPO 2009).

Jordan, a resource-poor country, imports about 95 percent of the energy it needs and has been significantly affected by swings in contemporary oil and natural gas prices (Luck 2010b). The Jordanian government intends to exploit newly discovered indigenous uranium deposits with the assistance of the French nuclear company Areva. It also recently signed a deal with the Korea Atomic Energy Research Institute (KAERI) and Daewoo of South Korea to construct a 5-megawatt (MW) research reactor, and is in the process of selecting a contractor to build a large 750–1,100 MW reactor near Aqaba. The three finalists are Areva-Mitsubishi (a French-Japanese consortium), AECL of Canada, and AtomStroyExport of Russia (*World Nuclear News* 2010a). The United States and Jordan are forging ahead with a separate 123 Agreement, which has been contentious because Jordan (unlike the UAE) insists on retaining the national right to enrich uranium in the future (Solomon 2010)— a right guaranteed by the Non-Proliferation Treaty.

Both Turkey and Vietnam recently selected reactor vendors. Turkey engaged AtomStroyExport to build four 1.2-gigawatt (GW) light water reactors in Akkuyu on the Mediterranean Sea at a projected cost of US$18–20 billion. Turkey plans for these reactors to begin operation between 2016 and 2019. The Russian company will own 51 percent of shares in the plant, provide the fuel, and take back spent fuel for reprocessing (*Hürriyet Daily News* 2010a; World Tribune.com 2010). Turkey also is considering an offer by KEPCo to build reactors at its Sinop site on the Black Sea (AFP 2010). Similar to Turkey, Vietnam plans to construct two plants—a northern one at Vinh Hai, for which the government signed an agreement with a Japanese consortium to build two reactors; and a southern plant at Phuoc Dinh with reactors slated to be built by AtomStroyExport. Vietnam expects to have the first plant operational by 2020, with the rest to follow in the 2021–2025 time frame (*World Nuclear News* 2010c). The United States is negotiating a 123 Agreement with Vietnam, which, like Turkey, insists on maintaining all potential fuel cycle technological opportunities, including enrichment and reprocessing (Steinglass 2010).

Of these five countries, Indonesia is probably the furthest away from realizing nuclear-powered electricity. The president stated that Indonesia will not have nuclear power any time soon (Lee 2010). A site proposed for Central Java island at Muria came under intense local opposition. As a result, the government is exploring a new site on Bangka Island. Indonesia has three operating research reactors, whereas Turkey and Vietnam each have one.

Buyers

What motivates countries to want to acquire nuclear power reactors? Though many countries have expressed interest in acquiring nuclear power, apparently they do not become serious buyers of power reactor technology unless their gross domestic product (GDP) is greater than US$87 billion a year (CIA 2009). This makes sense, given that a single large reactor costs roughly US$4 billion, or a significant percentage of the GDP of many buyer countries. In fact, countries that have a nominal GDP above US$87 billion tend to already have nuclear power, to have considered it and decided against, or to have made yet unsuccessful efforts to pursue it (Gourley and Stulberg, Chapter 1 in this volume). However, correlations between GDP or other objective indicators alone cannot explain the appeal of nuclear power, given the wide range of views held both across and within national communities. Therefore, in order to examine the discourse surrounding the appeal of nuclear energy, this analysis distinguishes the statements of government officials and scientists from buyer countries from those of analysts outside these countries. A number of recurring themes emerge from the wealth of writings on aspiring nuclear energy countries.

Motivations for Acquiring Reactors

All countries studied put the need to address future—and growing—energy demand near the top of their list of reasons to pursue nuclear power. These countries have projected their domestic electricity needs for a few decades and are alarmed by the increase in electricity that will be required to continue or ramp up the pace of economic development. For instance, a representative from Electricity of Vietnam projected that demand for electricity would increase rapidly in the future. They expect that by 2020 their coal and natural gas will be exhausted and their water to produce hydroelectricity will be fully utilized. Accordingly, the representative stated that it was necessary to find other ways to generate electricity, with nuclear power standing out as the best option (*Vietnam News* 2009).

Jordan's Atomic Energy Commission chair, Khaled Toukan, "pointed out that electricity demand is expected to double from the current 2,200 megawatts (MW) to 4,500 MW within the next decade, a number that is on pace to quadruple by 2030" (Luck 2010b). For resource-poor countries like Jordan that spend up to 13 percent of GDP on energy, nuclear power is expected to provide an important level of energy security (Luck 2010b).

For some countries, nuclear energy would provide economic security. The UAE intends to use its oil and natural gas resources to gain foreign currency and not to produce domestic electricity.[4] The UAE has the ability to cover the high capital costs of a nuclear power plant, so this strategy makes sense for them. Abu Dhabi intends to sell some of the electricity it produces to neighboring countries such as Saudi Arabia; Jordan has the same strategy (BBC 2010b). Other countries, such as Vietnam, intend to develop an indigenous self-sufficiency in nuclear energy technology and may eventually seek to export that technology:

> Vietnam aims to master nuclear power plant design technology during the final phase of the program. The country wants to partner with foreign companies to design its nuclear power plants with Vietnamese companies participating in nuclear power projects to account for 30–40% of the total construction value. (*World Nuclear News* 2010c)

Similarly, most nuclear energy aspirants mention the need to reduce carbon dioxide emissions as a reason to pursue nuclear power instead of fossil fuels. For a number of Middle Eastern countries, in particular, nuclear power supply offers a ready source of electricity for water desalination plants, especially as freshwater supplies begin to dwindle.[5]

Finally, prestige and political power play a large and often unacknowledged role in the desire for nuclear power. In an unexpected show of candor, a scientific advisor to the Vietnam agency for nuclear safety noted, "Eight nuclear reactors with a total capacity of 16,000 MW are expected to help

Vietnam join the 15 leading countries in the field of nuclear power. Everybody knows the respect a country receives once it owns nuclear power" (Hien 2009). Prestige is important both for international and domestic audiences, because it raises the standing of a country with its neighboring states and the larger international community—all of which plays well with domestic audiences.

Analysts in existing nuclear energy countries acknowledge some of the justifications for acquisition of reactors provided by the buyers, including the predicted growth in energy demand and the need for economic security and development. For instance, Dan Yurman suggests that "the UAE plans to build an estimated 4–5 GWe of nuclear-powered electricity by 2017 to meet three needs; 1) replace natural gas for water desalinization, 2) supply power to its growing aluminum industry, and 3) turn the UAE into a regional supplier of electricity especially to the Kingdom of Saudi Arabia" (Yurman 2009). These analysts also acknowledge the role of prestige in boosting the appeal of nuclear energy. As noted by one outside observer, "the UAE also gains prestige in the region, especially as it continues to shed Saudi dominance. It also serves as hefty leverage against Iran's growing clout in the region, empowering the UAE, while serving as a model for peaceful nuclear development" (Cala 2009).

Outside observers often view the situation differently, noting that civilian nuclear energy development offers a convenient hedge for nuclear weapons development. In particular, Middle Eastern countries are discussed as wanting to counterbalance Iran's desired nuclear weapons capabilities. For instance, analysts at the Center for American Progress claim: "Suddenly, after multiple energy crises over the 60 years of the nuclear age, these countries that control over one-fourth of the world's oil supplies are investing in nuclear power programs. This is not about energy; it is a nuclear hedge against Iran" (Cirincione 2007).

Arguments Against Acquisition

The arguments *against* acquiring nuclear reactors are perhaps as interesting as the reasons offered *for* obtaining them. Both foreign and domestic players have entered into the discourse against aspirant countries purchasing nuclear reactors. For example, both foreign and domestic opponents have cited the cost of the plants as reason not to purchase them.[6] Both types make claims about safety issues as well. These critiques focus on the absence of a safety culture among nuclear energy aspirants:

Foreign critique: Some states may diligently implement all the recommendations for safety, physical protection, and regulatory infrastructure, but they could lag in developing safety and security cultures, which are necessary for reliable and safe operation of nuclear power plants. (Squassoni 2009)

Domestic critique: However, some members of the Vietnamese National Assembly have voiced concerns over . . . Vietnam's lack of nuclear power experience and infrastructure. (*World Nuclear News* 2009)

The French have stepped into this debate by criticizing the foreign critics:

France on Monday called upon the developed world not to close the door on the havenots by restricting access to civil nuclear energy and termed the North's concerns about the inability of the South to safely manage atomic power "incredibly contemptuous." (Dikshit 2010)

Other safety concerns arise out of domestic fears about the effects of earthquakes on nuclear power plants and the potential for Chernobyl-type accidents (Trong and Barta 2009; Tanter and Ng 2010).

Security issues remain a central concern to those outside the buyer countries. The general issue is summed up by Sharon Squassoni, who argues: "New nuclear capabilities, particularly in some geographic locations, could increase the probability of proliferation and could pose security risks because of political instability or the existence of terrorist groups" (Squassoni 2009). Government corruption is a concern of domestic critics in Indonesia, where senior officials associated with the nuclear regulatory agency were jailed for corruption.[7]

The main foreign concern about the acquisition of nuclear energy in countries that do not yet possess the technology is focused on the link between nuclear energy and nuclear weapons. Some critics have even referred to nuclear power plants as "bomb starter kits" (Constantine 2010). These critics argue that the country in question could acquire the know-how to make nuclear weapons, since "the same people that help you design and build nuclear reactors have many of the skill sets you will need if you are going to build a nuclear weapon" (Murphy 2007). There is also an expectation that these skills can affect the politics in the neighborhood:

Even if the majority of new nuclear plans never come to fruition, mere high-level discussion of the nuclear energy option can lead neighboring states to develop nuclear technology themselves. The links between nuclear energy and nuclear weapons create strong incentives for states to respond to any nascent nuclear weapons capability in a rival by preparing against that eventuality. (Sasikumar 2009)

Equity

The issue of equity among countries plays a special role in the acquisition of nuclear power technology. Many nuclear energy aspirant countries have insisted on the right to peaceful nuclear technology conferred by the Non-Proliferation Treaty (Davutoglu 2009; *Xinhua News* 2009; al-Khalidi 2010). The nuclear energy countries have mostly ignored the issue of equity, with the exception of France, which has explicitly recognized the right of all countries to possess nuclear power. A top French diplomat stated, "France supports Jordan's right to enrich uranium as outlined in the nuclear Non-Proliferation Treaty" (Luck 2010a).

The equity issue became more complicated during negotiations between the United States and Jordan over the 123 Agreement. The United States initially insisted that Jordan give up its right to enrich uranium as the Emiratis did in their 123 Agreement with the United States.[8] Jordan, however, balked, as the government envisions selling nuclear fuel derived from indigenous uranium deposits at some point in the future. A senior Jordanian official stated, "Such an agreement would limit Jordan's ambition to become a 'regional nuclear fuel supply and export center'" (Solomon 2010). For Jordan, an additional concern was that it would become dependent on one supplier and therefore be subject to that supplier's whims. The head of Jordan's Atomic Energy Commission, Khaled Toukan, stated, "In this sense, Jordan will lose the source of strength in its nuclear program and depend on America in the enrichment process, consequently losing control over the development of the program" (BBC 2010a). In light of this staunch commitment, the United States was compelled to acknowledge, albeit reluctantly, Jordan's nuclear rights. As stated by Tom D'Agostino, U.S. Undersecretary for Nuclear Security, "We believe quite strongly that nations have the right to develop their civil programs for civil purposes . . . We are not trying to tell other nations that you can't have enrichment" (Tirone and Razzouk 2010).

Suppliers

Those who are looking to sell nuclear technology to countries that do not yet have it are motivated by a number of factors beyond the bottom line. Three main themes are apparent in the discourse of the nuclear industry: the ability of the vendor country to project power abroad; the link to other industries; and the ability to secure long-term, high-value contracts. In addition, the suppliers have developed unique strategies to market their products.

The major vendors in the nuclear industry and the governments that back them are a small group. They include reactor vendors, such as Areva (France), Rosatom/AtomStroyExport (Russia), KEPCo/KAERI/Daewoo (South Korea), Hitachi/Toshiba/Mitsubishi (Japan), Westinghouse/GE (U.S./Japan), and AECL (Canada). The Russian, South Korean, French, Canadian, and Japanese companies are all nationalized. As such, they generally and seamlessly represent the interests of the nations that back them. France and Japan have gone as far as to establish government agencies to initiate discussions with interested purchasers before engaging respective nuclear vendors (Campbell 2010). For these countries, reactor deals are often preceded by state visits from the prime ministers or presidents of the seller country.

As a result, the projection of political power is clearly tied to the sale of nuclear technology. Neil Alexander, president of the Organization of CANDU Industries, a Canadian group, articulated this connection when he noted, "If we can make a commercial success of that [reactor sales], we are guaranteed superpower status" (Spears 2010). President Nicolas Sarkozy of France stated, "these great national companies have not only the reputation and image of France in their hands, but also its economic and industrial future" (Hollinger 2010).

Countries use nuclear technology sales, nationalized or not, to send political messages to other nations. Both the French and the Americans hope to send a message to Iran through their agreements with the UAE. For instance, Vann Van Diepen, acting Assistant Secretary for International Security and Nonproliferation at the U.S. State Department, "called the proposed US-UAE nuclear sharing accord a 'significant non-proliferation achievement' and put it in 'marked contrast' to Iran" (Stanek 2009). One French government official noted that the agreement with the UAE ". . . is the best way to show Iran that we are not against the Middle East having nuclear technology" (Hollinger 2009).

Sometimes experts within the buyer countries are aware of the influence provided by nuclear deals. For instance, several Turkish scholars and politicians appreciate the influence that Russia may gain over Turkey through the sales of nuclear power plants. Emre Iseri, an academic at Kadir Has University in Istanbul, noted:

Turkey is 70 percent dependent on Russian natural gas . . . Giving the nuclear tender to Russia would mean a double dependency. One has to take into consideration that Moscow is using energy as a foreign-policy tool. So accepting the outcome of last year's tender [would have meant] that Turkey would have a hard time making policy without Russia's approval. (Bilgic 2009)

A number of nuclear technology deals are apparently associated with sales of military hardware, other energy resources, and political support. For instance, Russian reactor deals with Vietnam and India were accompanied by sales of fighter jets and other military equipment. Russia sold reactors to China at the same time that Beijing agreed to purchase natural gas from Russia. U.S. Secretary of State Hillary Clinton, while in talks with Vietnam over a 123 Agreement, lent support to Vietnam in its tiff with China over control of the South China Sea (Steinglass 2010; Matlack and Humber 2010). France explicitly acknowledged the connection between sales of nuclear technology and other technologies when a government official stated, "France also believes that there could be huge wider commercial gains to be had from nuclear deals, especially in defence and infrastructure" (Hollinger 2009).

The financial value of dependable, long-term contracts also cannot be understated. As Neil Alexander, the Canadian reactor supporter, noted, ". . . the real value in this business lies in selling, servicing and operating reactors" (Spears 2010). KEPCo, the South Korean company, is receiving roughly the same amount to build four reactors as to operate them for sixty years—US$20 billion. Sixty years is a very long-term contract that will supply the company with certainty in income. The large vendors in these cases are not just sharing the wealth. Smaller companies that subcontract to the large ones also see opportunities. For instance, the president of the U.S.-U.A.E. Business Council stated, "The relationships here are obviously going to be mostly in the area of being subcontractors, but getting certified and approved on the Korean supply chain would be a big part of what this initial thrust is about . . . We see this as a much bigger, broader opportunity in the long run" (Stanton 2010).

Observations

Based on the themes emerging from the discourse and on additional empirical analysis of the current situation, a number of observations can be made about the acquisition of nuclear technology by nuclear energy aspirants and their location within the larger geopolitical setting.

Focus of Buyers

Prestige looms large in the spectrum of reasons to acquire nuclear power, as it operates at both international and domestic levels. Much has been written about the prestige and allure of nuclear technology. Byrne and Hoffman note that "nuclear power continues to be evaluated in the "future tense", that is, in terms of what it will bring rather than what it has already wrought or what it requires from society to maintain operation" (Byrne and Hoffman 1996). Nuclear power carries with it a sense of modernity (even though it is a sixty-year-old technology) and a sense of power from its association with nuclear weapons. Kinsella (2005) notes that nuclear technology possesses an impression of mystery and secrecy: "Nuclear science, technologies, and policies, products of human discourse, are widely portrayed as arcane, difficult, and out of the intellectual reach of ordinary people." He points out that nuclear technologies do what is referred to in the science studies literature as "boundary-work" (Gieryn 1983) by establishing a cognitive line between those who have this technology and those who do not. Moreover, Kinsella states that "geopolitical hierarchies are driven by a competition for nuclear superiority, or at least by a striving for membership in the 'nuclear club' (symbolized by the possession of a nuclear 'club' of another kind)" (Kinsella 2005). Proops (2001) explains the allure of nuclear technology in comparison to other energy sources:

> Nuclear power offers 'control' over the very basic building blocks of nature; it is 'modern', being the latest technique of supplying electricity; it is 'clean', with no need to produce smoke and ash; it is 'assured', with small quantities of fuel being needed. Altogether it is an appropriate technique for a centralized, interventionist and modernizing state.

The desire for nuclear power, therefore, is not exclusive to wealthy and powerful nations, but also to those aspiring to acquire more power and wealth.

The allure of nuclear technology is strong because for a number of emerging nuclear energy countries, the current grid size is not suitable to acquisition of one of the existing large reactor models. To date, reactors have been constructed primarily in large sizes—above 750 megawatts-electric (MWe), with most over 1,000 MWe. Reactors like Areva's EPR, at 1,600 MWe, were actually designed for European and U.S. markets, not for developing countries (Hollinger 2010). For countries with national grids less than 10 gigawatts-electric (GWe), it will not be possible to add one of these reactors to the respective electricity mix. Jordan is a glaring example. With a national grid of only 2.2

GW, its grid capacity will need to expand significantly to accommodate a single reactor. In fact, developing nations are, in general, better suited for deploying small modular reactors with generating capacities between 100 and 300 MWe. Despite the feasibility of small modular reactors for less-developed nations, and growing industry interest in these reactors, their economic and technical viability are still not assured (Macfarlane 2010).

Prestige as a motivator for nuclear power acquisition is linked to the desire for equity, stated by a number of emerging nuclear countries. The prestige conferred by nuclear technology can bring a sense of parity with global powers. Access to this technology, with its links to the most powerful weapons in the world, brings with it entrée to secrets possessed by the rich and powerful.

Emerging nuclear energy countries may view the historical cases of acquisition of nuclear power technology as allegories for themselves. Beyond the experience of the nuclear weapons states, which could acquire nuclear energy technology without much technical difficulty, and those of the former Soviet Union, which had nuclear power technology "given" to them, the balance of countries that have acquired nuclear power technology[9] correlate with those countries that have had larger economies than those that have perpetually been in the "wannabe" class: Bangladesh, Egypt, Libya, Turkey, the Philippines (Surrey 1988). Accordingly, it may prove in the future that the countries which are most successful at acquiring a robust nuclear power program are those which possess equally robust economies.

In emerging nuclear energy countries, not all nations are created equal. Countries located in the Middle East have sensitivities to the proliferation risks associated with nuclear power that those in other regions do not. Most of the Middle Eastern countries, when referring to nuclear energy, use the term "peaceful." For instance, Hamad al-Kaabi, the UAE's permanent representative to the IAEA, noted "it was concluded that *peaceful* nuclear power-generation represents an environmentally promising and commercially competitive option that could make a significant contribution to the UAE's economy and future energy security" [emphasis added].[10] The head of the Jordanian Atomic Energy Agency stated, "The Kingdom's *peaceful* nuclear power programme will not only diversify the power mix . . ." [emphasis added] (Luck 2010b). Even actors from vendor countries use the term "peaceful" in addressing the acquisition of nuclear energy by these countries. For instance, Janet Sanderson of the U.S. State Department stated, "They are offering the international community an alternative example of how to move forward on *peaceful* nuclear power" [emphasis added] (Stanek 2009). By contrast, the term "peaceful" does not resonate in the discourse surrounding Asian countries' acquisition.

Several buyer countries are deciding whether to acquire nuclear power technology by allowing democratic debate on the issue; others are not. Significant public debate has occurred, for instance, in Indonesia (AFP 2007). The government has responded to the public's concerns about safety issues by both putting off any near-term decisions about adopting nuclear energy and considering an alternate locus for reactor siting (Lee 2010; Kusuma 2010). Turkey also has endured controversy over the acquisition of nuclear power. Significant demonstrations have occurred, with a number of protesters awaiting trial for "wearing clothes against nuclear energy" (*Hürriyet Daily News* 2010b). A few members of Vietnam's National Assembly have questioned the safety, potential environmental impact, and high costs of nuclear power, but no public opposition has been observed (Trong and Barta 2009; AFP 2009; *World Nuclear News* 2009). Jordan and the UAE are notable for their lack of dissenting opinions and democratic debate over acquisition of nuclear power.

Interestingly, in response to the accident in Fukushima, Japan, in March 2011, all five countries examined in this chapter reaffirmed their faith in nuclear power technology and plans to move forward (see, for example, Hang 2011). For instance, Jordan's Khaled Toukan, Minister of Energy and Mineral Resources, announced, "We are still set for our dates as previously envisioned and we are watching the Japan situation closely as it unfolds" (Luck 2011).

Indonesia and Turkey experienced the most conspicuous public outcry against nuclear power in reaction to the Fukushima Daiichi accident (for instance, see *Trend* 2011). Yet the Turkish government has remained steadfast in the pursuit of nuclear energy. Moreover, the UAE nuclear regulator required the contractor, KEPCo, to perform additional studies to ensure the safety of the planned reactors (Yee 2011).

The overwhelmingly positive response, in the face of public criticism and decisions by some countries (e.g., Germany and Switzerland) to abandon nuclear power altogether, affirmed the importance of acquiring nuclear power technology to the self-image of these countries, as well as the belief that they will somehow overcome the obstacles that confronted Japan, a highly technologically advanced country. Indeed, even though some of these countries are at risk for large-magnitude earthquakes and tsunamis (Indonesia and Turkey are located in seismically active regions), they remain confident in dealing with these challenges. For instance, Indonesia's Ferhat Aziz of the National Atomic Energy Agency boldly claimed, "There are many places in Indonesia that are safe . . . We are not worried. Japan is a different story" (Deutsch 2011). Such statements not only ignore the potential cultural, societal, and technical problems in Japan that may have contributed to this accident, but also betray a national myopia concerning plausible challenges that may lie ahead.

Focus of Suppliers

There is a stark contrast between the focuses of supplier nations. In national debates, those countries with nationalized nuclear industries tend to focus on selling their product. Other issues such as security and proliferation potential, though at times acknowledged, are not central. In the United States, the potential for nuclear aspirants to become weapons proliferators is central to the national discourse. In 2010, the U.S. House of Representatives held two hearings on the global expansion of nuclear power, and the debate was largely over whether these countries should be "allowed" to have access to this technology through the rubric of the 123 Agreements. Expert opinion in the United States mirrors this focus on proliferation. The U.S. nuclear industry, however, is generally confident that its solid nonproliferation credentials can hold and optimistic about developing novel technologies as a barrier to proliferation. It also presses Congress to remove legal liability hurdles that often undermine the competitiveness of U.S. companies in global nuclear technology markets (Banks et al. 2010).

In some of the vendor countries, little evidence of the promised nuclear renaissance can be found. Russia has eleven reactors under construction, while South Korea has five (IAEA 2010). These countries have an active nuclear industry. By contrast, in Japan, formerly with two reactors under construction, in France with one under construction, in the United States just beginning to break ground on two reactors, and in Canada with none under construction, the renaissance looks quite different. In fact, in the United States and much of Europe, the trend is to increase existing reactor capacity through upgrades and life extensions rather than by building new reactor capacity.[11] Many reactors in the United States, for instance, have received twenty-year life extensions over the forty years they were originally licensed to operate. Now the discussion is turning to an additional twenty-year extension—to eighty years for plant lifetimes (Szilard, Planchon, and Busby 2009). Economic recession has hit the industry hard as well (Pfeifer 2010), resulting in decreased energy demand. In the United States, the current and expected low price of natural gas due to the increase in shale gas extraction has led Exelon nuclear utility CEO John Rowe to predict a lack of new nuclear construction for at least a decade (*Bloomberg News* 2010). Failures on the back end of the nuclear fuel cycle in some vendor countries have compounded a sense of lack of progress. The Obama administration in the United States withdrew the license application for the Yucca Mountain high-level nuclear waste repository, and the startup of the Japanese spent fuel reprocessing plant in Rokkasho has been delayed yet again. Finally, in response to the Fukushima Daiichi accident, some countries, such as Germany and Switzerland, plan to opt out of nuclear power altogether once they secure alternative sources of electricity. For many of these supplier countries, the dire situation at home has forced the focus onto potential buyers, especially emerging nuclear energy countries. This is not the first time the nuclear industry has looked abroad to maintain the industry. For example, sales of plants to South Korea, Argentina, and China in the 1980s were "critically important" to supplier countries, which had few new orders from traditional customers in the aftermath of the energy spikes in the 1970s and the Three Mile Island accident (Surrey 1988, p. 464).

Back End of the Fuel Cycle
In the discourse on acquisition of nuclear power in emerging nuclear countries, one point of discussion is notable for the paucity of mention: the back end of the nuclear fuel cycle. In the past, the nuclear industry often ignored issues associated with nuclear waste disposal in the planning of new nuclear power plants, especially in the United States (Walker 2009). This tradition has continued in the United States, with reactor lifetime extensions granted without a final solution to the high-level radioactive waste estimated to be produced. Nonetheless, a few actors in some countries, all in Asia, have mentioned nuclear waste issues. An official from the Malaysian Nuclear Agency noted:

> We do have a waste management centre to cater to low and medium level nuclear waste. Countries like Finland, Sweden, and Switzerland have experimental plots for nuclear waste disposal. If we want to use nuclear power we have to look for suitable sites to dispose nuclear waste. (Menon 2010)

Some people, including this Malaysian official, talk about waste in relation to nuclear weapons through the reprocessing of spent nuclear fuel (Menon 2010; *Xinhua News* 2010). Still others have mentioned the closed fuel cycle as an avenue to secure future nuclear fuel: "We do not need to dispose of nuclear waste because it can be used again as a source of fuel for nuclear power plants after being stored for some time" (*Antara News* 2010). Russia plans to offer spent fuel take-back to its buyers, thus solving the waste problem for these customers (*World Nuclear News* 2010b).

Conclusions

This is an interesting moment in the history of nuclear power. Nuclear energy, an ambiguous technology designed for large, rich nations, is being sought after by lesser-developed countries. Perhaps this is the dawn of a nuclear renaissance, not in the countries that have traditionally owned nuclear reactors but in countries across Eurasia and the Middle East, some of which possess no nuclear power plants. This "displaced" renaissance results from the coalescence of a number of factors. The lack of a "promised" resurgence in the traditional markets has sent vendors searching for business elsewhere. Vendor countries see nuclear technology sales as a way to gain power and influence over buyer countries. The rising energy demand of a number of moderate-GDP countries and the desire to increase development, in conjunction with a global push for decreasing carbon dioxide emissions, has led these states to consider nuclear power. Yet each country examined in this study has its own set of reasons for pursuing nuclear power.

Despite all claims to the contrary, nuclear power remains an ambiguous technology with respect to its links to nuclear weapons. If it were not, then little attention would be paid to Iran's nuclear power plant, enrichment facilities, and associated industries. Much of the discourse surrounding acquisition of nuclear power by aspirants, both within and outside of buyer countries, focuses on the relationship of nuclear power and nuclear weapons.

Nuclear power also can be viewed as ambiguous because it represents a modern technology, bringing electricity that provides economic development. At the same time, as the experiences of Three Mile Island, Chernobyl, and now Fukushima Daiichi illustrate, it can be an extremely dangerous technology, with the potential to adversely affect large portions of the world.

Nuclear energy technology can bring prestige and power to a buyer, both by raising its image domestically and by demonstrating to neighbors and other nations that it has the ability to manage this complex and powerful technology. This prestige, in turn, is expected to translate into greater equity and economic prosperity for the aspirant country. As well, sales of nuclear technology provide suppliers with potential leverage over the buyer nations that, in turn, become indebted to them for a long period and may have to rely heavily on these suppliers to maintain and operate the facilities.

As a result, it is to the advantage of both buyers and suppliers to hype the power, prestige, and ambiguity associated with nuclear technology. Is acquisition of nuclear energy technology a prelude to acquisition of nuclear weapons? The answer "maybe" suits the buyers, as it increases power and prestige both within and outside their borders. "Maybe" also suits suppliers, who may use this ambiguity to sell their product. Nuclear energy technology is a way of buying ambiguity—in terms of political power. It is the ambiguity of nuclear energy technology that makes it of interest to non-nuclear nations. Without the existence of this ambiguity, nuclear power would be a much less sought-after energy technology.

Nuclear power is, after all, one of the most costly sources of baseload electricity on the market, as compared to natural gas, coal, and hydropower. Even wind is at least as competitive in some regions. New nuclear build suffers from significantly longer lead times for construction compared to fossil fuel plants, in addition to the years of regulatory planning and institutional requirements to establish a nuclear program in a country that presently lacks one. The associated potential liabilities from an accident, which always need to be underwritten by the government of the country hosting the reactors, are an additional drawback. Nonetheless, there is strong support for nuclear in the countries pursuing it. Nuclear promises prestige, increased economic advantage, power, and a playing field closer to level for many countries. It similarly assures money and power to those who sell it. It is this ambiguous nature of nuclear power that is finally attractive to all.

Notes

1. According to Jose Goldemberg, these prospective nuclear nations include Algeria, Bahrain, Bangladesh, Belarus, Bolivia, Chile, Croatia, Dominican Republic, Egypt, El Salvador, Estonia, Georgia, Ghana, Greece, Haiti, Indonesia, Israel, Jamaica, Jordan, Kazakhstan, Kenya, Kuwait, Latvia, Libya, Malaysia, Mongolia, Morocco, Myanmar (Burma), Namibia, Nigeria, Oman, Peru, Philippines, Poland, Qatar, Saudi Arabia, Senegal, Singapore, Sri Lanka, Sudan, Syria, Tanzania, Thailand, Tunisia, Turkey, United Arab Emirates, Uruguay, Venezuela, Vietnam, and Yemen (Goldemberg 2009). The list continues to grow—add Uganda (Mwasa 2009).

2. By "in the business" I mean to imply not only the nuclear industry, but also the policy experts, governmental officials, scholars, and interested public who have voiced opinions on this topic.

3. From section 123 of the U.S. Atomic Energy Act of 1954. These agreements are required to be signed before any transfer of nuclear technology can occur.

4. An economist at an Abu Dhabi-based bank: "These projects will of course enable the UAE to save its oil and gas wealth for future generations. This means the UAE will be able to export oil and gas for a long time and increase such exports to meet growing world demand in the long term as demand for both is projected to surge. By doing so, the UAE is preserving its wealth and at the same time maximizing its income in the long run" (Kawach 2009).

5. Luck, *Zawya*, September 17, 2009.

6. Dalberg Group Development Advisors, for the Nonproliferation Policy Education Center (World Nuclear News 2009).

7. Radio Australia, panel on "Indonesia's Govt revives interest in nuclear power plant plan," January 28, 2010.

8. Referred to as the "gold standard" 123 Agreement.

9. These include Argentina, Belgium, Brazil, Canada, Finland, Germany, Iran, Japan, Republic of Korea, Mexico, Netherlands, Spain, Sweden, Switzerland, and Taiwan. The former Soviet states with nuclear power plants are Armenia, Bulgaria, Czech Republic, Hungary, Romania, Slovakia, Slovenia, Ukraine. South Africa, India, and Pakistan are not listed, as they are or were nuclear weapons states.

10. Sambidge, Arabianbusiness.com, November 25, 2008.

11. Switzerland, Germany, Finland, Sweden, Spain, and Belgium have or are increasing generating capacity at their plants (WNA 2010).

References

AFP (Agence France-Presse). 2007. "Thousands Protest Against Indonesian Nuclear Plant." *ABC News* (Australia), June 12.

———. 2009. "Vietnam Approves First Nuclear Power Plants," November 25.

———. 2010. "S. Korea, Turkey Sign Deal on Nuclear Power Plant," March 10.

al-Khalidi, Suleiman. 2010. "Jordan Nuclear Deal Held Up by U.S. Curbs—Sources." *Reuters*, July 2.

Antara News. 2010. "House Okays Nuke Plants," March 16.

Banks, John P., Charles K. Ebinger, Michael M. Moodie, Lawrence Scheinman, and Sharon Squassoni. 2010. "Nonproliferation and the Nuclear 'Renaissance': The Contribution and Responsibilities of the Nuclear Industry." *Brookings Policy Brief* 10-01 (May).

BBC (British Broadcasting Corporation). 2010a. "Jordan Atomic Energy Official on Commitment to Nuclear Programme." *BBC News*, April 5.

———. 2010b. "Jordan's Programme Takes 'Centre Stage' at Regional Nuclear Summit." *BBC News*, March 23.

Bilgic, Taylan. 2009. "Turkey's Radioactive Waltz with Russia Comes to an End." *Radio Free Europe/Radio Liberty*, November 23.

Bloomberg News. 2010. "Low Natural Gas Prices Likely to Delay US Nuclear Plant Construction." *National Post*, September 11.

Byrne, John, and Steven Hoffman. 1996. "The Ideology of Progress and the Globalization of Nuclear Power." In *Governing the Atom: The Politics of Risk*, eds. John Byrne and Steven Hoffman. New Brunswick, Canada: Transaction Publishers.

Cala, Anres. 2009. "Editorial." *Energy Tribune*, December 30.

Campbell, Keith. 2010. "Nuclear Essential as a Future Energy Source, Says French Group." *Creamer Media's Engineering News*, March 8.

CIA (Central Intelligence Agency). 2009. *CIA World Factbook.* Langley, VA: Central Intelligence Agency.

Cirincione, Joseph, and Uri Leventer. 2007. "The Middle East's Nuclear Surge," Center for American Progress, August 21.

Constantine, Zoi. 2010. "UAE Meets Nuclear Gold Standard." *The National*, February 14.

Davutoglu, Ahmet. 2009. Interview with the Turkish Foreign Minister. *Press TV*, October 6.

Daya, Ayesha, and Shinye Kang. 2009. "Korea Electric Surges on $20 Billion U.A.E. Order." *Bloomberg.com*, December 28.

Deutsch, Anthony. 2011. "Indonesia Insists Nuclear Plans are Safe." *Financial Times*, March 17.

Dikshit, Sandeep. 2010. "Give South Access to Civil Nuclear Technology: France." *The Hindu*, March 9.

Gieryn, T. F. 1983. "Boundary-work and the Demarcation of Science from Nonscience: Strains and Interests in Professional Ideologies of Science." *American Sociological Review* 48 (6): 781–795.

Goldemberg, Jose. 2009. "Nuclear energy in developing countries." *Daedalus* 138 (4): 71–80.

Gusterson, Hugh. 2007. "Nuclear Weapons and the Other in the Western Imagination." In *People of the Bomb*, ed. Hugh Gusterson. Minneapolis: University of Minnesota Press.

Hang, Thu. 2011. "Vietnam to Proceed with Nuclear Power Plants." *Thanh Nien News*, March 17. Available at: http://www.thanhniennews.com/2010/Pages/20110317154038.aspx.

Hien, Pham Duy. 2009. Editorial. *Vietnam News*, December 13.

Hollinger, Peggy. 2009. "UAE's Ambitions Set Trend for Regional Players to Follow." *Financial Times*, September 11.

———. 2010. "Cooling Ambitions." *Financial Times*, October 20.

Hürriyet Daily News. 2010a. "Lawmakers Give Nod to Turkish-Russian Nuclear Plant Bill." Daily News and Economic Review, July 2.

———. 2010b. "Tea for Some Turkish Activists, Lawsuits for Others." Daily News and Economic Review, October 13.

IAEA 2010. *International Status and Prospects for Nuclear Power*. Vienna: IAEA.

Jasanoff, Sheila, and Sang-Hyun Kim. 2009. "Containing the Atom: SocioTechnical Imaginaries and Nuclear Power in the United States and South Korea." *Minerva* 47 (2): 120.

Kawach, Nadim. 2009. "UAE's Nuclear Project Will Save Its Oil Wealth." *Emirates Business 24/7*, December 30.

Kinsella, William. 2005. "One Hundred Years of Nuclear Discourse: Four Master Themes and Their Implications for Environmental Communication." In *The Environmental Communication Yearbook*, ed. Susan Senecah. Mahwah, NJ: Lawrence Erlbaum Associates.

Kusuma, Ririn Radiawati. 2010. "Indonesian Government Eyeing Bangka Island for 2 Nuclear Power Plants." *The Jakarta Globe*, October 28.

Lee, Lynn. 2010. "No Plans for Nuclear Power in Indonesia." *The Straits Times*, June 19.

Luck, Taylor. 2009. "Toukan stresses Jordan's right to peaceful nuclear programme." *Zawya*, September 17.

_____. 2010a. "France Stands by Jordan's Nuclear Programme." *Jordan Times*, July 14.

———. 2010b. "Jordan—Energy Comes Under the Spotlight." *Jordan Times*, May 11.

———. 2011. "Undaunted by Japan, Jordan Continues Nuclear Drive." *Jordan Times*, April 18.

Macfarlane, Allison. 2010. "Nuclear Power—A Panacea for Future Energy Needs?" *Environment Magazine* 52 (1): 34–46.

Matlack, Carol, and Yuriy Humber. 2010. "Cheap Nuclear Reactors Are Russia's Ace." *Bloomberg Businessweek*, September 30.

Menon, Rajeshwary. 2010. "Long Road to Nuclear Energy." *The Sun Daily*, February 4.

MIT (Massachusetts Institute of Technology). 2003. *The Future of Nuclear Power: An Interdisciplinary Study*. Cambridge, MA: MIT.

Murphy, Dan. 2007. "Middle East Racing to Nuclear Power." *Christian Science Monitor*, November 1.

Mwasa, Fred. 2009. "Experts laugh at Uganda's nuclear ambitions." *The Observer*, April 29.

Pfeifer, Sylvia. 2010. "Nuclear Power: A New Dawn for a Former Sunset Industry." *Financial Times*, October 29.

Proops, John. 2001. "The (Non-) Economics of the Nuclear Fuel Cycle: An Historical and Discourse Analysis." *Ecological Economics* 39 (1): 13–19.

Radio Australia. 2010. "Indonesia's govt revives interest in nuclear power plant plan," January 28. Available at: http://www.radioaustralia.net.au/international/radio/onairhighlights/indonesias-govt-revives-interest-in-nuclear-power-plant-plan.

Rappert, Brian. 2001. "The Distribution of and Resolution of Ambiguities of Technology, or Why Bobby Can't Spray." *Social Studies of Science* 31 (4): 570.

Sambidge, Andy. 2008. "UK poised to play key role in UAE nuclear energy." Arabian Business.com, November 25.

Sasikumar, Karthika. 2009. "Despite Economic Downturn, Nuclear Energy Commerce is Still Worrisome." *Bulletin of the Atomic Scientists* (online edition), December 1. Available at: http://www.thebulletin.org/web-edition/features/despite-economic-downturn-nuclear-energy-commerce-still-worrisome.

Schmid, Sonja D. 2011. "The Unbearable Ambiguity of Knowing: Making Sense of Fukushima." *Bulletin of the Atomic Scientists* (online edition), April 11. Available at: http://www.thebulletin.org/web-edition/features/the-unbearable-ambiguity-of-knowing-making-sense-of-fukushima.

Solomon, Jay. 2010. "Jordan's Nuclear Ambitions Pose Quandary for Obama." *Wall Street Journal*, June 14.

Spears, John. 2010. "Nukes Can Make Canada Energy 'Superpower' Says CANDU Backer." *The Star*, June 1.

Squassoni, Sharon. 2009. *Nuclear Energy: Rebirth or Resuscitation?* Washington, DC: Carnegie Endowment for International Peace.

Stanek, Steven. 2009. "US Hails UAE as Model for Nuclear Power." *The National*, October 8.

Stanton, Chris. 2010. "US Firms Chase Nuclear Deals." *The National*, February 21.

Steinglass, Matt. 2010. "Nuclear Power in Vietnam: The US and Russia Compete." *Financial Times*, September 6.

Surrey, John. 1988. "Nuclear Power: An Option for the Third World?" *Energy Policy* 16 (October): 461–479.

Szilard, R., P. Planchon, and J. Busby. 2009. "The Case for Extended Nuclear Reactor Operation." *Journal of the Minerals, Metals and Materials Society* 61 (7): 24–27.

Tanter, Richard, and Eileen Ng. 2010. "Malaysia's Proposed Nuclear Plant Comes Under Fire." *Bloomberg Businessweek*, May 5.

Tirone, Jonathan, and Nayla Razzouk. 2010. "U.S. Says Jordan, Other Nations Have Right to Enrich Uranium." *Bloomberg Businessweek*, September 22.

Trend. 2011. "Turks Protest Against Nuclear Power after Fukushima Accident," March 17. Available at: http://en.trend.az/regions/met/turkey/1847615.html.

Trong, Vu, and Patrick Barta. 2009. "Vietnam Assembly Approves Nuclear Plants." *Wall Street Journal*, November 26.

USGPO (United States Government Printing Office). 2009. "Proposed Agreement for Cooperation Between the Government of the United States of America and the Government of the United Arab Emirates Concerning Peaceful Uses of Nuclear Energy." Available at: http://www.fas.org/man/eprint/uae-nuclear.pdf.

Vietnam News. 2009. "Nation's Future Looks Nuclear," November 21.

Walker, J. Samuel. 2009. *The Road to Yucca Mountain: The Development of Radioactive Waste Policy in the United States.* Berkeley: University of California Press.

WNA (World Nuclear Association). 2010. "Plans for New Reactors Worldwide." Available at: http://www.world-nuclear.org/info/inf17.html.

World Nuclear News. 2009. "Vietnamese Congress Approves Nuclear Project," November 25.

———. 2010a. "Jordan Shortlists Reactor Designs," May 13.

————. 2010b. "Reactor and Fuel Take-back for Vietnam," September 9.

————. 2010c. "Vietnam Plans Ambitious Nuclear Program," June 24.

World Tribune.com. 2010. "Russia to Build, Own First Nuclear Power Plant for 'Strategic Partner' Turkey," May 14.

Wynne, Brian. 1988. "Unruly Technology: Practical Rules, Impractical Discourses and Public Understanding." *Social Studies of Science* 18 (1): 147–161.

Xinhua News. 2009. "Asian Parliamentary Assembly Supports Right to Develop Nuclear Power," December 11. Available at: http://news.xinhuanet.com/english/2009-12/11/content_12633344.htm.

————. 2010. "Indonesian Experts Prefer Renewable Source to Nuclear Power Plant," February 11.

Yee, April. 2011. "Nuclear Watchdog Seeks Japan Lessons." *The National,* April 1. Available at: http://www.thenational.ae/business/energy/nuclear-watchdog-seeks-japan-lessons.

Yurman, Dan. 2009. "UAE Creates Nuclear Regulatory Agency." *The Energy Collective,* October 5.

3 Nuclear Suppliers and the Renaissance in Nuclear Power

Matthew Fuhrmann

COUNTRIES HAVE RELIED ON THE PEACEFUL USES OF THE atom to meet their energy needs for more than fifty years. While the highly industrialized states were the first to build nuclear power plants, the use of the atom became widespread beginning in the 1970s. The nuclear accidents at Three Mile Island in 1979 and Chernobyl in 1986 led to a decline in global civilian nuclear development, but many countries began expressing a newfound interest in nuclear energy during the early 2000s. The future of nuclear power is uncertain in the wake of the accident at Japan's Fukushima Daiichi nuclear power plant in March 2011. This incident will probably make some countries reluctant to rely on nuclear energy to meet their electricity needs—especially if they are democratic or do not currently operate nuclear power plants (Fuhrmann 2012a; Macfarlane, Chapter 2 in this volume). Yet nuclear power will remain a viable option for many states in the coming decades. China, for example, appears to be building nuclear plants at a breakneck pace in the aftermath of Fukushima.

The so-called nuclear renaissance, whether real or perceived, has triggered a renewed interest in the peaceful use of the atom among both scholars and policy makers (e.g., Fuhrmann 2009a,b, 2012b; Miller and Sagan 2009; Ferguson 2010; Findlay 2011). Most of the other chapters in Part I of this book focus on general patterns of growth and on which states are moving forward with plans to begin or expand nuclear power programs. Somewhat lost in the extant literature, however, is the role played by the nuclear supplier countries such as France, Russia, and the United States.

This chapter analyzes the nuclear suppliers in the context of the looming nuclear renaissance. Unlike previous research on the subject (e.g., Fuhrmann 2009b), this chapter is less concerned with the relationship between the supplier and the recipient country (i.e., the dyad). Rather, the emphasis is on understanding the factors that motivate countries to enter the nuclear marketplace as suppliers. Why do nuclear supplier countries assist other states in developing nuclear energy programs?

As Allison Macfarlane hints in Chapter 2, this question is important because most states with nuclear ambitions, such as Vietnam, Saudi Arabia, and the United Arab Emirates (UAE), will require foreign assistance to get their nuclear programs off the ground. In the absence of such aid, the nuclear renaissance will not unfold as expected. Consequently, the world would not address the problem of global climate change by reducing greenhouse gas emissions (see Busby, Chapter 5 in this volume), and individual countries would be unable to enhance their energy security and reap the other benefits of nuclear power production (see Gourley and Stulberg, Chapter 1 in this volume).

Additionally, policy makers and scholars have long recognized a connection between the peaceful and military uses of the atom. Dwight D. Eisenhower, for example, acknowledged this in his historic "Atoms for Peace" address before the U.N. General Assembly in December 1953 when he said, "The United States pledges . . . to devote its entire heart and mind to finding the way by which the miraculous inventiveness of man shall not be dedicated to his death, but consecrated to his life."[1] In the 1960s and 1970s, analysts such as Albert Wohlstetter and his colleagues (1979) began to raise concerns about the diffusion of nuclear technology. The fear was that countries could come close to making bombs by developing civilian nuclear programs without violating any international commitments. More recent research suggests that this concern may have been justified by showing that there is a connection between peaceful nuclear assistance and nuclear weapons proliferation (Fuhrmann 2009a,b, 2012b). Countries receiving aid in developing a peaceful nuclear program appear to be more likely to pursue and acquire nuclear weapons, especially if they also experience militarized interstate conflict. Other research shows that "sensitive nuclear assistance"—defined as transfers of enrichment facilities, plutonium reprocessing centers, or significant quantities of bomb-grade material—increases the likelihood that states pursuing nuclear weapons will successfully develop the bomb (Kroenig 2009b). Much of this assistance is provided for military rather than civilian purposes, however. Debates persist about whether peaceful nuclear assistance will lead to nuclear proliferation (e.g., Bluth et al. 2010). A better understanding of the nuclear marketplace may help us obtain a more complete picture of how and why nuclear weapons spread—a point revisited in this chapter's conclusion.

Despite the importance of understanding why countries provide nuclear assistance, important gaps remain in our knowledge. Many scholars have discussed the supply side of nuclear proliferation, which focuses on technology diffusion and other factors that influence a state's capacity to build the bomb (e.g., Scheinman 1965; Barnaby 1969; Willrich 1973; OTA 1977; Gilinsky 1978; Wohlstetter et al. 1979; Potter 1982; Holdren 1983; Meyer 1984; Fuhrmann 2009a,b; Kroenig 2009b). Others have conducted important qualitative historical analyses to explain why particular countries supply nuclear technology or materials (e.g., Boardman and Keeley 1983; Potter 1990; Bratt 2006). Some studies have tested original arguments on why countries provide nuclear assistance in a large-n setting, examining variation in patterns between countries and over time (e.g., Fuhrmann 2009a; Kroenig 2009a). Yet we do not fully understand the factors that motivate countries to provide peaceful nuclear assistance. This is, in part, because much of the nuclear proliferation literature focuses on the demand side of the proliferation equation by exploring how factors such as international norms, security threats, economic liberalization, and leaders' psychological profiles affect countries' interest in bomb development (e.g., Sagan 1996/97; Paul 2000; Hymans 2006; Solingen 2007; Rublee 2009).

This chapter builds on existing supply-side research by examining the factors that motivate a country to supply nuclear technology, materials, or know-how, irrespective of its relationship to the recipient state. Focusing on the individual supplier (i.e., the monad) allows us to evaluate whether there are unique country-level characteristics that motivate states to supply nuclear technology for peaceful purposes. It also provides another venue for assessing the validity of arguments on the causes of peaceful nuclear assistance.

This chapter argues that suppliers enter the nuclear marketplace, in part, to enhance their influence in international politics. Statistical analysis using a dataset on bilateral civilian nuclear cooperation agreements (NCAs) signed between 1950 and 2000 lends empirical evidence in favor of this argument. The findings also reveal that economic considerations play a role, but we cannot fully understand this phenomenon without embracing political and strategic factors.

The next section of this chapter presents an argument on peaceful nuclear assistance and identifies two hypotheses that flow from it. Subsequently, the chapter outlines the empirical approach to evaluating the hypotheses. This is followed by a discussion of the results from the statistical analysis. The chapter concludes by highlighting the implications of the findings for the nuclear renaissance and nuclear weapons proliferation.

Theory and Hypotheses

There is no single answer to the question of why nuclear supplier countries assist other states in developing nuclear energy programs. Indeed, there are numerous reasons why countries might export nuclear technology, materials, and know-how. Perhaps the simplest motive for suppliers is to generate hard currency (see, e.g., Potter 1990; Bratt 2006). While the opportunity to make money and other economic factors affect the nuclear marketplace, the pursuit of political influence is one of the more significant causes of peaceful nuclear assistance. The remainder of this section briefly summarizes this argument and identifies the observable implications that stem from it. Readers interested in additional details may consult prior research where the argument is developed more comprehensively (Fuhrmann 2009a, 2012b).

Reactors and Influence in International Politics

The general argument is that countries use civilian nuclear assistance as an instrument of statecraft to forge or strengthen partnerships with recipient states and facilitate bilateral cooperation. Peaceful nuclear assistance is well suited to achieving these objectives. Countries tend to value civilian nuclear programs, because they are seen as symbols of prestige and modernity and can enhance energy security (Poneman 1982; see also Gourley and Stulberg, Chapter 1 in this volume; Macfarlane, Chapter 2 in this volume). At the same time, most states depend on other countries in order to reap the benefits of peaceful nuclear programs. Suppliers recognize the political value of civilian nuclear assistance. For example, when speaking of nuclear aid to India in the 1950s, former Canadian Undersecretary of State for External Affairs Jules Leger stated, "politically, it would do more to strengthen our relations with India than anything I could think of" (quoted in Donaghy 2007).

While atomic assistance is an effective instrument of statecraft, this argument does not imply that suppliers should shell it out indiscriminately. Countries recognize that in providing peaceful nuclear assistance they could inadvertently contribute to nuclear weapons proliferation, given that all the relevant technology and materials are dual-use in nature. Countries are more willing to accept these risks when they receive offsetting political and strategic benefits. According to this logic, suppliers provide aid for three main politico-strategic reasons: to strengthen their military alliances, to counter the influence of their enemies, and, if the supplier is democratic, to promote the development of democracies (see Fuhrmann 2009b, 2012b).[2]

This argument has been tested by analyzing the nature of relationships between supplier and recipient countries. Previous studies help us understand why the United States, for instance, helped India and Japan develop peaceful nuclear programs but did not provide similar aid to Libya or Poland. What we do not know is whether the argument helps us understand why countries enter the nuclear marketplace as suppliers in the first place. Can this logic help us understand why some countries (such as Russia and the United States) regularly provide peaceful nuclear assistance, while other states (such as South Korea) have provided limited amounts of aid and still others (such as Israel and Portugal) have shown little interest in becoming nuclear exporters?

The general implication is that countries enter the nuclear marketplace to influence world politics in ways that promote their politico-strategic interests. Recent examples support this proposition. The controversial 2006 U.S.-India nuclear deal illustrates that the United States views its nuclear exports as a tool of political influence. It agreed to transfer nuclear reactors and nuclear fuel—despite New Delhi's refusal to ratify the Non-Proliferation Treaty (NPT)—to enhance its influence in Asia vis-à-vis China. Not surprisingly, Beijing responded to this arrangement by signing an NCA with Pakistan (Blank 2010). Russia too made a push to reestablish itself as a major nuclear exporter, having recently signed NCAs with countries in Latin America, the Middle East, and Southeast Asia. Former Prime Minister and reelected President Vladimir Putin offered one explanation for this resurgence when he said in 2007 that expertise in nuclear power is part of "what makes Russia a great power" (quoted in Weir 2007). There are also indications that Australia views its uranium exports as a means to exercise political influence. Former Prime Minister John Howard asserted in 2006, for example, that the country was an "energy superpower" in part because of its ability to export uranium. This statement does not imply that economic considerations are irrelevant for Australia's uranium exports, but it does suggest that some elites in Canberra perceive a link between peaceful nuclear assistance and political influence (see Clarke, Fruhling, and O'Neil 2011).

If states become nuclear suppliers to enhance their international influence, what should we observe empirically? Those states with politico-strategic interests to preserve or promote should be more likely to enter the nuclear marketplace. One indication of having politico-strategic interests at stake is whether states are party to military alliances. Countries depend on military alliances for a variety of purposes, including deterring third-party aggression (e.g., Walt 1987). Yet states cannot always take the cooperation of an ally for granted. Recent research shows that allies do not provide support to one another in war roughly 25 percent of the time (Leeds, Long, and Mitchell 2000). This means that countries must continually work to maintain the strength of their alliances. Peaceful nuclear assistance is one tool that allows states to accomplish this objective. If strengthening military alliances is a major reason why countries provide nuclear assistance, we would expect states to enter the nuclear marketplace when they have alliances to preserve.

Generally, states with military alliances are more likely to have a stake in manipulating world politics; such incentives may have provided the impetus to forge alliances in the first place. The United States, for instance, has numerous military allies because it has a vested interest in politico-strategic stability around the world—especially in certain key regions such as Europe during the Cold War—whereas countries with neutral postures, such as Switzerland, are unlikely to form military alliances in part because they care less about the maintenance of politico-strategic stability. The preceding logic leads to the first hypothesis:

Hypothesis 1: Countries are more likely to enter the nuclear marketplace as the number of military alliances they are party to increases.

Countries with rivals also have a large stake in politico-strategic considerations such as the regional balance of power, because the prospect for war or other violent militarized conflict looms large. As one indication of this, countries often attempt to constrain their enemies by cultivating certain relationships with their rivals' enemies (e.g., Waltz 1979). States may provide civilian nuclear assistance to enemies of enemies in order to develop closer strategic ties with those states. China, for instance, provided military nuclear assistance to Pakistan in part to constrain India, a common enemy in this case (Paul 2003). Russia's nuclear assistance to Venezuela was motivated in part to constrain U.S. influence in its own backyard by cultivating closer ties with one of the United States' adversaries in South America (Fuhrmann 2012b). And India's peaceful nuclear assistance to Vietnam in the late 1990s was motivated in part to constrain the rising influence of China in Asia (Singh 2007; see also Fuhrmann 2009a: 189).

If countries experience relative peace, they do not have the same motivations to manipulate relationships in ways that promote their politico-strategic interests. This does not mean that countries will never enter the nuclear marketplace if they live in peaceful neighborhoods. Rather, such countries are *less likely* to become nuclear suppliers compared to states with many rivals, because they have less to gain from a salient benefit of peaceful nuclear assistance. This leads to the second hypothesis:

Hypothesis 2: Countries are more likely to enter the nuclear marketplace as they experience a greater number of rivalries with other states.

Research Design

Dataset

To test the two hypotheses outlined above, statistical analysis was used to explore the relationships between independent variables and peaceful nuclear assistance. The process drew from a standard time-series–cross-section dataset for the period 1953–2000.[3] The unit of analysis is the country-year, meaning that the dataset includes forty-eight observations for each state in the international system.

Dependent Variable

The dependent variable is based on a dataset of NCAs previously used to study the causes and consequences of peaceful nuclear assistance (Fuhrmann 2009a,b). Nuclear cooperation agreements are a reasonable measure of atomic aid, because countries typically conclude these deals before sharing nuclear technology, materials, or know-how. These agreements could lead to the transfer of a variety of items including nuclear materials such as enriched uranium or plutonium, nuclear power or research reactors, or other fuel cycle facilities such as plutonium reprocessing centers. Many NCAs also lead to joint research and development or the training of foreign scientists and

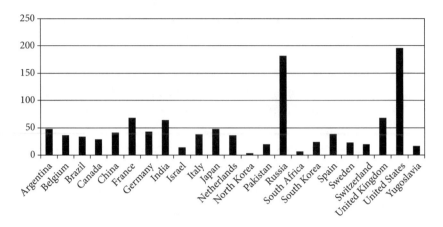

FIGURE 3.1 Number of supply agreements by country, 1953–2000

technicians. *Nuclear supplier* is coded 1 if a state signed an NCA authorizing nuclear exports in year $t + 1$, and is coded 0 otherwise.[4]

Figure 3.1 plots the distribution of the dependent variable to illustrate which countries have been the most active suppliers from 1953 to 2000. Notice that many countries provided nuclear assistance during this period, but there is interesting variation in the degree to which suppliers have participated in the nuclear marketplace.

Independent Variables

Two independent variables were created to test the hypotheses developed above. To measure the number of military alliances a state is party to, the Correlates of War's formal alliance data (Gibler and Sarkees 2004) was consulted to create *military alliances*, which measures the total number of alliances a state has in force in a given year.[5] Rivalry involvement is measured using a comprehensive database of all interstate rivalries between 1816 and 2001 (Klein, Goertz, and Diehl 2006).[6] The variable *rivalries* measures the total number of rivals a state has in year t.

Control Variables

A number of factors unrelated to politico-strategic influence could affect whether a state supplies nuclear technology, materials, or know-how. To facilitate cross-study comparison, the same controls used in other studies of peaceful nuclear assistance were included whenever appropriate. A state's level of development is likely to have some influence on whether it provides nuclear assistance. Underdeveloped states such as Burkina Faso simply lack the capability to enter the nuclear marketplace as a supplier. To account for the effects of economic development on nuclear assistance, *GDP* [gross domestic product] *per capita* was included as a proxy for a country's wealth.[7] A state's existing nuclear-related resources are also likely to influence nuclear assistance. States with greater indigenous nuclear capabilities might have a greater opportunity to export nuclear technology. *Nuclear reactors* measures the total number of nuclear power reactors that a country has in operation in year t.[8]

Other economic factors could also motivate states to become nuclear suppliers. Economists (e.g., Krugman 1980) have argued that countries trade because of the cost reductions that result from increased production (i.e., economies of scale). In short, trade is welfare-enhancing because it is most efficient to concentrate production of particular commodities in a small number of locations. The problem of economies of scale also could influence the nuclear marketplace (e.g., Hofhansel 1996; Bratt 2006). Nuclear industries must meet some minimum threshold of production in order to remain competitive. If industries cannot meet their production needs through domestic demand, they are forced to export nuclear technology in order to stay afloat. To control for this argument, the variable *export pressure* is included, which measures the number of nuclear power reactors per capita in the exporting country. This variable is calculated by dividing the number of power plants by a country's population and multiplying this factor by 100 for the purposes of rescaling.

The NPT might influence nuclear assistance. One of the "grand bargains" of the treaty is that countries share nuclear technology with states that forswear nuclear weapons. In particular, Article IV of the treaty states: "All the Parties to the Treaty undertake to facilitate, and have the right to participate in, the fullest possible exchange of equipment, materials and scientific and technological information for the peaceful uses of nuclear energy."[9] Suppliers, of course, are only bound by this bargain if they enter the regime. We might expect, therefore, that NPT members would be more likely to become nuclear suppliers. *NPT* is a dichotomous variable coded 1 if a state is part of the NPT in year t, and coded 0 otherwise.[10]

The nuclear accident at Chernobyl in 1986 had a devastating effect on nuclear industries around the world. To account for the decline in demand for nuclear power following this disaster, a dichotomous variable, *Chernobyl*, is included and coded 1 if the year is after 1986 and coded 0 otherwise. The price of oil could also influence nuclear assistance. In particular, countries might be more enticed to enter the market as nuclear suppliers when oil prices are high, because demand for nuclear power might be greater. *Oil price*, thus, is included as a measure of the price of a barrel of oil in U.S. dollars in year t.[11] To account for any effect that a state's regime type might have on its interest in supplying nuclear technology, *polity* is included to measures a state's score on the widely used Polity IV scale (Marshall and Jaggers 2007).[12] Finally, to control for temporal dependence, a variable counting the number of years that pass without a state offering nuclear assistance is included, along with three cubic splines (Beck, Katz, and Tucker 1998).

Method

Since the dependent variable is dichotomous, logit analysis is used for the multivariate statistical analysis. Robust standard errors clustered by country are used to account for heteroskedastic error variance and serial correlation within the panel.

Results

Before turning to the multivariate statistical analysis, a simple cross-tabulation analysis is conducted to reveal underlying patterns in the data. Table 3.1 displays the results of a cross-tabulation analysis of nuclear assistance against the number of a state's military allies. This table indicates that, consistent with Hypothesis 1, the likelihood of a state supplying nuclear technology increases as the number of allies rises. Note, however, that having a military alliance is not a necessary condition for entering the nuclear marketplace. In cases where a military alliance is not present, nuclear assistance occurs about 3 percent of the time.[13] States with between one and ten military allies are more likely to share nuclear technology, materials, or know-how; at this level of alignment, we see nuclear assistance occur in roughly 9 percent of the cases. The chances of supply become even greater when states have between eleven and twenty allies, although we do not see a further increase when states have between twenty-one and thirty allies. At each of these levels of alignment, nuclear assistance occurs in roughly 13 percent of the observations in the sample. When the number of allies rises above thirty, another significant spike occurs in the sharing of nuclear technology. Compared to states that do not have a single ally, countries at this level of alignment are 360 percent more likely to offer nuclear assistance. Yet states achieve this level of alignment in only 5 percent of the observations in the dataset.[14]

Table 3.2 displays the results of a cross-tabulation analysis of nuclear assistance against the number of rivals. The data displayed in this table are also quite revealing. Just as some states supply in the absence of a single military alliance, having a rival is not a necessary condition for nuclear assistance. Atomic aid occurs in about 6 percent of the country-year observations where states do not possess a single rival. Consistent with Hypothesis 2, states are more likely to supply in the nuclear marketplace as the number of rivals increases. Having just one or two rivals increases the likelihood of nuclear assistance by about 50 percent. The probability of nuclear assistance continues to increase as the number of rivals rises. In cases where a state has more than six

TABLE 3.1 Cross-tabulation analysis of military alliances and nuclear assistance

		Number of military allies					
		0	1–10	11–20	21–30	30	Total
Nuclear supply	No	2,284 (96.78%)	1,429 (90.73%)	1,814 (86.96%)	598 (87.17%)	397 (85.19%)	6,522 (90.92%)
	Yes	76 (3.22%)	146 (9.27%)	272 (13.04%)	88 (12.83%)	69 (14.81%)	651 (9.08%)
	Total	2,360 (100%)	1,575 (100%)	2,086 (100%)	686 (100%)	466 (100%)	7,173 (100%)

Pearson $\chi^2 = 168.09$ $p < .0001$

TABLE 3.2 Cross-tabulation analysis of rivalries and nuclear assistance

		Number of rivals					
		0	1–2	3–4	5–6	> 6	Total
Nuclear supply	No	3,733 (94.15%)	2,225 (91.26%)	402 (84.28%)	71 (75.53%)	91 (45.73%)	6,522 (90.92%)
	Yes	232 (5.85%)	213 (8.74%)	75 (15.72%)	23 (24.47%)	108 (54.27%)	651 (9.08%)
	Total	3,965 (100%)	2,438 (100%)	477 (100%)	94 (100%)	199 (100%)	7,173 (100%)

Pearson $\chi^2 = 595.44$ $p < .0001$

rivals in a given year, the sharing of nuclear expertise and technology occurs about 55 percent of the time. Thus, countries with a large number of rivals are 845 percent more likely to enter the nuclear marketplace than states that do not have a rival.[15]

The cross-tabulation analysis lends preliminary support in favor of both hypotheses. The relationships uncovered above, however, might be spurious. It could be, for instance, that we see a strong relationship between rivals and nuclear assistance because countries that become involved in militarized conflict also tend to be economically developed. The next step is to examine whether the links between nuclear assistance, alliances, and rivalries hold up once we account for confounding variables.

Table 3.3 displays the results of the multivariate statistical analysis. Model 1, which includes all of the variables discussed above, represents the core test of the hypotheses. *Military alliances* is positively associated with nuclear exports, and this relationship is statistically significant. It suggests that the likelihood of nuclear assistance rises as states become more aligned. *Rivalries* is also statistically significant in the positive direction, indicating that the probability of a state entering the nuclear marketplace rises as the number of its enemies increases. These results demonstrate that politico-strategic considerations remain salient even when accounting for the other factors that could influence peaceful nuclear assistance.

How substantively important are these two variables in shaping the probability of peaceful nuclear assistance? To address this question, Figure 3.2 illustrates how the predicted probability of supplying nuclear technology, materials, or know-how changes as *military alliances* and *rivalries* increase from their minimum to maximum values and all other factors are held constant. Notice that the probability of nuclear aid is close to zero when states do not have a single ally, but that this likelihood rises as suppliers become more aligned. A modest increase in this variable (from 0 to 5) results in nearly a 30 percent spike in the probability of a supplier providing aid. Increasing the value of *military alliances* from its minimum value (0) to its maximum value (57) raises the probability of aid by more than 2,000 percent. The absolute probability of nuclear aid remains fairly small (around 0.07) when *military alliances* is set to its maximum value. This is in part a function of the dataset used for this analysis. These probabilities tell us what the chance is that a particular country will provide assistance in a given year; the probability that it would provide aid over a ten-year period, for instance, would be greater than the probabilities reported here.

TABLE 3.3 Correlates of peaceful nuclear assistance, 1953–2000

	(1) Baseline	(2) Intangible NCAs	(3) Material NCAs	(4) Technology NCAs	(5) U.S. & Russia excluded	(6) Post–Cold War
Military alliances	0.053*** (0.018)	0.040*** (0.014)	0.016 (0.015)	0.040*** (0.014)	0.055*** (0.019)	0.051 (0.032)
Rivalries	0.286*** (0.070)	0.196*** (0.043)	0.188*** (0.062)	0.261*** (0.062)	0.268*** (0.079)	0.657*** (0.151)
GDP per capita	0.000*** (0.000)	0.000*** (0.000)	0.000** (0.000)	0.000** (0.000)	0.000** (0.000)	−0.000 (0.000)
Nuclear reactors	0.013 (0.015)	0.009 (0.011)	−0.010 (0.007)	−0.025*** (0.008)	0.019 (0.014)	0.001 (0.018)
Export pressure	0.455 (3.304)	1.997 (4.072)	10.978*** (4.256)	6.970 (5.097)	−0.454 (3.032)	8.738** (4.237)
NPT	−0.257 (0.261)	−0.535* (0.285)	−0.715** (0.355)	−0.529* (0.272)	−0.274 (0.259)	0.117 (0.425)
Polity	0.034* (0.020)	0.054*** (0.020)	0.021 (0.024)	0.026 (0.019)	0.037* (0.021)	0.126*** (0.037)
Chernobyl	−0.935*** (0.190)	−0.930*** (0.197)	−0.184 (0.407)	−0.393 (0.289)	−0.996*** (0.180)	
Oil price	0.008 (0.010)	0.016 (0.010)	0.012 (0.014)	0.016** (0.008)	0.010 (0.010)	0.031 (0.022)
No NCA years	−0.665*** (0.071)	−0.501*** (0.061)	−0.288*** (0.089)	−0.357*** (0.076)	−0.654*** (0.073)	0.059 (0.248)
Spline 1	−0.003** (0.001)	−0.003** (0.001)	−0.001 (0.001)	−0.001 (0.001)	−0.003* (0.001)	0.058** (0.027)
Spline 2	0.001 (0.001)	0.002 (0.001)	0.000 (0.001)	−0.000 (0.001)	0.000 (0.001)	−0.081** (0.037)
Spline 3	0.000 (0.001)	−0.001 (0.001)	0.000 (0.000)	0.001 (0.000)	0.000 (0.001)	0.069** (0.031)
Constant	−0.781*** (0.279)	−1.406*** (0.233)	−2.930*** (0.561)	−1.839*** (0.312)	−0.822*** (0.298)	−3.308*** (0.937)
Observations	5,985	5,985	5,985	5,985	5,887	1,574

NOTE: $*p < .1$, $**p < .05$, $***p < .01$; robust standard errors in parentheses; GDP = gross domestic product; NCA = nuclear cooperation agreement; NPT = Non-Proliferation Treaty.

Figure 3.2 reveals that *rivalries* has a much larger substantive effect on nuclear assistance than *military alliances*. Increasing the number of interstate rivals a state has from 0 to 5 while holding all other factors constant raises the probability of assistance by almost 300 percent. When this variable shifts from its minimum value (0) to its maximum value (20), the probability

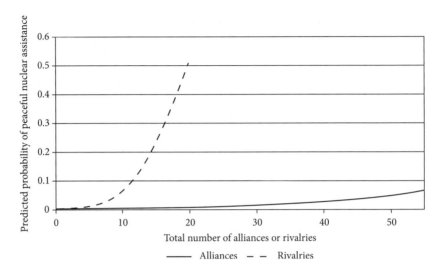

FIGURE 3.2 Substantive effects of alliances and rivalries on probability of nuclear assistance

increases by approximately 13,000 percent! From an absolute perspective, the probability of a supplier providing aid is roughly 0.5 when *rivalries* is set to its maximum value. Thus, the likelihood that states with an extreme number of enemies will provide assistance in a given year is greater than the likelihood that they will not offer aid.

Alliances and rivalries are not the only variables that shape the nuclear marketplace. Some of the control variables are also statistically significant. *GDP per capita* is correlated with nuclear assistance in the positive direction. Not surprisingly, this indicates that countries cannot offer nuclear assistance if they lack the technological wherewithal to enter the marketplace.[16] *Chernobyl* has a statistically significant and negative relationship with nuclear assistance, indicating that countries are less likely to offer nuclear assistance following this major nuclear accident. *Polity* is the third control variable that achieves conventional levels of statistical significance. It is positively associated with providing nuclear assistance, indicating the movement towards democracy increases the probability that a state will become a nuclear supplier. The other controls are statistically insignificant in Model 1.

The findings lend support for Hypotheses 1 and 2. Yet readers could raise a few objections to the initial statistical test. One possible concern is that the dependent variable used in the analysis captures all types of nuclear exports ranging from sensitive fuel cycle facilities to the training of foreign scientists. Some NCAs might be better suited than others for the purpose of enhancing suppliers' politico-strategic interests. If this were true, we might expect that the findings would vary based on the type of assistance that suppliers are providing. To explore whether this is the case, three disaggregated dependent variables were created.[17] *Intangible nuclear supplier* is coded 1 if a state signed an NCA dealing with training or research and development in year t+1 and coded 0 otherwise. Similarly, *nuclear material nuclear supplier* is coded 1 if a state signed an NCA dealing exclusively with nuclear materials in year t+1 and coded 0 otherwise, while *technology nuclear supplier* is coded 1 if a state signed an agreement to transfer reactors or fuel cycle facilities in year t+1 and coded 0 otherwise. Model 1 was replicated using these disaggregated dependent variables (see Models 2–4). Most of the findings are substantively similar, indicating that the type of assistance does not have a major effect on the motives of exporting countries.[18] In terms of the control variables, *GDP per capita* remains positive and statistically significant, but many of the other findings vary across the models. *NPT* is negatively correlated with nuclear assistance in Models 2–4, suggesting that countries entering the NPT are statistically less likely to share nuclear technology, materials, or know-how for peaceful purposes despite the spirit of Article IV.[19] The other controls are significant in just one of the models employing a disaggregated dependent variable.

Another possibility is that the findings reported in Model 1 are driven by Russia and the United States. These two countries were involved in many rivalries and military alliances from 1953 to 2000. A quick glance at Figure 3.1 reveals that they were by far the most active nuclear suppliers during this period. Russia and the United States may be especially likely to use foreign assistance—including nuclear exports—to influence international politics, because they have substantial political and strategic interests to defend. Other suppliers, such as Belgium and Sweden, may be less interested in using nuclear exports to enhance their international influence, given that they are less powerful militarily. From a qualitative perspective, Russia and the United States appear to offer the strongest evidence in favor of the argument. One can identify many cases—such as Russia's contemporary cooperation with Iran and Venezuela (Pape 2005) and America's assistance to Iran during the 1960s and 1970s (Fuhrmann 2012b: 82–89)—where politico-strategic interests played a key role in motivating the supply activities of these two countries.

The findings reported in Model 5, however, suggest that there is also empirical support for the argument among countries that are not superpowers. *Military alliances* and *rivalries* remain positive and statistically significant even when Russia and the United States are excluded from the dataset. Some may find this surprising, but a close look at historical cases reveals that politico-strategic factors often play an important role in influencing the supply activities of middle powers. To cite one example, Canada provided peaceful nuclear assistance to Romania beginning in the 1970s, in part to contribute to America's détente with the Soviet Union and drive Bucharest away from Moscow. Economic factors may have played a role in this cooperation as well, but they appear to have been secondary to Canadian political objectives (Bratt 2006; Fuhrmann 2012b: 94–102). This does not imply that middle powers *always* behave in a manner consistent with the argument. South Korea's interest in nuclear cooperation with the UAE, for example, appears to be largely economic in nature (see Early 2010).

It is also conceivable that the results are an artifact of the Cold War period. Indeed, there are three reasons to question whether the argument explains the behavior of nuclear suppliers in the post–Cold War era. First, the end of the Cold War might have influenced nuclear transactions by reducing the importance of balance-of-power politics. With the collapse of the Soviet Union, the United States and other suppliers may have felt less compelled to strengthen bilateral relationships with certain key "battleground states" through the use of atomic assistance. Second, shocks to the system that occurred during the Cold War might have had an effect on the nuclear marketplace. Most significant, in 1974, India conducted a test of a nuclear explosive device using technology it imported from Canada for "peaceful" purposes. According to conventional wisdom, this highlighted the proliferation risks associated with nuclear commerce and discouraged suppliers to modify their practices. In the late 1970s, a group of countries formed the Nuclear Suppliers Group (NSG) to harmonize export practices among the major suppliers and reduce the proliferation risks associated with peaceful nuclear assistance. Third, there are many more capable suppliers in the world today than there were in the early days of the nuclear age. This is potentially significant because one might expect that a state's ability to enhance its international influence by exporting nuclear technology would decrease as more suppliers enter the arena.

The results show that there are some differences in the post–Cold War period when it comes to providing peaceful nuclear assistance (see Model 6).

Most important, *military alliances* is no longer statistically significant, suggesting that strengthening alliances is not a compelling reason to enter the nuclear marketplace after the collapse of the Soviet Union. This is consistent with an earlier study, which found that states were less likely to provide nuclear assistance to their allies after 1991 (Fuhrmann 2009b). On the other hand, *rivalries* remains positive and statistically significant. This is important because it indicates that politico-strategic motives to enter the nuclear marketplace have not subsided with the end of the Cold War.

The other findings are generally consistent with those reported in Model 1, although *export pressure* is positive and statistically significant in Model 6. This finding lends credence to the notion that the saturation of domestic demand for nuclear power motivates states to provide civilian nuclear assistance in the post–Cold War period.

Conclusion

This chapter indicates that countries provide peaceful nuclear assistance partly for politico-strategic reasons. *Military allies* is positively related to nuclear assistance, indicating that states are more likely to supply nuclear items when they are highly aligned. *Rivals* is also positively associated with atomic aid. The likelihood that a country will offer assistance rises dramatically as its number of enemies increases. The relationships between these two politico-strategic variables and nuclear assistance are probabilistic; having allies or rivals is neither necessary nor sufficient for nuclear aid to occur. Further analysis reveals that there are some differences in the motivations for nuclear assistance across agreement type, although politico-strategic factors influence the markets in nuclear technology, intangibles, and materials. The general patterns held when Russia and the United States were removed from the dataset, indicating that the findings were not driven by superpowers, representing the "easy" cases for the argument. States' incentives for entering the nuclear marketplace appear to have evolved slightly over time. There is not a statistically significant relationship between alliances and nuclear assistance in the post–Cold War era, for example. However, countries with more rivals remain more likely to provide nuclear assistance in this period, indicating that politico-strategic factors remain important even after the collapse of the Soviet Union.

Other factors are also salient in explaining nuclear assistance, indicating that the nuclear marketplace is shaped by multiple factors. Economic development, in particular, plays a major role in the nuclear marketplace. Gross domestic product per capita is highly correlated with nuclear supply in the positive direction. A state's nuclear-specific resources are generally unrelated to civilian nuclear assistance, but the likelihood that suppliers will enter into technology NCAs declines as the number of domestic reactors increases. The findings also reveal that countries were less likely to offer nuclear aid after the Chernobyl disaster. There is some evidence that democracies are more likely to become nuclear suppliers, but this finding is sensitive to the type of assistance that is provided. Sustaining the domestic nuclear industry appears to motivate states to provide nuclear aid—but only in the post–Cold War era. Preserving one of the "grand bargains" of the NPT does not appear to motivate nuclear suppliers. There is actually some evidence that NPT members are less likely to provide nuclear assistance. The price of oil is also generally unrelated to the provision of nuclear assistance, but suppliers are more likely to sign technology NCAs when the oil prices increase.

These findings have some important implications for theory and policy, although we need to be cautious when basing future projections on the past, as Christopher Way and Dan Reiter point out in this book (Chapters 6 and 13, respectively). While military alliances have less of an influence on nuclear assistance today than they did during the Cold War, the salience of rivalries indicates that politico-strategic factors continue to shape the nuclear marketplace. Since many countries continue to be involved in rivalries, incentives to share nuclear technology are likely to remain for the foreseeable future. New suppliers may even emerge if states with reasonable levels of development face security threats in the coming years. Yet suppliers are not equally likely to share technology with all countries (Fuhrmann 2009b). Consider the behavior of the United States between 2005 and 2009. It signed NCAs with India, Saudi Arabia, and the UAE in large part because it was able to extract politico-strategic benefits. During the same period, there were other states seeking help in developing a nuclear power program—such as Belarus, Tanzania, and Venezuela—that the United States did not attempt to assist.

Countries will be unable to move forward with their nuclear power programs only if there is not a single supplier that has politico-strategic incentives to assist them. This is not the case for many of the current aspiring nuclear power states, including those that the United States has denied nuclear assistance. Russia, for example, has concluded NCAs with Belarus and Venezuela. And China recently signed an NCA with Tanzania as it seeks to expand its influence in Africa (Gill, Huang, and Morrison 2007). There are few countries among the current aspirants (see Miller and Sagan 2009) that are likely to face major difficulties in securing nuclear assistance. One possibility is Syria, particularly in light of the ongoing civil strife in that country.[20]

Ultimately, the primacy of politico-strategic motives in the nuclear marketplace is unlikely to significantly stymie the nuclear renaissance, given the current set of nuclear power aspirants. This could change if other states become interested in nuclear power, since it is theoretically possible for countries not to present politico-strategic opportunities to any supplier state. The supply side will influence the renaissance mostly by affecting *where*—not *if*—countries are able to obtain nuclear assistance. This conclusion is not trivial, given that some suppliers are able to offer more reliable technology than others. Moreover, emerging suppliers might be willing to engage in transactions that are riskier from a proliferation standpoint in order to break into the marketplace.

The findings also have implications for the future of the nuclear nonproliferation regime. In some respects, the NPT has been effective in limiting proliferation (e.g., Dunn 2009). The treaty has been weakened, however, by the perception that the nuclear powers have not met their obligations by freely sharing nuclear technology and making "good faith efforts" toward the eventual elimination of nuclear weapons.[21] Research has shown that these perceptions are at least partially correct, because states that ratify the NPT are no more likely than those that do not to receive peaceful nuclear assistance (Fuhrmann 2009a). This chapter does not directly test this proposition, but the findings lend credence to the notion that the nonproliferation regime has little influence on the nuclear marketplace. Given the historical patterns discussed in this chapter, it is unlikely that peaceful nuclear assistance will serve as an effective lynchpin of nonproliferation arrangements like the NPT in the future. To preserve these institutions, nuclear powers such as the United States must do more to demonstrate their commitment to nonproliferation.

This chapter does not directly evaluate whether the nuclear renaissance will lead to nuclear weapons proliferation, but the findings tell us something about when and why the bomb spreads. Research shows that countries receiving peaceful nuclear assistance are more likely to pursue and acquire nuclear weapons—especially if they also face security threats (Fuhrmann 2009b, 2012b). Assuming that this remains true, this chapter lends support to the notion that nuclear weapons spread because suppliers use atomic aid as a means of pursuing short-term politico-strategic objectives, often overlooking long-term proliferation risks. Many nuclear power aspirants (e.g., states in the Middle East) are likely to face a security threat in the future, which only enhances this possibility.

That the nuclear renaissance will contribute to further nuclear proliferation is not a foregone conclusion. Alexander Montgomery (Chapter 7 in this volume), for example, suggests that the renaissance may not fuel proliferation if recipient countries lack the capacity to absorb critical technologies.[22] Scholars should continue to devote attention to the connection between nuclear energy and nuclear weapons to inform critical contemporary policy debates.

There are still gaps in our knowledge of the causes of peaceful nuclear assistance. This chapter provides evidence that both superpowers and non-superpowers provide aid partially to enhance their influence. Additional case studies of middle-power suppliers, such as South Korea, would be welcome, as they could shed further light on the relative importance of political and economic variables in the nuclear marketplace when it comes to non-superpowers. It would be fruitful to further probe the ways in which country-specific factors—such as the supplier's regime type—might affect the degree to which politico-strategic interests matter. Future research should also devote more attention to the ways in which international norms influence the nuclear marketplace. What is the relationship between the nonproliferation regime and the supply of nuclear technology? While this chapter and earlier work on the subject (Fuhrmann 2009a, 2012b) indicate that the regime—including the NPT and the NSG—has had less of an effect on nuclear assistance than is commonly assumed, this is a question that warrants additional consideration. It is possible that norms and international institutions matter in ways that have not been fully captured by research. Another avenue for future research has to do with the consequences of peaceful nuclear assistance. Christopher Way notes in Chapter 6 that we still lack a complete understanding of whether aid of this nature buys influence. Does nuclear assistance actually strengthen military alliances and constrain the influence of enemies? If so, in what ways? These are important questions to be addressed in future studies.

Notes

1. The full text of the address is available at http://www.iaea.org/About/history_speech.html.

2. Fuhrmann (2012b) also shows that suppliers provide aid to enhance their energy security by bartering nuclear technology for oil, but only when oil prices spike sharply.

3. The analysis begins in 1953 because this is when U.S. President Dwight D. Eisenhower made his historic "Atoms for Peace" address. Before this speech took place, peaceful nuclear assistance rarely occurred.

4. This variable would not capture cases where countries signed NCAs as recipients of nuclear assistance.

5. This variable captures three types of agreement: defense pacts, neutrality agreements, and ententes.

6. This dataset classifies states as rivals if they experienced at least three militarized interstate disputes between 1816 and 2001. The three disputes must have been fought over a related issue.

7. These data are obtained from Singh and Way (2004), who compile GDP data from the Penn World Tables (Heston, Summers, and Aten 2002).

8. Data are obtained from the IAEA (2009).

9. The full text of the treaty is available at: http://www.un.org/events/npt2005/npttreaty.html.

10. This variable is coded based on a list compiled by the James Martin Center for Nonproliferation Studies (CNS 2008).

11. These data come from the *Historical Statistics of the United States* (Carter et al. 2006).

12. This scale ranges from −10 to 10, with higher scores indicating more democratic.

13. This modest figure emerges primarily because India, Sweden, and Switzerland became nuclear suppliers despite being nonaligned for most of the post–World War II period.

14. States that achieve this level of alignment are all part of the Organization of American States defense pact.

15. States with more than six rivals at various points between 1953 and 2000 include China, Iraq, Israel, Russia, Turkey, the United Kingdom, the United States, and Yugoslavia.

16. As a robustness check, Model 1 was reestimated in a sample that only included countries that had a nuclear reactor in operation for at least five years. The substantive interpretation of the results is similar. Most important, *military alliances* and *rivalries* remain statistically significant in the positive direction.

17. For more on the disaggregation of NCAs, see Fuhrmann (2012b).

18. The one difference is that *military alliances* is statistically insignificant in Model 3.

19. This finding is consistent with prior research on nuclear assistance in a dyadic setting (Fuhrmann 2009b). Many countries, including Argentina, Brazil, China, France, and Spain, shared nuclear technology, materials, or know-how before ratifying the NPT.

20. Prior to the Arab Spring, Turkey reportedly expressed some interest in engaging in nuclear cooperation with Damascus (Reuters 2008).

21. The NPT may not explicitly require states to share nuclear technology with treaty members, but failing to do so is inconsistent with the spirit of the nonproliferation regime.

22. See also Hymans 2012.

References

Barnaby, C. F. 1969. "The Development of Nuclear Energy Programs." In *Preventing the Spread of Nuclear Weapons*, ed. C. F. Barnaby. London: Souvenir.

Beck, Nathaniel, Jonathan Katz, and Richard Tucker. 1998. "Taking Time Seriously: Time-Series–Cross-Section Analysis with a Binary Dependent Variable." *American Journal of Political Science* 42 (4): 1260–1288.

Blank, Stephen. 2010. "China Puts Down Marker in Nuclear Power Race." *Asia Times*, June 16.

Bluth, Christopher, Matthew Kroenig, Rensselaer Lee, William C. Sailor, and Matthew Fuhrmann. 2010. "Correspondence: Civilian Nuclear Cooperation and the Proliferation of Nuclear Weapons." *International Security* 35 (1): 184–200.

Boardman, Robert, and James Keeley. Eds. 1983. *Nuclear Exports and World Politics*. New York: St. Martin's.

Bratt, Duane. 2006. *The Politics of CANDU Exports*. Toronto: University of Toronto Press.

Carter, Susan, Scott Sigmund Gartner, Michael Haines, Alan Olmstead, Richard Sutch, and Gavin Wright. 2006. "Table Db56–59 Crude Petroleum—Average Value, Foreign Trade, and Proved Reserves: 1859–2001." *Historical Statistics of the United States*. Cambridge, UK: Cambridge University Press.

Clarke, Michael, Stephan Fruhling, and Andrew O'Neil. Eds. 2011. *Australia's Uranium Trade: The Domestic and Foreign Policy Challenges of a Contentious Export*. London: Ashgate.

CNS (James Martin Center for Nonproliferation Studies). 2008. "NPT Membership." *Inventory of International Nonproliferation Organizations and Regimes*. Monterey, CA: James Martin Center for Nonproliferation Studies.

Donaghy, Greg. 2007. "Nehru's Reactor: The Origins of Indo-Canadian Nuclear Cooperation, 1955–1959." In *Canada's Global Engagements and Relations with India*, eds. Christopher Sam Raj and Abdul Nafey, pp. 267–278. New Delhi, India: Manak.

Dunn, Lewis. 2009. "The NPT: Assessing the Past, Building the Future." *Nonproliferation Review* 16 (2): 143–172.

Early, Bryan. 2010. "Acquiring Foreign Nuclear Assistance in the Middle East." *The Nonproliferation Review* 17 (2): 259–280.

Ferguson, Charles. 2010. "The Long Road to Zero: Overcoming the Obstacles to a Nuclear-Free World." *Foreign Affairs* 89 (1): 86–94.

Findlay, Trevor. 2011. *Nuclear Energy and Global Governance: Ensuring Safety, Security, and Non-Proliferation*. London: Routledge.

Fuhrmann, Matthew. 2009a. "Taking a Walk on the Supply Side: The Determinants of Civilian Nuclear Cooperation." *Journal of Conflict Resolution* 53 (2): 181–208.

———. 2009b. "Spreading Temptation: Proliferation and Peaceful Nuclear Cooperation Agreements." *International Security* 34 (1): 7–41.

———. 2012a. "Splitting Atoms: Why Do Countries Build Nuclear Power Plants?" *International Interactions* 38 (1): 29–57.

———. 2012b. *Atomic Assistance: How "Atoms for Peace" Programs Cause Nuclear Insecurity*. Ithaca, NY: Cornell University Press.

Gibler, Douglas M., and Meredith Sarkees. 2004. "Measuring Alliances: The Correlates of War Formal Interstate Alliance Data Set, 1816–2000." *Journal of Peace Research* 41 (2): 211–222.

Gilinsky, Victor. 1978. "Nuclear Energy and the Proliferation of Nuclear Weapons." In *Nuclear Policies: Fuel without the Bomb*, eds. Albert Wohlstetter, Victor Gilinsky, Robert Gillette, and Roberta Wohlstetter. Cambridge, MA: Ballinger.

Gill, Bates, Chin-hao Huang, and J. Stephenson Morrison. 2007. "Assessing China's Growing Influence in Africa." *China Security* 3 (3): 3–21.

Heston, Alan, Robert Summers, and Bettina Aten. 2002. *Penn World Table, Version 6.1*. Philadelphia: University of Pennsylvania, Center for International Comparisons.

Hofhansel, Claus. 1996. *Commercial Competition and National Security: Comparing U.S. and German Export Control Policies*. Westport, CT: Praeger.

Holdren, John. 1983. "Nuclear Power and Nuclear Weapons: The Connection Is Dangerous." *Bulletin of the Atomic Scientists* 39 (1): 40–45.

Hymans, Jacques E. C. 2006. *The Psychology of Nuclear Proliferation: Identity, Emotions, and Foreign Policy*. New York: Cambridge University Press.

———. 2012. *Achieving Nuclear Ambitions: Scientists, Politicians, and Proliferation*. New York: Cambridge University Press.

IAEA. 2009. *Nuclear Power Reactors in the World*. Vienna: IAEA.

Klein, James, Gary Goertz, and Paul Diehl. 2006. "The New Rivalry Dataset: Procedures and Patterns." *Journal of Peace Research* 43 (3): 331–348.

Kroenig, Matthew. 2009a. "Exporting the Bomb: Why States Provide Sensitive Nuclear Assistance." *American Political Science Review* 103 (1): 113–133.

———. 2009b. "Importing the Bomb: Sensitive Nuclear Assistance and Nuclear Proliferation." *Journal of Conflict Resolution* 53 (2): 161–180.

Krugman, Paul. 1980. "Scale Economies, Product Differentiation, and the Pattern of Trade." *American Economic Review* 70 (5): 950–959.

Leeds, Brett Ashley, Andrew Long, and Sara McLaughlin Mitchell. 2000. "Reevaluating Alliance Reliability: Specific Threats, Specific Promises." *Journal of Conflict Resolution* 44 (5): 686–699.

Marshall, Monty, and Keith Jaggers. 2007. "Polity IV Project: Political Regime Characteristics and Transitions." Fairfax, VA: George Mason University.

Meyer, Stephen M. 1984. *The Dynamics of Nuclear Proliferation*. Chicago: University of Chicago Press.

Miller, Steven E., and Scott D. Sagan. 2009. "Nuclear Power Without Nuclear Proliferation?" *Daedalus* 138 (4): 7–18.

OTA (Office of Technology Assessment). 1977. *Nuclear Proliferation and Safeguards*. New York: Praeger.

Pape, Robert. 2005. "Soft Balancing against the United States." *International Security* 30 (1): 7–45.

Paul, T. V. 2000. *Power versus Prudence: Why Nations Forgo Nuclear Weapons*. Montreal: McGill-Queen's University Press.

———. 2003. "Chinese-Pakistani Nuclear/Missile Ties and the Balance of Power." *Nonproliferation Review* 10 (2): 1–9.

Poneman, Daniel. 1982. *Nuclear Power in the Developing World*. London: George Allen & Unwin.

Potter, William C. 1982. *Nuclear Power and Nonproliferation: An Interdisciplinary Perspective*. Cambridge, MA: Oelgeschlager, Gunn & Hain.

———. Ed. 1990. *International Nuclear Trade and Nonproliferation: The Challenge of the Emerging Nuclear Suppliers*. Lexington, MA: Lexington Books.

Reuters. 2008. "Turkey, Syria Eye Nuclear Energy Cooperation," June 13.

Rublee, Maria Rost. 2009. *Nonproliferation Norms: Why States Choose Nuclear Restraint*. Athens: University of Georgia Press.

Sagan, Scott D. 1996/97. "Why Do States Build Nuclear Weapons? Three Models in Search of a Bomb." *International Security* 21 (3): 54–86.

Scheinman, Lawrence. 1965. *Atomic Energy Policy in France under the Fourth Republic*. Princeton, NJ: Princeton University Press.

Singh, Sonali, and Christopher R. Way. 2004. "The Correlates of Nuclear Proliferation: A Quantitative Test." *Journal of Conflict Resolution* 48 (6): 859–885.

Singh, Yogendra. 2007. *India-Vietnam Relations: The Road Ahead*. New Delhi, India: Institute of Peace and Conflict Studies.

Solingen, Etel. 2007. *Nuclear Logics: Contrasting Paths in East Asia and the Middle East*. Princeton, NJ: Princeton University Press.

Walt, Stephen. 1987. *The Origins of Alliances*. Ithaca, NY: Cornell University Press.

Waltz, Kenneth N. 1979. *Theory of International Politics*. Boston: McGraw-Hill.

Weir, Fred. 2007. "Russia Plans Big Nuclear Expansion." *Christian Science Monitor*, July 17.

Willrich, Mason. 1973. *Global Politics of Nuclear Energy*. New York: Praeger.

Wohlstetter, Albert, Thomas Brown, Gregory Jones, David McGarvey, Henry Rowen, Vince Taylor, and Roberta Wohlstetter. 1979. *Swords from Ploughshares: The Military Potential of Civilian Nuclear Energy*. Chicago: University of Chicago Press.

4 Internationalization of the Fuel Cycle and the Nuclear Energy Renaissance

Confronting the Credible Commitment Problem

Adam N. Stulberg

SINCE THE DAWNING OF THE NUCLEAR ERA, THE INTERNA-tional community has struggled to spread the benefits of peaceful nuclear activities while restricting weapons-usable material and expertise. Because technical activities stem from a single nuclear fuel cycle, the focus historically has centered on crafting institutional firebreaks to bolster confidence and resilience of commercial supply relations while simultaneously limiting access to the most sensitive dual-use technology, specifically uranium enrichment and plutonium reprocessing. With renewed concerns that the proliferation of these technologies and know-how would be an Achilles' heel to nuclear energy expansion in the twenty-first century, policy makers worldwide again are seriously considering "internationalization" of the fuel cycle.

Yet the wisdom of multilateral nuclear approaches (MNAs) remains hotly contested. On one hand, proponents extol mutual interests among customers and suppliers in expanding commercial ties, stemming weapons proliferation, and moving beyond technology denial and international safeguards as elements that are especially conducive to institutionalizing nuclear energy cooperation (Scheinman 1981; Vieira de Jesus 2011). Multilateral nuclear approaches can reassure market mechanisms and redress proliferation "tough nuts," as existing suppliers can scale up operations to meet growing demand. Should the nuclear weapons states make real progress toward eliminating their arsenals—but accentuating concerns about latent military programs— the demand for extraterritorial fuel cycle facilities arguably will become more pressing (Glaser 2009). On the other hand, critics bemoan pursuit of MNAs as futile and unnecessary, if not dangerous. States generally resist dependence on fuel imports out of concerns for energy security or prestige, as suggested by the meager progress toward implementing MNAs. Should MNAs materialize, they could jeopardize smoothly running global markets and lower the costs of reenrichment for states with nefarious ambitions, as is widely suspected of Iran (Glinsky, Miller, and Hubbard 2004).

This debate, however, is exceedingly selective on empirical evidence and narrow in analysis of the strategic challenges to extending credible commitments to international fuel cycle cooperation. Neither side can systematically account for the variation in MNAs with respect to goals, forms, and practical effects. Proponents overstate the economic rationale and challenges posed by market uncertainty, but understate the risks of relying on foreign supply. Difficulties with signaling trustworthy intentions are typically conflated with perverse incentives to renege on international bargains confronting even benignly motivated states. Critics, however, are too quick to assume irreconcilable differences and treat MNAs as stand-alone nonproliferation instruments. They also cannot explain the traction of select nuclear fuel agreements that do not bring states closer to the brink of making bombs.

This chapter develops the critique above in four parts. The first section notes the checkered record of MNAs, highlighting problems posed for mainstream strategic, economic, and technical accounts of international bargaining. The second part deconstructs the commitment problems associated with MNAs. The central argument is that requirements for credibility differ for specific nuclear fuel suppliers and customers. Although prospective customers are sensitive to cost-benefit calculations, they may assess the value and risks of their nuclear fuel cycle choices differently, depending on their projected reliance on nuclear energy and the market position of specific suppliers. Accordingly, the credibility and impact of a particular MNA turn on the fit with specific combinations of power asymmetry and vulnerability among the bargaining parties. This is illustrated by the contemporary postures toward MNAs adopted by Kazakhstan, South Africa, South Korea, and the United Arab Emirates (UAE). These episodes vary in bargaining contexts and outcomes, as well as offer insights into cases that are integral to forecasting the significance of MNAs for global expansion of nuclear energy. The conclusion offers lessons for theories of international bargaining and practice.

The Mixed Record of MNAs

Multilateral nuclear approaches consist of voluntary, reciprocal guarantees by nuclear energy suppliers and customers. Suppliers pledge to offer, on commercially competitive terms, nuclear fuel cycle services to states that do not otherwise exercise full sovereign rights over these sensitive technologies or that experience supply interruptions unconnected to proliferation concerns. Customers, in return, promise to forgo constructing sensitive national nuclear fuel cycle facilities, and to uphold international safety and nonproliferation norms with expansion of peaceful energy activity.[1] Accordingly, these ironclad international guarantees should bolster the security of supply for customers by providing attractive alternatives to building sensitive nuclear fuel cycle facilities that are simultaneously attuned to technical specifications of reactor types, market dynamics, potential for politically motivated supply interruptions, and dangers associated with the proliferation of near-weapons capabilities (Braun 2006).

Diverse Landscape of Internationalization

Multilateral nuclear approaches vary across several dimensions. Specific initiatives prioritize different objectives. Fuel banks (e.g., insurance mechanisms) and "cradle-to-grave" measures (e.g., multinational or regional fuel centers or spent fuel repositories) redress political motivations for weapons proliferation and can circumscribe the national sovereignty of participating states. Alternatively, pooling arrangements and early-warning mechanisms promote nuclear power by improving comparative advantages and reinforcing markets (Goldschmidt and Kratzer 1978; Neff and Jacoby 1979; Yager 1981).

Multilateral nuclear approaches also come in different forms and levels of commitment. They range from virtual promises (e.g., reflagging procedures, market assessments, performance bonds) to coordinated national policies and physical guarantees (e.g., international fuel pool and dedicated fuel banks), to cooperative ventures (e.g., jointly managed centers, extraterritorial enrichment or reprocessing facilities). Cooperative ventures, in turn, can embody different distributions of rights, such as consortia with equal ownership and control over sensitive technologies and products (e.g., the consortium of operational enrichment plants in Europe [URENCO]), or joint stock companies that entitle members to share profits and market data but "black-box" sensitive technologies (e.g., European Gaseous Diffusion Uranium Enrichment

Consortium [EURODIF] and the International Uranium Enrichment Center in Russia) (Nikitin, Andrews, and Holt 2011).

In addition, MNAs vary in their practical effects. First, there are feasibility studies and generic proposals for multilateral control over the nuclear fuel cycle that do not go beyond rhetorical or evaluation stages (Scheinman 1981). Second, there are MNAs, such as the fuel bank proposal by the Nuclear Threat Initiative (NTI, a U.S.-based nongovernmental organization) and the British proposal for "enrichment bonds" that specify technologies, facilities, financing, or legally binding guarantees. While these proposals present concrete assurance mechanisms and have been formally approved by the International Atomic Energy Agency (IAEA), implementation remains incomplete owing to ambiguities on important practical issues, such as release and hosting criteria for backup supply, modalities of IAEA control and approval, enforcement mechanisms, and division between national and international jurisdictions (Harvey 2011; Nikitin, Andrews, and Holt 2011). Third, there are MNAs that are fully operational and in force, such as established fuel banks by the United States and Russia, as well as URENCO and EURODIF that consist of multinational membership and a variety of institutional forms.

Finally, there are robust MNAs that are reinforced by formal restrictions on national rights. Russia passed domestic legislation that removed the International Uranium Enrichment Center (IUEC) from the list of sensitive enterprises and placed it under IAEA inspections. Russia also ratified the Additional Protocol that paved the way for the IAEA's intrusive safeguards on the fuel bank hosted at the facility. Neither of these national measures was stipulated by Russia's formal nonproliferation obligations, given its stature as a nuclear weapons state. Similarly, there have been concessions made by nuclear energy aspirants, such as the UAE, that codify diplomatic pledges to forsake rights to sensitive indigenous facilities in domestic law.

Explaining MNAs

The checkered pattern of specific MNAs challenges the scholarly literature. That customers are willing not only to depend on foreign supply of a strategic good, but also to extend formal concessions that forswear sovereign rights to indigenous ownership of sensitive technologies and facilities, counter expectations rooted in realpolitik. It is especially surprising that by 2011 Russia was in close partnership on the IUEC with Kazakhstan, Armenia, and Ukraine; all states with otherwise strained energy relations with Moscow.

Neomercantilist accounts are taxed by evidence that nuclear energy statecraft does not afford uniform advantages to dominant suppliers, and that to date there have been no reactor shutdowns owing to disrupted fuel supply (Yudin 2009). In practice, it was the United States' market dominance that stoked (not discouraged) European pursuit of independent expansion in the early 1970s. This "burden of hegemony," coupled with domestic political struggles over privatization, effectively subverted the favorable commercial standing of the national industry and American leverage over the nuclear programs of even close allies, spurring foreign competition in the enrichment field (Wonder 1977; Brenner 1981).

Neoliberal arguments do not fare much better. Progress toward globalization and liberalization of energy markets has not nourished a uniform rush to MNAs (Stein et al. 2004). Failure to implement concepts that pose the least infringement on the sovereign rights of nuclear aspirants—such as a German proposal for regional fuel centers that includes entitlement clauses—is especially perplexing. Why, for example, do states such as Algeria, Brazil, South Africa, and Egypt continue to frame international fuel assurances as affronts to their inalienable rights to nuclear energy, even as participating suppliers and customers openly acknowledge that MNAs should be provided "without prejudice to the rights of participating states," and in some cases undertake domestic legal action to reinforce diplomatic pledges for voluntary and nondiscriminatory MNAs (IFNEC 2010)? This points to deep suspicions surrounding the nuclear energy trade not readily captured by market uncertainty or assumptions about expected utility-maximizing behavior common to theories of international cooperation (Lorenz and Kidd 2010).[2]

Classic accounts of strategic interaction also are taken to task, as the variety of MNAs entail both coordination and collaboration scenarios. Initiatives to assure supplies—such as the U.S. national fuel reserve, the enrichment bond concept, and Japan's early-warning procedures—require at most short-term coordination of national policies to avert the proliferation of dangerous nuclear technologies. However, not all of these efforts have been fully implemented, with the Japanese proposal for states to voluntarily share information on a range of respective fuel cycle activities yet to be approved by the IAEA. In contrast, Austria's proposal to establish cradle-to-grave data systems and multinational nuclear fuel cycle facilities, the IAEA (NTI-inspired) fuel bank, and the German proposal require member states to share strategic information, procure new physical infrastructure, allocate financial resources, and make difficult political and security compromises regarding the modalities of international ownership and access to sensitive nuclear materials (Yager 1981; Yudin 2009).[3] These initiatives necessitate contracts that specify duties, distribute costs and benefits, and stipulate enforcement among the parties. Yet why has the IAEA fuel bank made more progress transcending incentives to free ride, while the others have languished? Furthermore, the mix of democratic (e.g., United States and URENCO members) and neopatrimonial regimes (e.g., UAE, Kazakhstan, Russia, Ukraine) in various MNAs reveals that domestic institutional distinctions alone are insufficient to explain the variation in international fuel supply cooperation (Gourley and Stulberg, Chapter 1 in this volume; Hastings, Chapter 9 in this volume; Montgomery, Chapter 7 in this volume).

Given the diversity of customer responses, it is also difficult to discern the prestige associated with different stages of the nuclear fuel cycle. As discussed by MacFarlane (Chapter 2 in this volume), states value nuclear energy very differently. But why is nuclear status associated with domestic production of nuclear energy for some states, but for others it is garnered specifically from indigenous development of enrichment and reprocessing capabilities or even nuclear weapons possession? Why does Brazil root the legitimacy of fuel cycle activity at the national level, while Austria claims that appropriate solutions rest with "inclusive, transparent, and verifiable multilateral systems" (Austria 2009; Vieira de Jesus 2011)?

The same holds for reputational considerations. Some scholars argue that reputational costs inhibit cooperation, especially among leaders who face significant political costs for reneging on promises to develop national nuclear energy programs (Fearon 1995; Powell 2006; Sechser 2010). But which reputations are decisive for advancing MNAs? Sweden, for example, has historically cultivated a reputation for restraint in developing sensitive fuel cycle capabilities while advancing nuclear power to reduce oil import dependence and recently to fight global warming (Bergenas 2009). This contrasts starkly with the reputational concerns of Algeria, Egypt, and South Africa. These states have remained critical of MNAs largely to preserve reputations as bulwarks among the Non-Aligned Movement for nuclear equity and nondiscrimination, and to avert dangerous precedents for eroding perceived "inalienable" peaceful nuclear rights (Horner and Meier 2009). Thus, it is not clear a priori what the meaning of reputation is for a customer state, whether it works as a single identity, how states manage multiple reputations across different issue areas, and which reputation matters most for nuclear energy bargaining (Downs and Jones 2002).

The checkered past of MNAs also exposes limitations to traditional economic analyses. Although MNAs may constitute unnecessary subsidies—given that fuel costs represent only 5 percent of total costs of producing nuclear energy, and that for states intent on producing at least 8–10 gigawatts-electric (GWe) of electricity annually it may be cost-effective to develop an indigenous enrichment capacity—pooling resources and co-locating facilities in multilateral fuel centers may generate net gains by constraining negative safety and security externalities. Economies of scale and diversification are difficult to discern and can generate conflicting commercial incentives, depending on the assessment of absolute versus relative costs and direct versus opportunity costs (Tomas 2005; Sokolski 2007; Habib et al. 2006; Kidd 2010). Also, the projected retirement of obsolete gaseous diffusion technology and replacement by more-efficient centrifuge facilities could cut two ways—significantly raising or lowering market capacity and price—that would generate conflicting incentives for MNAs to assure optimal long-term commercial investment and nonproliferation (Rothwell and Braun 2008). Furthermore, focus on commercial incentives for MNAs conflates economic with political considerations. While fuel costs are modest and can be spread out or passed on to consumers once national nuclear facilities are operational, decisions to develop indigenous programs require that policy makers embrace significant up-front political commitments and risks.

It is intriguing that some states without secure uranium conversion or fuel fabrication capacity (e.g., UAE) have accepted MNAs for low enriched uranium—rendering them potentially more dependent on foreign supply and vulnerable to short-term disruptions—while others with such capacities (e.g., Brazil) have balked at such assurances. Given the traditional asset specificity of enrichment technologies, it is not surprising that more progress has been made at forging international cooperation on front-end nuclear fuel cycle issues than with respect to plutonium reprocessing. As some scholars note, such distinctions may be blurring with advanced enrichment engineering processes and technologies that are expanding into other sectors of the modern economy (Glaser 2009). Yet why do we still see more progress with MNAs regarding enrichment services than with back-end activities involving mature and diffused reprocessing technologies and depository services (McCombie and Isaacs 2010)?

MNAs and Credible Commitments

Why, then, have rational suppliers and prospective customers experienced only mixed success at reaching efficient outcomes? The answer rests largely with solving for trust in international relations. Nuclear energy aspirants remain deeply suspicious that fuel assurances will be taken as first steps toward eroding sovereign rights or establishing predatory supplier cartels. Once customers operationalize nuclear power programs, they become dependent upon predictable deliveries specific to fuel fabrication and reactor design requirements (Lorenz and Kidd 2010).[4] They also stand to face difficult economic and political challenges, not to mention long lead times, with mustering the necessary domestic resources to shift course in response to blackmail. Suppliers, too, are reticent about embracing measures that can confound smoothly functioning fuel cycle markets, or that can be exploited to expedite or diffuse latent military capabilities. By spreading dual-use materials, lowering technical hurdles, and building up the indigenous knowledge base, nuclear cooperation could eventually lower the expected costs of developing a weapons program for both deceitful and insecure customers (Fuhrmann 2009).

This predicament is tantamount to the commitment problem in international bargaining (Fearon 1995; Powell 2006). Because the decision to form a given agreement depends on expectations regarding the likelihood that it will be fulfilled, success rests on the credibility of mutual commitments. It is confounded, however, by asymmetric distributions of information (i.e., each party knows more about its own intentions than the other's), and incentives *ex post* for unilaterally reneging on promises. Assurances by an actor to behave cooperatively may not be credible if the other does not trust it (Kydd 2005). The credible commitment problem, therefore, looms large for interactions between states whose choices are contingent and have no way of distinguishing benign from malevolent intentions of the other party, as well as where fulfillment of initial promises cannot be enforced. This is distinct from pure signaling problems that turn on challenges of communicating intentions *ex ante*, as credible commitments entail solving for time-inconsistent preferences, whereby a state must convince the other that it will cooperate in the future even if it may be rational to renege opportunistically *ex post* (Fearon 1997; Morrow 1999; Martin 2005).[5]

Although they are pervasive, credible commitment problems do not unconditionally stymie international cooperation. Actors who experience high domestic audience costs from breaking commitments, surrender a bond to a third party in case of defection, or derive legitimacy from an international reputation for trustworthiness should be well poised to go beyond "cheap talk." By incurring the costs of either giving up sovereign decision-making authority or "tying their hands" *ex ante*, states may raise the expected political costs of defection to make their commitments more credible at the outset (Martin 1993; Fearon 1995; Tomz 2007). Information asymmetries also may be less daunting in the nuclear energy realm, given the history of efficient fuel cycle markets, diversity of established trading relationships, and web of nonproliferation obligations across the sector. These factors afford opportunities for states to develop mutual understandings of nuclear ambitions, strategies, and capabilities, reducing the burden of conveying trustworthiness behind each deal (Fearon 1995; Powell 2006).

These mitigating factors likely carry less weight for MNAs. The ambiguity surrounding reputational issues and diversity of participating regime types complicate the ability of nuclear suppliers and customers to convince one another of the normative or domestic political costs that they would incur by reneging on nuclear obligations. States also cannot irrevocably "tie their hands" *ex ante*. A sober review of nuclear fuel transactions suggests that suppliers and customers can experience unexpected changes in political leadership and market and security settings, presenting even benignly motivated leaderships with rational opportunities to renege on commitments made under fundamentally different conditions (Neff and Jacoby 1979). Because of asymmetries between nuclear suppliers and customers, the value of implementing nuclear fuel cycle agreements also varies. It follows that if disparities in power and vulnerability influence the likelihood that agreements will be fulfilled, they should affect the probability of MNAs entering into force.

Risk, Power, and the Credibility of MNAs

Multilateral nuclear approaches also involve risk. This is analytically distinct from bargaining under conditions of uncertainty, where the probabilities of outcomes are generally unknown. Risk calculations also focus on the value of outcomes, measured in terms of magnitude of potential losses or gains from a reference point, as opposed to expected utilities derived from weighing overall costs, benefits, and probabilities of different options (Farnham 1994; McDermott 1998; Taliaferro 2004). This is especially apropos of the nuclear sector, as states historically have canceled or postponed construction of nuclear power plants even under sound economic conditions, in response to high investment and financial risks.[6] In the MNA context, suppliers seek assurances primarily to mitigate risks of clandestine development and proliferation of sensitive material, rather than to address the uncertainty of receiving payment for deliveries. Similarly, customers are mainly concerned about avoiding significant losses due to political disruptions, rather than insulating themselves from market perturbations and transaction costs of switching to alternative suppliers.

Risk perceptions are affected by cognitive, group, cultural, or situational factors. When it comes to nuclear trading, however, situational factors seem directly relevant, given the collective and protracted character of related decisions. The mixed traction of MNAs also points to low correlations between specific national institutions, cultural biases, and patterns of risk taking for nuclear cooperation (Douglas and Wildavsky 1983). In contrast, situational factors travel well, and if sufficiently specified they can offer sound basis for comparative analysis of national nuclear risk taking.

Prospect theory, for example, tells us that national risk taking varies with how decision makers frame their circumstances. In practice, they evaluate outcomes with respect to deviations from a benchmark rather than with respect to net asset levels. They also give more weight to losses than to comparable gains, and are generally risk-averse with respect to gains and risk-accepting with respect to losses (Levy 1994). Accordingly, decision makers are prone to take risks when framing choices among outcomes considered as nearly certain losses from a reference point, while they tend to be risk-averse when facing choices among uncertain gains.

These insights alone lack predictive power for international fuel cycle bargaining. Which a priori conditions shape how nuclear energy aspirant states frame reference points and evaluate prospective outcomes (Boettcher 1995; O'Neill 2001)? Which situational factors affect practical, intangible considerations of probabilistic versus certain outcomes associated with reliance on the import of nuclear fuel? How do these considerations influence the likelihood of forming an MNA in the first place? Can risk-prone states be more inclined to gamble on MNAs than on developing sensitive indigenous facilities?

A full accounting of the impact of risk perceptions for MNAs, therefore, necessitates identifying conditions that shape credible nuclear energy commitments. For customers, a crucial reference point for framing nuclear supply options comes from the value of the sector for the nation's energy security strategy. This is captured by the fraction of domestic electricity generation or additional hydrocarbon exports that the state projects for nuclear power over the strategic planning period.[7] The more reliant a state expects to be on nuclear power for its energy security, the more important it will become to secure steady fuel supplies. The pure economics of nuclear energy markets, however, tend to understate the costs of disruptions in foreign supply, especially if a customer has made a large commitment to nuclear energy and the alternative is to concede sovereign control over its strategic energy decisions (Neff and Jacoby 1979; Harding 2007).[8] Even with economies of scale of indigenous production, spare international capacity, and enhanced fuel supplier competition, import dependence becomes a vulnerability for a state with lofty nuclear energy ambitions, given the acute need for predictable supply to generate baseload power. Conversely, customers with a modest national commitment to nuclear power generation for their energy security would be less affected by the short- to medium-term costs of disruption. Though sensitive to transaction costs imposed by import dependency, they could turn to alternative energy resources or suppliers to compensate for shortfalls without suffering dramatic political or economic costs. Thus, customer states are likely to assess the value of different contingencies for fuel cycle supply in terms of deviations from their projected reliance on the sector for national energy security.

At the same time, power asymmetries can distort mutual trust and the extension of credible commitments (Farrell 2004; Powell 2006; Sechser 2010). When one party holds too much power over another, as available options afford it disproportionate advantages to breaking off an agreement, the relationship can be insufficient to bind it to act in the interests of both parties. The significantly stronger state has neither an incentive not to renege *ex post* nor capacity to convince *ex ante* the weaker party that it encapsulates the latter's interest or will refrain from making additional demands. Because the relationship is relatively meaningless, it becomes too powerful to extend credible commitments to cooperation, even if it does not harbor future designs to exploit the weaker party. By the same token, gross power asymmetries drive out expectations that the stronger state can be trusted to attend to the interests of the weaker party. Where the weaker party cannot trust the stronger, its calculations about the future will depend increasingly on error-prone—if not worst-case—judgments about the certainty of being exploited by an opportunistic stronger party (Kramer 2004; Sechser 2010). This compounds fears of future losses and reduces the value assigned to risky negative prospects, leaving the weaker state with little incentive to act in a trustworthy or risk-averse fashion; and the strong state realizes this. Consequently, extreme power differentials leave neither strong nor weak parties reason to trust each other, irrespective of mutual interests in cooperation.

In the nuclear energy trade, the market position of a supplier is integral to determining the power balance. Market power enables a supplier both to charge prices higher than costs and to extract concessions from customers. This can be measured in terms of both aggregate percentages of global supply and competitive advantages at delivering nuclear fuel to specific customers. A state is traditionally considered to wield significant market power if it controls nearly half of the aggregate supply of a good (Drezner 1999: 15). However, the "relevant" aggregate share of the global market is much lower when it comes to nuclear fuel supply. This is because nuclear fuel must be fabricated to specific fuel assembly and reactor design requirements, and because increasing returns to scale and concentrated features of related fuel cycle markets create barriers to entry and reduce market discipline. The absorption of excess capacity, retirement of diffusion technology, depletion of stockpiles and secondary supplies, and high rates of government intervention in home markets also reduce the projected elasticity of the global enrichment market associated even with a modest nuclear energy resurgence (Rothwell 2009).[9] Consequently, it is estimated here that a supplier can wield significant market power if it claims roughly 25 percent of the aggregate supply market, in conjunction with holding competitive advantages at servicing the technical requirements demanded by the infrastructure of a specific customer.

A Taxonomy of MNAs for the Contemporary Nuclear Landscape

As depicted in Figure 4.1, combining insights from prospect theory and asymmetrical bargaining offers a prism for understanding the relative appeal of specific MNAs for contemporary nuclear energy aspirants. Together they can yield four possible outcomes.

South Africa's Risky Defiance

One scenario that militates against international fuel assurances is where the market power of the specific supplier is so great that neither it nor the

Nuclear reliance

+	**TOO RISKY** *South Africa (1998–2008)* MNAs least likely (rhetorical critique/ambivalence)	**HIGHLY UNCERTAIN** *Kazakhstan* MNAs possible (formation/implementation) Tie hands/third-party hosting
−	**RISKY** *South Korea* MNAs possible (formation/implementation) Subsidized inducement Reciprocal investment	**OPPORTUNISTIC** *United Arab Emirates* MNAs probable (formation/implementation/extra commitment) Coordination of national policies Minimum inducement

Market power asymmetries

FIGURE 4.1 Conceptual framework

customer can be trusted, and the customer cannot afford to incur the anticipated losses of being exploited. The unfavorable power balance and import vulnerability render customers nearly insensitive to promises by suppliers to uphold commitments. Acceding to an MNA thus becomes a losing prospect for even a benignly motivated but risk-prone customer.

Prior to 2009, signing onto any type of MNA was a dangerous gamble for South Africa. Successive national energy strategies in 1998 and 2008 codified lofty ambitions for nuclear power to grow from 5 percent to 25 percent of national electricity generation by 2030, propelled by construction of up to twenty-four additional reactors, including a commercial-size pebble bed modular reactor (PBMR). The nuclear industry was expected to cover at least half of the projected doubling of national electricity generation, reducing the country's reliance on depleting coal reserves by nearly 20 percent (Department of Minerals and Energy 2008; WNA 2010a). This expansion was deemed especially significant for supplying electricity to the Western Cape region, and was heralded as a panacea for blackouts in rural communities across the country that otherwise lacked reliable baseload power (Figg 2006). Moreover, growth of national nuclear power generation was expected to satisfy 60 percent of the increasing demand for electricity across the continent, via interconnected regional power grids, as well as to add significant value to the world's fourth-largest uranium mining industry.

But the South African government remained protective of the industry. Notwithstanding dependence on foreign trade, the country's difficult experience with OPEC and apartheid sanctions by U.S. and European suppliers (which at the time controlled nearly 70 percent of the fresh fuel market) left the leadership acutely anxious about collusion among international energy suppliers. Coupled with concerns about Russia's capacity to provide reliable fuel for the prospective PBMR and the legacy of earlier military and commercial enrichment programs, this stoked a drive for independence in the nuclear sector, including pursuit of a complete but inefficiently developed fuel cycle. To the extent that the government was interested in international engagement, it was as a source of foreign investment to develop these national facilities (Figg 2006; Department of Minerals and Energy 2008). Ironically, this impulse stunted the national nuclear resurgence, as the 2009 downturn in the economy forced Pretoria to scale back construction of new reactors by 80 percent and to extend indefinitely the timeline for realizing the national energy program.

South Africa's projected nuclear reliance and commitment to possessing a self-sufficient but regionally integrated fuel cycle ultimately framed the government's resistance to MNAs. Although willing to import fuel with the shutdown of commercial enrichment in 1995, MNAs simply constituted a bridge too far, especially given prevailing inequities in the nonproliferation regime. The government castigated MNAs in the name of promoting the independent "nuclear rights" of the Non-Aligned Movement. This was evidenced most vividly by Ambassador Abdul Minty's unwavering support for the inalienable rights to peaceful uses of nuclear energy for all states, and his blistering criticism of MNAs as instruments for circumscribing these rights in multiple disarmament and nonproliferation forums. Even as suppliers dropped "conditionality clauses" and it became obvious that the country could not go it alone with its nuclear program, Minty and other South African officials consistently railed against international supplier arrangements as encroachments on the rights of nuclear aspirants, deepening dependence and discrimination in the global nuclear regime (Minty 2007; Horner 2009).[10]

UAE's Cheap Talk
Conversely, as captured by the lower right cell, even robust MNAs are likely to obtain under conditions with little impact on a nuclear resurgence or renaissance; where a specific supplier does not wield significant market power, and

the customer does not expect to be reliant on nuclear energy. The invulnerable customer can afford to be opportunistic with cooperation. Neither side must significantly compensate the other for accepting its assurance, because the supplier lacks capacity to reap disproportionate gains by reneging, and the risk-averse customer does not have much to lose from being exploited. However, because both trustworthy and untrustworthy customers may have little at stake with cooperation, even successful implementation of robust MNAs will be neither decisive for spurring national nuclear programs nor effective at illuminating the nuclear ambitions of the parties.

As part of a bilateral nuclear pact with the United States, the UAE formally renounced rights to indigenous enrichment and reprocessing facilities (and heavy water production) in favor of reliance on international fuel supplies (USGPO 2009). In this 123 Agreement, the UAE promised to uphold the highest nonproliferation standards, including adherence to the Additional Protocol to IAEA safeguards, and to return relevant nuclear technology to the providers if it was found in violation of these provisions. Abu Dhabi subsequently pledged to make such obligations, as well as self-imposed restraints on the transfer of spent nuclear fuel, unilaterally binding via accompanying domestic legislation. To underscore the commitment to internationalization, the UAE then solicited joint ventures for construction of reactors and committed to relying on foreign contractors to manage initial facilities, as well as contributed US$10 million in support of the IAEA fuel reserve (Early 2010; WNA 2010c). These gestures were touted worldwide as exemplars of the positive link between MNAs and widening access to peaceful nuclear power for nuclear energy aspirants in the Middle East and beyond. The UAE, too, heralded them for demonstrating the transparency of the country's civilian nuclear ambitions (Blanchard and Kerr 2009).

The UAE's commitments were much less groundbreaking than conventionally presumed. The embrace of MNAs presented little risk, given that the UAE depends on natural gas for generating 98 percent of domestic electricity and holds only modest objectives for the national nuclear program by comparison. Notwithstanding the country's determination to field a "fleet of reactors" by 2020 (as many as fourteen plants producing 20 GWe) to cover half of the projected 9 percent annual increase in demand for electricity, the national energy strategy envisions deepening the state's overwhelming dependence on natural gas for both domestic power generation and export earnings. Although supportive of a regional nuclear power program, the UAE maintained a keen interest in directing these efforts toward development of a desalination program aimed at facilitating expansion of the national gas sector (WNA 2010c).

At the same time, the UAE remained largely unconstrained in pursuing its nuclear suitors. Through 1999, Abu Dhabi solicited nine bids for new reactor construction and then short-listed three foreign consortia comprised of vendors from the United States, Japan, France, and South Korea. Ultimately the contract was competitively awarded to the South Korean consortium that demonstrated "the highest capacity factor, lowest construction cost and shortest construction time among the bidders" (WNA 2010b). Similarly, the UAE remained open to purchasing fuel via open tenders. In this spirit, it complemented the agreement with the United States with a series of memoranda of understandings (MOUs) with Japan, France, South Korea, and Russia. Most of these MOUs did not include unilateral pledges to forswear indigenous fabrication of nuclear fuel or to return controlled materials, virtually undercutting the practical significance of the commitments to the United States. With little at stake in terms of the projected trajectory of the domestic nuclear program, and freedom to exploit competitive bids by prospective suppliers, Abu Dhabi did not have much to lose materially by setting the "gold standard" for MNAs. Instead, this provided a cheap opportunity to counter the country's tarnished image as a weak link in the nonproliferation regime and to signal interest in engaging in open trade (Early 2010).

Kazakhstan: Forging Ahead with Cautious Optimism
In between the polar scenarios of South Africa and the UAE are conditions that can go either way, depending on how specific nuclear fuel assurance mechanisms are crafted. Where there is a gross power imbalance involving a dominant supplier and a risk-averse customer, the success of the MNA will rest on how effective the supplier is at mitigating uncertainty owing to its market advantages. Because invulnerable customers are less likely to fear losses from *ex post* exploitation, distrust endemic to the power differential can be assuaged by conspicuous efforts on the part of the supplier to restrain its market power and proprietary control over specified institutional mechanisms. This can include offers to construct jointly managed or owned enrichment facilities, establish market sharing or diversified supply relationships, or accept unanimous voting on release authority to "tie the hands" and dilute the significant market power of the supplier (Ribcoff 1976). This scenario is depicted

in the upper-right cell of Figure 4.1.Kazakhstan's cooperation with Russia in the IUEC and other enrichment arrangements dovetails with this predicament. Like the UAE, Kazakhstan does not project reliance on nuclear power generation for energy security, because it possesses abundant natural gas and oil reserves, as well as significant wind, hydroelectric, solar, and biomass potential. Instead, the government embraces expansion of the nuclear sector in order to move up the value chain in global nuclear fuel cycle markets. Strategic sights are set on doubling mining capacity to become the world's largest supplier of natural uranium (capturing 30 percent of the foreign market), as well as on enlarging its international footprint in the conversion (12 percent) and fuel fabrication (30 percent) markets by 2020. By combining these fuel cycle services, along with collaborating in reactor development and sales, Kazakhstan seeks to boost its competitive advantages in key expanding markets, such as Japan, China, South Korea, and India (Kassenova 2009; WNA 2010d; Gleason 2011).

At the same time, Kazakhstan is heavily beholden to Russia for nuclear fuel supply. The Soviet infrastructural legacy left it without a national electricity grid, rendering the northern parts of the country dependent on Russian electrical supply and southern regions intertwined with power generation in Uzbekistan and Kyrgyzstan (Stulberg 2007; Kassenova 2009). Moreover, Kazakhstan sends the lion's share of mined uranium for conversion and enrichment to Russia, which in turn is projected to control nearly 50 percent of the concentrated enrichment supply market for the foreseeable future (Rothwell 2009). Kazakhstan then fabricates the fuel pellets and sends them back to Russia for final production of fuel rods. Accordingly, Russia's stature looms large in Kazakhstan's strategy for leveraging the indigenous nuclear sector to expand and diversify its export portfolio.

Against this backdrop, it has been neither difficult for Russia to entice Kazakhstan nor too risky for Kazakhstan to sign onto the IUEC. In order to allay possible anxieties of greater reliance on Russian fuel supply and to set a positive precedent for future partners, Russia signaled self-restraint by offering Kazakhstan a 10 percent ownership stake in the IUEC. Although Kazakhstan accepted arrangements that "black-boxed" enrichment technologies and committed to indigenous enrichment capabilities, it acquired full voting rights over all financial and managerial decisions. This was reinforced by several joint ventures that enhanced the payoffs to Kazakhstan of collaborating with Russia both on enrichment and related transactions. In particular, the two countries agreed to construct a gas centrifuge enrichment plant in Russia on a fifty-fifty ownership basis. This offers to secure for Kazakhstan a flow of enriched uranium and will entitle it to sell excess fuel derived from its natural uranium, adding value to its future exports. Russia, in turn, committed to investing in Kazakhstan's growing mining industry. It also partnered with Kazakhstan to develop and market its small and medium-size reactors, without requiring the latter to forsake cooperation with other foreign reactor vendors (Sokova and Chuen 2007; Loukianova 2008; Kassenova 2009). Together these inducements not only improved transparency and raised the costs to Russia of breaking off future supplies of enriched fuel, but also made deepening cooperation both low cost and potentially lucrative—in commercial and nonproliferation terms—for an otherwise risk-averse Kazakh nuclear establishment intent on expanding its share in select fuel cycle markets.

South Korea: Gambling on Restraint

Under conditions marked by vulnerable customers and involving a more diversified supply market (or less dominant supplier), the key to a successful MNA turns on whether it represents an attractive gamble to the customer. Because customers are highly risk prone, the potential upside of the institutionalized fuel cycle arrangement must be greater than the downside of being exploited. Although difficult to achieve, cooperation is possible, because the absence of a gross power asymmetry creates opportunity to convey credible commitments to enhance risky positive prospects. Proposals that offer prospects for significant gains, including subsidized fuel cycle services, reciprocal investment in supplier fuel cycle facilities, and access to highly prized commercial or security externalities, may be the most credible. What matters most, however, is that suppliers tailor proposals to compensate for the magnitude of risk assumed by the vulnerable customer; neither "cheap talk" nor offers of modest gains will suffice. As long as suppliers fashion fuel assurance proposals to accommodate the risk propensity of a customer, even failed MNAs can be constructive at illuminating preferences among the parties.

The situation confronting South Korea reflects this predicament. Shortly after construction of its first reactor in 1971, South Korea turned to nuclear energy as a strategic priority for the national energy strategy aimed at sustaining economic growth amid domestic hydrocarbon scarcity and dependence on oil imports. Under the current strategy, the government projects that the share of electricity generated by the sector will jump from 48 percent in 2008 to as high as 60 percent by 2030. This calls for doubling reactor construction and developing advanced technologies for pyroprocessing spent nuclear fuel technology to close the nuclear fuel cycle, thus putting the domestic industry on track to become self-sufficient and among the top five in the world by the end of the period. Buoyed by the UAE deal, South Korea also has targeted owning 50 percent stakes in large uranium mining projects (e.g., Canada, Africa, and South America), as well as boosting foreign reactor sales to established nuclear energy consumers (e.g., U.S., France) and aspirant states (especially Jordan, Turkey, Romania, and Ukraine) as the most lucrative element of its overall trade policy after exports of automobiles, semiconductors, and shipbuilding. This is complemented by designs for capturing a greater share of the projected US$78 billion reactor operation, repair, and service market (WNA 2010b; Stott 2010). In short, South Korea has become the world's sixth-largest nuclear power–generating state and is committed to expanding its footprint both at home and abroad in uranium mining, reactor development, and backend processing.

South Korea has not developed a sensitive nuclear fuel facility and remains dependent on the international commercial uranium and uranium enrichment service markets to supply its significant and growing fuel needs. To date, nuclear fuel supply has come from multiple sources, including the United States and France. However, the country's deepening reliance on nuclear power generation and goals for capturing significant shares of reactor markets have made it vulnerable to foreign supply disruptions and resistant to officially forsaking its national rights to peaceful nuclear energy development. It has become especially concerned about prospective competitive disadvantages at selling its reactors relative to commercial rivals that can include fresh fuel in their bids. Looking forward, South Korea also rejects a narrow preoccupation with establishing mechanisms that redress anxieties from a static market perspective. Rather, consistent with objectives of expanding sales to nuclear energy aspirants, South Korea remains wary of restrictions on the global demand side of the market that may compromise its ability to break into this growing sector (ROK 2009).

Notwithstanding concerns about MNAs born of deepening nuclear reliance and dependence on global fuel markets, South Korea has resisted development of sensitive nuclear enrichment facilities and even signed onto several foreign initiatives that impose modest restraint. This includes membership in the U.S. Global Nuclear Energy Partnership program and official reaffirmation of pledges to forsake domestic enrichment during successive sessions of the 2010 NPT review conference. However, this restraint has been cultivated by concerted international efforts to sweeten the positive risk prospects of cooperation. Notably, the United States cemented cooperation not only by demonstrating the security benefits of the bilateral relationship during successive nuclear crises with North Korea, but also by offering inducements to share novel Generation IV reactor technology and initially endorsing joint development of reprocessing technology, including pyroprocessing. As well, the potential positive payoffs associated with engaging France on supply contracts were complemented by the acquisition of ownership stakes in France's new Beese II enrichment facility. Seoul also secured greater ownership stakes in joint ventures to develop uranium mines in Niger and Canada that significantly improved the upside of front-end cooperation (WNA 2010b).

Implications

The mixed success of MNAs raises important theoretical and practical issues often overlooked by proponents and critics alike. Recasting the basic analytical challenges in terms of international credible commitment problems confronting nuclear energy suppliers and prospective customers offers a chart to help navigate these shoals. Most of the scholarly research in this vein treats the central bargaining problem in terms of uncertainty and expected utility maximization that has yielded important theoretical and empirical insights. However, as applied to the nuclear domain, where calculations of risk loom particularly large, this myopia creates a conspicuous blind spot. Because MNAs must redress both information problems and concerns about vulnerability, success depends on how well proposals encapsulate both *ex ante* motivations of the actors and fears of exploitation *ex post*. By considering different combinations of market power and nuclear reliance confronting customers, it seems that MNAs are most likely to advance nuclear energy programs when they embody solutions to gross power asymmetries or the high-risk propensity of a customer, but not to both. At the same time, they are more apt to attract opportunistic rather than risk-prone customers.

   This framework suggests ways to integrate alternative assumptions about rational decision making into strategic bargaining theories. Because states must contend with risk as well as uncertainty, factoring in assessments of vulnerability offers a productive avenue for explaining the value-maximizing choices that may otherwise appear to be suboptimal from a utility-maximizing approach. By focusing on situational conditions, it offers insight into applying prospect theory beyond ad hoc (if not post hoc) and narrow decision-making analyses of a specific state's foreign policy.

The argument also complements research that demonstrates the potentially counterintuitive implications of bargaining among asymmetrical players that disadvantage stronger states. Whereas recent attention has been devoted to highlighting the impact of power asymmetry on the efficacy of coercive threats, this analysis underscores how such disparities can complicate international cooperation. Even benignly motivated actors may be too strong to trust. Rather than facilitating collective action, hegemonic power may be a liability for engaging risk-prone actors. It also highlights the importance of power disparities for shaping how actors frame and evaluate their choices, as opposed to affecting strictly reputational dynamics.

This chapter underscores that not all MNAs are created equal or carry the equivalent implications for alternative nuclear futures. Some MNAs, for example, can gain traction among strictly opportunistic customers that pursue them for cheap gains. As suggested by the UAE, although cooperative fuel agreements may codify nonproliferation interests, because they do not significantly impact the nuclear energy ambitions of the customer, they are not likely to be decisive for the trajectory of growth. Accordingly, the success of related MNAs may be less crucial to a broadening of a nuclear energy renaissance than is commonly projected by critics and opponents alike. Alternatively, MNAs may prove most difficult to forge among those states that are likely to be the most reliant on nuclear energy. Vulnerable to losses associated with political disruptions in supplies and prone to worst-case thinking in the face of concentrated markets, these states may be too consumed by the negative risk prospects to be assuaged. The proliferation of related cases would suggest that the efficacy of future market-neutral MNAs, therefore, will have little impact on a future nuclear resurgence; they are more appropriate to states with modest interests in nuclear energy than to those that expect to deepen reliance on the nuclear sector for national energy security.

In addition, the promise of MNAs rests on the fit with specific circumstances. Others note that MNAs must address customer concerns about conditionality clauses, dependency, equal rights, nonexclusive eligibility, and multinational ownership and control. However, the argument here suggests that such concerns are neither uniform nor require equal redress in specific proposals. Because customers are attracted to MNAs out of different concerns about risk, as well as the issues above, the appeal of MNAs varies. For opportunistic customers, the mere offer of engagement may suffice, rendering moot the modalities of release and access. Alternatively, for states such as South Korea, the inducements for cooperation may require offers of reciprocal investment opportunities or provision of subsidies and preferred commercial access to a customer that may conflict with the market-neutral interests of suppliers.

Finally, the value of MNAs may extend beyond tangible commercial and nonproliferation contributions. As suggested by the Gourley/Stulberg, Kroenig, and Montgomery chapters in this volume (Chapters 1, 8, and 7, respectively), MNAs constitute only one instrument for spurring global nuclear energy growth and stemming weapons proliferation; they are not panaceas for what are otherwise economic, technical and political challenges. Indeed, the real contribution of MNAs may extend beyond providing an institutional break between the peaceful and military dimensions to the fuel cycle and turn on improving transparency among nuclear energy suppliers and aspirants. If crafted appropriately to reassure the specific uncertainties and risks confronting customers, MNA proposals can obviate benign imperatives for indigenous enrichment and reprocessing technologies, as well as expose less pragmatic, if not belligerent, motivations of nuclear energy aspirants. Accordingly, even if they fail to take effect, such proposals will be important for distinguishing trustworthy from untrustworthy nuclear energy aspirants. This alone will make an important contribution to a safe and secure global expansion of nuclear energy under any scenario.

Notes

1. MNAs differ from international safeguards that focus on detecting the misappropriation of sensitive technology, material, and knowledge, in that their central thrust is to discourage respective indigenous development in the first place.

2. Tensions among interpretations of MNAs are vivid in statements issued at the 2010 NPT Review Conference. On one hand, working papers by Sweden, Austria, and "the Vienna Group of 10," as well as the approved final draft document, explicitly endorsed voluntary, nondiscriminatory principles for all future MNAs. On the other hand, repeated statements issued by Egyptian, Brazilian, and Algerian representatives noted inherent restrictions imposed by MNAs on the sovereign rights of states to develop full nuclear fuel cycles.

3. By 2010, the United States had also publicly endorsed exploration of an international cradle-to-grave nuclear fuel management framework.

4. Given impracticalities of stockpiling more than one or two reactor loads on site and holding fabricated fuel in reserve (due to specific reactor designs), customers that do not develop indigenous facilities cannot insulate themselves from bargaining issues.

5. This also differs from circumstances where suppliers and customers either have harmonious interests or are deadlocked without overlapping interests.

6. As evidenced by the impact of the accidents at Three Mile Island and Chernobyl on the global sector, the prospects for significant loss can outweigh the expected utilities of probabilistic outcomes.

7. Nuclear reliance is embodied in a nation's overall energy security strategy, as opposed to the estimated aggregate annual growth rates of nuclear power generation, electricity generation, or export earnings, or even the likelihood of realizing such projections. This is distinguished from other definitions that focus on the significance of meeting only one aspect of a state's energy security concerns, such as electricity demand (Nelson 2010).

8. The conservative planning for fuel supply is reflected in the standard long-term contracting for enriched uranium sales.

9. Market slack and fuel prices alone do not determine a prospective nuclear energy customer's vulnerability, owing to the combination of technical, political, and economic features associated with exploration and production, relationships among existing suppliers, and the interdependence of different stages of the nuclear fuel cycle. With respect to the concentration of critical stages of the nuclear fuel cycle, four companies (based in Russia, France, the United States, and Canada) account for 88 percent of the conversion market; five uranium enrichers (based in Russia, France, the Netherlands, the United Kingdom, and the United States) account for 95 percent of the global market (with a possibly duopoly on the horizon with Russia and France); and four companies control 84 percent of the fuel fabrication market (based in France, Russia, the United States, and Japan).

10. For example, in 2009 the United States and South Africa signed an agreement on cooperation on nuclear energy research and development related to PBMR and Generation IV technologies that did not include a conditionality clause.

References

Austria. 2009. *Multilateralization of the Nuclear Fuel Cycle: Increasing Transparency and Sustainable Activity.* Working paper submitted by Austria to the Preparation Committee for the 2010 Review Conference of the Parties to the Treaty on the Non-Proliferation of Nuclear Weapons. NPT/CONF.2010/PC.III/WP.34. May 13, 2009.

Bergenas, Johan. 2009. "Sweden Reverses Nuclear Phase-Out Policy." NTI Analysis, 9 November 2009. Available at: http://www.nti.org/analysis/articles/sweden-reverses-nuclear-phase-out/.

Blanchard, Christopher M., and Paul K. Kerr. 2009. "The United Arab Emirates Nuclear Program and Proposal for U.S. Nuclear Cooperation." *Congressional Research Service Report 7-5700*, October 28.

Boettcher, William A., III. 1995. "Context, Methods, Numbers, and Words." *Journal of Conflict Resolution* 39 (3): 561–583.

Braun, Chaim. 2006. "Nuclear Energy Market and the Nonproliferation Regime," *Nonproliferation Review* 13 (3): 627–644.

Brenner, Michael J. 1981. *Nuclear Power and Non-Proliferation: The Remaking of U.S. Policy.* New York: Cambridge University Press.

Department of Minerals and Energy (DME). 2008. *Nuclear Energy Policy for the Republic of South Africa.* Available at: http://www.info.gov.za/view/DownloadFileAction?id=72522.

Douglas, Mary, and Aaron Wildavsky. 1983. *Risk and Culture.* Berkeley: University of California Press.

Downs, George W., and Michael A. Jones. 2002. "Reputation, Compliance, and International Law." *Journal of Legal Studies* 31: 95–114.

Drezner, Daniel. 1999. *The Sanctions Paradox: Economic Statecraft and International Relations.* New York: Cambridge University Press.

Early, Bryan. 2010. "Acquiring Foreign Nuclear Assistance in the Middle East." *The Nonproliferation Review* 17 (2): 259–280.

Farnham, Barbara. Ed. 1994. *Avoiding Losses/Taking Risks.* Ann Arbor: University of Michigan Press.

Farrell, Henry. 2004. "Trust, Distrust, and Power," In *Distrust*, ed. Russell Hardin. New York: Russell Sage.

Fearon, James D. 1995. "Rationalist Explanations of War." *International Organization* 49 (3): 379–414.

———. 1997. "Signaling Foreign Policy Interests: Tying Hands versus Sinking Costs." *Journal of Conflict Resolution* 41 (1): 68–90.

Figg, David. 2006. "Political Fission: South Africa's Nuclear Program." *Energy & Environment* 17 (3): 457–467.

Fuhrmann, Matthew. 2009. "Spreading Temptation: Proliferation and Peaceful Nuclear Cooperation Agreements." *International Security* 34 (1): 7–41.

Gilinsky, Victor, Marvin Miller, and Harmon Hubbard. 2004. "A Fresh Examination of the Proliferation Dangers of Light Water Reactors." Washington, DC: Nonproliferation Policy Education Center.

Glaser, Alexander. 2009. "Internationalization of the Nuclear Fuel Cycle." International Commission on Nuclear Non-proliferation and Disarmament, *ICNND Research Paper*, No. 9. February.

Gleason, Gregory. 2011. "Kazakhstan's Uranium Industry and Nuclear Nonproliferation." *Central Asia-Caucasus Institute Analyst*, January 19. Available at: http://cacianalyst.org/?Q=node/5477/print.

Goldschmidt, Betrand, and Myron B. Kratzer. 1978. "Peaceful Nuclear Relations: A Study of the Creation and the Erosion of Confidence." *International Consultative Group on Nuclear Energy.* London: RIIS.

Habib, Babur, Sunil Jain, Richard Johnson, Ilan Jones, R. Scott Kemp, Andrew Kovacs, David Malkin, Marya Nachinkina, Bart Szewczyk, and Pei Tsia. 2006. *Stemming the Spread of Enrichment Technology: Fuel-Supply Guarantees and the Development of Objective Criteria for Restricting Enrichment.* Princeton, NJ: Princeton University, Woodrow Wilson School of Public Policy.

Harding, Jim. 2007. "Economics of Nuclear Power and Proliferation Risks in a Carbon-Constrained World." *The Electricity Journal* 20 (10): 65–76.

Harvey, Cole J. 2011. "From Theory to Reality: The Evolution of Multilateral Assurance of Nuclear Fuel." *NTI Issue Brief,* March 24. Available at: http://www.nti .org/e_research/e3_fuel_cycle.html.

Horner, Daniel. 2009. *Accord on New Rules Eludes Nuclear Suppliers, Arms Control Today* (July/August). Washington, DC: Arms Control Association. Available at: http://www.armscontrol.org/print/3729.

Horner, Daniel, and Oliver Meier. 2009. "Talks on Fuel Banks Stalled." *Arms Control Today,* October. Washington, DC: Arms Control Association.

IFNC (International Framework for Nuclear Cooperation). 2010. "Executive Joint Statement." *First IFNC Executive Committee Meeting.* King Hussein Bin Talal Convention Center, November 4. Sweimeh, Jordan.

Kassenova, Togzhan. 2009. "Kazakhstan's Nuclear Renaissance." *Saint Anthony's International Review* 4 (2): 51–74.

Kidd, Steve. 2010. "Nuclear Fuel: Myths and Realities," in *Nuclear Power's Global Expansion: Weighing Its Costs and Risks,* ed. Henry D. Sokolski. Carlisle, PA: U.S. Army War College, Strategic Studies Institute.

Kramer, Roderick M. 2004. "Collective Paranoia: Distrust Between Social Groups." In *Distrust,* ed. Russell Hardin. New York: Russell Sage.

Kydd, Andrew H. 2005. *Trust and Mistrust in International Relations.* Princeton, NJ: Princeton University Press.

Levy, Jack. 1994. "An Introduction to Prospect Theory." In *Avoiding Losses/Taking Risks,* ed. Barbara Farnham. Ann Arbor: University of Michigan Press.

Lorenz, Thomas and Joanna Kidd. 2010. "An Uncertain Future for International Fuel Banks." *Bulletin of the Atomic Scientists* 66 (3): 44–49.

Loukianova, Anya. 2008. "The International Uranium Enrichment Center at Angarsk: A Step Towards Assured Fuel Supply?" NTI Issue Brief (November). Available at: http://www.nti.org/analysis/articles/uranium-enrichment-angarsk/.

Martin, Lisa. 1993. "Credibility, Costs, and Institutions: Cooperation on Economic Sanctions." *World Politics* 45 (3): 406–432.

———. 2005. "The President and International Commitments: Treaties as Signaling Devices." *Presidential Studies Quarterly* 35 (3): 440–465.

McCombie, Charles, and Thomas Isaacs. 2010. "The Key Role of the Back-end in the Nuclear Fuel Cycle." *Daedalus* 139 (1): 32–43.

McDermott, Rose. 1998. *Risk-Taking in International Relations: Prospect Theory in American Foreign Policy.* Ann Arbor: University of Michigan Press.

Minty, Ambassador Abdul Samad, Special Representative for Disarmament at the Department of Foreign Affairs, Republic of South Africa. 2007. First Session of the Preparatory Committee for the 2010 Review Conference of the Parties to the Treaty on the Nonproliferation of Nuclear Weapons. "Agenda Item 4: General Debate on Issues Related to All Aspects of the Work of the Preparatory Committee." South Africa Committee II 5/10/10. May 1.

Morrow, James D. 1999. "The Strategic Setting of Choice: Signaling Commitment, and Negotiation in International Relations." In *Strategic Choice and International Relations*, eds. David A. Lake and Robert Powell. Princeton, NJ: Princeton University Press.

Neff, Thomas, and Henry Jacoby. 1979. "Supply Assurances in the Nuclear Fuel Cycle." *Annual Review of Energy* 4: 260–263.

Nelson, Paul. 2010. "An Empirical Assessment of Elements of the Future of Civil Nuclear Energy." NSSPI-10-001. College Station, TX: Nuclear Security Science & Policy Institute, Texas A&M.

Nikitin, Mary Beth, Anthon Andrews, and Mark Holt. 2011. "Managing the Nuclear Fuel Cycle: Policy Implications and Expanding Global Access to Nuclear Energy." *CRS Report for Congress 7-5700*. March 2. Washington, DC.

O'Neill, Barry. 2001. "Risk Aversion in International Relations Theory." *International Studies Quarterly* 45: 617–640.

Powell, Robert. 2006. "War as a Commitment Problem." *International Organization* 60 (1): 169–203.

Ribcoff, Abraham A. 1976. "A Market-Sharing Approach to the World Nuclear Sales Problem." *Foreign Affairs* 54 (4): 763.

ROK (Republic of South Korea). 2009. *Multilateral Approaches to the Nuclear Fuel Cycle*. Working paper submitted by the Republic of South Korea to The Preparatory Committee for the 2010 Review Conference of the Parties to the Treaty on the Non-Proliferation of Nuclear Weapons. May 2009.

Rothwell, Geoffrey. 2009. "Market Power in Uranium Enrichment." *Science and Global Security* 17: 132–154.

Rothwell, Geoffrey, and Chaim Braun. 2008. "The Cost Structure of International Uranium Enrichment Service Supply." Presented at the Workshop on Internationalization of Uranium Enrichment Facilities, Cambridge, MA. October 20–21.

Scheinman, Lawrence. 1981. "Multinational Alternatives and Nuclear Non-proliferation." *International Organization* 35 (1): 77–102.

Sechser, Todd S. 2010. "Goliath's Curse: Asymmetric Power and the Effectiveness of Coercive Threats." *International Organization* 64 (4): 627–660.

Sokolski, Henry. 2007. "Market Fortified Nonproliferation." In *Breaking the Nuclear Impasse*, eds. Jeffrey Laurenti and Carl Robichaud. New York: Century Foundation.

Sokova, Elena, and Cristina Hansell Chuen. 2007. "Nuclear Power Broker." *Bulletin of the Atomic Scientist* 63 (5): 51–54.

Stein, Marius, Gotthard Stein, Bernard Richter, and Caroline Jorant. 2004. "Multi- or Internationalization of the Nuclear Fuel Cycle: Revisiting the Issue." *Journal of Nuclear Materials Management* 32 (4): 53–58.

Stott, David Adam. 2010. "South Korea's Global Nuclear Ambitions." *The Asia-Pacific Journal.* Available at: http://www.japanfocus.org/-David_Adam-Stott/3322.

Stulberg. Adam N. 2007. *Well-Oiled Diplomacy.* Albany: State University of New York Press.

Taliaferro, Jeffrey W. 2004. *Balancing Risk: Great Power Intervention in the Periphery.* Ithaca, NY: Cornell University Press.

Tomas, Steve. 2005. "The Economics of Nuclear Power." *Nuclear Issues Paper,* No. 5. December.

Tomz, Michael. 2007. "Domestic Audience Costs in International Relations: An Experimental Approach." *International Organization* 61: 821–840.

USGPO (United States Government Printing Office). 2009. "Proposed Agreement for Cooperation Between the Government of the United States of America and the Government of the United Arab Emirates Concerning Peaceful Uses of Nuclear Energy." Available at: http://www.fas.org/man/eprint/uae-nuclear.pdf.

Vieira de Jesus, Diego Santos. 2011. "Building Trust and Flexibility: A Brazilian View of the Fuel Swap with Iran." *The Washington Quarterly* 34 (2): 61–75.

Wonder, Edward F. 1977. *Nuclear Fuel and American Foreign Policy.* Boulder, CO: Westview Press/Atlantic Council Paperback Series.

WNA. 2010a. *Nuclear Power in South Africa.* Available at: http://www.world-nuclear .org/info/inf88.html.

———. 2010b. *Nuclear Power in South Korea.* Available at: http://www.world-nuclear .org/info/inf81.html.

———. 2010c. *Nuclear Power in the United Arab Emirates.* Available at: http://www .world-nuclear.org/info/UAE_nuclear_power_inf123.html.

———. 2010d. *Uranium and Nuclear Power in Kazakhstan.* Available at: http://www .world-nuclear.org/info/inf89.html.

Yager, Joseph A. 1981. *International Cooperation in Nuclear Energy.* Washington, DC: The Brookings Institution.

Yudin, Yury. 2009. "Multilateral Approaches to the Nuclear Fuel Cycle." *UNIDIR Report.* New York: United Nations Publications.

5   Vaunted Hopes

Climate Change and the Unlikely Nuclear Renaissance

Joshua William Busby

FTER YEARS OF STAGNATION, NUCLEAR POWER IS ON THE table again. Although the sector suffered a serious blow in the wake of the Fukushima Daiichi nuclear meltdown that occurred in Japan in early 2011, a renewed global interest in nuclear power persists, driven in part by climate concerns and worries about soaring energy demand. As one of the few relatively carbon-free sources of energy, nuclear power is being reconsidered, even by some in the environmental community, as a possible option to combat climate change. As engineers and analysts have projected the potential contribution of nuclear power to limiting global greenhouse gas emissions, they have been confronted by the limits in efficiency that wind, water, and solar power can provide to prevent greenhouse gas emissions from rising above twice pre-industrial levels.

What would constitute a nuclear power renaissance? In 1979, at the peak of the nuclear power sector's growth, 233 power reactors were simultaneously under construction. By 1987, that number had fallen to 120. As of February 2012, 435 nuclear reactors were operable globally, capable of producing roughly 372 gigawatts (GW) of electricity (WNA 2012). Some analysts suggest that, with the average age of current nuclear plants at twenty-four years, more than 170 reactors would need to be built just to maintain the current number in operation (Schneider et al. 2009a).[1] As discussed in the Introduction to this volume, merely besting the current number of reactors would not constitute a renaissance. When analysts refer to a nuclear renaissance, they not only imply that nuclear power will experience a revival of plant construction on the order of thirty new reactors per year, similar to the sector's heyday in the 1960s and early 1970s, but also that the collective growth in nuclear power capacity will be sufficient to offset a significant share of global emissions of greenhouse gases that otherwise would have been emitted from the burning of fossil fuels. Whatever reservations people have about nuclear power—the high cost of reactor construction, the possibility of accidents and nuclear proliferation, issues associated with the disposal of nuclear waste—the potential for nuclear power to partially address the problem of climate change has given the industry a new lease on life after decades of increasing marginalization.

Proponents of nuclear power are often willing to look past the sector's defects and assume that the benefits are large enough and the barriers tractable enough that the imperative for a greenhouse gas solution will ultimately create adequate political will to see through the technological and economic challenges. We can call this line of argument the *nuclear technological optimists* position (examples include IAEA 2000; IEA 2010b). Critics, for their part, seize on negative information—cost overruns on new plant construction, the relative affordability of alternatives (such as natural gas), reports of accidents and stoppages at existing plants, thefts of nuclear material—to pour cold water on the nuclear renaissance. We can refer to this as the *nuclear alarmists* position (some examples include Greenpeace n.d.; Stoett 2003).

Both advocates and opponents have plenty of material to use in bolstering their arguments. A number of countries are again constructing nuclear power plants. Some, such as Finland and France, are experiencing cost overruns and delays. Even before Fukushima, Japan had experienced several worrying accidents around its nuclear facilities. The United States, too, had canceled the waste disposal site at Yucca Mountain. At the same time, after a period in which new construction starts dwindled to a trickle, more than sixty nuclear reactors are being built, with possibly hundreds more on the way. This chapter evaluates the disparate evidence, analyzing the technological possibilities for emissions reductions while recognizing practical challenges facing the sector.

In the wake of Fukushima, it appears that *residual domestic political opposition* in many wealthy Western countries and several middle-income countries elsewhere in the world will complicate strategies for supporting nuclear energy. This relates to countries building new nuclear plants at home, as well as their ability to promote international strategies to support nuclear power through such instruments as the Kyoto Protocol's Clean Development

Mechanism (CDM). At the same time, lingering *technological barriers, capacity issues, and safety concerns* may slow the construction of new nuclear plants even in countries that are otherwise enthusiastic about nuclear power. Other reasons may limit the supply and demand for nuclear power. Indeed, as Christopher Way argues in Chapter 6 of this volume, concerns about proliferation may lead nuclear fuel suppliers to try to regulate access by nuclear aspirants. Concerns about the credibility of commitments of fuel may, in turn, lead would-be nuclear power states to scale back their own demand. The net consequence of countervailing pressure for and against nuclear power will be more nuclear power plant construction but perhaps significantly less than renaissance supporters project. As such, much-vaunted plans for plant construction may never fully materialize.[2]

This chapter unfolds in three parts. The first section reviews the putative potential for nuclear power to offer a significant contribution to reduced greenhouse gas emissions, as well as other reasons for renewed interest in nuclear energy. The second section assesses the likelihood that nuclear power will fulfill the range of aspirations ascribed to it. While the nuclear renaissance ultimately depends on the decisions of states and private investors, the landscape for construction of new nuclear plants may be affected by climate change negotiations and the decisions by international organizations. The third section, therefore, reviews the role of nuclear power in international climate negotiations and assesses the implications of renewed interest in nuclear power for global climate governance.

Climate Change and the Nuclear Renaissance: The Potential

Nuclear power is one of the few nearly carbon-free sources of energy. For example, in the United States, nuclear power was responsible for nearly 70 percent of the country's low-carbon energy in 2008 (Pew Center on Global Climate Change 2009). While the extraction of uranium and the construction process of nuclear power plants release some greenhouse gases, emissions are modest—not quite as advantageous as renewables or hydropower, but far superior to gas and especially coal.

Nuclear power remains an attractive proposition for a number of countries, not least of which is the prospect for an energy source that has an extremely low carbon footprint. For countries reliant on imported fuel sources (particularly those with uranium reserves), diversification through nuclear power potentially provides a source of reassurance for reasons of energy security. This is more the case for countries that import natural gas than it is for oil importers, as oil currently has limited use in the electricity sector where nuclear is deployed. That said, the prospects for increased use of electric vehicles in the transport sector could make low-carbon energy from nuclear power an important way to offset reliance on imported oil. Nuclear power currently provides a significant share of existing power needs in the electricity sector. As of 2012, 435 commercial nuclear reactors, operating in thirty countries, produced 372 GW of electricity, roughly 13.8 percent of the world's total electricity needs (WNA 2012). Of this total, 80 percent is concentrated in just eight countries: the United States, France, Japan, Germany, Russia, South Korea, Ukraine, and Canada (IPFM 2007: 82). Moreover, 63 percent of total world capacity is produced in North America and Western Europe (von Hippel 2010). Some positive trends have buoyed the industry in recent years. In a number of countries, the efficiency of existing nuclear power plants has improved considerably. For example, nuclear plants in the United States have operated at an average fleet capacity of 90 percent since 2003 (MIT 2009). Moreover, though a number of nuclear plants were to be shuttered after twenty years of use, U.S. officials were extending the planned lives of nuclear plants from forty to sixty years (Joskow and Parsons 2009: 49). Prior to the Fukushima disaster, officials in other countries had made similar determinations.

The existing fleet of nuclear power plants is already responsible for significant emissions savings of greenhouse gases. Lester and Rosner estimate that the avoided greenhouse gas emissions from the current nuclear fleet total 650 million tons of carbon, or nearly 9 percent of the current global total (Lester and Rosner 2009: 24).[3] In addition, nuclear power prospectively offers great potential to lower a significant share of future greenhouse gas emissions.

This section reviews three growth trajectories for nuclear power and estimates the emissions savings potential under each scenario. In the "wedge" scenario, nuclear power provides 700 GW of power in 2050. In the MIT scenario, nuclear power provides 1,000 GW of power by midcentury. In the BLUE Map scenario generated by the International Energy Agency (IEA), nuclear provides 1,200 GW of power.

None of these scenarios implies either a continuation of the status quo (nuclear stagnation) or a modest decline in the contribution of nuclear to overall energy needs. The wedge strategy is the closest to what the Introduction describes as a "resurgence" of nuclear power, with a deepening of construction by Korea, Russia, India, and China. Two of the three scenarios—the MIT and BLUE Map— imply a "renaissance" of nuclear power, including substantial construction by the aforementioned states and a revival in nations such as the United States and Japan, as well as significant construction by new nuclear aspirants.

In their 2009 analysis, Socolow and Glaser note that humans currently emit about thirty billion tons of carbon dioxide (CO_2) per year. Some business-as-usual scenarios put 2050 emissions at sixty billion tons per year.[4] In their view, we would be fortunate if 2050 emissions could be stabilized at current levels. This would require a variety of strategies to collectively reduce emissions over projected business-as-usual strategies by thirty billion tons (Socolow and Glaser 2009). In this portfolio of strategies, or what Pacala and Socolow refer to as a "wedge" strategy, each represents about four billion tons of avoided CO_2 emissions (or about 13 percent of total emission savings that are needed) (MIT 2003). Energy efficiency, renewables, reduced deforestation, carbon capture and sequestration, and fuel switching from high-carbon to low-carbon sources are among the possible wedges that could deliver such emissions reductions. No single strategy will be enough to deliver sufficient emissions savings, nor is any particular wedge strategy essential. Of about fifteen different possibilities, we will need to use a combination of at least seven or eight of them (Pacala and Socolow 2004).

Nuclear power was one of the promising wedge strategies. In Socolow's original paper with Pacala, they estimated the emissions savings of substituting 700 GW of nuclear power, roughly twice the size of the current nuclear power sector, for 700 GW of coal-fired power plants. Socolow and Glaser explained further: a nuclear wedge would equal about 700 large baseload nuclear power plants on the scene in 2050, substituting for 700 coal plants that otherwise would have been built. A large baseload nuclear plant would generate 1 GW of electricity and operate roughly 8,000 hours a year. A 1-GW nuclear power plant can provide electricity to a U.S. city of 500,000 people, slightly less than the population of Washington, D.C. (Ferguson 2007). The baseload coal plant that each nuclear power plant would replace would be marginally more efficient than contemporary coal plants, emitting 800 grams of CO_2 per kilowatt-hour of electricity, or 6.4 million tons per year (this assumes a 1-GW power plant operating 8,000 hours per year producing 800 grams of CO_2 per kilowatt-hour). Pacala and Socolow suggested the full life-cycle emissions of nuclear power were 50 grams of CO_2 per kilowatt-hour, sixteen times less than coal plants (Kleiner 2008; Sovacool 2008). Accordingly, they estimated that 700 nuclear plants would emit roughly four billion tons of CO_2 per year *less* than 700 coal plants (without carbon capture and sequestration). If nuclear were to offset natural gas plants instead of coal plants, which are roughly 50 percent less greenhouse gas intensive than coal plants, nuclear plants would generate CO_2 savings of roughly two million tons per year (see Table 5.1) (Pacala and Socolow 2004: 42).

In a 2003 report, scholars from MIT assessed the requirements for increasing nuclear power production globally to 1,000 GW, a more aggressive nuclear growth strategy than the wedge approach. If we again assume that nuclear exclusively replaces coal, then 1,000 1-GW nuclear plants would produce six billion tons of CO_2 less than 1,000 coal-burning power plants. This would be about 20 percent of the thirty-billion-ton reduction needed to maintain emissions at contemporary levels (about a wedge and a half).

An even more aggressive pro-nuclear scenario was developed by the IEA. The BLUE Map scenario for 2050 depicts a world in which emissions in energy-related CO_2 emissions fall by 50 percent below 2005 levels. In this world, nuclear power grows from providing 370 GW to 1,200 GW. The share of global electricity generated by nuclear increases from 14 percent to 24 percent, while total electricity use doubles from 20,000 terawatts-hours (TWh) in 2007 to 41,000 TWh by 2050. China's percentage of global nuclear capacity would rise from 3 percent today to 27 percent in 2050; India's proportion would rise from 2 percent to 11 percent (IEA 2010b). Assuming that 1,200 GW of nuclear power only replaces coal power plants, the emissions savings from nuclear would reduce emissions by 7.2 billion tons a year. This would constitute 24 percent of the cumulative emissions reductions needed to maintain emissions at current levels (almost two wedges) but only about 16.7 percent for a strategy intended to reduce emissions 50 percent below 2005 levels. In all likelihood, the emissions savings predicted in this scenario are optimistic, as some nuclear plants would displace natural-gas-fired plants; the savings would nevertheless be more significant than in the other scenarios, as depicted in Table 5.2.

How many nuclear plants would be needed to deliver significant greenhouse gas emissions savings? If each new plant produced roughly 1 GW, the BLUE Map scenario would imply an additional 830 GW of nuclear plants, more than double the current capacity. However, most of the current nuclear fleet will be decommissioned by 2050. With the extended life of existing

TABLE 5.1 Comparison of emissions from different sources

Fuel source	Baseload plant capacity	Yearly operating	CO_2 emissions/kilowatt-hour	Number of plants	CO_2 emissions tons/year (1,000,000 grams = 1 metric ton)
	×	×	×	×	÷ 1,000,000
Coal	1 gigawatt (= 1 million kilowatts)	8,000 hours per year	800 grams per kilowatt-hour	700 plants	4,480,000,000 tons
Nuclear	1 gigawatt	8,000 hours per year	50 grams per kilowatt-hour	700 plants	280,000,000 tons
Gas	1 gigawatt	8,000 hours per year	400 grams per kilowatt-hour	700 plants	2,480,000,000 tons
Nuclear – coal difference					–4,200,000,000 tons
Nuclear – gas difference					–2,100,000,000 tons

TABLE 5.2 Comparison of emissions savings between Wedge, MIT, and BLUE Map scenarios

Fuel source	Gigawatt (GW) nuclear	Emissions savings over coal (tons)	% of 30 billion tons reduction per year (stabilization strategy)	% of 43 billion tons per year reduction (50% below 2005)
Wedge	700	−4,200,000	14.0	9.8
MIT	1,000	−6,000,000	20.0	14.0
BLUE Map	1,200	−7,200,000	25.0	16.7

nuclear power plants, the IEA estimates that up to 60 GW of existing plant capacity would likely still be on line in 2050, meaning that 1,140 1-GW plants would need to be constructed between 2012 and 2050 to reach 1,200 GW, roughly 28 plants per year. The IEA suggests that new plant size potential is more likely to be in the 1.2 to 1.7 GW range. If plant size averaged 1.2 GW, this would imply an additional 950 new nuclear plants, roughly 24 per year over the next forty years. At the industry's peak in the 1970s and 1980s, construction starts briefly exceeded thirty plants per year. Throughout the 1990s, construction starts were five or fewer in most years. Since 2005, a modest boom in plant construction has been observed, with ten or more plants beginning construction in recent years (IEA 2010c: 20). Even the 1,000 GW strategy of the MIT study would require 940 1-GW plants (or more than 780 plants of 1.2 GW average size). The more modest wedge strategy would imply 700 plants of 1 GW operating in 2050. If we accept the IEA estimate that 60 GW of current capacity will still be around by midcentury, then 640 new plants of 1 GW will have to be built over the next forty years—sixteen a year—for nuclear to provide one wedge of climate mitigation.

While the unit of analysis varies among different studies and the range of emissions differs across energy sources, the core assumptions that truly matter are the projected size of the nuclear sector, total projected energy demand, and the extent to which nuclear replaces coal or natural gas. Ultimately, the ability of nuclear power to displace coal as a fuel source and to generate significant emissions reductions hinges upon a rapid acceleration in nuclear power plant construction. The next section reviews the reasons why such a building spree may ultimately be less than the optimists envision.

The Nuclear Revival: A Reality Check

What is the likelihood that nuclear could contribute emissions savings any-where near what the wedge strategy, the MIT study, or the BLUE Map scenario suggest might be possible? If technological optimists are correct, then none of the problems previously observed by the nuclear industry—accidents, cost overruns, proliferation concerns, waste disposal issues, public opposition—should matter all that much. New designs should make plants safer, cheaper, faster to construct, harder to proliferate; third- and possibly fourth-generation reactors, as well as the need for low-carbon energy, ought to alleviate public opposition. All the nuclear industry needs is another start, and even if there are early teething problems, construction firms will be able to learn by doing. If these problems persist, however, then the optimists will have engaged in wishful thinking and fewer plants ultimately will be built. If the alarmists are correct, we would expect troubles to befall the nuclear industry, a repeat of the 1970s and 1980s, with serious accidents, soaring costs, and problems with storage that reenergize public opposition, even in states such as China, and ultimately poison investor and political support.

In between these poles is a more realistic scenario, based on some nuclear plants being built but persistent problems dogging the industry, such that instead of a wedge of emissions reductions we will just get a slice. There are a number of reasons to be skeptical that the renewed interest in nuclear energy will deliver the emissions savings that proponents of nuclear power tout. As the 2009 update to the MIT study concluded: "Even if all the announced plans for new nuclear power plant construction are realized, the total will be well behind that needed for reaching a thousand gigawatts of new capacity worldwide by 2050" (MIT 2009: 4).

As of March 2012, sixty nuclear power reactors were under construction according to the World Nuclear Association (WNA) (WNA 2012), with a total of about 60.8 GW capacity. Nearly 50 percent of that added capacity was being constructed in China and Taiwan. In 2009, eleven plants began construction; nine began in China and another two began in Russia. In 2008, of the ten construction starts, six were in China and two were in South Korea and Russia (see Table 5.3 for a list of countries with reactors under construction).

Given that it takes between seven and ten years for plants to be constructed, the net capacity in the nuclear sector by 2020 will likely be around 432 GW (370 GW of current capacity plus 61.6 GW of plants under construction), assuming

TABLE 5.3 Countries with nuclear power reactors under construction as of February 2012

Location	Number of units	Gross capacity (MWe)[a]
Argentina	1	745
Brazil	1	1,405
Canada	3	2,190
China	26	27,640
Finland	1	1,700
France	1	1,720
India	6	4,600
Japan	2	2,756
Korea (South)	3	3,800
Pakistan	1	340
Russia	10	9,160
Slovakia	2	880
Taiwan	2	2,700
United States	1	1,218
Total	**60**	**60,854**

SOURCE: World Nuclear Association 2012.
[a]MWe = megawatt electrical (as distinct from thermal).

all the current plants are built. This accounts for the reduction of Japan's nuclear sector with the closure of Fukushima's four reactors (which reduced Japan's nuclear capacity by 2.7 GW) and the closure of eight German nuclear reactors after Fukushima (about 8 GW capacity reduction). This estimate does not include plans to close the remaining nine German reactors by 2022 (about 12 GW of capacity) or Switzerland's five reactors (another 3.2 GW), nor does it include projections on Japan's nuclear sector, nearly all of which, as of early 2012, remained in temporary shutdown pending approval by local municipalities. It remains an open question whether Japan's nuclear plants will restart (JEA 2012). Even before Fukushima, the WNA estimated that sixty of the existing nuclear reactors would likely be closed by 2030.

Beyond the plants currently under construction, the WNA has documented the number of planned and proposed reactors worldwide. Forty-five countries (including Taiwan) have plans and proposals to build nuclear reactors, and other countries have expressed interest in nuclear power. If all these reactors were built, the total would be nearly 495 additional reactors with gross capacity of nearly 558 GW.[5] With the 61 GW of plants under construction, this would still be 80 GW (or about 12 percent) short of the additional capacity needed by 2050 to contribute fully to one of the Socolow wedges. If we assume that an additional 60 GW of existing facilities were still on line in 2050, then the world would be about 3 percent short of a wedge. However, this total would be 32 percent below the 1,000 GW MIT target, and about 43 percent below the 1,200 GW BLUE Map scenario (see Table 5.4).

TABLE 5.4 Reactors planned and proposed as of February 2012

Location	Planned	Gross capacity (MWe)[a]	Proposed	Gross capacity (MWe)[a]
Argentina	2	773	1	740
Armenia	1	1,060	0	0
Bangladesh	2	2,000	0	0
Belarus	2	2,000	2	2,000
Brazil	0	0	4	4,000
Bulgaria	2	1,900	0	0
Canada	3	3,300	3	3,800
Chile	0	0	4	4,400
China	51	57,480	120	123,000
Czech Republic	2	2,400	1	1,200
Egypt	1	1,000	1	1,000
Finland	0	0	2	3,000
France	1	1,720	1	1,100
Hungary	0	0	2	2,200
India	17	15,000	40	49,000
Indonesia	2	2,000	4	4,000
Iran	2	2,000	1	300
Israel	0	0	1	1,200
Italy	0	0	10	17,000
Japan	10	13,772	5	6,760
Jordan	1	1,000	0	0

(*continued*)

TABLE 5.4 (*Continued*)

Location	Planned	Gross capacity (MWe)[a]	Proposed	Gross capacity (MWe)[a]
Kazakhstan	2	600	2	600
Korea (North)	0	0	1	950
Korea (South)	6	8,400	0	0
Lithuania	1	1,350	0	0
Malaysia	0	0	2	2,000
Mexico	0	0	2	2,000
Netherlands	0	0	1	1,000
Pakistan	1	340	2	2,000
Poland	6	6,000	0	0
Romania	2	1,310	1	655
Russia	14	16,000	30	28,000
Saudi Arabia	0	0	16	20,000
Slovakia	0	0	1	1,200
Slovenia	0	0	1	1,000
South Africa	0	0	6	9,600
Switzerland	0	0	3	4,000
Taiwan	0	0	1	1,350
Thailand	0	0	5	5,000
Turkey	4	4,800	4	5,600
Ukraine	2	1,900	11	12,000
United Arab Emirates	4	5,600	10	14,400
United Kingdom	4	6,680	9	12,000
United States	11	13,260	19	25,500
Vietnam	4	4,000	6	6,700
Total	**160**	**177,645**	**335**	**380,255**

SOURCE: World Nuclear Association 2012.

[a]MWe = megawatt electrical (as distinct from thermal).

Attaining the Socolow wedge would require that the countries with the most ambitious plans for nuclear plant construction are able to achieve or exceed their goals, and/or that other countries without plans and proposals to build nuclear plants embrace nuclear power. Yet, the vaunted hopes for a nuclear renaissance may remain unfulfilled, for a number of reasons, including:

1. The pace of construction is currently too slow to realize the gains, particularly in such as like India that are expected to be major locations for new plant construction;

2. Public resistance to nuclear power remains embedded in several Western countries, as well as in some middle-income countries such as Thailand and Indonesia;

3. Cost overruns and delays in Western countries such as Finland and France, where resistance to nuclear power is less strong, have the potential to dampen enthusiasm for nuclear power;

4. The decline of oil prices from historic highs of several years ago, high up-front costs of plant construction, the more favorable costs for natural gas, and the financial crisis have rendered nuclear power less economical or affordable in some places;

5. The current nuclear fleet is aging and likely to be retired in the next twenty years, requiring a significant investment in construction just to maintain the level of nuclear energy provided today;

6. Limits to the number of trained personnel and producers of nuclear equipment make it difficult to implement a large-scale nuclear renaissance, even in countries like China that are prepared to significantly expand plant construction;

7. The unresolved issue of nuclear waste disposal feeds into public and official distrust of nuclear power;

8. Some announced and prospective candidates for nuclear power may be, because of small economies or small power grids, poor candidates for nuclear power;

9. A nuclear accident or act of sabotage anywhere, as Fukushima demonstrated, has major implications for the industry everywhere, making the dispersion of nuclear power technology to inexperienced and unstable countries potentially risky for the nuclear industry across the globe; and, perhaps most important,

10. The proliferation risks associated with nuclear power make nuclear power potentially dangerous for peace and security.

How a number of these issues may affect the actual construction of nuclear plants can be illustrated by country examples.

China

For countries with ambitious plans to build nuclear power plants, the question becomes, Will all the plants planned and proposed actually be built? Will the Chinese build more than 170 reactors over the next fifteen years as their plans suggest? As of March 2012, China has fifteen reactors in operation and, according to the WNA, twenty-six under construction. Will China be able to build on average more than ten a year for fifteen years? Has the enthusiasm for new plant construction dimmed in the aftermath of Japan's nuclear disaster?

In China, the political obstacles to new plant construction are much less daunting than in other places, where local communities have a "not in my backyard" (NIMBY) attitude toward nuclear plant construction and nuclear firms face lengthy permitting processes. The Chinese state possesses more siting capacity for nuclear facilities and is able to provide nuclear companies with land and other amenities at low cost and via an expeditious approval process.[6] Moreover, Chinese communities in general are more supportive of the economic opportunities provided by the nuclear sector. Since the mid-2000s, China has been at a breakneck pace to construct new power plants, adding as much as 70 GW in capacity in successive years, most of it coal-fired power plants (MIT 2007).

However, China's ambitions for the nuclear sector may be more difficult to achieve, or could come at a cost of plant safety and design. Though the country has not experienced a major nuclear power plant accident, the head of China's National Nuclear Safety Administration warned in 2009 that the country might have difficulty with construction and operational safety if it is not careful. In a country that had already experienced scandal for inadequate oversight in drugs, toys, and food, such a warning raised international concern. In August 2009, the president of China National Nuclear Corporation was detained in a US$260 million corruption scandal. In October 2009, China's premier announced that the country would increase the number of nuclear safety inspectors from around 200 to more than 1,000. Although China has demonstrated a willingness to cooperate with international inspectors to ensure nuclear plant safety, there are serious concerns that future safety incidents could upend its aggressive growth plans (Bradsher 2009).

Should China ever experience a serious nuclear incident, the reputational consequences would likely reverberate around the world. Nuclear power safety is what public goods scholars call a "weakest link" type of problem (Sandler 2004). To the extent that a serious accident anywhere will dampen enthusiasm for nuclear power everywhere, the nuclear industry is vulnerable to the negative reputational externalities of international nuclear accidents. The incidents at Three Mile Island in 1979 and Chernobyl in 1986 had such an effect. The nuclear industry likes to tout its subsequent safety record. While newer nuclear power plants are both different from the Chernobyl design and are considered to be safer, it is unclear if the international public will react to a serious accident in China, for example, by differentiating between the kinds of nuclear plants or the practices of a foreign government, particularly since many of the designs employed by China are derived from those developed in Western countries.

The Fukushima disaster did not fundamentally dampen enthusiasm for nuclear power in China. The leadership's immediate response was to introduce a strategic pause in new plant construction, while existing facilities went through rigorous safety inspections. This was projected to impose a modest delay in China's timetable for new plant construction, and was not expected to have a major effect on China's nuclear ambitions (Busby 2011; Kong and Lampton 2011). As discussed below, this contrasted with the developments in other countries, such as Germany, where public opinion turned decisively against nuclear power and the leadership opted to phase out the sector entirely.

Despite China's sustained interest in new nuclear plant construction, its demands for specialized nuclear equipment may face technical bottlenecks, owing to the lack of nuclear parts suppliers and skilled expertise. While nuclear optimists assume that credible demand signals from China will generate the necessary supply of parts and skilled nuclear technicians, any barriers to a nuclear expansion may make it difficult for any of the aggressive nuclear growth strategies—wedge, MIT, and BLUE Map—to meet their aims. The challenges of nuclear construction are twofold: There are only a handful of companies that provide some of the specialized equipment for nuclear reactors, and there is a shortage of people who are skilled nuclear professionals, with many of those who used to work in the industry in the West having retired from the field without being replaced. For example, only one firm,

Japan Steel Works, can cast forgings for particular types of reactor vessels (Schneider et al. 2009b). It had a two-year waiting list for forgings, and even with an expansion to be completed in 2010 would only be able to complete eight reactors a year. China's own capacities for casting are unclear (Squassoni 2008a, 2008b). Many of the training staff in countries like the United States and France are on the verge of retirement. The assertion that a large proportion of nuclear power plant workers are five to ten years from retirement has become a common refrain in the industry (Berr 2010). The situation in France was similar. One study noted that in 1980 there were sixty-five nuclear engineering programs in the United States, but by 2008, there were only thirty-one (Schneider et al. 2009b). An IAEA official estimated that there were about 200 nuclear graduates from U.S. universities per year and a similar number from all European universities combined. He noted numerous years in Germany during the 1990s when there were no new nuclear graduates. The situation in China was thought to be less severe but still significant. While China is preparing large numbers of engineers and scientists (360,000), a small proportion of them are nuclear specialists. Therefore, China may need more than 13,000 nuclear engineers by 2020 (Kadak 2006; Kubota 2009).

India

Will India build the nearly sixty reactors it has planned and proposed? As of March 2012, India had twenty reactors in operation and six under construction. Since the United States and India signed a deal sanctioning cooperation on civilian nuclear power in 2005, the Indian parliament has struggled with the contentious issue of whether foreign firms would have limited liability in the event of an accident. This was thought to be a necessary change in India's laws to attract foreign investment, and is a particularly charged issue, given the 1984 chemical accident at the Dow Chemical facility in Bhopal, India. After a long, contentious debate, the Indian parliament finally passed an investor indemnity law in August 2010, but the law did not go as far as foreign investors had hoped, providing only partial legal liability for foreign firms— up to eighty years for suppliers of nuclear equipment, raw materials, and services in the event of an accident. Some suggested that India's supplier liability was unprecedented: Twenty-eight other national laws and three international nuclear treaties all placed liability on operators with limited commercial liability for suppliers. While state-owned firms like France's Areva corporation may be less affected by legal challenges, American nuclear providers, as private firms, could not rely on U.S. government financial backing in the event of an accident (Platts 2010). The Obama administration reportedly had encouraged the Indian government to revise the law, though this was seen as unlikely in the wake of the Fukushima disaster (Devraj 2011). It remains an open question whether this will dampen enthusiasm for investing in India's nuclear sector (Kazmin 2010; *Nuclear Power Daily* 2010).

As in China, the initial impact of the Fukushima accident on India's nuclear power expansion plans was modest. While ordering a safety review, India's Prime Minister Manmohan Singh reaffirmed the country's support for nuclear power (PTI 2011). It remains unclear, however, how long the status quo can hold. Despite assertions of confidence in the sector, the Fukushima accident has emboldened anti-nuclear activists and opposition parties in India (Sasikumar 2011). Of particular concern are siting issues associated with the approved Jaitapur nuclear power plant, located along the coast in Maharashtra state, which with six reactors and a total 9,900 MW capacity is slated to be the largest nuclear facility in the world (Bajaj 2011). In the wake of the government's April 2011 decision not to review the earlier approval of the Jaitapur plant, protests turned violent after 700 demonstrators attacked a police station (*India Today* 2011).

Finland, Bulgaria, and France

Other countries, particularly in Europe, that have decided to build new nuclear plants have experienced considerable cost overruns and delays in the construction of new facilities. Critics also point to the experience of recent power plant construction in Western advanced industrialized countries. The MIT update notes that most plans for construction of nuclear power plants estimate completion in four and a half to five years on paper. Many plants in practice, such as Finland's Olkiluoto plant and France's Flamanville plant, are taking considerably longer. In the Finnish case, the plant, under construction by France's Areva corporation, is likely to take at least seven years to bring to fruition, and the costs have doubled from the initial 3 billion Euros price tag (roughly USD$3.6 billion). The Olkiluoto plant was supposed to herald a European nuclear revival. Placed in 2003, it was the first order in Western Europe and North America since France's Civaux-2 from 1993. Despite the cost overruns, a second plant is slated to begin construction at Olkiluoto in 2012. The Flamanville plant in France, which began construction in December 2007, also was projected to come in between 700 million and 1 billion

Euros (roughly USD$860 million to $1.2 billion) over budget after experiencing problems in the concrete base mat (Schneider et al. 2009a, 2009b). In Bulgaria, two nuclear reactors built with Russian assistance were supposed to cost less than US$4.0 billion but costs have soared to US$11.4 billion (Kanter 2010). If nuclear power providers fail to standardize construction models and costs, with each plant subject to lengthy delays and cost overruns, governments and investors will likely be unable to afford as many reactors, and the reactors will not all be built in a timely fashion to realize the expected emissions savings. Both governments and investors, therefore, may ultimately rethink their commitments to nuclear power.

The Fukushima accident further complicated these governments' nuclear calculations. In June 2011, the Bulgarians reached an agreement with Russia to further delay its decision on constructing a new nuclear project until October, while it continued to review the financial and safety details of the proposed facility (Tsolova 2011). The Finnish coalition government that came into power in June 2011 appointed a Green environment minister and agreed that it would not approve any permits for new nuclear plants (Tanner 2011). In June 2011, France's leader Nicolas Sarkozy pledged more than 1 billion Euros (about USD$1.2 billion) in new investments in fourth-generation nuclear technology (*France 24* 2011). However, he faced difficult reelection prospects in May 2012.

The United States

The 2003 MIT study on nuclear power assessed the emissions saving potential of an increase in nuclear power from 340 to 1,000 GW, implying an expansion in the United States from 100 GW in 2000 to 300 GW at midcentury (MIT 2009: 3). Though the United States has plans to build thirty new nuclear plants over the next fifteen years, progress on actual construction has been slow. Between the 2003 MIT report and a 2009 update, no new nuclear units had begun construction. Only one refurbished unit had been restarted, and one previously ordered reactor that had not been fully constructed was being completed (MIT 2009: 5). Though a cap on carbon would make nuclear more cost-competitive with coal and to a lesser extent with natural gas, the 2009 MIT report also concluded that nuclear power was still not cost-competitive with either. Indeed, nuclear power would become competitive if it could eliminate the risk premium it has to pay on construction. However, as the report noted, the estimated construction costs for large-scale power projects have doubled since 2003, outpacing otherwise rising costs for coal and gas plants (MIT 2009: 6).

The parlous state of the country's economy and financial markets may make it difficult for putative nuclear power producers to secure private financing. Even investments in renewables have been hit hard by the recession, with major projects like T. Boone Pickens' proposed wind farms scaled back or put on hold. Long-time critics of nuclear power like Amory Lovins see investors voting with their feet, shunning nuclear power in favor of natural gas, conservation, distributed power, and renewables, which he argues offer greater emissions reductions at lower cost, given the speed with which such projects can be deployed. In his view, nuclear power will never be able to compete with other energy sources; the up-front capital costs are still so high, the construction periods so long, and the costs and regulatory environment so uncertain that investors will only look to nuclear if there is a vast public subsidy (Lovins and Sheikh 2008; Lovins, Sheikh, and Markevich 2008; Sokolski 2010).

The Obama administration heeded the advice of the MIT study and announced US$54.5 billion in loan guarantees to jolt the U.S. nuclear industry out of its inertia. The animating idea behind the loan guarantees was that the United States needed experience again building nuclear power plants. Only after a few new plants were built could the industry standardize construction costs and drive costs down, thereby minimizing the risk and legitimating the promise of nuclear power for the broader private sector. In February 2010, the Obama administration provided US$8.3 billion in loan guarantees to the Southern Company for construction of two new nuclear plants in Georgia (Shear and Mufson 2010). In May 2010, the Department of Energy offered a second US$2 billion loan guarantee to the French firm Areva to build a nuclear enrichment facility in Idaho (Fehrenbacher 2010).

In the aftermath of the Fukushima disaster, the Obama administration, even as it stepped up efforts to assure the safety of the U.S. nuclear power sector, reaffirmed its support for nuclear power (Hennessey 2011). That said, private sector enthusiasm for nuclear power had already diminished in the face of depressed prices of natural gas and further cooled after Fukushima. Moreover, nearly half of the US$17.5 billion in loan guarantees approved in 2005 had not been claimed (Wald 2011). A project in Maryland was canceled in 2010 (Behr 2010), and after the Fukushima accident, expansion of a nuclear facility in south Texas was canceled (Price and Toohey 2011).

Even as the Obama administration embraced the idea of nuclear power, it rejected the key storage site for nuclear waste, Nevada's Yucca Mountain.

The Obama administration in 2009 effectively mothballed the permanent disposal site of Yucca Mountain by reducing funding of the site to almost negligible levels (Farrell 2010). A presidential commission report from January 2012 recommended that the United States begin pursuing an alternative to Yucca Mountain (Blue Ribbon Commission 2012). While on-site storage in pools and more permanent storage in cement-lined bunkers remain options, the volume of waste in a world of expanded nuclear power has scarcely been thought through. Yucca Mountain, for example, was estimated to be able to hold 140,000 metric tons (MT) of spent fuel equivalent, though its legal limit was restricted to 70,000 MT. The MIT study noted that a nuclear revival on the order of 1,000 GW would require an additional waste disposal site of Yucca Mountain's capacity every three to four years. A threefold increase in nuclear power production in the United States would generate enough waste to require another waste disposal site of Yucca Mountain's legal capacity in twelve years, and of its physical capacity in twenty-five years (MIT 2003: 10, 61).[7]

No country has yet resolved the challenge of permanent nuclear waste disposal storage sites. In advanced democracies, siting issues for storage facilities remain subject to potent NIMBY backlashes. Finland is preparing a storage site at Olkiluoto, which is expected to be operational by 2020. However, if the regulatory uncertainty for waste storage continues for nuclear power producers, it may complicate investor enthusiasm for new nuclear construction, providing yet another reason for plans, particularly in Europe and North America, to be modest and less than what renaissance proponents desire.

Germany

Countries with extensive nuclear power sectors, particularly in Europe, were proposing to build few new reactors even before the Japan nuclear disaster. France had plans to build only two new reactors, with one under construction that was behind schedule and over budget. The country's efforts to export nuclear expertise to the United Arab Emirates were dampened in 2000 when France lost out on the bid for a contract to a South Korea firm that came in with a much less expensive offer. After Japan's nuclear accident, a number of European countries, notably Germany and Switzerland, moved to phase out nuclear power entirely (Sokolski 2011).

Not too long ago, some of those same countries were delicately maneuvering in the other direction. Before Fukushima, several countries with nuclear power plants—including Germany, Spain, Sweden, and Belgium—slowly walked away from plans to shutter their nuclear power sector, and none had plans to build new ones. Fukushima notwithstanding, whether these countries would have been able to extend the lives of the nuclear plants remained deeply contested politically for countries with vibrant Green political constituencies and those possessing parliamentary democracies that allow small parties to become swing coalition partners. In Germany, Chancellor Angela Merkel struggled to reverse the planned closure of the country's seventeen nuclear plants, which provided 20 GW of electricity, about 28 percent of the country's electricity (von Hippel 2010). The four firms that produce Germany's nuclear power vigorously lobbied to reverse the decision, which was made in 2002 by the coalition government comprised of the Social Democratic Party and the Greens. In September 2010, Merkel's government decided to extend the life of Germany's nuclear power sector, with plants built before 1980 having an additional eight years and those built after 1980 receiving an additional fourteen years (Thomas 2010).[8] While Germany embraced an extension of the life of its existing nuclear power sector, the reprieve even before the Fukushima disaster was potentially temporary if the Christian Democrats lost power and the Greens became swing coalition partners again.

In this difficult political environment, the nuclear volte-face in Germany was extraordinary. After Fukushima, Merkel in March 2011 ordered a three-month suspension of operations at the country's seven oldest nuclear reactors (Wiesmann 2011). With German public opinion rallying against nuclear power and her party poised to lose power, Merkel announced in May 2011 that those plants would not be reopened and Germany's entire nuclear power sector would be phased out by 2022 (Buergin and Parkin 2011).

In sum, proponents of nuclear power will not only have to convince investors and the international community to complete the construction of planned nuclear power plants, but also they will have to hope that countries such as China ultimately are overachievers, that countries like Germany reverse course, and that a number of other aspirants prove capable of building new plants.

Nuclear Power and International Climate Negotiations

The ability of some countries to secure adequate financing to build nuclear plants may depend on decisions about nuclear power's eligibility for valuable, tradable emissions credits. Heretofore, nuclear power was excluded from that market. Whether nuclear power will receive significant attention in future international climate negotiations is uncertain. While nuclear power issues have periodically been part of the backdrop of climate negotiations, they have not entered in as a major topic of discussion, consistently overshadowed by more divisive issues concerning national emissions targets and financial support for developing countries. Should those issues be resolved, nuclear power could become a more important agenda item. Of particular importance will be whether the Kyoto Protocol's rules (or those of a successor agreement) are altered to allow nuclear power to be eligible for emissions reductions through the CDM and whether the World Bank prohibition against lending for nuclear power will continue and be extended to new instruments, such as the Green Climate Fund agreed at the 2009 Copenhagen climate negotiations.

Nuclear power was specifically excluded from CDM credits under the Kyoto Protocol. The CDM was one of the flexibility mechanisms established under the Kyoto Protocol that permit companies in advanced industrialized countries (so-called Annex I countries) to pay for emissions reductions in developing countries (so-called Annex B countries). At the follow-on meeting of the Sixth Conference of the Parties held in Bonn, Germany, in July 2001, delegates fleshed out the rules that specified eligibility for certified emissions reductions under the CDM and prohibited Annex I countries from meeting their commitments through nuclear power (UNFCCC 2001).

Most environmental organizations, a number of countries in Europe (including staunch anti-nuclear states such as Austria), and many developing countries (including the low-lying island states) historically have opposed nuclear power's eligibility for emissions credits through the CDM. A few nuclear supplier states such as Japan, France, and Australia have periodically supported a stronger role for nuclear power but have been outflanked by opponents of nuclear power. In the 2000s, diehard opposition by the environmental community to nuclear power fractured as the climate problem became more imminent and dire, with prominent environmentalists including Greenpeace founder Patrick Moore and *Whole Earth Catalog* founder Stewart Brand advocating for nuclear power. With European countries divided and the United States having failed to ratify the Kyoto Protocol, there were few powerful advocates to support revision of Kyoto's rules to include nuclear power. While the Copenhagen climate negotiations in December 2009 were intended to reach an accord on the post-2012 commitment period, higher-order concerns including country commitments; a long-term target;

financing for developing countries; and measurement, reporting, and verification dominated the discussion. The meeting ended with a political accord, with the post-2012 commitment period under the Kyoto Protocol or a successor agreement put off for later discussion. As a consequence, nuclear power's eligibility under the CDM remained as it was in the lead-up to Copenhagen. The draft negotiating text considered in August 2010 in Bonn included the same text of options for nuclear power, including (option 1) maintaining the current rules, (option 2) preventing Annex I countries from meeting their commitments through nuclear power but allowing non–Annex I countries to claim credits, and (option 3) allowing countries to pursue credits from nuclear power for activities beginning January 1, 2008, or later (UNFCCC 2010a). Whether these changes are pursued is bound up with the larger status of the Kyoto Protocol and the CDM. In the interim, climate negotiations in Bonn in June 2011—the Fukushima accident notwithstanding—revived calls to include nuclear power in projects eligible for CDM credits (Climate Action Network 2011).

At the Copenhagen climate negotiations, donor countries agreed to provide up to US$30 billion in fast-start finance to developing countries between 2010 and 2012, and committed to mobilizing up to US$100 billion in public and private sources by 2020. One of the instruments created to transfer these funds was the Green Climate Fund. At Copenhagen, it remained unclear which entity would administer this fund, its likely size, the activities it would finance, and the specific countries that would be the beneficiaries (Busby 2010).[9] At the 2010 climate change conference in Cancun, Mexico, it was agreed after much deliberation that the World Bank would serve as the interim trustee for the fund, though the fund would be governed by its own board of twenty-four members, with developing and developed countries retaining equal representation. Further design details were concluded by the Durban, South Africa, climate negotiations in December 2011, although much remained unsettled even after the conference, including respective financing commitments (UNFCCC 2010b).

The World Bank has long had a policy of not loaning funds for new nuclear power plant construction. The last nuclear project it financed was a reactor in Italy in 1959. The Bank adopted a more official policy proscription against loans for nuclear plants in 1996, though the it has supported modernization of existing nuclear plants and supporting orders to advance the decommissioning of facilities and improve safety. Despite a renewed call in

March 2010 by French president Nicolas Sarkozy to amend the Bank's rules by 2013, a Bank spokesman suggested that it had no plans to support nuclear power in the immediate future (Hollinger and Crooks 2010; Yurman 2010). However, should Bank shareholders make support for nuclear power a priority, the policy could change, though division between pro- and anti-nuclear states makes the maintaining the status quo ban on Bank lending more likely.

In early 2010, the Bank reviewed the rules for energy lending for the next decade with a controversial draft report discussed in April 2011; as of late 2011, a rift over phasing out support for coal in middle-income countries left the strategy in limbo. No change in nuclear's eligibility for Bank lending was ultimately expected (Bretton Woods Project 2011). With lending for coal plants becoming increasingly controversial as part of the Bank's portfolio (particularly after the 2010 decision to support South Africa's Medupi coal plant), it was unclear if nuclear might benefit from the push for low-carbon energy sources. The Bank could conceivably reject funding of future coal-burning power plants, but with a ban on support for nuclear and coal, that would leave it relegated to supporting renewables, potentially marginalizing its influence in middle-income countries. Middle-income countries are especially important to the financial health of the Bank. Even as they have been able to tap private markets for finance, the Bank has been able to retain influence through continued lending to those countries but also through the imprimatur that World Bank support often signals to the private sector. A move to ban support for coal while lifting the prohibition against support for nuclear might be too difficult politically for the Bank's shareholders to reach agreement (Friedman 2010). At the same time, as developing countries seek financing for their power sectors, the World Bank's decision to extend its current moratorium on lending for nuclear power, or a decision to phase out support for coal, could affect not only the direct support countries receive, but also the types of private sector financing that often look to the Bank as a signal of creditworthiness.

Conclusion

Given the grave climate risks worldwide, the environmental community is in the unenviable position of having to put a lot of options on the table, including nuclear power. No single answer is likely to be successful on its own, but there will be room for nuclear in a mix with energy efficiency, renewables, hybrid cars and their successors, combined-cycle gas plants, and even clean coal and carbon sequestration. However, the various scenarios for nuclear power to play a large role in reducing greenhouse gases are conditioned by exceeding ambitious plans for new nuclear power construction. A number of barriers—both political and technical—may undercut the ability for resurgent nuclear power to provide even a wedge of emissions reductions. Lingering doubts about costs, safety, and security make it difficult for advocates of nuclear power to revise international rules to facilitate the sector's renaissance.

For technological optimists, these concerns will yield to the necessity of low-carbon energy. For alarmists, they are enough to stop construction of nuclear power plants. In reality, a considerable number of new nuclear plants will be built. The challenge, however, is to sustain construction of twenty or more plants a year, every year for forty years. Such construction rates were only achieved for a few years at the peak of the nuclear boom before the accidents, cost overruns, and proliferation concerns came to be fully appreciated. For the technological optimists to prevail (and for the far-reaching goals for nuclear power to be met), none of these issues or any other supply constraints can significantly dampen the willingness of governments and investors to support nuclear power. Although the challenges posed by climate change may become so stark as to leaven concerns about nuclear power, political opposition and the technical obstacles attendant to building out the nuclear sector so quickly will likely lead to a partial nuclear resurgence at best.

Notes

1. Schneider et al. note that that the average age of the units that were previously shut down was twenty-two years. They reach their estimates assuming that the existing plants are shut down, on average, after forty years and that new plants under construction have a forty-year operational lifetime (Schneider et al. 2009b).

2. The views presented in this chapter are largely consistent with those of Christopher Way in Chapter 6 of this volume, though he is more pessimistic about the potential resurgence of nuclear power. These differences may be a function of different judgments about China's potential to stay on course with its ambitious nuclear build plans.

3. This assumes that nuclear power would exclusively displace coal-burning power plants, which likely overstates the case, as some nuclear plants may displace natural gas.

4. The IEA's estimate for 2007 was 28.8 gigatons of CO_2 a year, with emissions projected to increase in its baseline scenario to 57.0 gigatons (IEA 2009, 2010a).

5. Planned plants are those that have approval, funding, or a major commitment and are likely to be built in eight to ten years, and proposed plants are those that are likely to be built within fifteen years.

6. For a review of these advantages in the renewables sector, see Bradsher 2010.

7. Yucca Mountain's legal limit was 70,000 MT of nuclear waste.

8. The four nuclear power companies were to pay a new tax from 2011 to 2016 that would go into the country's general budget, expected to bring in 2.3 billion Euros (about USD$2.8 billion) a year. They were also to pay 300 million Euros (USD$370 million) in 2011 and 2012 into a fund to support renewable energy, with payments reduced to 200 million Euros (about USD$250 million) a year for the period 2013–2016.

9. Discussion centered on the poorest countries and China, acknowledging that it would not be an initial beneficiary of climate finance.

References

Bajaj, Vikas. 2011. "Resistance to Jaitapur Nuclear Plant Grows in India." *New York Times*, April 13. Available at: http://www.nytimes.com/2011/04/15/business/global/15nuke.html?pagewanted=all.

Behr, Peter. 2010. "Constellation Pullout From Md. Nuclear Venture Leaves Industry Future Uncertain." *New York Times*, October 11.

Berr, Jonathan. 2010. "Nuclear Power Industry Faces Critical Labor Shortage." *Daily Finance*, March 1. Available at: http://www.dailyfinance.com/2010/03/01/nuclear-power-industry-faces-critical-labor-shortage/.

Blue Ribbon Commission on America's Nuclear Future. 2012. Available at: http://brc.gov/.

Bradsher, Keith. 2009. "Nuclear Power Expansion in China Stirs Concerns." *New York Times*, December 15. Available at: http://www.nytimes.com/2009/12/16/business/global/16chinanuke.html?pagewanted=all.

———. 2010. "Government Aid Puts China Ahead in Clean Energy." *New York Times*, September 8. Available at: http://www.nytimes.com/2010/09/09/business/global/09trade.html?partner=rss&emc=rss.

Bretton Woods Project. 2011. *World Bank Energy Strategy Stalled*, June 14. Available at: http://www.brettonwoodsproject.org/art-568577.

Buergin, Rainer, and Brian Parkin. 2011. "Merkel Will Scrap German Nuclear Plants by 2022 After Fukushima Disaster." *Bloomberg*, May 30. Available at: http://www.bloomberg.com/news/2011-05-30/merkel-s-coalition-agrees-to-shut-all-of-germany-s-nuclear-plants-by-2022.html.

Busby, Joshua. 2010. *After Copenhagen: Climate Governance and the Road Ahead*. New York: Council on Foreign Relations. Available at: http://www.cfr.org/publication/22726/after_copenhagen.html.

———. 2011. *Time for a Safety Check: China's Nuclear Power Sector after Fukushima.* Cambridge, MA: Long Term Strategy Group.

Climate Action Network. 2011. *No Nuclear for Mitigation*, June 13. Available at: http://www.climatenetwork.org/blog/no-nuclear-mitigation.

Devraj, Ranjit. 2011. *INDIA: Fukushima Revives Debate Over Nuclear Liability*. IPS (Inter Press Service News Agency), March 30. Available at: http://ipsnews.net/news.asp?idnews=55065.

Farrell, Michael B. 2010. "Nuclear Waste Storage in Limbo as Obama Axes Yucca Mountain Funds." *Christian Science Monitor*, February 1. Available at: http://www.csmonitor.com/USA/2010/0201/Nuclear-waste-storage-in-limbo-as-Obama-axes-Yucca-Mountain-funds.

Fehrenbacher, Katie. 2010. "DoE Backs 2nd Nuclear Project with Loan Guarantee." *earth2tech*, May 21. Available at: http://gigaom.com/cleantech/doe-backs-2nd-nuclear-project-with-loan-guarantee/.

Ferguson, Charles. 2007. "Nuclear Energy: Balancing Benefits and Risks." *Council Special Report*. New York: Council on Foreign Relations.

France 24. 2011. *Sarkozy Eyes Re-election with Reshuffled Cabinet*, June 30. Available at: http://www.france24.com/en/20110630-sarkozy-prepares-2012-war-cabinet-presidential-election-baroin-centrists#.

Friedman, Lisa. 2010. "Industrial Nations Divide on Future World Bank Anti-Carbon Policy." *ClimateWire*, August 17. Available at: http://www.nytimes.com/cwire/2010/08/17/17climatewire-industrial-nations-divide-on-future-world-ba-71337.html?pagewanted=2.

Greenpeace. n.d. "End the Nuclear Age." Available at: http://www.greenpeace.org/international/en/campaigns/nuclear/.

Hennessey, Kathleen. 2011. "Energy Secretary Steven Chu says Obama Administration Remains Committed to Nuclear Power." *Los Angeles Times*, March 15. Available at: http://articles.latimes.com/2011/mar/15/news/sc-dc-chu-nuclear-energy-20110316.

Hollinger, Peggy, and Ed Crooks. 2010. "Sarkozy Makes Nuclear Energy Plea." *Financial Times*, March 8. Available at: http://www.ft.com/intl/cms/s/0/fbd1c6f0-2aec-11df-886b-00144feabdco.html.

IAEA (International Atomic Energy Agency). 2000. *Climate Change and Nuclear Power 2008*. Vienna: IAEA. Available at: http://www.iaea.org/OurWork/ST/NE/Pess/assets/08-33461-CCNP-Brochure.pdf.

IEA (International Energy Agency). 2009. *World Energy Outlook*. Available at: http://web.archive.org/web/20110720074945/http://www.worldenergyoutlook.org/docs/weo2009/climate_change_excerpt.pdf.

———. 2010a. *Energy Technology Perspectives*. Available at: http://www.iea.org/techno/etp/index.asp.

———. 2010b. *Expansion of Nuclear Energy Is a Key Contributor to Combating Climate Change*, June 16. Available at: http://www.iea.org/press/pressdetail.asp?PRESS_REL_ID=393.

———. 2010c. *Technology Roadmap: Nuclear Energy*, June 16. Available at: http://www.iea.org/papers/2010/nuclear_roadmap.pdf.

India Today. 2011. *Jaitapur Nuclear Plant Protest: 1 Killed in Police Firing*, April 18. Available at: http://indiatoday.intoday.in/site/story/jaitapur-nuclear-plant-protest-1-killed-in-police-firing/1/135638.html.

IPFM (International Panel on Fissile Materials). 2007. *Global Fissile Material Report 2007.* Princeton, NJ: IPFM.

JEA (Japan Electric Association). 2012. "Capacity Factor at Nuclear Power Stations Falls Under 10%," March 6. Available at: http://www.eco-business.com/news/capacity-factor-of-nuclear-power-stations-falls-under-10/.

Joskow, Paul, and John Parsons. 2009. "The Economic Future of Nuclear Power." *Daedalus* 138: 45–59.

Kadak, Andrew C. 2006. "Nuclear Power: 'Made in China.'" Cambridge, MA: MIT, Department of Nuclear Science and Engineering.

Kanter, James. 2010. "New Warnings About Costs of Nuclear Power." *New York Times*, August 31. Available at: http://green.blogs.nytimes.com/2010/08/31/new-warnings-about-costs-of-nuclear-power/.

Kazmin, Amy. 2010. "India Business Wary Over Nuclear Law." *Financial Times*, August 25. Available at: http://www.ft.com/cms/s/0/cd2e4990-b02f-11df-939d-00144feabdc0.html.

Kleiner, Kurt. 2008. "Nuclear Energy: Accessing the Emissions." *Nature Reports: Climate Change*, September 24. Available at: http://www.nature.com/climate/2008/0810/full/climate.2008.99.html.

Kong, Bo, and David Lampton. 2011. "How Safely Will China Go Nuclear?" *China US Focus*, April 6. Available at: http://www.chinausfocus.com/energy-environment/how-safely-will-china-go-nuclear/.

Kubota, Hideo. 2009. "China's Nuclear Industry at a Turning Point." *European Journal of Advanced Maintenance* 1 (3): GA6.

Lester, Richard, and Robert Rosner. 2009. "The Growth of Nuclear Power: Drivers and Constraints." *Daedalus* 138: 19–29.

Lovins, Amory B., and Imran Sheikh. 2008. "The Nuclear Illusion." *Ambio.* Available at: http://www.rmi.org/rmi/Library/E08-01_NuclearIllusion.

Lovins, Amory B., Imran Sheikh, and Alex Markevich. 2008. "Forget Nuclear." *Solutions.* Available at: http://www.rmi.org/rmi/Library/E08-04_ForgetNuclear.

MIT (Massachusetts Institute of Technology). 2003. *The Future of Nuclear Power: An Interdisciplinary Study.* Cambridge, MA: MIT.

———. 2007. *The Future of Coal.* Cambridge, MA: MIT.

———. 2009. *Update of the MIT 2003 Future of Nuclear Power.* Cambridge, MA: MIT.

Nuclear Power Daily. 2010. "Indian Nuclear Bill Wins Final Approval," August 31. Available at: http://www.nuclearpowerdaily.com/reports/Indian_nuclear_bill_wins_final_approval_999.html.

Pacala, S., and R. Socolow. 2004. "Stabilization Wedges: Solving the Climate Problem for the Next 50 Years with Current Technologies." *Science* 305 (5686): 968–972.

Pew Center on Global Climate Change. 2009. "Nuclear Power." *Pew Fact Sheet*. Available at: http://web.archive.org/web/20100813165022/http://www.pewclimate.org/docUploads/Nuclear%2009%2008%2027_clean.pdf.

Platts. 2010. *French Areva Confident Liability Law Won't Stop Indian Contract*, September 7. Available at: http://www.platts.com/RSSFeedDetailedNews/RSSFeed/HeadlineNews/Nuclear/8923881.

Price, Asher, and Marty Toohey. 2011. "NRG Pulls Financial Support for South Texas Nuclear Plant Expansion." *Austin American-Statesman*, April 20. Available at: http://www.statesman.com/news/local/nrg-pulls-financial-support-for-south-texas-nuclear-1417445.html.

PTI. 2011. "India Committed to Harnessing Nuclear Energy: Manmohan Singh." *DNA—Daily News & Analysis*, May 22. Available at: http://www.dnaindia.com/india/report_india-committed-to-harnessing-nuclear-energy-manmohan-singh_1546353.

Sandler, Todd. 2004. *Global Collective Action*. Cambridge, UK: Cambridge University Press.

Sasikumar, Karthika. 2011. "The Global Future of Nuclear Power after Fukushima—India." Belfer Center for Science and International Affairs, March 16. Available at: http://belfercenter.ksg.harvard.edu/power/2011/03/16/the-global-future-of-nuclear-power-after-fukushima/.

Schneider, Mycle, Steve Thomas, Antony Froggatt, and Doug Koplow. 2009a. "2009 World Nuclear Industry Status Report." [Summary] *Bulletin of the Atomic Scientists* 65 (6): 1–19.

Schneider, Mycle, Steve Thomas, Antony Froggatt, and Doug Koplow. 2009b. *The World Nuclear Industry Status Report: With Particular Emphasis on Economic Issues*. Paper commissioned by the German Federal Ministry of Environment, Nature Conservation and Reactor Safety.

Shear, Michael D., and Steven Mufson. 2010. "Obama Offers Loan to Help Fund Two Nuclear Reactors." *Washington Post*, February 17. Available at: http://www.washingtonpost.com/wp-dyn/content/article/2010/02/16/AR2010021601302.html.

Socolow, Robert, and Alexander Glaser. 2009. "Balancing Risks: Nuclear Energy & Climate Change." *Daedalus*. 138 (4): 31–44.

Sokolski, Henry. 2010. "The High and Hidden Costs of Nuclear Power." *Policy Review* 162 (August 1). Available at: http://www.hoover.org/publications/policy-review/article/43316.

———. 2011. "Europe's Anti-Nuclear Power Outburst." *Weekly Standard* (blog), June 30. Available at: http://www.weeklystandard.com/blogs/europe-s-anti-nuclear-power-outburst_575938.html.

Sovacool, Benjamin. 2008. "Valuing the Greenhouse Gas Emissions from Nuclear Power: A Critical Survey." *Energy Policy* 36 (8): 2950–2963.

Squassoni, Sharon. 2008a. *The Realities of Nuclear Expansion*. Carnegie Endowment for International Peace, March 12. Available at: http://www.carnegieendowment.org/files/squassoni_testimony_20080312.pdf.

————. 2008b. "Nuclear Renaissance: Is it Coming? Should It?" *Carnegie Endowment for International Peace Report on Foreign Policy for the Next President*, October. Available at: http://www.carnegieendowment.org/files/nuclear_renaissance1.pdf.

Stoett, Peter. 2003. "Toward Renewed Legitimacy? Nuclear Power, Global Warming, and Security." *Global Environmental Politics* 3 (1): 99–116.

Tanner, Jari. 2011. "6-party Government in Finland after Lengthy Talks." *Bloomberg Businessweek*, June 17. Available at: http://www.businessweek.com/ap/financial-news/D9NTR0481.htm.

Thomas, Andrea. 2010. "Germany Delays Decision on Fuel-Rod Levy." *Wall Street Journal*, August 18. Available at: http://online.wsj.com/article/SB100014240527487 03649004575437683179343538.html?mod=googlenews_wsj.

Tsolova, Tsvetelia. 2011. "Bulgaria Seeks New Delay for Belene Nuclear Deal." *London South East*, June 17. Available at: http://www.lse.co.uk/FinanceNews.asp?Ar ticleCode=xl9y5jkv756qxbz&ArticleHeadline=Bulgaria_seeks_new_delay_for_ Belene_nuclear_deal.

UNFCCC (United Nations Framework Convention on Climate Change). 2001. *Report of the Conference of the Parties on the Second Part of Its Sixth Session, Held At Bonn from 16 to 27 July 2001*. Available at: http://www.unfccc.int/resource/docs/cop6s ecpart/05.pdf.

————. 2010a. *Ad Hoc Working Group on Further Commitments for Annex I Parties under the Kyoto Protocol*, August 6. Available at: http://unfccc.int/files/kyoto_ protocol/application/pdf/draft_proposal.pdf.

————. 2010b. *The Cancun Agreements: Financial, Technology and Capacity-Building Support*. Available at: http://cancun.unfccc.int/financial-technology-and-capacity-building-support/new-long-term-funding-arrangements/.

von Hippel, Frank. Ed. 2010. *The Uncertain Future of Nuclear Energy*. Princeton, NJ: International Panel on Fissile Materials.

Wald, Matthew. 2011. "Despite Bipartisan Support, Nuclear Reactor Projects Falter." *New York Times*, April 28. Available at: http://www.nytimes.com/2011/04/29/business/ energy-environment/29utility.html.

Wiesmann, Gerrit. 2011. "Oldest German Nuclear Plants to Stay Closed." *Financial Times*, May 27. Available at: http://www.ft.com/intl/cms/s/0/186a4d98-8864-11e0-a1c3-00144feabdc0.html.

WNA (World Nuclear Association). 2012. *World Nuclear Power Reactors & Uranium Requirements*. Available at: http://www.world-nuclear.org/info/reactors.html.

Yurman, Dan. 2010. "World Bank Nixes Nuclear Power." *The Energy Collective* (blog), April 11. Available at: http://theenergycollective.com/djysrv/34453/world-bank-nixes-nuclear-energy.

6 The Politics of the Nuclear Renaissance

A Comment

Christopher Way

ALLISON MACFARLANE (CHAPTER 2 IN THIS VOLUME) analyzes nuclear energy as an "ambiguous technology," meaning that many aspects of the technology—its meaning, function, and effects—are contested. It is a fitting phrase for a book on a possible "nuclear renaissance," for the nuclear renaissance is nothing if ambiguous and contested. Will it actually happen? Will nuclear technology play a role in saving the planet from environmental disaster? Or perhaps in causing environmental disaster, a fear exacerbated by the uncertain consequences of the Fukushima accident? Will it make the world a more, or less, secure place? Will the renaissance be accomplished by the spread of nuclear technology to a new set of less-developed countries (and if so, can they handle it securely and safely?), or by a deepening in countries that already have it? The meaning and reality of the nuclear renaissance is certainly contested.

Prior to questions about its consequences, however, are questions about the renaissance's reality. Is a nuclear energy revival actually taking place? If so, will it be large enough to affect climate change, economic development, or international security? Which countries will build new reactors, and why? These are the questions addressed by the preceding five chapters, and in many ways they precede the remainder of the volume: If a nuclear revival fails to occur, discussions about its consequences are putting the cart before the horse.

In addressing these questions, the preceding five chapters at first glance seem diverse. Joshua Busby (Chapter 5) presents a careful analysis of the likelihood that nuclear energy can make a meaningful contribution to re-ducing carbon emissions, whereas Bernard Gourley and Adam Stulberg (Chapter 1) provide a quantitative analysis of the drivers of nuclear energy acquisition. Matthew Fuhrmann (Chapter 3) describes a quantitative analysis of the history of the supply of nuclear assistance by technologically advanced countries, complemented by Adam Stulberg's analysis (Chapter 4) of the stra-tegic interaction between suppliers and buyers in the context of multilateral nuclear approaches (MNAs). Allison Macfarlane (Chapter 2) analyzes the dis-courses of both buyers and suppliers about the acquisition of nuclear energy technology. Superficially, these papers appear to be a disparate lot. Yet despite the divergence in methods of inquiry, they converge in placing a spotlight on the role of politics in driving or limiting the incipient nuclear revival. Many analyses of the nuclear revival focus on environmental, economic, and tech-nological themes. Those are not missing here, particularly in Busby's chapter. But a common denominator of these chapters is the primacy of politics. These chapters agree that powerful political factors will play a much greater role in the (potential) nuclear energy renaissance than many discussions allow.

An emphasis on politics is not novel, although political scientists have tended to focus much more on the politics of nuclear weapons than on nuclear energy. A vast literature explores the drivers of weapons proliferation. Some of this work, although not specifically addressing the spread of nuclear energy, offers arguments of potential relevance to the politics of energy technology (Betts 1993; Hymans 2006; Solingen 2007; Rublee 2009). For example, Jacques Hymans (2006) argues convincingly that leaders' psychology—in particular, what he calls their "national identity conception"—is important for under-standing attitudes toward nuclear weapons. Might not leader psychology also shape attitudes toward nuclear energy, particularly in terms of the emphasis placed on the prestige and energy autonomy potentially conferred by such technology? For the most part, these five chapters leave possible insights from the nuclear weapons proliferation literature undeveloped, missing an opportunity—a point to which I return later in the chapter. Compared to the voluminous work on the spread of nuclear weapons, the political science literature exploring the politics of nuclear energy expansion is smaller, and it is to this literature that this volume adds. This literature has covered concerns about the spillover of energy technology (particularly that pertaining to sen-sitive parts of the fuel cycle) to weapons (Wohlstetter et al. 1979; Potter 1982), the politics of nuclear energy in both developed and developing countries

(DeLeon 1980; Poneman 1982; Jasper 1990; Kapur 1993; Delmas and Heiman 2001; Nelson and Sprecher 2008; Toth 2008; Nelson 2010; Jewell 2011), and the politics of international trade in nuclear technology (Wonder 1977; Boardman and Keeley 1983; Potter 1990; Brenner 1991; Bratt 2006). The five chapters here build upon this literature, update it, and take a more quantitative bent than most of it. In doing so, they offer a more systematic analysis of the role of politics in the spread of nuclear energy technology than much of the earlier work in the field. This promises a heightened ability to detect systematic relationships. Among other advantages, quantitative analyses avoid the pitfall of "sampling on the dependent variable" (looking only at cases where a positive outcome occurred), a problem that can lead to incorrect inferences about the relationship between variables. However, these methods are not without limitations of their own—a point which I highlight in the final section of this chapter.

In this commentary, I focus on four features of the politics of the nuclear energy revival highlighted by the previous chapters, followed by a discussion of what remains to be done in terms of unpacking the way politics will shape the nuclear resurgence.

Will the Supply of Technology Constrain the Nuclear Revival?

Any renaissance of nuclear energy will entail the spread of nuclear power to a new tier of countries. This means both the introduction of power reactors to countries lacking any experience with nuclear energy—such as the United Arab Emirates (UAE), Turkey, and Vietnam—and a rapid, large-scale expansion of plants in countries currently possessing a limited nuclear infrastructure (such as India, South Africa, and China). To accomplish this spread and deepening of nuclear power quickly, safely, and economically, access to nuclear technology needs to be relatively free and easy. As Gourley and Stulberg observe in Chapter 1, hardly any of the leading nuclear aspirants are capable of building and operating power plants without foreign assistance. The papers agree that this, at least, should not be an obstacle.

Fuhrmann's analysis of the history of nuclear assistance (Chapter 3) indicates that great powers possessing nuclear know-how are willing to share technology with others, especially those in whom they have geostrategic interest. It is not just the great powers that play this game, according to

Fuhrmann, but any state with broad interests beyond its borders. His paper shows that states engaged in enduring rivalries or involved in a network of military alliances are, on average, more likely to provide nuclear assistance to other states.[1] Extrapolating the results of Fuhrmann's quantitative-historical analysis—admittedly an exercise fraught with peril, since relationships that held true in the past may not hold in the future—suggests that two ongoing trends augur an abundant supply of nuclear assistance. First, the transition toward a multipolar system implies that a growing number of states may have the kind of wide-ranging interests that have historically been drivers of nuclear supply: In the past, the United States, the USSR/Russia, France, and the United Kingdom fit Fuhrmann's profile to a tee; in the future, China, India, Brazil, and South Africa may do so as well. Second, the number of countries with nuclear know-how to share has expanded. Just as the potential suppliers of nuclear weapons–related technology and knowledge has expanded to a second "tier" of proliferators (Braun and Chyba 2004), so has the set of potential suppliers of nuclear energy–related technology and knowledge. In brief, the group of willing and able suppliers is expanding, easing supply-side constraints. An important question to ask, however, is whether Fuhrman's analysis will apply to the middle powers of the future. Whether countries like Brazil and South Africa will have the same portfolio of geostrategic interests, and pursue them in the same way, as did members of the Cold War alliances that drive Fuhrman's results is unclear. Indeed, Fuhrman's example of a middle power following geostrategic interests in its nuclear supply policy—Canada's interaction with Romania—is one of Cold War alliance dynamics, as Canada sought to contribute to *America's* détente policy (emphasis added). Again, this offers an important reminder that our ability to extrapolate past patterns into the future depends on the future being like the past. (It also depends on state type, something I will have more to say about later in the chapter.)[2]

Allison Macfarlane's emphasis on the discourse of nuclear buyers (Chapter 2) nicely complements this argument. The evolution of the nuclear regime has provided potential buyers with effective rhetorical resources in arguing for open access. As Macfarlane chronicles, aspirant nuclear energy producers emphasize themes of equity and fairness in their discourse. Under the Non-Proliferation Treaty (NPT) regime, these arguments are difficult to counter because the NPT *does* guarantee access to nuclear energy technology, including the entire fuel cycle, under the provisions of Article IV. This right is, like most legal rights, a conditional one: It is conditional upon compliance with

Articles I and II (Sagan 2010). Countries in good standing that desire nuclear energy technology have a strong case under current international law, and it will take considerable persuasive and rhetorical powers to deny it to them without appearing hypocritical. Potential buyers will not be shy about making this case, as Jordan's resistance to following the UAE's example in giving up its right to enrich uranium shows, and in this effort they can take advantage of divisions among potential suppliers (most notably, France). Nuclear aspirants have an impressive tool kit of strategies available to them in efforts to overcome hesitation to strike nuclear cooperation agreements (NCAs) with them, not least by playing off potential suppliers against one another (Early 2010).

Putting together Fuhrmann's analysis of the drivers of nuclear supply and Macfarlane's chronicle of the rhetorical tools available to nuclear buyers implies that countries desiring access to nuclear assistance will get it, with very few exceptions. Given the emergence of a larger number of globally, or at least regionally, engaged powers able to serve as suppliers, efforts by one or several great powers to deny nuclear technology to any particular recipient are likely to fail. A large body of literature in international relations argues that the fewer the relevant players and the more coincident their interests, the easier it is to achieve cooperation. In the realm of nuclear technology, the number of relevant states is growing and their interests are diverging. And recipient countries have strong arguments, in terms of equity and rights embodied in treaty law, on their side. From a policy standpoint, this means that efforts to deny nuclear energy technology, including fuel cycle technology, to specific countries will face an uphill battle. Hopes by some that the United States could make the UAE's 123 Agreement a template for future NCAs will most likely be disappointed.[3] The logic of embargoes kicks in here: Without unified participation by all potential suppliers, unilateral efforts (or those by a subgroup of countries) to deny technology will be undercut by substitute providers. The UAE's agreements provide a telling example. As Stulberg points out, although the UAE's agreement with the United States may appear as a model, the UAE also completed a series of memoranda of understandings with other counties, and most of these did not include provisions forswearing indigenous fuel fabrication, "virtually undercutting the practical significance of the commitments to the United States" (Stulberg, Chapter 4 in this volume).

Moreover, the agreement contains provisions allowing the UAE to request renegotiation of the agreement in the event that other states in the region (such as Jordan) do not follow its lead in agreeing to forgo enrichment and reprocessing (USGPO 2009, Agreed Minute p. 17–18). Thus, for good or for ill, the nuclear energy revival will probably not be slowed by limited access to necessary technology and knowledge.

Nuclear Power and Power Politics

Many discussions of the nuclear revival focus on its environmental or economic aspects. When politics appear, it is usually in guise of potential domestic political opposition to nuclear power. Joshua Busby in Chapter 5, for example, argues that China's ability to expand nuclear energy production is enhanced by the state's greater capacity to site facilities compared to democratic countries such as India (where the ability of protestors in West Bengal to block an auto plant should give pause to advocates of nuclear energy). Alternatively, politics sometimes enters the discussion when assessing the challenges facing negotiation of a successor accord to the Kyoto Protocol. Missing from many of these discussions, however, is the politics of power, influence, and status. The previous subsection brought power politics back in from the standpoint of suppliers; this subsection considers it from the viewpoint of buyers.

Great powers have long used conventional arms flow, foreign aid allocation, and economic exchange as means of gaining influence and deepening alliances. Conventional arms sales, for example, have been linked to geopolitical calculations (Pierre 1982; Krause 1991). On the receiving end, buyers often seek arms as a way of cementing a great power's commitment to them, or of enhancing their own status and prestige. From the viewpoint of political scientists, these sorts of exchange not only underpin commitments and deepen relationships, but also open up avenues of influence. Albert Hirschman argued decades ago that even apparently innocuous economic exchanges open up potential avenues of influence: Asymmetrical interdependence is a potential source of power between states (Hirschman 1945/1980). According to this logic, when the gains from economic exchange are unequally distributed between two actors, the less dependent party gains bargaining power because it faces lower "exit costs" from ending the relationship. The distributional implications of cooperation are often as important as its attainment (Krasner 1991; Gruber 2000).

Stulberg analyzes the logic of MNAs through this power-political lens, arguing that major nuclear suppliers have, to put it simply, a commitment problem. From a buyer country's perspective, committing to nuclear energy without control over the fuel supply leaves them vulnerable to what economists call the "hold-up problem." Having sunk investments into nuclear energy, buyers are vulnerable to threatened disruptions from suppliers. To assuage these fears, suppliers need to make a credible commitment not to take advantage of this asymmetric interdependence; but it can be difficult to do so, because it may be tempting for them to take advantage of their position in the future (perhaps under circumstances difficult or impossible to foresee) even if their current intentions are completely benign. As Stulberg chronicles, suppliers can try to create credible commitments by offering shared ownership of enrichment facilities and relevant companies, but these strategies can fail to reassure when the dependence of the buyer is great.

This analysis is important, because it suggests that the political constraint on the nuclear revival may come from the demand side rather than the supply side. Whereas nuclear suppliers may always be found, that supply often comes with a price; and the price may be too high for many buyers. Stulberg's four cases are suggestive. Unwilling to depend on others for fuel supplies, South Africa has scaled back its nuclear plans dramatically. The UAE, never intending to depend on nuclear energy for essential electricity needs in the first place, agreed to forgo domestic fuel fabrication (but still leaves a back door open just in case). Kazakhstan and South Korea, exemplifying intermediate cases, did work out arrangements with suppliers though for different reasons. These four cases indicate that buyers of nuclear technology may ultimately limit the extent of the nuclear revival unless they are sufficiently reassured that their supply of nuclear materials will not be subject to politically motivated disruptions.

This analysis has a number of additional implications for the nuclear revival. Multilateral nuclear approaches may be easiest to achieve where they are least needed. Presumably, they would be most valuable for states that would potentially come to depend the most on nuclear energy. This is true not just for the state in question, but also for hopes that nuclear energy can provide one of the "wedges" necessary to contain global carbon emissions (Busby, Chapter 5 in this volume). Yet precisely because those states would be the most vulnerable to supply disruptions, they would be the most cautious in their approach to MNAs. From an environmental standpoint, the states we most need to embrace nuclear energy may be the most hesitant to sign on unless they are allowed to control the fuel cycle. A related point is that nuclear aspirants who are shunned by some suppliers (perhaps for political reasons related to potential weapons proliferation) will be all the more vulnerable to the small number of suppliers willing to work with them. Shunning by some suppliers will have the effect of exaggerating the market share of the remaining ones, and in the extreme turning them into de facto monopolists. The consequence of this is to heighten the supplier's temptation to use the asymmetric relationship as a power resource (thus making it harder for them to provide a credible commitment to uninterrupted supply), with the further consequence that the buyer should beware of accepting their overtures. The price of nuclear energy dependence, in terms of creating a political vulnerability, increases for nuclear aspirants in these situations. This somewhat offsets the logic of embargoes discussed in the previous section, providing a countervailing mechanism that suggests a greater possibility for limiting the spread of nuclear technology (at least assuming that everyone agrees to withhold enrichment technology, a perhaps dubious assumption).

The Fuhrmann and Macfarlane chapters also emphasize the important role of power and influence considerations, although they both also point to gaps in our knowledge about the precise mechanisms and consequences of political calculations in the spread of nuclear energy. For Fuhrmann, political motives are central in driving countries to become nuclear suppliers. States with wide-ranging strategic interests seek to deepen military alliances, gain influence, and undercut or constrain their enemies by providing peaceful nuclear assistance. For example, India is said to have offered assistance to Vietnam partly to constrain the rising influence of China. Consistent with Stulberg's theoretical analysis of asymmetric vulnerabilities, Macfarlane's empirical analysis implies that Russia may extend its well-known energy politics to the nuclear realm. In some cases, this may generate power for the supplier—a possibility driving Turkish concerns about dependence upon Russia. In other cases, it may allow buyers to play potential suppliers against one another.

Here, however, we know less than we would like. Fuhrmann documents a (historic) correlation between wide-ranging strategic interests and willingness to supply nuclear assistance, and Macfarlane documents some concerns about potential nuclear influence. But there is scant good evidence about consequences: *If* states are seeking influence via the provision of nuclear energy assistance, do they actually *get* it? Is nuclear energy assistance a fungible good? Can it be converted into other desired outcomes? Strengthening military alliances may well be, as Fuhrman posits in Chapter 3, a "major reason why countries provide nuclear assistance," but we do not know if provision actually does strengthen military alliances. Providers may hope that recipients will have a hard time making policy without their approval, but will they? The question of actual consequences is important from a policy perspective. Before embarking on a policy of using nuclear energy supply as a means of influence, policy makers would like to know whether it actually achieves that goal. Should U.S. policy makers worry about attempts by Russia and China to use access to nuclear energy technology as a diplomatic tool? The answer depends on whether it works. Stulberg in Chapter 4 provides four illustrative cases that begin to provide some answers, but we don't know whether they represent the broader universe: More systematic analysis is needed. These questions of nuclear power supply and influence are important avenues for future research, and the answers have important implications for policy makers.

So far, this discussion has focused on attempts by suppliers to use nuclear energy as a means of influence over recipient states. But buyers also are motivated by power (and not just the electric kind). As Macfarlane documents in Chapter 2, prestige seems to loom large among the motivations of new nuclear aspirants. And prestige, in turn, is often seen as a marker of power, modernity, and wealth, as well as a means to those ends. But does it deliver them? And how important is it among the hierarchy of motives? Here again, as with the question of influence for providers, we need to know more. As Gourley and Stulberg observe (Chapter 1 in this volume), prestige is notoriously difficult to study empirically and systematically, and it is hard to gauge its importance as a driver of nuclear energy acquisition. But, even assuming it is a key driver, do countries actually gain a status boost from operating nuclear power reactors? Does it confer prestige on them, and what are the tangible benefits of enjoying such prestige? Again, firmer knowledge on this point would be useful. For nuclear aspirants chasing prestige, knowing whether or not nuclear energy delivers it would be important, especially if Macfarlane is right about prestige's importance among reasons for acquiring nuclear power. From the standpoint of nuclear suppliers, if nuclear energy delivers prestige, then supplying technology to a given state in effect confers prestige on the recipient—this would be an intrinsic part of the transaction. Better knowledge about the consequences of providing nuclear energy technology—in terms of power, prestige, and status—would be helpful for parties on both sides of the transaction.

The Revival Cannot be Limited to Current Nuclear Haves

Even if one accepts the need for nuclear power to provide one of the wedges of carbon dioxide (CO_2) reductions by providing enough energy to replace four billion tons of emissions, we still might hope that most of the required 640 new plants (as calculated by Joshua Busby in Chapter 5) would come from current nuclear power operators. After all, the newly aspiring nuclear power states are on average more corrupt, less stable politically, score lower on regulatory indices, and are nondemocratic (Miller and Sagan 2009). Wouldn't it be better to restrict expansion to those who already have a track record of operating power plants? This almost seems feasible: Of the planned and proposed nuclear plants listed by Busby, just eight countries account for 70 percent of the total. And for the moment, the vast majority of activity is concentrated in a group of four countries that we might dub (borrowing from Goldman Sachs' coining of the BRICs category) the KRICs: Korea, Russia, India, and China.

The chapters here, however, imply that this will not be possible. It is not just that the participation of additional countries is necessary to meet the carbon replacement levels called for by the wedge strategy. It is rather, once again, the politics of the matter. For if rising powers such as India and China, joined by countries such as Korea and perhaps South Africa, lead the nuclear energy charge, this will only reinforce the symbolic linking of nuclear power to modernity, ambition, rising power, and status. In short, it will strengthen one of the chief motives for acquiring nuclear power technology. Any efforts to restrict access would only make matters worse. By in effect saying "nuclear power is fine for China, India, and South Africa but not for you," efforts to limit the spread would only reinforce the message that nuclear energy is associated with status and arrival on the world scene as a great power or modern nation. Just as statements by nuclear weapons powers implying that nuclear weapons are useful only fuel the idea that such weapons are desirable (President Jacques Chirac's praise in a 2006 speech of nuclear weapons as the "ultimate guarantor of our security" come to mind), so an association of nuclear energy with rising powers only furthers the linkage of reactors with development and rising status. In brief, we cannot have it both ways: We cannot encourage full-tilt nuclear power expansion in some countries while seeking to avoid it in others. Either the nuclear revival both deepens *and* spreads nuclear energy, or it in all likelihood does neither.

And Nuclear Power Probably Won't Save the World . . .

Will politics undercut the possibility of a nuclear renaissance? The five chapters in this volume suggest a contingent answer. On one hand, the dynamics of power politics in an emerging multipolar world will ensure ready suppliers for (nearly) any aspiring country (as implied by Fuhrmann, Chapter 3 in this volume). Prestige motivations will ensure that aspirant countries are attracted to nuclear energy even if the economics do not quite add up (or even if the existing energy grid is not ready!). Moreover, the logic of prestige politics ensures that if countries like China and India start building reactors at a rapid clip, more and more nuclear aspirants will be attracted to the technology. On the other hand, the allure of prestige motivations must be weighed against the implications of energy dependence for recipients, as highlighted in Stulberg's strategic interaction framework in Chapter 4. Whether prestige motivations trump concerns about political vulnerabilities remains an open question, and as Gourley and Stulberg argue in Chapter 1, prestige is an elusive concept for empirical study.

On balance, nuclear power will probably end up hard pressed to meet the minimal requirements of providing one of the anti-carbon wedges discussed by Busby. Seven hundred plants providing 700 GW by 2050 is probably the upper limit on what could be achieved. Where does the limitation come from? From all the obvious places—cost overruns and delays, difficulties in scaling up production fast enough and safely enough, unresolved issues about nuclear waste, the consequences of the Fukushima accident (see Busby, Chapter 5 in this volume)—but once again, politics looms large. As Busby emphasizes, political support for nuclear energy is often fragile, lacking, or vulnerable to a negative publicity shock from an accident, sabotage, or terror incident. And here I am even more pessimistic than Busby. One of the bright spots in most surveys of nuclear energy potential is China's ability to overcome siting constraints and "not in my backyard" attitudes. Yet while this may be true of the past, it is far from clear that it will be true of the future (or is of the present).

As a recent study of dam projects makes clear, the politics of large-scale infrastructure projects in China has changed quickly and dramatically. Only a decade ago, the possibility of media, grassroots movements, and local politicians blocking major projects was almost unimaginable; now it is a reality (Mertha 2011; Stern 2011). Similarly, Chinese authorities have recently been forced by protests to shut down or relocate chemical plants producing paraxylene (Anderlini 2011). As the examples of the politics of dams and chemical plants suggest, the ability of the Chinese state to steamroller opposition in building some 120 or more reactors in the next decades might not be as assured as nuclear optimists suppose. And if China is the great hope of nuclear optimists, the prospect of building projected numbers of plants in countries such as India and elsewhere can only be worse. Indeed, India's plans for nuclear expansion have hit new obstacles post-Fukushima, with West Bengal's scrapping of a proposed nuclear power plant (on environmental grounds) portending a likely slowdown in construction. Public support for nuclear power is thin and fragile in most countries for which we have data, and survey takers often have to go to great lengths in terms of strategic survey construction to generate substantial support (Goldacre 2010). If the public gains more influence over energy policy in an increasing number of countries, the domestic politics of the nuclear renaissance will in all likelihood begin to look less promising.

The counterpoint to this pessimism might be the non-finding about domestic regime type in Gourley and Stulberg's analysis of the drivers of nuclear power plant construction. They find that two drivers matter a lot: the size of the domestic economy, and energy security (defined as dependence on imported energy sources).[4] Politics is notable by its absence: Neither a standard scale of democracy–authoritarian regime type nor an indicator of regime durability seems to matter for nuclear power plant construction. Yet this non-finding can be taken a number of ways. It could mean that the domestic politics of nuclear energy does not really matter on the assumption that, if it did, democracies should be different from nondemocracies in their propensity to rely on nuclear energy. But the non-finding is equally consistent with the possibility that domestic politics matters everywhere. What the analysis shows is a lack of difference *between* regime types on one particular indicator of democracy. This result does not show that politics does not matter; just that there is no discernible difference between regime types. The non-finding could also be interpreted, as noted by Gourley and Stulberg, that the Polity index simply does not capture the *relevant* aspect of politics. It may not be, for example, just executive autonomy that matters, but the extent to which political arrangements are capable of shaping public risk perceptions about nuclear energy. This is definitely an area ripe for further research.

Furthermore, for nuclear power to be cost-competitive with other sources of electricity, a substantial carbon charge for CO_2 emissions would be necessary (Joskow and Parsons 2009). This would likely have to be driven by an international climate accord; many countries, not least the United States, lack the political will to impose carbon charges without some kind of treaty-mandated goal. Aside from the issue, discussed by Busby, of nuclear power's eligibility for emissions reduction credits in any future accord is the question of the likelihood of successful negotiation of such an accord. Again, the political prospects look bleak. There is a trade-off between the depth and breadth of international cooperation and regulations (Drezner 2007). Any effective accord definition, under the auspices of the United Nations, would have to be broad; this implies shallow depth in terms of demands placed on countries. Yet what is needed here is depth and breadth. Again, the political odds are long.

Bringing Politics Back In: More to Do

The five chapters thus illuminate several political aspects that will help shape the contours of any revival or resurgence in nuclear energy. Although the papers advance our knowledge, they also stop short of answering several important questions about the politics of the nuclear resurgence.

Gourley and Stulberg's and Fuhrmann's analyses provide interesting findings about the relationship between regime type and nuclear technology. Fuhrmann finds that democracies are more likely to supply nuclear technology to other states, whereas Gourley and Stulberg find no relationship between democracy or regime durability and the acquisition of nuclear energy plants. Neither of these chapters yields a clear conclusion about the causal effects of regime type for a simple reason: They were not designed to do so. As is typical of many studies of nuclear proliferation (both of weapons and energy), these chapters follow a "causes of effects" approach in which the goal is to maximize the amount of variation explained in the dependent variable rather than identify the causal effect of a specific independent variable (for example, regime type). However, this common research strategy works against finding regime type effects: Including variables that are themselves potentially consequences of regime type—"post-treatment" variables that are likely to be influenced by regime type—can result in biased estimates of the true effects of regime type. If we are interested in the effects of regime type, then including variables that may themselves be influenced by regime type (such as conflict propensity or economic outcomes) can obscure the effects of regime type. This is similar to a problem commonly encountered in labor economics: One cannot accurately assess the effect of education on earnings if one also controls for occupation. Since education causes occupation—in other words, occupation is post-treatment—it is a "bad control" for a study interested in the causal effect of education (King and Zeng 2007b; Angrist and Pischke 2008). This problem of post-treatment bias is common in international relations research, but recognition of it is less common (King and Zeng 2007a).

In practice, this means we cannot place a causal interpretation on the findings about regime type presented in these two chapters, as the authors note. Given the likelihood that regime type or durability is linked to other variables such as gross domestic product per capita, alliance behavior, conflict propensity, timing of NPT membership, economic openness, and perhaps other included variables, we cannot infer the net effect of regime type on outcomes from these models. This catch-all "causes of effects" approach contrasts with an "effects of causes" strategy in which one tries to evaluate the (causal) relationship between a specific variable of interest and an outcome of interest. The findings (including non-findings) on correlations reported here are thus suggestive; but in order to explore further, and more precisely, the causal relationship between regime type and nuclear policy, there is a lot more to do.

More is also in play here than questions about research design and causal inference. The chapters here tend to focus on the differences between democracies and autocracies. This is not surprising: After all, the democratic peace literature has been one of the most active and influential in international relations in recent years. As is common in the democratic peace literature, the two quantitative chapters here use the Polity scale as their indicator of regime type and couch their discussion in terms of "democracy." But there is much more to regime type than the democracy–dictatorship, and research in comparative politics has increasingly investigated the variation of institutions across both democratic and authoritarian regimes. For example, the growing literature on the politics of authoritarianism has shown great variation in the domestic institutional structure of dictatorships, with important consequences for a variety of domestic and international outcomes.[5] A deeper understanding of the (possible) relationship between regime type/domestic politics and nuclear policy can be gained by moving beyond the Polity scale's emphasis on the democracy/dictatorship distinction to explore these richer types of institutional variation.

As an example, consider one of the most consequential ways that dictatorships (and political systems in general) vary: the ability of domestic institutions to constrain individual leaders, and the extent to which an individual leader holds the levers of power. In some authoritarian regimes—known variously as despotic, personalistic, or sultanistic—a paramount leader enjoys control over government decisions to an extent unseen even in other dictatorships. Policy decisions lay mainly at his or her discretion, and institutions such as the military or any political parties have been eviscerated to the point that they have little independent power (Geddes 2003). These leaders face few constraints on their policy decisions. As well, their motives differ systematically from those of other leaders. As psychological analyses of "tyrants" have shown, the types of leaders who become personalist dictators often suffer from intense narcissism, leading to grandiose ambitions (Glad 2002). They may well be especially likely to exhibit the type of "national identity conception" that Jacques Hymans has linked to the desire for nuclear weapons technology (Hymans 2006).

For these reasons, personalist regimes are likely to have distinctive patterns of nuclear technology policy. As Macfarlane's chapter documents, the prestige motive is strongly associated with the pursuit of nuclear energy. Given that personalist leaders are more strongly driven by status goals and the desire for national autonomy (Hymans 2006) and tend to have grandiose self-images (Post 1993) that can be validated by large-scale technological projects, it is reasonable to expect this type of regime to have a strong attraction to nuclear energy technology. Moreover, the implications extend beyond the desire for nuclear power. Because personalist regimes tend to eviscerate institutions that might foster alternative sources of power, they are likely to be unusually inept and ineffective in the pursuit of large-scale scientific projects (Hymans 2008; Montgomery, Chapter 7 in this volume). Thus, in personalist regimes we have a political recipe for an unusually strong interest in nuclear energy combined with a singular ineptitude in ability to handle such projects in due course—surely an important political implication of regime type. But the important point is that this implication is obscured by a focus on the Polity scale and the democratic/dictatorship distinction. Once again, exploring that distinction provides a starting point to understanding the politics of nuclear energy, but there is a lot more to do: More refined understandings of regime type will yield richer insights into the spread of nuclear energy.

Finally, there is also more to do in terms of identifying and understanding the domestic political drivers that help determine how factors such as strategic considerations, desires for influence, or prestige motivations play out in practice. For the most part, these chapters "black-box" the state when considering how states respond to various incentives. This is perhaps most easily seen in the quantitative papers. Their implicit assumption is that all states respond in the same way to various external situations (such as alliances or rivalries) and internal situations (such as economic development or export pressure). In statistical language, they assume that the relationship between these explanatory variables and the outcome of interest features the same slope for all states, across both space and time.

But is this unstated assumption reasonable? In part, this is another way of raising the caveat that "past performance does not guarantee future returns" (as the mutual fund industry is required by law to remind us). Will future middle powers such as Brazil and South Africa fit Fuhrmann's description of the behavior of great powers of the past? It is far from clear that they will, even if they face similar external environments. For one thing, it is well established in the comparative and international political economy literatures that domestic structure affects the way states respond to similar challenges. Differences in bureaucratic structure, state–society relations, and historical trajectories that impart a distinctive sense of purpose to national policies all shape how states will respond to similar situations and incentives. Whether or not future nuclear suppliers will behave like past ones depends not just upon whether they become great powers, but also on their state structures— something missing from the current discussion.

Equally important is the question of whether we can expect states to have the same reaction functions to opportunities. Is the slope of influence or prestige variables really the same across different types of states? Take prestige motivations. The discussions of Macfarlane and Gourley and Stulberg agree that prestige features fairly prominently in the language of nuclear aspirants, although it is difficult to quantify. Even if we grant that mastery of nuclear energy technology is widely believed to confer prestige, surely it does not follow that all states will find this appeal equally attractive. Domestic political factors will mediate the effect of prestige as a driver of interest in nuclear energy.

The same logic applies to other variables discussed in these chapters. Will a country favor its allies with access to nuclear technology? Again, the effect is likely to be mediated by domestic political/state-type factors. In other words, the effect is going to be conditional on state structure. Will a state seek to use access to energy technology as a source of influence? Yet again, the likelihood that a state will take advantage of such opportunities depends on its domestic structure. Turkey's concerns about dependence on Russian supply of energy technology is certainly not just due to Russia's (former) great power status; rather, it has everything to do with the domestic structure of the Russian state and the nature of its political elite. This general idea—that the effect of many variables will be conditional upon elements of a state's domestic politics and structure—provides a way of bridging some of the gap between quantitative and qualitative analyses of nuclear energy and proliferation. In emphasizing systematic analysis and relationships, it retains the generalizing impulse of quantitative research; in emphasizing the conditionality of the effects of systematic variables, it retains the emphasis of qualitative scholars on context-specific analyses. It also offers a more nuanced way of understanding the role of politics in shaping the spread of nuclear energy, pointing toward a path forward in building upon the analyses offered in these chapters.

These five chapters go a long way toward advancing our understanding of the role of politics in the resurgence of nuclear energy, building on the earlier and growing literature on the politics of nuclear energy, trade in nuclear technology, and concerns about the spillover of energy technology to weapons programs. They add to that literature and point several ways forward to obtaining a more nuanced understanding of the role of politics in the nuclear resurgence.

Conclusion

Many discussions of the nuclear power renaissance focus on economic, environmental, or technological issues. To the extent that politics feature in these discussions, they fit in terms of either the potential for nuclear energy to fuel the spread of nuclear weapons or of domestic politics to pose a constraint on the expansion of nuclear energy. The chapters here, however, argue for a much greater role for political factors in understanding the likelihood, extent, and dynamics of the nuclear energy revival. Political-power motivations will drive the supply of nuclear assistance to aspirant states, and in all likelihood will assure that most aspirants find willing patrons. Prestige and power motivations will drive the demand for nuclear energy technology from aspirant states. Considering prestige, the faster the expansion goes in countries such as China and India, the greater will be those demands from aspirant states. Yet concerns about opening themselves up to political vulnerabilities by depending on foreign suppliers for fuel could well put a brake on the demand for nuclear energy. In short, the nuclear renaissance features political drivers and faces political constraints, and analysts and policy makers who ignore the political aspects will miss a large part of the picture.

Notes

1. Fuhrmann's analysis seems to show that this is less true for assistance pertaining to nuclear materials and fuel, but one should be cautious about drawing that conclusion from his results. His analysis tests the relationship between provision of materials assistance and security factors against a null hypothesis of zero effect, but the relevant comparison is between the provision of materials agreements and other types of nuclear assistance agreements: Is there any discernible difference between types of assistance? Without proper statistical tests of these differences, the results presented cannot help us conclude that materials cooperation is "special" in any way.

2. An additional caveat here is the relative lack of attention to changes over time in export control regimes, and the possibility that future changes to export policies could alter the implications of his analysis.

3. After the UAE's accord was struck, some observers and many politicians hoped it could be emulated with other countries: "the positive reception the UAE's approach received from the nuclear supplier community suggests that it could become the path of least resistance for other countries seeking nuclear assistance" (Early 2010). Many members of the U.S. Congress were also enthusiastic about this possibility: After the deal's conclusion, several contacted the State Department's Office of Nuclear Energy, Safety and Security expressing their desire to see the UAE's 123 Agreement become a model for future ones. One example of this is remarks made by Richard Stratford, Undersecretary for International Security and Nonproliferation, at the National Academy of Science's workshop on Improving the Assessment of Proliferation Risk of Nuclear Fuel Cycles on August 1, 2011.

4. Here it would be interesting to see a comparison between the effect of the energy security variable and a more familiar energy or electricity demand variable. It is difficult to know how important the security aspect is unless it is compared with the demand aspect.

5. The literature here is vast. For an overview of typologies, see Ezrow and Frantz 2011. Some important recent entries in the literature include Wintrobe 1998; Brooker

2000; Geddes 2003; Brownlee 2007; Magaloni 2008; Pepinsky 2008; Levitsky and Way 2010.

References

Anderlini, James. 2011. "Protest Closes Factory in China." *Financial Times*, August 15. Available at: http://www.ft.com/intl/cms/s/0/92a73bf0-c682-11e0-bb50-00144 feabdco.html.

Angrist, Joshua D., and Jorn-Steffen Pischke. 2008. *Mostly Harmless Econometrics: An Empiricist's Companion.* Princeton, NJ: Princeton University Press.

Betts, Richard K. 1993. "Paranoids, Pygmies, Pariahs and Nonproliferation Revisited." In *The Proliferation Puzzle: Why Nuclear Weapons Spread (And What Results)*, eds. Z. S Davis and B. Frankel. Portland, OR: Frank Cass & Company.

Boardman, Robert, and James Keeley. Eds. 1983. *Nuclear Exports and World Politics.* New York: St. Martin's.

Bratt, Duane. 2006. *The Politics of CANDU Exports.* Toronto: University of Toronto Press.

Braun, Chaim, and Christopher F. Chyba. 2004. "Proliferation Rings: New Challenges to the Nuclear Nonproliferation Regime." *International Security* 29 (2): 5–49.

Brenner, Michael J. 1981. *Nuclear Power and Non-Proliferation: The Remaking of U.S. Policy.* New York: Cambridge University Press.

Brooker, Paul. 2000. *Non-Democratic Regimes: Theory, Government, and Politics.* New York: St. Martin's.

Brownlee, Jason. 2007. *Authoritarianism in an Age of Democratization.* New York: Cambridge University Press.

DeLeon, Peter. 1980. "Comparative Technology and Public Policy: The Development of the Nuclear Power Reactor in Six Nations." *Policy Sciences* 11 (3): 285–307.

Delmas, Magali, and Bruce Heiman. 2001. "Government Credible Commitment to the French and American Nuclear Power Industries." *Journal of Policy Analysis and Management* 20 (3): 433–456.

Drezner, Daniel. 2007. *All Politics Is Global: Explaining International Regulatory Regimes.* Princeton, NJ: Princeton University Press.

Early, Bryan. 2010. "Acquiring Foreign Nuclear Assistance in the Middle East." *The Nonproliferation Review* 17 (2): 259–280.

Ezrow, Natasha M., and Frantz, Erica. 2011. *Dictators and Dictatorships: Understanding Authoritarian Regimes and Their Leaders.* New York: Continuum.

Geddes, Barbara. 2003. *Paradigms and Sand Castles: Theory Building and Research Design in Comparative Politics.* Ann Arbor: University of Michigan Press.

Glad, Betty. 2002. "Why Tyrants Go Too Far: Malignant Narcissism and Absolute Power." *Political Psychology* 23 (1): 1–2.

Goldacre, Ben. 2010. "How to Make People 'Love' Nuclear Power." *Guardian*, November 20. Available at: http://www.guardian.co.uk/commentisfree/2010/nov/20/ben-goldacre-bad-science-nuclear.

Gruber, Lloyd. 2000. *Ruling the World: Power Politics and the Rise of Supranational Institutions.* Princeton, NJ: Princeton University Press.

Hirschman, Albert O. 1945/1980. *National Power and the Structure of Foreign Trade.* Berkeley: University of California Press.

Hymans, Jacques E. C. 2006. *The Psychology of Nuclear Proliferation: Identity, Emotions, and Foreign Policy.* New York: Cambridge University Press.

———. 2008. "Assessing North Korean Nuclear Intentions and Capacities: A New Approach." *Journal of East Asian Studies* 8 (2): 259–292.

Jasper, James M. 1990. *Nuclear Politics: Energy and the State in the United States, Sweden, and France.* Princeton, NJ: Princeton University Press.

Jewell, Jessica. 2011. "Ready for Nuclear Energy? An Assessment of Capacities and Motivation for Launching New National Nuclear Programs." *Energy Policy* 39 (3): 1041–1055.

Joskow, Paul, and John Parsons. 2009. "The Economic Future of Nuclear Power." *Daedalus* 138: 45–59.

Kapur, K. D. 1993. *Nuclear Non-Proliferation Diplomacy: Nuclear Power Programmes in the Third World.* Columbia, MO: South Asia Books.

King, Gary, and Langche Zeng. 2007a. "Detecting Model Dependence in Statistical Inference: A Response." *International Studies Quarterly* 51 (1): 231–241.

———. 2007b. "When Can History Be Our Guide? The Pitfalls of Counterfactual Inference." *International Studies Quarterly* 51 (1): 183–210.

Krasner, Stephen D. 1991. "Global Communications and National Power: Life on the Pareto Frontier." *World Politics* 43 (3): 336–366.

Krause, Keith. 1991. "Military Statecraft: Power and Influence in Soviet and American Arms Transfer Relationships." *International Studies Quarterly* 35 (3): 313–336.

Levitsky, Steven, and Lucan A. Way. 2010. *Competitive Authoritarianism: Hybrid Regimes After the Cold War.* New York: Cambridge University Press.

Magaloni, Beatriz. 2008. "Credible Power-Sharing and the Longevity of Authoritarian Rule." *Comparative Political Studies* 41 (4–5): 715–741.

Mertha, Andrew. 2011. *China's Water Warriors: Citizen Action and Policy Change.* Ithaca, NY: Cornell University Press.

Miller, Steven E., and Scott D. Sagan. 2009. "Nuclear Power Without Nuclear Proliferation?" *Daedalus* 138 (4): 7–18.

Nelson, Paul. 2010. "Reassessing the Nuclear Renaissance." *Bulletin of the Atomic Scientists* 66: 11–22.

Nelson, Paul, and Christopher Sprecher. 2008. "What Determines the Extent of National Reliance on Civil Nuclear Power?" NSSPI-08-014. College Station, TX: Nuclear Security Science & Policy Institute, Texas A&M.

Pepinsky, Thomas B. 2008. "Capital Mobility and Coalitional Politics: Authoritarian Regimes and Economic Adjustment in Southeast Asia." *World Politics* 60 (3): 438–474.

Pierre, Andrew J. 1982. *The Global Politics of Arms Sales.* Princeton, NJ: Princeton University Press.

Poneman, Daniel. 1982. *Nuclear Power in the Developing World*. London: George Allen & Unwin.

Post, Jerrold M. 1993. "Current Concepts of the Narcissistic Personality: Implications for Political Psychology." *Political Psychology* 14 (1): 99–121.

Potter, William C. 1982. *Nuclear Power and Nonproliferation: An Interdisciplinary Perspective*. Cambridge, MA: Oelgeschlager, Gunn & Hain.

———. Ed. 1990. *International Nuclear Trade and Nonproliferation: The Challenge of the Emerging Nuclear Suppliers*. Lexington, MA: Lexington Books.

Rublee, Maria Rost. 2009. *Nonproliferation Norms: Why States Choose Nuclear Restraint*. Athens: University of Georgia Press.

Sagan, Scott D. 2010. *Nuclear Power, Nuclear Proliferation, and the NPT*. Paper presented at the 2010 Annual Meeting of the American Political Science Association. Washington, DC, September 2–5.

Solingen, Etel. 2007. *Nuclear Logics: Contrasting Paths in East Asia and the Middle East*. Princeton, NJ: Princeton University Press.

Stern, Rachel E. 2011. "From Dispute to Decision: Suing Polluters in China." *The China Quarterly* 206: 294–312.

Toth, Ferenc. 2008. "Prospects for Nuclear Power in the 21st Century: A World Tour." *International Journal of Global Energy Issues* 30 (1): 3–27.

USGPO (United States Government Printing Office). 2009. "Proposed Agreement for Cooperation Between the Government of the United States of America and the Government of the United Arab Emirates Concern Peaceful Uses of Nuclear Energy." Available at: http://www.fas.org/man/eprint/uae-nuclear.pdf.

Wintrobe, R. 1998. "Some Lessons on the Efficiency of Democracy from a Study of Dictatorship." In *The Political Dimension of Economic Growth*, eds. S. Borner and M. Paldam. New York: Macmillan.

Wohlstetter, Albert, Thomas Brown, Gregory Jones, David McGarvey, Henry Rowen, Vince Taylor, and Roberta Wohlstetter. 1979. *Swords from Ploughshares: The Military Potential of Civilian Nuclear Energy*. Chicago: University of Chicago Press.

Wonder, Edward F. 1977. *Nuclear Fuel and American Foreign Policy*. Boulder, CO: Westview Press/Atlantic Council Paperback Series.

II THE NUCLEAR RENAISSANCE AND NUCLEAR WEAPONS PROLIFERATION

7   Stop Helping Me

When Nuclear Assistance Impedes Nuclear Programs

Alexander H. Montgomery

U NTIL RECENTLY, THEORIES OF HOW DIFFERENT FACTORS influence the supply of nuclear technologies have not been as well developed as theories of demand for nuclear weapons. For example, most quantitative studies of nuclear weapons development have used indicators that reflected national resources without including technology transfers from other states (Kegley 1980; Meyer 1984; Singh and Way 2004; Jo and Gartzke 2007). Part of this lack of attention to nuclear technology transfer may be due to the perception that many of the initial nuclear weapons programs attempted to rely on primarily internal, domestic sources of knowledge, technology, and resources for fissile material production and were thus structured as top-down "hierarchies." More recent programs have relied on imports of all three components either in an attempt to cut development times or simply because one or more of these necessary components were not available domestically (Braun and Chyba 2004; Montgomery 2005). With these later nuclear aspirants, domestic capabilities and direct assistance or international proliferation networks were combined to create a supply of nuclear technologies. Recent nuclear programs thus are structured more like networks than hierarchies, although the technical characteristics of nuclear proliferation and the nonproliferation regime have prevented a full-blown market from arising.[1] Publications have lamented the A. Q. Khan network and its deleterious effects on proliferation, emphasizing its clandestine nature and effectiveness and predicting an ominous end to existing nuclear nonproliferation institutions.[2]

Recent work by Fuhrmann (2008, 2009a,b) and Kroenig (2009a,b, 2010) has attempted to tackle both the causes and effects of the supply of both sensitive and peaceful nuclear technologies. The bargain of the nonproliferation regime also seems to be broken: Kroenig finds that sensitive nuclear assistance is more likely to be given by states in the Nuclear Suppliers Group (although Non-Proliferation Treaty [NPT] members are less likely to do so), and Fuhrmann finds that peaceful nuclear cooperation is less likely to be given to states that are part of the NPT. Kroenig argues that countries who receive sensitive nuclear assistance—that is, technologies that are necessary for the construction of a nuclear weapons arsenal, including uranium enrichment, plutonium reprocessing, and nuclear weapons designs—are more likely to start nuclear programs and acquire weapons. Fuhrmann argues that there are several pathways through which civilian nuclear assistance can affect proliferation, including acquisition of dual-use technology and knowledge as well as the creation of bureaucratic interests. Their quantitative findings so far have been disturbing: Both types of nuclear transfer seem to increase the probability that a state will start a nuclear program and that it will succeed.

However, the apparently significant effect of these variables on the likelihood of proliferation is due in part to the use of a model specification that includes a large number of countries in the pool for nuclear acquisition that have never even tried to start a nuclear program. When the pool is limited to countries that have been actively seeking nuclear weapons, the effect is inverted: Instead of increasing proliferation, both sensitive and peaceful nuclear assistance appear to decrease the probability that countries which are pursuing nuclear weapons will succeed.

This counterintuitive result can be explained in part by the inclusion of theories previously excluded from quantitative studies but found in the qualitative literature: the ability of the recipient of such aid to turn it into a bomb. A nuclear weapons program is a large-scale sociotechnical system that requires a long-term investment in multiple technologies, each with its own unique hurdles to overcome. While it is certainly theoretically possible for any state with a sufficient level of industrial capability to construct a nuclear weapon, some states may simply take much longer than others, and some states may have a sufficiently pathological scientific infrastructure as to retard or prevent a program from taking off. In particular, countries that have neopatrimonial ruling structures seek shortcuts through importing nuclear weapons technologies without being able to absorb them properly and so end up taking longer than they would otherwise. This appearance of a negative relationship between assistance and acquisition success is thus due to the inability of certain regimes to absorb inappropriate technologies rather than this being a general effect of nuclear assistance.

Jacques Hymans' (2008) work on the relationship between neopatrimonial ruling structures and an inability to complete large-scale nuclear projects is particularly relevant here. Neopatrimonial regimes are those that undermine traditional bureaucratic structures and rely on individual, personalized rule, with little or no accountability to others.[3] Hymans argues that

> such regimes will (1) alienate or even eliminate their best scientists, promote political hacks, and generally engage in routine, counterproductive churning of personnel; (2) make suboptimal, shifting, and even bizarre technical choices, while undermining efforts to develop a long-term, coherent action plan and indeed setting various wings of the effort at odds with each other; and (3) exhaust the program and its resources through repeated "crash" efforts with unreasonable deadlines and distracting side projects (274).

Consequently, such regimes will take a much longer time to complete nuclear weapons projects, if they do at all. Neopatrimonialism is conceptually different from underdevelopment, although both have a significant effect on proliferation. Underdeveloped countries may not be able to afford certain technologies and may struggle to conduct large-scale projects because of a lack of underlying infrastructure or the materials to build them. By contrast, neopatrimonial regimes are incompetent rather than poor. They lack the ability to develop professional scientific establishments, run projects efficiently, or get good advice on which pathway to the bomb they should take.

Such regimes also will be less able to absorb assistance from other countries. Neither peaceful nuclear cooperation nor sensitive technical assistance have generally increased the likelihood of proliferation, owing to the inability of most regimes that are seeking nuclear weapons to absorb such assistance. Indeed, such assistance may end up setting certain countries back even further than they would be without such assistance by encouraging "crash" efforts based on the imported technologies rather than slowly working on an indigenous program. In part, this is because tacit knowledge, a crucial element of successful nuclear weapons programs, is more difficult to attain when attempting to adapt foreign technologies than when programs are allowed to build from the ground up and experiment through trial and error.[4] To be sure, this is not to argue that assistance, in general, should be given to all countries without any concern. Cases where assistance was given to a country that had governing structures that allowed for the timely completion of large-scale projects, such as Israel, did seem to benefit from it. Hence, past experience with assistance to neopatrimonial regimes should not be taken as a license to spread nuclear technologies to all countries.

Methodology

This paper uses a quantitative model, adopting the Singh and Way (2004) data as the base model, following Fuhrmann (2009a,b) and Kroenig (2009a,b). Singh and Way measure nuclear status along a continuum with four "degrees of nuclearness" (2004: 866): no program, exploration, pursuit, and acquisition. The first degree is no interest in nuclear weapons. The second degree is exploration, which is "demonstrated by political authorization to explore the option or by linking research to defense agencies that would oversee any potential weapons development" (Singh and Way 2004: 867). To qualify as pursuing nuclear weapons, the third degree, states must take steps such as "a political decision by cabinet-level officials, movement toward weaponization, or development of single-use, dedicated technology" (Singh and Way 2004: 866). Finally, states are coded fourth degree, having fully acquired weapons, if they either test or possess a "functional nuclear weapon" (Singh and Way 2004: 866).

Consequently, the factors that lead states in general to explore a nuclear option can be directly compared with factors that lead states to move from exploration to pursuit and from pursuit to acquisition. The transitions in this dataset are diagrammed in Figure 7.1. Not counting the United States (since the dataset starts in 1945), nineteen states have explored a nuclear option; of these, twelve have actively pursued nuclear weapons, while three states (according to their dataset) moved directly to pursuing nuclear weapons. Of the fifteen states that have pursued nuclear weapons, eight are widely considered to have built nuclear weapons by 2000. Ukraine, Belarus, and Kazakhstan are excluded because they acquired weapons without first starting a program.

There are four different types of transition pictured in Figure 7.1: From 0 to 1 (No Program → Explore), from 0 to 2 (No Program → Pursue), from 1

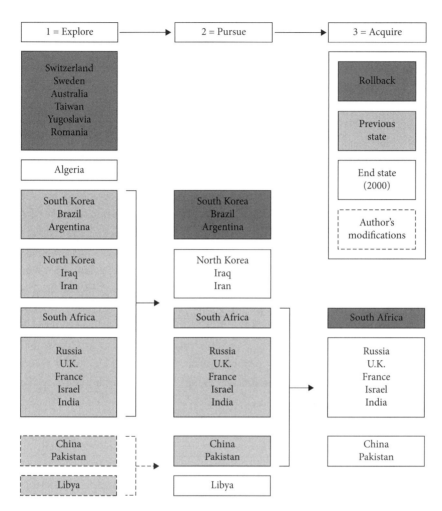

FIGURE 7.1 Proliferation transitions, Singh and Way dataset

NOTE: The United States is not included because of acquisition before the first year in the dataset.

to 2 (Explore → Pursue), and from 2 to 3 (Pursue → Acquire). The total number of countries is low for each transition. In order to give the algorithm the most information possible, a year of exploration was added for China, Pakistan, and Libya before the first year of pursuit, consistent with Montgomery and Sagan (2009). This adds three observations of states moving from 0 to 1, and three from 1 to 2, albeit within a single year, while eliminating the problematic category of moving from 0 to 2. This reflects the much more rapid movement of these three programs and is conceptually consistent with these three states possessing factors that moved them rapidly to pursuing nuclear weapons.

Three different sets of hazard models were thus tested: Model set E(xplore): 0 to 1; Model set P(ursue): 1 to 2; and Model set A(cquire): 2 to 3. In each case, the observations are censored based on the current status of the program, following Jo and Gartzke (2007) and Montgomery and Sagan (2009). A hazard model for each level (1, 2, 3) with the pool restricted to states at the previous level of development (0, 1, 2) is the most empirically relevant way to analyze this data, because it models each level as a prerequisite for the next. Since no state moves from acquiring or pursuing weapons to simply exploring them, the pools for Model set E include only states that have no program; similarly, for Model set P, only states that are exploring nuclear weapons (including Libya, Pakistan, and China for one year) are included, and for Model set A, only states that are pursuing nuclear weapons are included. This contrasts with Singh and Way's, Fuhrmann's, and most of Kroenig's models, which include all countries in all analyses.[5] In these analyses, even states that have no nuclear program are included in their models of nuclear acquisition. Yet states cannot acquire weapons without first pursuing them, and it seems unlikely that states will pursue nuclear weapons without first exploring the option, even if only for a short period of time.

Independent Variables

The variable *sensitive nuclear assistance*, "a dichotomous variable measuring whether a state has ever received the key materials and technologies necessary for the construction of a nuclear-weapons arsenal from a capable nuclear-supplier state" was adopted from Kroenig (2009b: 168). The variable *peaceful nuclear cooperation*, which "measures the aggregate number of [Nuclear Cooperation Agreements] that a state signed in a given year entitling it to nuclear technology, materials, or knowledge from another country," was adopted from Fuhrmann (2009b: 25).

In addition to these two variables, a variable *Neopatrimonialism*[6] was constructed, drawn from the individual component variables of the Polity IV dataset (Marshall and Jaggers 2009). One (1) or zero (0) was added to the variable based on the following assessments: if Competitiveness of Executive Recruitment is coded as unregulated or by selection; if Executive Constraints are coded as unlimited authority; and if Competitiveness of Participation is coded as unregulated, repressed, or suppressed. Three component variables (openness of executive recruitment, regulation of chief executive recruitment and participation) were omitted, since any coding is potentially compatible with a neopatrimonial system. While openness of executive recruitment could plausibly fit the definition, the coding of this variable seems to be suspect. For example, North Korea is coded as "open" recruitment, despite the Kims being in power since 1948. Consequently, it is excluded. This creates a variable with a range from 0 to 3. The variable was then lagged by a year, since Polity scores are based on the regime in place on December 31 of a year.

To give a few examples from the countries in the pool for acquiring nuclear weapons, France scores 0, South Africa scores 1, Iran averages 1.63, and Iraq and Libya score 3. At first glance the scores seem to be appropriate. Hymans does not provide a comprehensive list but discusses Iraq, Libya, North Korea, and Romania. All but Romania are coded 3; Romania only receives a 2 since it was coded 2 instead of a 1 on Executive Constraints (out of 7). Iran's average is brought down by a *neopatrimonialism* score of 0 after the election of Mohammad Khatami; however, this is actually consistent with the argument regarding Iran's success in its nuclear program. Until Khatami's election, the Atomic Energy Organization of Iran (AEOI) was run by "the incompetent Reza Amrollahi and a team chosen more for their revolutionary credentials than their technical skills." As a result "the Iranian nuclear program had stumbled along despite the considerable resources lavished upon it" (Pollack 2004: 362).

Neopatrimonialism, while not the opposite of democracy, nonetheless has a correlation of −0.82 with *polity* (which ranges from −10 for an autocracy to +10 for a democracy) in the overall sample, and a correlation of −0.88 in the subset of states that pursued nuclear weapons. Figure 7.2 demonstrates the relationship between *neopatrimonialism* and the standard *polity* score. In this figure, each *x*-axis runs from −10 (total autocracy) on the left to 10 (total democracy) on the right. Each of the four graphs demonstrates the distribution of *polity* given a certain level of *neopatrimonialism*, from 0 (no neopatrimonial characteristics) to 3 (all neopatrimonial characteristics). The height of the graph thus indicates the frequency distribution of different polity scores within a particular *neopatrimonialism* score. The modal democracy score of states with no neopatrimonial characteristics is 10, while the modal score for states with 2 of the 3 neopatrimonial characteristics have an autocracy score of −7. The modal polity score for a completely neopatrimonial state is −9, although −7 is close.

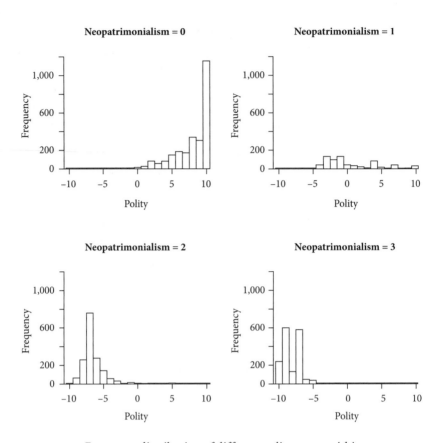

FIGURE 7.2 Frequency distribution of different polity scores within a particular neopatrimonialism score

Control Variables

All of Singh and Way's reported variables are adopted as controls. They employ three technological determinants that represent the domestic capability of a state: *GDP per capita, GDP per capita squared,* and *industrial capacity threshold.* They also include three external determinants: whether a state is involved in an *enduring rivalry,* the average number of *militarized disputes* a state is involved in over a five-year period, and whether a state is in an *alliance* with a nuclear-armed state.[7] Finally, they include five internal determinants: the *polity* score of a state in Polity IV (referred to by Singh and Way as *democracy*), a measure of *democratization* (the change in a state's polity score over a five-year period), the *percentage of democracies* in the international system, *economic openness* to trade, and a measure of *economic liberalization* (the change in trade openness over a five-year period).[8] *NPT membership* is also included in the regressions for exploration, included in Fuhrmann's models. Although it is unclear how to interpret this variable due to the mixed motives of states as they join it (see Montgomery and Sagan 2009), to exclude it entirely could introduce bias.[9]

Results

For each set of models, a base model was first run with only control variables, then each of the three above variables added in individually, then collectively, to each of the three sets of regressions (Explore, Pursue, and Acquire). Below, only regressions in which one or more of these three variables were significant are reported. Each of the control variables with the highest *p* value were eliminated one by one until all of the remaining variables were significant at the 0.10 level or below. A hazard model was used with a Weibull distribution and robust standard errors clustered on individual countries, because it gives additional information in the form of the ancillary parameter *p*.[10] The results are reported as hazard rates, so values above 1 indicate an increase in the likelihood of moving to the next level (e.g., 1.1 indicates a 10 percent increase when that variable is increased by one unit), whereas values below 1 indicate a decrease (e.g., 0.9 indicates a 10 percent decrease when that variable is increased by one unit). Table 7.1 summarizes the statistically significant findings for states moving from no program to exploring nuclear weapons, Table 7.2 from exploring to pursuing, while Tables 7.3 and 7.4 summarize the findings for states moving from pursuing to acquiring nuclear weapons.

For the transition from No Program to Explore, not all of Singh and Way's original findings are significant; for example, *GDP per capita* and its square are insignificant. However, with adding *sensitive nuclear assistance*, the *economic openness* variable seems to have a dampening effect; while neither *militarized disputes* nor *NPT membership* were originally significant in this corrected model, in the process of dropping insignificant variables, it becomes significant in Model E3. This does appear to be good news for promoters of the NPT, as membership decreases the onset of exploration by two-thirds. Neither *peaceful nuclear cooperation*, whether interacted with *militarized disputes* or not, nor *neopatrimonialism* are significant in causing countries to start exploring nuclear weapons programs. *Sensitive nuclear assistance*,

TABLE 7.1 Exploration of nuclear weapons, 1945–2000

	No program → Explore		
	E1	E2	E3
Sensitive nuclear assistance		6.2554**	3.7861*
		(0.8812)	(0.7936)
GDP per capita	1.0004	1.0004	
	(3.00E–04)	(3.00E–04)	
GDP per capita squared	1	1	
	(2.00E–08)	(1.90E–08)	
Industrial capacity index	7.8134***	7.9515**	8.6845****
	(0.7893)	(0.8221)	(0.6102)
Enduring rivalry	4.1752****	4.4275***	4.7194****
	(0.4283)	(0.4592)	(0.4056)
Militarized disputes	1.101	1.1041	
	(0.0663)	(0.0687)	
Alliance	0.58825	0.54819	
	(0.5953)	(0.624)	
Polity	1.0088	1.0082	
	(0.0355)	(0.0357)	
Democratization	0.96156	0.95883	
	(0.0552)	(0.0519)	
Percentage of democracies	0.96953	0.94372	
	(0.0412)	(0.0471)	
Economic openness	0.9865	0.98225**	0.98451**
	(0.0103)	(0.009)	(0.0076)
Economic liberalization	0.96191**	0.96027***	0.95686***
	(0.0166)	(0.0146)	(0.0157)
NPT membership	0.42602	0.50492	0.34153**
	(0.6253)	(0.5602)	(0.5243)
Ancillary parameter p	0.5905***	0.52738***	0.51848***
	(0.193)	(0.1975)	(0.207)
N	5,402	5,402	5,501

NOTE: $*p < .1$, $**p < .05$, $***p < .01$, $****p < .001$; Models E1–3 have Explore as the dependent variable.

however, appears at first glance to be highly significant, increasing the hazard rate in Model E2 by 526 percent, although this drops to 279 percent in Model E3 once insignificant variables are excluded. The results for sensitive assistance increasing exploration are due entirely to three cases: Iran, Iraq, and Taiwan, which received assistance in 1984, 1976, and 1975, respectively, with

t
Stop Helping Me   187

TABLE 7.2 Pursuit of nuclear weapons, 1945–2000

	Explore → Pursue		
	P1	P2	P3
Peaceful nuclear cooperation		1.0869* (0.0456)	1.0677** (0.0281)
GDP per capita	1.0004 (5.00E–04)	1.0004 (6.70E–04)	
GDP per capita squared	1 (3.40E–08)	1 (5.00E–08)	
Industrial capacity index	4.9369 (1.799)	3.3117 (1.797)	
Enduring rivalry	4.9109 (1.255)	5.2034 (1.187)	6.6611** (0.7952)
Militarized disputes	1.4334*** (0.1319)	1.4853**** (0.1054)	1.3046*** (0.0809)
Alliance	0.87103 (0.5056)	1.115 (0.7184)	
Polity	1.0232 (0.05)	1.0449 (0.0797)	
Democratization	0.90431 (0.0953)	0.91283 (0.0744)	
Percentage of democracies	0.87503 (0.1158)	0.86038 (0.1629)	
Economic openness	1.003 (0.0256)	1.0221 (0.028)	
Economic liberalization	1.0033 (0.029)	1.0002 (0.0272)	
Ancillary parameter p	1.7494 (0.3553)	1.5507 (0.3739)	1.4342* (0.1894)
N	250	250	250

NOTE: $^*p < .1$, $^{**}p < .05$, $^{***}p < .01$, $^{****}p < .001$; Models P1–3 have Pursue as the dependent variable.

the latter coding only affecting Taiwan's second nuclear weapons program in 1987, since it was already exploring nuclear weapons during its first program (1967–1977). In Model E3 of Table 7.1, the parameter p is 0.52; after ten years of not exploring nuclear weapons, a country is 9.52 times less likely to fail than after one year, which is good news for the nonproliferation regime: The longer that states do not explore nuclear weapons, the less likely it is that they will ever do so.

TABLE 7.3 Acquisition of nuclear weapons, 1945–2000, single-variable models

	Pursue → Acquire			
	A1	*A2*	*A3*	*A4*
Sensitive nuclear assistance		0.2941* (0.6391)		
Peaceful nuclear cooperation			0.8298** (0.0755)	
Neopatrimonialism				0.5186† (0.3898)
GDP per capita	1 (9.80E–04)	0.9998 (0.001)	1.001 (0.0013)	1 (0.0011)
GDP per capita squared	1 (7.80E–08)	1 (8.00E–08)	1 (9.50E–08)	1 (8.30E–08)
Industrial capacity index	3.1e+07**** (1.306)	2.2e+07**** (1.342)	2.3e+08**** (2.162)	1.2e+07**** (1.398)
Enduring rivalry	4.282 (1.373)	3.264 (1.437)	3.227 (1.446)	4.722 (1.306)
Dispute involvement	1.09 (0.1867)	1.192 (0.1917)	0.9832 (0.205)	1.076 (0.1783)
Alliance	1.057 (1.116)	1.304 (1.209)	1.992 (2.168)	0.894 (1.141)
Polity	1.109 (0.0803)	1.068 (0.0762)	1.276*** (0.0759)	
Democratization	0.9421 (0.0725)	0.9733 (0.0772)	0.9944 (0.1243)	0.9469 (0.0729)
Percentage of democracies	0.9509 (0.1994)	0.9554 (0.1932)	0.7917 (0.1838)	0.9648 (0.1992)
Economic openness	0.9856 (0.0285)	1.004 (0.0339)	0.907 (0.0647)	0.9853 (0.0303)
Economic liberalization	0.9746 (0.0285)	0.9741 (0.0314)	0.9632 (0.0315)	0.9749 (0.0278)
Ancillary parameter *p*	2.152**** (0.2065)	2.264**** (0.1904)	4.584**** (0.3745)	2.095*** (0.236)
N	210	210	210	210

NOTE: *$p < .1$, **$p < .05$, ***$p < .01$, ****$p < .001$; Models A1–4 have Acquire as the dependent variable.

TABLE 7.4 Acquisition of nuclear weapons, 1945–2000, combined models

	Pursue → Acquire			
	A5	A6	A7	A8
Sensitive nuclear assistance	0.1101** (0.8654)	0.2078** (0.7497)	0.7069 (0.5564)	
Peaceful nuclear cooperation	0.7526*** (0.0989)	0.8853**** (0.0258)		0.9271*** (0.0287)
Neopatrimonialism	0.1686*** (0.5441)	0.3166*** (0.4157)	0.6236 (0.3478)	1.793* (0.3515)
Neopatrimonialism* Sensitive nuclear assistance			0.7162 (0.5129)	
Neopatrimonialism* Peaceful nuclear cooperation				0.6561*** (0.134)
GDP per capita	1.001 (0.0017)			
GDP per capita squared	1 (1.20E–07)			
Industrial capacity index	5.7e+07**** (2.899)	1.1e+07**** (0.7429)	6.6e+06**** (0.877)	1.9e+07**** (1.063)
Enduring rivalry	1.864 (1.644)			
Dispute involvement	0.996 (0.1749)			
Alliance	1.005 (2.243)			
Polity				
Democratization	1.165 (0.1432)			
Percentage of democracies	0.7714 (0.2133)			
Economic openness	0.9137 (0.0842)			
Economic liberalization	0.9629 (0.0521)			
Ancillary parameter p	5.838**** (0.3565)	3.169**** (0.2498)	1.836**** (0.1637)	3.133**** (0.2066)
N	210	210	210	210

NOTE: *p < .1, **p < .05, ***p < .01, ****p < .001; Models A5–8 have Acquire as the dependent variable.

Moving from Explore to Pursue, very few of Singh and Way's original findings persist; only *militarized disputes* are significant in Model P1, although *enduring rivalry* becomes significant by Model P3. Neither *neopatrimonialism* nor *sensitive nuclear assistance* affect the rate of moving from exploration to pursuit; however, an increase in *peaceful nuclear cooperation* by one unit increases the hazard rate by 8.7 and 6.8 percent in Models P2 and P3, respectively. An interaction term between *peaceful nuclear cooperation* and *militarized disputes*, significant in Fuhrmann's original findings, is insignificant for Model P2. Including a variable for the NPT as per Fuhrmann's specification in Models P2 and P3 does make a *peaceful cooperation–militarized disputes* interaction term significant while making both lower-order terms insignificant, commensurate with his original findings. Here, the news in the ancillary parameter is less favorable: When exploring a nuclear weapons program, after ten years a country is 2.72 times more likely to pursue in Model P3 than after just one year. Modeling a two-step instead of a three-step model produces results similar to Fuhrmann's original results (unsurprising, since half of his models test precisely that proposition), while providing no new significant coefficients for *neopatrimonialism* or *sensitive nuclear assistance*.

Moving from pursuit to acquisition in Table 7.4, few control variables are still significant: Only *industrial capacity index* is consistent, although *polity* is briefly significant in Model A3. This is probably due to the negative correlation between *neopatrimonialism* and *polity*. Both *sensitive nuclear assistance* and *peaceful nuclear cooperation* are significant—but in the opposite expected direction. In Model A2, *sensitive nuclear assistance* decreases the hazard rate by 70 percent, while a one-unit increase in *peaceful nuclear cooperation* in Model A3 decreases it by 17 percent. Moreover, *neopatrimonialism* decreases the hazard rate by 48 percent in Model A4. When run together with all of the controls in Model A5 in Table 7.4, they decrease the hazard rate even further, by 89, 25, and 83 percent, respectively. Since the *industrial capacity index* has such an overwhelming effect here, a separate model was run with just the three independent variables; all were significant at the 0.05 level, and decreased the hazard rate by 84, 12, and 72 percent, respectively.

Because of the low number of observations, it is difficult to determine statistically whether there is a quantitatively observable interaction effect between *neopatrimonialism* and nuclear assistance. Although interaction terms were generally in the expected direction, they were frequently insignificant. In a model (A7) with only *neopatrimonialism, sensitive nuclear assistance*, the interaction between the two, and *industrial capacity*, all coefficients were in the expected direction but insignificant; that is, states that were neopatrimonial and received assistance did even worse than would be expected from either of those alone. When combining *neopatrimonialism, peaceful nuclear cooperation*, the interaction between the two, and *industrial capacity*, the results were significant, although there appears to be a strange neopatrimonial bonus if they receive no cooperation at all. This would presumably be the rare weapons-seeking state that did not seek external peaceful assistance as well, and is caused by the inclusion of the Soviet Union and China (and the exclusion of the United States) in the dataset; without those two observations, no bonus exists.

Finally, there does seem to be some urgency around stopping serious nuclear programs early; in Model A6, according to the ancillary parameter, a country still pursuing nuclear weapons after ten years is 147 times more likely to acquire them than after one year. This is likely a partial artifact of the physical reality that even the most accelerated nuclear weapons program takes a significant amount of time.

Discussion

Table 7.5 lists the characteristics of every state that pursued nuclear acquisition and offers some significant clues to the puzzle of why nuclear assistance seems to backfire. Among the top group, states that had no assistance took less time to complete their successful nuclear development program; the average number of years in the pool regardless of success or failure for states receiving assistance is 18.0, versus 8.3 for those not receiving it. Those successful without assistance took an average of about 7.3 years, while those with assistance took double the time: about 14.6 years. This compares poorly with the 6.5-year estimate by Harney et al. for a first nuclear weapon in a country with a low level of resources (Harney et al. 2006). Note that the Acquire Pool Years may in some cases seem inaccurate. Iraq's program could be reasonably coded as ending in 1991 instead of post-2000. North Korea's plutonium program was effectively suspended as of 1994, so it was only 14.0 instead of 20.0 years in development by 2000. Iran's program as of 2010 would be 25.0 years in with still no bomb. India's program could be seen as a "double-dip" as far as the variables go, but if the United States were included instead, that would be a wash for two of the three variables in question and would intensify the effect of peaceful

TABLE 7.5 Characteristics of success and failure (Singh and Way dataset)

Country	Acquire pool years	Years in pool	Assist year	Neopat. (mean)	NCA to date (mean)	Main method	2000 result
Russia	1945–1949	5		3.00	0.0	Pu	Success
United Kingdom	1947–1952	6		0.00	0.0	Pu	Success
France	1954–1960	7		0.00	6.7	Pu	Success
China	1955–1964	10	1958	2.00	1.9	HEU-GD	Success
Israel	1958–1972	15	1959	0.00	4.5	Pu	Success
India (1)	1964–1974	11		0.00	21.7	Pu	Success
India (2)	1980–1988	9		0.00	21.7	Pu	Success
Pakistan	1972–1990	19	1974	1.58	16.6	HEU-Cent	Success
South Africa	1974–1979	6		1.00	3.7	HEU-Aero	Success
Average success		**9.8**		**0.76**	**7.7**		
Korea (South)	1970–1978	9		2.00	4.3	Pu	Quit
Libya	1970–	31	1997	3.00	9.8	HEU-Cent	Still trying (quit 2003)
Argentina	1978–1990	13		1.38	37.6	HEU-GD	Quit
Brazil	1978–1990	13	1979	1.00	45.1	HEU-Cent	Quit
Korea (North)	1980–	21	1997	3.00	3.5	Pu	Still trying (test 2006)
Iraq	1982–	19	1976	3.00	9.9	HEU-Cent	Still trying (invaded 2003)
Iran	1985–	16	1984	1.63	15.7	HEU-Cent	Still trying
Average failure		**17.4**		**2.14**	**18.0**		

NOTE: NCA = nuclear cooperation agreement. Main methods are plutonium (Pu) or highly enriched uranium (HEU), of which there are three variants here: centrifuges (Cent), gaseous diffusion (GD), and aerodynamic separation (Aero).

nuclear cooperation dampening the likelihood of acquisition. However, none of the possible modifications would significantly alter the patterns in the table or regressions. The same applies to civilian nuclear assistance. Comparing the top and bottom groups, those that received less civilian nuclear aid were more likely to succeed (7.7 nuclear cooperation agreements [NCAs] versus 18.0 NCAs). What explains these counterintuitive results for nuclear assistance?

First, sensitive assistance tends to be given to states that are at least weakly neopatrimonial; out of the twelve cases of sensitive assistance in total, only three had neopatrimonial scores of 0 at the time (Israel, Japan, and Pakistan); five had a score of 2 (Iran, Taiwan, Egypt, Brazil, and China), and four had a score of 3 (North Korea, Algeria, Iraq, and Libya). The average neopatrimonial level of a state that succeeded was far less (0.76) than those that failed (2.14). Put another way, every state except China that had a neopatrimonial score of 2 or higher at the time of assistance failed to develop nuclear weapons by the end of the data sample.

How do *neopatrimonialism* and *sensitive assistance* combine to slow countries down? Given that China managed to do so despite this combination, it bears a closer look. China, to a certain extent, managed to develop nuclear weapons despite the constant internal political interference in their program and despite the assistance that was first given to them, then removed, by the Soviet Union. According to Lewis and Xue, the Soviets refused to train Chinese engineers in their gaseous diffusion plants and refused to give access to the original blueprints. Chinese workers then "wantonly" attempted to modify nuclear industrial equipment supplied by the Soviet Union due to political pressures from well-connected individuals during the Great Leap Forward, causing over 290 accidents. The minister in charge had to appeal directly to Mao Zedong in order to stop the workers from modifying the equipment (Lewis and Xue 1988: 117–125).

Combining sensitive assistance with a neopatrimonial system that could not absorb it led to a lack of tacit knowledge on the shop floor, which significantly delayed the Chinese program. The Soviets simply refused to train workers. A Chinese survey in 1961 after the advisors left discovered 1,395 technical problem areas, the most troublesome of which resulted from the "inexperience and low technical level of most of the staff" (Lewis and Xue 1988: 124). The pumps had to be lubricated specially to prevent corrosion from uranium hexafluoride; the Soviets had locked away these special lubricants and took them with them when they left the country, leading to a frantic mission to find a suitable replacement. Moving from an external supplier's technology to indigenous technology cost the Chinese an estimated 700 days, a length comparable to the time that the Soviet advisors had "assisted" the Chinese (Lewis and Xue 1988: 117–125). Although it is difficult to spin out the full counterfactual, it is certainly plausible that if the Chinese had relied on building up indigenous technologies instead of having to reverse engineer lubricants and re-create missing blueprints, it would have taken them less time overall. Hymans argues that China is the exception that proves the rule for neopatrimonial states, since the nuclear program was protected by "military and party heavyweights" (Hymans 2008: 276).

The Chinese may have gotten lucky. Most proliferators who received (or stole) foreign assistance stuck with the technological paths that their supposed benefactors started them on, even when they were abandoned (North Korea is a notable exception, which may be why they ultimately succeeded). Those that were given relatively straightforward, if inefficient, technologies succeeded (the Chinese and Israelis), while those that were given centrifuges stuck with them—to their probable detriment. Centrifuges are "self-disassembling" machines that require a number of high-precision parts and careful trial-and-error experiments in order to operate correctly. Those who adopted centrifuges have spent on average 19.6 years in the pool, with a single success (Pakistan). Gaseous diffusion is a much better choice; if the United States were in the pool, the average number of years in the pool would be 9.0, with two successes. Even this number is deceptively high, since Argentina announced its facility in 1983, although it is unclear at what level, if any, it worked at (Montgomery and Mount 2010). Plutonium from natural uranium reactors is also a good choice, with 10.4 average years in the pool and a 75 percent success rate, although the former is somewhat inflated by continuing to count North Korea's program during the Agreed Framework, which froze the Democratic People's Republic of Korea's plutonium program. Rolling your own technology seems to work even better: South Africa completed its first device in only 6.0 years, although Pretoria did not produce fully weaponized devices for a couple more years.

Poor technology choice can be exacerbated not only by assistance (which creates and reinforces poor technological paths) but also by neopatrimonial government (which undermines competent administration). The Iraqis tried practically every technology, dividing efforts and minimizing progress; the Libyans proved incapable even at setting up the centrifuges that they received from the A. Q. Khan network; the Iranians put an incompetent political appointee in charge of their program; and the North Koreans failed to produce a full nuclear yield from either of their tests.[11] Pakistan took 19.0 years in the dataset (most of it as a neopatrimonial state) to develop a nuclear capability despite having more recorded assistance than any other country. Recently,

A. Q. Khan has claimed that China transferred not only uranium enrichment technology, plutonium reprocessing assistance, and a nuclear weapons design to Pakistan, but also 50 kilograms of highly enriched uranium (Smith and Warrick 2009). Even if this were not true, the Pakistani program probably received more help than any other—and yet still took more years than any other successful country in the dataset.

Israel is the only case in which sensitive nuclear assistance was given and seemed to fully succeed; it is also the only case of assistance in which the government was free of neopatrimonial pathologies. Consequently, it is also the case to be most wary of for nonproliferation. Sustained assistance with proven technologies from a friendly foreign government that was already on the verge of exploding its own nuclear weapon seems to have helped the program; yet it still took a longer period than any country other than Pakistan to acquire nuclear capability. Conversely, other datasets argue for periods up to six years shorter (1966 or 1967), although even with more optimistic dates, the Israeli program is at best average in completion time. Nonetheless, Israel's strategy was risky as well; the French government delayed the project twice for a significant period, and when Charles de Gaulle decided to cancel nuclear assistance, the Israelis had to convince the French government to allow the French contractor to finish Dimona (Cohen 1998: 75).

There are other risks involved in seeking foreign assistance for nuclear programs, in that the help that may be received—especially parts—can be sabotaged. The quality of parts given through clandestine nuclear assistance—especially those transmitted through proliferation networks—is even worse than the quality of the vehicles sold by unscrupulous used car salesman. The centrifuges spread through the A. Q. Khan network were probably used rejects from their program, evidenced by traces of highly enriched uranium on the Iranian imports. When the United States refused to assist Israel in bombing the Iranian program in 2008, it impressed upon the Israelis that they were actively sabotaging the Iranian program (Sanger 2009). The United States has had a long history of attempting to misguide Iran; even in the days of the Shah, the United States permitted the export of lasers intended for uranium enrichment, since U.S. government specialists had concluded that the technology in question was unworkable (Spector and Smith 1990: 207). Of course, even sabotage can backfire. James Risen has claimed that the Central Intelligence Agency leaked part of a nuclear weapons design to the Iranians with an intentional flaw that might have been discovered, thereby accelerating the program (Risen 2006).

What about peaceful nuclear assistance? It is clear that the states that had succeeded by 2000 had a very low average assistance (7.7) compared to the failed group, which had a great deal of assistance (averaging 18.0). The only additional success since then has been North Korea, the state with the fewest average NCAs in the failure pool. It is also worth reexamining the two states that had the highest levels of civilian nuclear assistance and still succeeded in developing nuclear weapons: Pakistan and India. Despite extensive peaceful nuclear assistance, both of them took a lengthy amount of time to finish their nuclear programs. While Pakistan received a great deal of peaceful nuclear assistance with their plutonium program, it was ultimately the uranium route which they chose, where most of the assistance they received was helping themselves: A. Q. Khan stole blueprints for centrifuges from the consortium of operational enrichment plants in Europe (URENCO) then built them by creating a clandestine network to produce parts that could not be made at home. Hardly peaceful nuclear assistance!

India is, if anything, the poster child for how peaceful nuclear assistance can lead to proliferation. At the same time, India's experiences also demonstrate the problems of attempting to import nuclear technology for proliferation instead of building technologies indigenously. Bhabha predicted in 1965 that India could produce a nuclear explosive in eighteen months; instead, it took nine years. The Phoenix plutonium extraction plant, built by Indians with U.S. blueprints and assistance, suffered from explosions and was "wholly dependent on the availability and utilization of fittings and supplies from the USA or elsewhere." India had severe difficulties building and operating heavy water reactors after it was cut off: The successor to the Cirus reactor, the Dhruva, had severe vibrations in the reactor core and had to be shut down soon after starting operation. It did not reach full operating capacity until 1988, two and a half years after it went critical (Perkovich 1999: 95).

This is not to argue that India was held back by peaceful nuclear assistance. Rather, India's experience demonstrates that there are significant problems in relying on foreign assistance, and that those areas of foreign assistance that are most useful are easily identified. The controls on the spread of plutonium separation technology and heavy water reactors that are known as bomb factories have probably helped significantly. Further, India still lacked crucial components for building a larger, deliverable arsenal; the 1974 test was a device that weighed 1,000 kilograms, and Indian scientists did not develop a smaller weapon until 1982. Yet India still could not produce a sufficient amount of heavy water indigenously and lacked a domestic supply of beryllium. Had the Germans not had such lax export controls, India could have been denied one or both—since India had to smuggle Chinese heavy water through a German source in the early 1980s and simply bought beryllium from a German company in 1984 (Perkovich 1999: 242, 250, 271).

Finally, these variables have emphasized primarily the quantity of help, not the quality. Some types of nuclear assistance are much more likely than others to advance nuclear weapons programs. Heavy water reactors, such as the one used by India as the source of the plutonium for their first atomic explosive, certainly help more than safety assistance or large, light water power reactors. Kroenig found that peaceful nuclear assistance in the form of research or power reactors decreases the probability of a nuclear weapons program (Kroenig 2009b: 178, fn. 21). Even within the category of sensitive assistance, some types of assistance are likely to help more than others; a nuclear weapons design or transferred sensitive nuclear materials are more likely to lead to proliferation than more generic help, such as smaller hot cells capable of reprocessing plutonium in small, but not industrial-size, quantities.

Conclusion

While it is clear that the spread of both sensitive and peaceful nuclear assistance has had much less of an impact on nuclear proliferation than generally has been thought, this does not imply that peaceful or sensitive nuclear assistance should be spread throughout the world without concern. It does indicate that such assistance may be less likely to cause nuclear proliferation than has been previously thought. The bargain of the nonproliferation regime seems to be holding, at least in part, since the net effect of increased peaceful assistance seems to be a decrease in the overall likelihood of the country acquiring a nuclear weapon. The results from models of exploration also offer some hope, since NPT membership in the final model decreased the likelihood of exploration of a nuclear option by two-thirds. Also, the longer a country abstains from exploring nuclear weapons programs, the less likely it is to start. Outside of the models here, it is worth noting that the spread of peaceful nuclear assistance is a valuable bargaining tool. For example, since nuclear technology brings prestige to countries, substituting nuclear prestige in the form of light water power plants for nuclear prestige in the form of nuclear weapons seems like a pretty good bargain. However, as more countries develop governing structures that can competently handle large-scale projects, the value (and danger) of nuclear assistance is likely to increase. For these states, nuclear assistance could truncate timelines for an existing nuclear weapons program and, perhaps, increase countries' incentives to pursue nuclear weapons in the first place.

Conclusions here are similar to those of Kroenig (Chapter 8 in this volume) but for very different reasons. He finds no support for the proposition that countries trade sensitive nuclear technologies for economic motives; rather, it is only under specific and rare circumstances that countries will supply such technologies. Consequently, we do not need to fear at least this mechanism for nuclear proliferation if a nuclear renaissance occurs.

This chapter's conclusions agree, with a second argument added: The lack of apparently harmful effects is simply due to the inability of countries to absorb technologies. This is particularly the case for neopatrimonial regimes, which are less likely to be able to successfully complete a nuclear weapons program than are other countries. The dual problem of developing the requisite tacit knowledge for fissile materials production combined with the difficulty of competently building and running large-scale technological systems is too much for these countries. When countries are run by fear and management positions are handed out as patronage, good scientific advice and management are very hard to attain. Such countries do not have the patience or ability to cycle through the expensive trial-and-error learning that is required to develop the requisite tacit knowledge. In these situations, importing nuclear technology is less likely to lead to nuclear weapons programs, or even effective nuclear power programs. Yet this does not mean that such countries are entirely incapable of producing either. The example of China is instructive: It managed to succeed despite assistance, and despite the usual neopatrimonial governing structures. Similarly, North Korea succeeded, but only after trying for a very long time. In part, both of these cases succeeded because they chose their technologies well, adopting simpler methods. These cases also point to a caution: While tacit knowledge and neopatrimonialism may slow the spread of some technologies, others are less constrained. For example, while plutonium reprocessing in a neopatrimonial state such as North Korea may be dirty, slow, and inefficient, it will still work. An omitted variable that undoubtedly affects these results is the question of how hard different countries are trying—perhaps many of these regimes are not succeeding simply because they are not nearly as pressed as others are.

The potential broadening of worldwide nuclear power should not be a concern for proliferation to regimes that lack the governance structures to develop weapons. However, regimes that have the requisite structures may still be at risk for proliferation. By the same token, the Fukushima accident is a reminder that even the most seemingly competent regimes can make errors in their deployment of large-scale technologies; even such states may struggle to translate outside assistance into effective nuclear energy programs, let alone nuclear weapons. The nonproliferation regime has adapted over time to prevent the most proliferation-prone types of dual-use technology, making peaceful nuclear assistance even safer than before. If any future expansion of nuclear power takes the form that it has in the more recent past—that is, primarily light water nuclear power reactors—then nuclear weapons proliferation will likely remain as it has been in the past, if not slower. To adopt Kenneth Waltz's phrase, it will hardly be proliferation; at most, it will be glacial spread (Sagan, Waltz, and Betts 2007: 136).

Notes

1. On the market/hierarchy distinction, see Williamson 1985; on network forms of transactions, see Powell 1990, Podolny and Page 1998. On the relationship between the transaction types and proliferation, see Montgomery 2008. See Montgomery 2005 on how these characteristics have limited proliferation.

2. This literature is exemplified by Langewiesche 2007; for an incisive critique, see Bunn 2007.

3. Hymans draws his characterization from Eisenstadt 1973, Clapham 1985, Chehabi and Linz 1998.

4. MacKenzie and Spinardi 1995, MacKenzie 1999, Montgomery 2005.

5. Model 4 of Table 2 of Kroenig (2009b) on p. 171 includes a censored hazard model, although oddly enough, the list of states that could acquire nuclear weapons was obtained from a different dataset (Jo and Gartzke 2007).

6. Thanks to Bryan Nakayama for his original construction of the variable.

7. Since Fuhrmann 2009a,b recalculates their disputes variable and uses the new calculation to create interaction effects, his version of the disputes variable was used.

8. The percentage of democracies is a systemic variable rather than an internal one.

9. This variable was only significant for one regression in Explore and none for Pursue or Acquire, so it is included only in the Explore results.

10. When $p > 1$, the hazard increases over time; when $p < 1$, it decreases over time. Cox models turned out statistically similar results, with no changes in the significance of the results for almost all models, including the last (and probably best) model for exploration, pursuit, and acquisition.

11. On North Korea, Libya, and Iraq, see Hymans 2008; on troubles with tacit knowledge and nuclear networks with North Korea, Libya, and Iran, see Montgomery 2005. On the North Korean tests, see Garwin and von Hippel 2006 and Shanker and Broad 2009.

References

Braun, Chaim, and Christopher F. Chyba. 2004. "Proliferation Rings: New Challenges to the Nuclear Nonproliferation Regime." *International Security* 29 (2): 5–49.

Bunn, Matthew. 2007. "Bombs We Can Stop." *American Scientist* 95 (5): 452–454.

Chehabi, Houchang E., and Juan J. Linz. 1998. *Sultanistic Regimes.* Baltimore, MD: Johns Hopkins University Press.

Clapham, Christopher S. 1985. *Third World Politics: An Introduction.* Madison: University of Wisconsin Press.

Cohen, Avner. 1998. *Israel and the Bomb.* New York: Columbia University Press.

Eisenstadt, Shmuel N. 1973. *Traditional Patrimonialism and Modern Neopatrimonialism.* Beverly Hills, CA: Sage Publications.

Fuhrmann, Matthew. 2008. "Exporting Mass Destruction? The Determinants of Dual-Use Trade." *Journal of Peace Research* 45 (5): 633–652.

———. 2009a. "Taking a Walk on the Supply Side: The Determinants of Civilian Nuclear Cooperation." *Journal of Conflict Resolution* 53 (2): 181–208.

———. 2009b. "Spreading Temptation: Proliferation and Peaceful Nuclear Cooperation Agreements." *International Security* 34 (1): 7–41.

Garwin, Richard L., and Frank N. von Hippel. 2006. "A Technical Analysis of North Korea's Oct. 9 Nuclear Test." *Arms Control Today* 36 (9): 3.

Harney, Robert, Gerald Brown, Matthew Carlyle, Eric Skroch, and Kevin Wood. 2006. "Anatomy of a Project to Produce a First Nuclear Weapon." *Science and Global Security* 14 (2–3): 163–182.

Hymans, Jacques E. C. 2008. "Assessing North Korean Nuclear Intentions and Capacities: A New Approach." *Journal of East Asian Studies* 8 (2): 259–292.

Jo, Dong-Joon, and Erik Gartzke. 2007. "Determinants of Nuclear Weapons Proliferation." *Journal of Conflict Resolution* 51 (1): 1–28.

Kegley, Charles W. 1980. "International and Domestic Correlates of Nuclear Proliferation: A Comparative Analysis." *Korea and World Affairs* 4: 5–37.

Kroenig, Matthew. 2009a. "Exporting the Bomb: Why States Provide Sensitive Nuclear Assistance." *American Political Science Review* 103 (1): 113–133.

———. 2009b. "Importing the Bomb: Sensitive Nuclear Assistance and Nuclear Proliferation." *Journal of Conflict Resolution* 53 (2): 161–180.

———. 2010. *Exporting the Bomb: Technology Transfer and the Spread of Nuclear Weapons.* Ithaca, NY: Cornell University Press.

Langewiesche, William. 2007. *The Atomic Bazaar: The Rise of the Nuclear Poor.* New York: Farrar, Straus.

Lewis, John Wilson, and Litai Xue. 1988. *China Builds the Bomb*. Stanford, CA: Stanford University Press.

MacKenzie, Donald. 1999. "Theories of Technology and the Abolition of Nuclear Weapons." In *The Social Shaping of Technology*, eds. D. A. MacKenzie and J. Wajcman. Philadelphia, PA: Open University Press.

MacKenzie, Donald, and Graham Spinardi. 1995. "Tacit Knowledge, Weapons Design, and the Uninvention of Nuclear Weapons." *American Journal of Sociology* 101 (1): 44–99.

Marshall, Monty, and Keith Jaggers. 2009. "Polity IV Project: Political Regime Characteristics and Transitions, 1800–2007." Severn, MD: Center for Systematic Peace.

Meyer, Stephen M. 1984. *The Dynamics of Nuclear Proliferation*. Chicago: University of Chicago Press.

Montgomery, Alexander H. 2005. "Ringing in Proliferation: How to Dismantle an Atomic Bomb Network." *International Security* 30 (2): 153–187.

———. 2008. "Proliferation Networks in Theory and Practice." In *Globalization and WMD Proliferation: Terrorism, Transnational Networks, and International Security*, eds. J. A. Russell and J. J. Wirtz. London: Routledge.

Montgomery, Alexander H., and Scott D. Sagan. 2009. "The Perils of Predicting Proliferation." *Journal of Conflict Resolution* 53 (2): 302–328.

Montgomery, Alexander H., and Adam J. Mount. 2010. "Misunderestimation: Explaining US Failures to Predict Nuclear Weapons Programs." Paper presented at the Intelligence and Nuclear Proliferation Conference. London, UK. June 3–4.

Perkovich, George. 1999. *India's Nuclear Bomb: The Impact on Global Proliferation*. Berkeley: University of California Press.

Podolny, Joel M., and Karen L. Page. 1998. "Network Forms of Organization." *Annual Review of Sociology* 24: 57–76.

Pollack, Kenneth M. 2004. *The Persian Puzzle: The Conflict between Iran and America*. New York: Random House.

Powell, Robert. 1990. *Nuclear Deterrence Theory: The Search for Credibility*. New York: Cambridge University Press.

Risen, James. 2006. "George Bush Insists that Iran Must Not Be Allowed to Develop Nuclear Weapons. So Why, Six Years Ago, Did the CIA Give the Iranians Blueprints to Build a Bomb?" *Guardian*, January 5. Available at: http://www.guardian.co.uk/environment/2006/jan/05/energy.g2/print.

Sagan, Scott D, Kenneth Waltz, and Richard K. Betts. 2007. "A Nuclear Iran: Promoting Stability or Courting Disaster?" *Journal of International Affairs* 60 (2): 135–150.

Sanger, David E. 2009. "U.S. Rejected Aid for Israeli Raid on Nuclear Site." *New York Times*, January 11. Available at: http://www.nytimes.com/2009/01/11/washington/11iran.html?pagewanted=all.

Shanker, Thom, and William J. Broad. 2009. "Seismic Readings Point to a Small Nuclear Test." *New York Times*, May 26. Available at: http://www.nytimes.com/2009/05/26/world/asia/26threat.html.

Singh, Sonali, and Christopher Way. 2004. "The Correlates of Nuclear Proliferation: A Quantitative Test." *Journal of Conflict Resolution* 48 (6): 859–885.

Smith, R. Jeffrey, and Joby Warrick. 2009. "A Nuclear Power's Act of Proliferation." *Washington Post*, November 13. Available at: http://www.washingtonpost.com/wp-dyn/content/article/2009/11/12/AR2009111211060.html.

Spector, Leonard S., and Jacqueline R. Smith. 1990. *Nuclear Ambitions: The Spread of Nuclear Weapons, 1989–1990*. Boulder, CO: Westview Press.

Williamson, Oliver E. 1985. *The Economic Institutions of Capitalism: Firms, Markets, Relational Contracting*. New York: Free Press.

8 The Nuclear Renaissance, Sensitive Nuclear Assistance, and Nuclear Weapons Proliferation

Matthew Kroenig

MANY ANALYSTS ARGUE THAT THE NUCLEAR RENAISSANCE could lead to the international spread of nuclear weapons.[1] While there are considerable distinctions among the arguments made by these authors, the essential logic linking the nuclear renaissance to nuclear weapons proliferation is fairly straightforward.[2] If the international demand for nuclear energy remains high, countries with nuclear energy programs will need access to nuclear fuel (Gourley and Stulberg, Chapter 1 in this volume). While countries can receive nuclear fuel cycle services from other states, those with strong interests in nuclear energy may prefer to produce nuclear fuel domestically in order to insulate themselves from the vagaries of strategic bargaining and the international market (Stulberg, Chapter 4 in this volume). Most of the countries interested in producing nuclear fuel domestically will not be able to develop these sophisticated nuclear technologies indigenously and will, therefore, need to acquire assistance from other, more advanced nuclear suppliers. Because the existing nuclear suppliers have strong economic incentives to export sensitive nuclear materials and technology, these states should be able to secure international help (e.g., Potter 1982; Braun and Chyba 2004). Finally, after having acquired sensitive dual-use nuclear technologies—such as uranium enrichment and plutonium reprocessing technologies that can be used to produce fuel for nuclear power plants, or nuclear weapons, or both—many countries might eventually opt to build nuclear weapons arsenals (e.g., Miller and Sagan 2009: 13). In short, the nuclear renaissance could lead to nuclear proliferation.

This chapter argues that the claim of a link between the nuclear renaissance and widespread nuclear weapons proliferation is misguided. While many countries might want sensitive nuclear fuel cycle capabilities, few will be able to acquire them. Nuclear suppliers are unwilling to transfer sensitive nuclear technologies to any country willing to pay the price. Rather, they are most likely to provide sensitive nuclear assistance under relatively rare strategic conditions (Kroenig 2009a, 2010). While a small number of countries might receive sensitive nuclear help, the majority of states will be unlikely to secure an international supplier. Without access to nuclear fuel cycle facilities, countries—even those that badly want to join the nuclear club—will not be able to build nuclear weapons.

Although this chapter argues that the nuclear renaissance is unlikely to result in a proliferation cascade, it in no way seeks to minimize the threat of nuclear proliferation. The spread of nuclear weapons remains one of the greatest threats to U.S. national security—as well as security around the world. As of 2012, Iran's nuclear program continued to advance, and U.S. government officials speculated that nuclear weapons in Iran could have grave consequences for U.S. national security, including enhancing Iranian hegemonic ambitions; providing a cover under which Iran can step up support for proxy groups or to engage in more aggressive coercive diplomacy; encouraging other states in the Middle East to go nuclear and weakening the global nonproliferation regime; and, most worryingly, triggering possible nuclear war between Iran and Israel, or Iran and the United States. Even a single instance of nuclear proliferation, therefore, provides a significant cause of concern. It is indeed possible that over the course of the coming decades a renaissance in nuclear energy could result in a small number of additional countries joining the nuclear club. This chapter, therefore, does not imply that we should not be worried about these cases. Rather, the argument here is that, even in the midst of a global nuclear renaissance, the forces that moderate the behavior of the nuclear suppliers will provide a check against the widespread diffusion of nuclear weapons.

The rest of the chapter elaborates on this argument in four parts. The first reviews the logic linking the nuclear renaissance to the diffusion of sensitive fuel cycle technologies and eventually to nuclear weapons proliferation. The second reviews the evidence supporting the argument that strategic conditions heavily condition the transfer of sensitive nuclear materials and technology. The third applies these findings to the question of whether the nuclear renaissance will result in nuclear proliferation. The conclusion recaps the argument and discusses the implications for policy makers interested in stemming the spread of nuclear weapons.

The Nuclear Renaissance and Nuclear Proliferation

The idea that the nuclear renaissance will result in widespread nuclear weapons proliferation rests on four propositions:

1. *The nuclear renaissance will result in an increased demand for nuclear fuel.* If the nuclear renaissance comes to fruition and many more countries around the world possess nuclear power programs, and the existing countries with nuclear energy programs increase their share of domestic energy provided by nuclear power, then there will be an increased demand for nuclear fuel. The logic is simple: More countries operating more nuclear power reactors will result in a greater need for nuclear fuel.

The production of nuclear fuel requires a series of technically sophisticated steps. Enriched uranium fuel is the result of a process that begins by mining natural uranium, milling the natural uranium into a dry powder known as "yellowcake," converting the powder into uranium hexafluoride gas, enriching the uranium (that is, separating the nonfissionable U-238 isotopes of uranium from the fissionable U-235 isotopes), chemically converting the enriched uranium hexafluoride gas into uranium metal or uranium dioxide, then finally fabricating the enriched uranium into solid pellets that are packed into metal nuclear fuel rods.

Plutonium can also be used as a nuclear fuel. PU-239 is a by-product of a nuclear reaction. Spent fuel rods that have passed through a nuclear reactor therefore contain some plutonium. The plutonium can be separated from the other elements of the spent fuel using a chemical process and then converted into plutonium fuel rods.

In order to acquire nuclear fuel made from either uranium or plutonium, countries have two broad options. They can operate nuclear fuel cycle facilities domestically—either uranium enrichment or plutonium reprocessing, or both—and produce their own nuclear fuel. Alternatively, if they lack domestic fuel cycle capabilities, they can have another country or international body provide them with fuel services. Nuclear fuel providers, such as France and Russia, ship recipient countries nuclear fuel for use in nuclear power reactors and then reclaim the spent fuel for reprocessing or storage. By contracting for nuclear fuel services, countries can enjoy the benefits of a nuclear power program without developing, maintaining, and operating their own domestic fuel cycle capabilities. There are costs, however, to depending on the international market for nuclear fuel.

2. *Countries will prefer to possess the ability to produce nuclear fuel indigenously rather than be vulnerable to international fuel supplies.* Many analysts argue that countries will tend to prefer to produce fuel indigenously for two reasons. First, they would like to produce nuclear fuel themselves for reasons of energy security (Stulberg, Chapter 4 in this volume). Relying on international suppliers to meet their core energy needs leaves countries vulnerable. A halt in the shipment of much-needed nuclear fuel because of changing economic or political incentives in the nuclear supplier countries could cripple a country's economy. As Stulberg points out, policy makers and analysts recognize this problem and are attempting to devise means to guarantee countries access to international nuclear fuel supplies through international nuclear fuel banks and fuel assurances. As Stulberg also notes, however, there are inherent challenges to making these promises credible. Indeed, on a few occasions in the past, countries have had their nuclear fuel supplies threatened, and many aspiring nuclear nations are skeptical about promises of international nuclear aid being consistently kept.

Second, some countries might seek to develop a domestic fuel cycle capability as a security strategy to hedge against an uncertain future. Nuclear fuel cycle facilities can be used to produce nuclear fuel for reactors or for nuclear weapons. Countries may seek to acquire capabilities under the guise of a nuclear energy program in the near future in order to develop and maintain the ability to dash to a nuclear weapons program down the road (Macfarlane, Chapter 2 in this volume). Many analysts believe that future nuclear power countries will prefer to produce fuel domestically for reasons of energy security, and/or to keep the nuclear weapons option open.

3. *Countries will be able to acquire sensitive nuclear fuel cycle technologies with relative ease in the international nuclear marketplace.* Wanting nuclear capabilities and having them are separate matters (Gartzke and Kroenig 2009). The majority of countries that might want nuclear fuel cycle facilities will not be able to produce them indigenously. Indeed, the countries that currently

express interest in developing a nuclear energy infrastructure, such as Jordan, Vietnam, and Kazakhstan, among many others, possess low levels of technical and industrial capacity. If these countries are to develop a nuclear fuel cycle capability, they will require international assistance.

Many analysts (e.g., Potter 1982; Jones 1990) suggest that international nuclear assistance can be readily secured. They claim that nuclear supplier states can earn handsome profits by exporting uranium enrichment and plutonium reprocessing technologies to the highest bidder. Some scholars (e.g., Chestnut 2007) have argued that North Korea's economy, for example, is in such poor shape that the country would be willing to export anything, including sensitive nuclear technology, in order to earn hard currency. Others (e.g., Braun and Chyba 2004) argue that even if state suppliers are unwilling to provide sensitive nuclear assistance, nonstate proliferation rings, exemplified by the former A. Q. Khan network in Pakistan, are more than willing to transfer sensitive nuclear technologies. According to this line of thought, the nuclear renaissance will lead to a significant increase in the number of countries with a fully developed nuclear fuel cycle.

4. *Countries that receive sensitive nuclear assistance will be able to produce nuclear weapons.* The international spread of nuclear facilities could lead to many potential security challenges, including concerns about nuclear safety, sabotage of nuclear facilities, terrorist theft of nuclear materials, nuclear weapons proliferation, and destruction of nuclear facilities in a conventional war (Miller and Sagan 2010: 126).

As more countries acquire sensitive fuel cycle facilities, more countries will have the ability to produce nuclear weapons. The most difficult part of building a nuclear weapon is producing the weapons-grade fissile material (either highly enriched uranium or separated plutonium) that forms the core of the nuclear device. Sensitive nuclear technologies, uranium enrichment and plutonium reprocessing technologies in particular, are dual-use technologies that can be used to produce nuclear fuel for either nuclear power reactors or nuclear weapons. In fact, once countries have mastered the ability to produce nuclear fuel, some analysts argue that they are no more than a few screwdriver turns away from possessing nuclear weapons. As Mohamed ElBaradei (2003), the Director General of the International Atomic Energy Agency, averred, "should a state with a fully-developed fuel-cycle capability decide, for whatever reason, to break away from its non-proliferation commitments, most experts believe it could produce a nuclear weapon within a matter of months." Similarly, Steven Miller and Scott Sagan (2009: 13) write, "Indeed, the connection between power and weapons is somewhat inevitable because key technologies in the nuclear sector—notably, uranium enrichment and plutonium reprocessing capabilities—are relevant to both."

Countries that possess fuel cycle technologies, therefore, exist in a state of "nuclear latency" (Sagan 2010). They have the ability to produce nuclear weapons in short order if they chose to do so. While many countries might remain latent nuclear powers for an extended period, the spread of sensitive nuclear technologies greatly increases the risk that additional countries will eventually engage in overt nuclear proliferation. Again, according to Miller and Sagan (2009: 13), depending on which "capabilities spread to which states, especially regarding uranium enrichment and plutonium reprocessing, a world of widely spread nuclear technologies could be . . . a world where more states possess nuclear weapons." Indeed, as shown in previous research, states that receive sensitive nuclear assistance from more-advanced nuclear suppliers are five and a half times more likely to acquire nuclear weapons than similar states that do not get outside help (Kroenig 2010: 171).

This chapter focuses on sensitive nuclear technologies because there is a widespread scientific and policy consensus on a direct link between the possession of sensitive fuel cycle technologies and the ability to produce nuclear weapons. Other, less-sensitive types of nuclear technology, such as light water nuclear power reactors, are more proliferation resistant. Matthew Fuhrmann (2009) proposes that all nuclear transfers, regardless of their level of sensitivity, contribute to proliferation, but these claims are based on an analysis of nuclear cooperation agreements (many of which are subsequently canceled), not on actual nuclear transfers. Data on transfers of nuclear technology that have actually occurred show instead that there is no statistical link between the receipt of civilian nuclear assistance and the probability that a country subsequently goes nuclear (Kroenig 2010: 159–169). The reason is simple: While some recipients of civilian nuclear assistance, such as India, went on to build the bomb, many more, including Australia, Belgium, Egypt, Finland, Peru, Vietnam, and others, have not.[3] A consideration of less-sensitive nuclear technologies and the nuclear renaissance can be found elsewhere in this volume (Fuhrmann, Chapter 3).

The four propositions above combine to suggest that the nuclear renaissance will lead to a significant increase in the number of countries with a fully developed nuclear fuel cycle and, in turn, to the proliferation of nuclear weapons.[4] The underlying logic of this argument is sound, but not all of the key propositions on which the argument rests stand up to empirical scrutiny. In Chapter 4 in this volume, Stulberg questions whether countries will prefer to produce nuclear fuel domestically and identifies conditions under which the international community can provide credible fuel assurances that are likely to convince future nuclear power states to accept international fuel-supply arrangements. Alexander Montgomery (Chapter 7 in this volume) challenges the evidence underlying the belief that sensitive nuclear assistance causes nuclear proliferation. The remainder of this chapter, in contrast, presents evidence that undermines proposition three, in that countries interested in developing a domestic nuclear fuel cycle capability will struggle to find an international supplier. Sensitive nuclear materials and technologies are not freely available on the international nuclear marketplace. Nuclear suppliers are selective in the provision of sensitive nuclear assistance, and this greatly complicates state efforts to acquire sensitive nuclear technology. As seen in the next section, states are most likely to provide sensitive nuclear assistance and technology only under relatively rare strategic conditions.

The Strategic Logic of Nuclear Assistance

Exporting the Bomb: Technology Transfer and the Spread of Nuclear Weapons (Kroenig 2010) presents the results of the first systematic analysis of why countries export sensitive nuclear materials and technology. This section of this chapter highlights four findings that are particularly relevant to the assessment of whether the nuclear renaissance will result in a cascade of nuclear weapons proliferation.

First, the state-sponsored transfer of sensitive nuclear materials and technology is extremely rare. Since 1945 there have been only fourteen instances in which capable nuclear suppliers have transferred sensitive nuclear materials and technology to non-nuclear weapon states. Twenty countries that could provide sensitive nuclear materials and technology and nearly two hundred potential recipient countries have been identified. Yet, despite the tens of thousands of potential situations in which nuclear transfers could have occurred, there have been slightly more than a dozen instances of sensitive nuclear transfer.

Second, the substate smuggling of significant quantities of sensitive nuclear materials and technologies is also extremely rare. Some scholars (e.g., Braun and Chyba 2004) warn of future proliferation rings, in which rogue scientists and private enterprises transfer the means of producing nuclear weapons without the authorization or even knowledge of national governments. But, as underscored by other chapters in this volume, such predictions are overblown owing to logistical problems confronted by illicit trafficking networks (Hastings, Chapter 9 in this volume) and the challenges of absorbing tacit nuclear weapons–related knowledge (Montgomery, Chapter 7 in this volume). Moreover, since 1945, there has only been one instance in which a significant transfer of sensitive nuclear materials or technology occurred without government knowledge.[5] There have been many failed attempts and a few actual transfers of small quantities of fissile materials from secure nuclear facilities across national borders, but these small-scale transfers are relatively insignificant and do not suggest that the large-scale transfer of sensitive nuclear materials and technology are likely.[6]

Arguments about future proliferation rings are generally extrapolations from the experience of the A. Q. Khan-led nuclear transfers from Pakistan to Iran, Libya, and North Korea from 1987 to 2002. Analysts cite this case as an example of how a rogue scientist acting without the authorization of a national government could transfer nuclear materials and technologies to other countries. As shown in *Exporting the Bomb*, however, the A. Q. Khan transfers, especially during the early phases, were the project of the Pakistani state (Kroenig 2010). A. Q. Khan's proliferation ring could not have developed without the support of—and its early incarnation indeed was an official policy of—the Pakistani government. Moreover, as discussed in the Chapter 9 of this volume by Hastings, once the network was deprived of access to state prerogatives, both the structure and vulnerability changed. Thus, if the A. Q. Khan case is a harbinger of things to come, it suggests that we should be most concerned about state decisions to export sensitive nuclear material and technology, not substate proliferation rings.

Third, as demonstrated in *Exporting the Bomb* and contrary to conventional wisdom, there is no systematic relationship between economic factors and patterns of sensitive nuclear assistance. States like North Korea, which are economically underdeveloped or suffering through periods of poor economic performance, are neither more nor less likely to export sensitive nuclear materials. In addition, economic considerations are often far from the minds of state leaders who decide to provide sensitive nuclear assistance. This makes sense, given that sensitive nuclear assistance does not generally result in large economic gains for the supplier. This is not to say that economic considerations are irrelevant. States do sometimes seek economic payment in exchange for sensitive nuclear transfers, but they are only likely to do so when such transfers are consistent with an underlying strategic logic.

Fourth, research suggests that strategy, not economics, largely determines countries' willingness to export sensitive nuclear materials and technology. Nuclear suppliers are most likely to provide sensitive nuclear assistance when doing so would threaten an enemy but not threaten themselves. When is a country most threatened by nuclear proliferation? The spread of nuclear weapons threatens powerful states more than it threatens weak states. This is because nuclear weapons proliferation constrains the military freedom of action of powerful states. They can threaten or promise to protect other states; but when other states acquire nuclear weapons, these threats to do harm, or promises to provide protection, lose their credibility. This fact leads to three strategic conditions under which states are most likely to provide sensitive nuclear assistance. First, the less powerful a state is relative to a potential nuclear recipient, the more likely it is to provide sensitive nuclear assistance to that state. The logic is simple: States avoid constraining their own military freedom of action. Second, states are most likely to provide sensitive nuclear assistance to states with which they share a common enemy. By providing nuclear assistance to these states, they can impose strategic constraints on other, more powerful rivals. Third, states that depend on superpower protection to provide for their own security are unlikely to provide sensitive nuclear assistance. These states judge that the costs of antagonizing a superpower patron outweigh any benefits of participating in sensitive nuclear transactions.

The strategic conditions that facilitate sensitive nuclear transfers can be illustrated by the case of Chinese nuclear assistance to Pakistan (Kroenig 2010: 112–120). From 1981 to 1986, China helped Pakistan construct and operate uranium enrichment facilities, transferred enough highly enriched uranium for two nuclear weapons, and shared a nuclear bomb design. Due to geographic constraints and a lack of airlift and amphibious invasion capabilities, China lacked the ability to project power over Pakistan, meaning that its own military freedom of action would not be constrained if Pakistan acquired the bomb. In addition, by providing nuclear assistance to Pakistan, China could impose strategic costs on its longtime regional rival, India, a country that had the ability to project power against Pakistan. Finally, as a nuclear weapon state, China enjoyed a measure of security independence and did not need to worry that sensitive nuclear exports would hurt its relationship with a superpower security provider.

In Chapter 10 of this volume, Gartkze suggests additional motives for sensitive nuclear transfers. He claims that states will be more willing to provide sensitive nuclear assistance to states that are likely to acquire nuclear weapons anyway, regardless of whether they get help. In this way, the supplier can garner some influence over the recipient without significantly contributing to proliferation. In addition, Gartzke suggests that non-nuclear weapon states with advanced nuclear technology will be more likely than nuclear weapon states to provide sensitive nuclear assistance, because nuclear weapon states have an incentive to limit the size of the nuclear club. His conjectures are plausible, but the empirical record demonstrates that they are incorrect. A careful look at the most important cases of sensitive nuclear assistance does not turn up a single instance of a policy maker choosing to provide nuclear assistance because he or she believed the recipient was bound to proliferate anyway. In fact, leaders often provide nuclear assistance because they believe that the recipient would not be able to proliferate without their help. As Guy Mollet, the Prime Minister behind France's nuclear assistance to Israel, explained, "When my government came to power, Israel asked for French assistance; I did my duty as a democrat and a Frenchman by supplying this endangered country with the arms it needed to survive" (as quoted in Troen and Shemesh 1990: 131). Indeed, while some things may seem preordained in hindsight, there was nothing inevitable about China, Israel, Pakistan, or North Korea joining the nuclear club. In fact, without external help it is possible that some of these countries would not possess nuclear weapons today. Moreover, Gartzke's explanation raises the question as to why a supplier should reasonably expect that the provision of unneeded help should buy any influence. Finally, contrary to Gartzke's other claim, it has been systematically demonstrated that nuclear weapon states are more, not less, likely to provide nuclear assistance than are capable non-nuclear weapon states (Kroenig 2010: 5, 178). This is because nuclear-armed states enjoy a degree of security independence and need to worry less about incurring the wrath of the international community.

Sensitive Nuclear Assistance and the Nuclear Renaissance

The above analysis of historical patterns of sensitive nuclear assistance has important implications for current attempts to understand the nuclear renaissance. One should be cautious about blindly extrapolating historical trends into the future; it is always possible that a radical discontinuity could emerge, creating a future that will be utterly unrecognizable from our current temporal perch. As the Danish physicist Niels Bohr is reported to have said, "Prediction is very difficult, especially about the future." Nevertheless, past is often prologue, and much of social science is based on the idea that historical data can help us better understand the workings of enduring social phenomena. In addition to conjectures by informed analysts, therefore, the findings of careful social science research can provide a valuable tool in helping to forecast the possible proliferation consequences of the nuclear renaissance.

This research demonstrates that the idea that so-called proliferation rings are an important driving force for future nuclear proliferation exists more in the imagination of analysts than in reality. The substate smuggling of significant quantities of sensitive nuclear materials and technology has been virtually nonexistent in the past. It is unlikely, therefore, that countries will be able to produce functioning nuclear fuel cycle facilities with help from non-state actors. Some may object that while substate proliferation rings leading to significant nuclear transfers have been rare historically, they could become more common in the future due to globalization, the diffusion of nuclear know-how, and worldwide reductions in technological barriers to entry in the nuclear field. There are, however, reasons to be skeptical of this claim. Governments have strong political, economic, and strategic incentives to maintain tight control over their most sensitive nuclear technologies. This has been true in the past and it will likely remain so in the future. Granted, some key component parts for the uranium enrichment facilities exported by A. Q. Khan's Pakistan were produced by private firms in Malaysia, Switzerland, and South Africa. But these actors could not have been important nodes in a global nonproliferation network had it not been for strong state support on both the recipient and *supplier* side of the transactions. As pointed out above, A. Q. Khan's nuclear supply network was supported by the Pakistani state through and through. And the recipients, Iran, Libya, and North Korea, were eager to receive sensitive nuclear help. Experience suggests, therefore, that we should be much more concerned about the *state-sponsored* transfer of sensitive nuclear materials and technology than we should about substate proliferation rings.

We also saw above, however, that state-sponsored transfer of sensitive nuclear materials and technology also has been rare. It is unlikely, therefore, that any particular new nuclear power state will receive sensitive nuclear assistance from other states. Since 1945, there have been only fourteen instances of sensitive nuclear assistance. Moreover, some of these transfers were to the same recipient state. Since 1945, only twelve countries have been fortunate enough to receive sensitive nuclear assistance from a more advanced nuclear supplier state. Many others have tried to obtain such assistance and failed. For example, while exploring the nuclear option in the 1960s, Egypt requested sensitive nuclear assistance from France, the Soviet Union, and China, only to be rebuffed each time. There is good reason to believe, therefore, that countries seeking sensitive nuclear assistance today will also encounter great difficulties.

While future sensitive nuclear transfers are unlikely, the above analysis suggests the conditions under which they will be most likely to occur. Despite conventional wisdom to the contrary, states do not provide sensitive nuclear assistance for economic reasons. Capable nuclear suppliers experiencing economic underdevelopment, or slow or negative growth rates, are not more likely to export sensitive nuclear materials and technology than their wealthier counterparts. One thus would be ill advised to make predictions about the future of the nuclear renaissance by identifying relationships between economically desperate nuclear suppliers, such as North Korea, and deep-pocketed aspirants, such as Saudi Arabia.

Rather, sensitive nuclear transfers are driven by a strategic logic. If we seek to identify whether the nuclear renaissance will lead to nuclear weapons proliferation and which countries will be most likely to acquire nuclear weapons in a future nuclear renaissance, we must focus on these strategic conditions. The nuclear supplier–nuclear recipient dyads that could engage in sensitive nuclear cooperation are those in which the supplier lacks the ability to project military power over the latter, the states possess a common enemy, and neither state depends on the United States to provide for its core security needs.

Focusing on the last condition first, it is evident that many capable nuclear suppliers are protected by the U.S. security umbrella and will therefore be unlikely to provide sensitive nuclear assistance. These countries will prefer to avoid jeopardizing an important security relationship by antagonizing the United States on this important political issue. Table 8.1 lists the twenty states capable of providing sensitive nuclear assistance in the world today. Looking at the table, we can see that over half of the countries (twelve of twenty) share a close military relationship with the United States. That leaves the remaining countries as the nuclear suppliers of special concern. In other words, only

TABLE 8.1 Capable nuclear suppliers

Country	Year	Country	Year
Argentina[a]	1969	Japan[a]	1977
Belgium[a]	1966	Netherlands[a]	1971
Brazil[a]	1988	North Korea	1993
China	1964	Norway[a]	1961
France[a]	1958	Pakistan	1986
Germany[a]	1969	USSR/Russia	1949
India	1964	South Africa	1977
Iran	2009	United Kingdom[a]	1951
Israel[a]	1966	United States[a]	1945
Italy[a]	1970	Yugoslavia/Serbia	1966

[a]Capable nuclear suppliers that share a formal military alliance with the United States. These countries are unlikely to provide sensitive nuclear assistance to non-nuclear weapon states. Although not joined in a formal alliance, Israel is included in the list due to its strong and enduring security relationship with the United States.

eight countries in the world today are at a heightened risk of providing sensitive nuclear assistance.

Additional strategic factors will shape how these countries view the attractiveness of nuclear exports. Returning to the first strategic condition shaping nuclear assistance, we can infer that these eight nuclear suppliers will be unlikely to provide sensitive nuclear assistance to countries against which they can project military power; they will prefer to avoid constraining their own military freedom of action. This consideration limits the pool of potential nuclear suppliers for would-be proliferators even further. China, for example, would be unlikely to provide sensitive nuclear assistance to other states in Asia because it desires to maintain its military predominance in this region. Similarly, Iran would be reluctant to export sensitive nuclear materials to other actors in the Middle East. Any country seeking to acquire sensitive nuclear materials and technology, therefore, will generally be forced to search for one of a handful of capable nuclear suppliers beyond its own geographic region.

Finally, we turn to the second condition. Taking this condition seriously suggests that future sensitive nuclear transfers will most likely occur between nuclear suppliers and nuclear recipients that share a common enemy. In these situations, nuclear suppliers could provide nuclear assistance in order to constrain a powerful rival. Considering the remaining pool of supplier states, we can identify only a small number of supplier–recipient dyads that meet this criterion. Some of the remaining nuclear suppliers, for example, have a history of antagonism and political-military competition with the United States. Countries such as Russia, China, Iran, and North Korea could conceivably provide sensitive nuclear assistance to states that are hostile to the United States in an effort to constrain U.S. military power. Potential recipients that fit this description could include Bolivia, Burma, Syria, or Venezuela.

North Korea has already begun to provide nuclear assistance to some of these recipient states. From 2001 to 2007, for example, North Korea helped Syria construct a plutonium-producing reactor, before Israel destroyed the facility in a preventative military attack in September 2007. As far as we know, North Korea did not export fuel cycle technologies to Syria, but the nuclear reactor may have been the first step in what was intended to be a broader nuclear relationship. Also, according to recent reports (e.g., Borgder 2009), North Korea may also be providing nuclear assistance to Burma. True to the pattern of sensitive nuclear transfers identified above, North Korea's nuclear exports may be driven in part by a desire to constrain American power. In a recent interview with a Japanese journalist, a high-ranking North Korean official explained the strategic goals behind North Korea's transfers. He claimed: "If we spread our nuclear weapons to other countries . . . the power of the U.S. would be relatively decreased" (Abe 2009). He continued to argue that nuclear proliferation to other countries improves North Korea's relative standing because "Once the U.S. is not able to be predominant over others, then we can be on equal footing." Given the continued animosity between the United States and North Korea, there is little reason to believe that North Korea's nuclear generosity to America's rivals will end any time soon. Indeed, the North Korean official threatened that the country will continue "to sell our nuclear arms to countries which hate the U.S."

India is also a country at risk of exporting sensitive nuclear materials and technology. Given its historical rivalry with China, India could conceivably provide sensitive nuclear assistance to small states on China's border in order to constrain China's military freedom of action. Illustrating this type of thinking, Bahrat Karnad, Research Professor of National Security Studies at the Centre for Policy Research in India, argued that New Delhi should provide sensitive nuclear assistance to Vietnam and Taiwan. In a recent book, Karnad

(2002) writes, "India should, likewise, create precisely the kind of dilemmas for China that Beijing has created for it with respect to a nuclear weapons and missile-equipped Pakistan by arming Vietnam with strategic weapons" and by "cooperating with Taiwan in the nuclear and missile fields." While Karnad's views do not represent the official policy of the Indian government, they demonstrate that the factors that have motivated sensitive nuclear assistance in the past also could fuel them under special conditions in future cases.

Given our understanding of why states have provided sensitive nuclear assistance, there is good reason to believe that the international transfer of sensitive nuclear materials and technology will remain uncommon. There are only a handful of nuclear supplier–nuclear recipient dyads for which the conditions that encourage sensitive nuclear transfers are in place. Over the next few decades, therefore, it is reasonable to expect that there might be a few—but only a few—instances in which capable nuclear suppliers might provide sensitive nuclear assistances to non-nuclear weapon states. This analysis strongly suggests that predictions that the nuclear renaissance will lead to the widespread diffusion of sensitive nuclear materials and technology that in turn results in a cascade of nuclear weapons proliferation are likely exaggerated.

Conclusion

This chapter examines whether the nuclear renaissance will result in the international spread of nuclear weapons, starting with the idea that whether the nuclear renaissance will fuel future nuclear proliferation rests on four propositions: that the nuclear renaissance will lead to an increased demand for nuclear fuel; that countries will prefer to possess domestic nuclear fuel cycle facilities rather than receive international fuel services; that countries will be able to acquire sensitive nuclear assistance from other states; and that once countries receive sensitive nuclear assistance, they will be more likely to produce nuclear weapons.

The chapter argues that the nuclear renaissance is unlikely to result in nuclear weapons proliferation because the third of these four propositions is not true. Acquiring sensitive nuclear assistance and technology is difficult. Drawing on previous analysis of the causes of sensitive nuclear assistance, the chapter demonstrates that the international transfer of sensitive nuclear materials and technology is uncommon and is most likely to occur only under relatively rare strategic conditions. For this reason, countries—even countries that badly want to build domestic fuel cycle facilities—will struggle to identify a willing foreign supplier. And, without international aid, countries will be less able to produce nuclear weapons.

When combined with the other chapters in this volume, the findings of this analysis give us further reason to doubt the conventional wisdom about a direct renaissance–proliferation link. Four assumptions underlie this proposition, but the chapters of this volume suggest that at least three of these four assumptions are problematic. Stulberg (Chapter 4) argues that it might be possible to design a system that provides a credible commitment to recipients of nuclear fuel cycle services. If Stulberg is correct, many future nuclear power states will be willing to accept international fuel supplies and will forgo the construction of domestic fuel cycle facilities. This chapter demonstrates that the countries that do decide to build domestic fuel cycle facilities will be unlikely to succeed because they will struggle to secure international help. And finally, Montgomery (Chapter 7) claims that even if countries receive sensitive nuclear assistance, they will be unable to construct nuclear weapons because, for a variety of reasons, international nuclear aid might actually impede a country's nuclear development. There is good reason to be skeptical of these claims. Previous research (Kroenig 2009b, 2010) has systematically demonstrated that countries that receive sensitive nuclear assistance are more likely to acquire nuclear weapons. Nevertheless, Montgomery's chapter makes some thought-provoking claims that give us reason to suspect that sensitive nuclear assistance might provide a bigger boost to nuclear programs in certain types of recipient states than in others.

In March 2011, an earthquake and tsunami triggered a nuclear meltdown at the Fukushima Daiichi nuclear power plant in Japan. This unexpected disaster might influence the development of the nuclear renaissance, as other authors in this volume point out, but it does not greatly affect our expectations about future patterns of sensitive nuclear transfers. Nuclear reactors produce sustained nuclear chain reactions that can generate tremendous power, but they can also result in devastating accidents. For this reason, nuclear reactors have been the incubators of history's worst nuclear disasters, including Fukushima. In addition, the spent fuel rods at Fukushima underwent a partial meltdown when the water levels in the spent fuel pools dropped. This has led to calls for more plutonium reprocessing, which could reduce the density of spent fuel rods left cooling in pools and, in turn, the risk of meltdown. While the Fukushima nuclear accident, therefore, could dampen leaders' willingness to build nuclear reactors in their own countries and could increase the demand for reprocessing capabilities in countries currently operating reactors, this chapter's analysis of the causes of sensitive nuclear assistance gives us little reason to believe that these considerations will greatly affect the calculations of the potential suppliers to export fuel cycle technologies.

This chapter not only draws lessons from past cases of nuclear assistance, but also it identifies a small number of cases in which future nuclear transfers could occur. Of particular concern are the small number of capable nuclear suppliers that do not enjoy a close strategic relationship with the United States and that could conceivably benefit from additional constraints on American military power. China, Iran, Russia, and North Korea are at the top of the list of nuclear suppliers that might make such a strategic calculation. The respective leaderships might be tempted to export the bomb to some of the United States' enemies interested in developing nuclear programs, including Bolivia, Burma, Syria, or Venezuela. Intelligence analysts and policy makers must closely watch these countries for signs of fledgling nuclear relationships and adopt measures now to prevent sensitive transfers before they occur.

There are a number of steps that the United States can take to ward off future nuclear transfers. To begin, the development of nuclear fuel guarantees could help to satisfy demand for nuclear fuel in new nuclear power states without generating a corresponding risk of nuclear proliferation. For this reason, the development of a credible international fuel services system is of paramount importance. Accordingly, Stulberg's recommendations (Chapter 4 in this volume) should be read with great attention.

Contrary to the belief of many, tightening national export controls is only a small part of the overall solution. While export controls are an important policy tool, their utility rests on the assumption that proliferation is a problem that results from firms or bureaucracies exporting dual-use items without the knowledge or authorization of the central government. But analysis suggests that this is rarely a problem. The most important historical cases of sensitive nuclear transfer—those that have led to the proliferation of nuclear weapons—were the result of strategic decisions by national governments to help another country acquire sensitive nuclear facilities. When central governments make such a strategic decision, they can simply choose to override their own export control systems. Tightening export controls will not help address this problem.

What is needed is an effort to alter the cost/benefit calculus of states that might be tempted to make the strategic decision to export sensitive nuclear materials and technology. There are a number of carrots and sticks that might be useful for such a purpose. Among the carrots, the United States could seek to extend security guarantees to nuclear suppliers who are not yet under the U.S. security umbrella. We have seen that countries that depend on the United States for their core security needs are less likely to export sensitive nuclear materials or technology. Therefore, the United States could, for example, encourage Serbia to join the North Atlantic Treaty Organization and could continue to expand and deepen its current strategic partnership with Pakistan. If these countries come to rely on the United States' protection, they will be more likely to think twice before conducting future sensitive nuclear transfers.

In some cases, however, carrots will fail to entice and the United States will need to reach for sticks. In these cases, the United States should turn to threats in order to deter the international transfer of sensitive nuclear materials and technology. A declaratory policy to hold responsible states that transfer sensitive nuclear material and technology, visibly strengthened nuclear forensics capabilities, and improved capabilities to interdict illicit nuclear shipments should induce caution in potential nuclear suppliers. This portfolio of policies will help to ensure that the nuclear renaissance will not allow many more countries to possess the world's most dangerous weapon.

Notes

1. See, for example, Nutall 2004; Schmid 2006; Allison 2008; Goldschmidt 2008; Shea and Zentner 2008; Barnaby 2009; Fuhrmann 2009; Lauvergeon 2009; Miller and Sagan 2009; Tagarinski 2009.

2. This is the author of this chapter's best articulation of the causal chain between the renaissance and proliferation and does not necessarily represent the views of any or all of the authors cited in footnote 1.

3. For more on this debate, see Bluth et al. (2010).

4. On the dangers of nuclear proliferation, see Beardsley and Asal, Chapter 11 in this volume; Horowitz, Chapter 12 in this volume.

5. While working in the Netherlands in the late 1970s, Pakistani scientist A. Q. Khan was able to smuggle designs and key component parts for uranium enrichment facilities from Holland to Pakistan without the knowledge or authorization of the Dutch government. This transfer was made possible by the combination of a recipient

with strong nuclear weapons ambitions, with a competent and nationalistic nuclear scientist placed in the laboratories of a nuclear-capable foreign country, which was relatively new to the operation of sensitive nuclear facilities and that did not yet have adequate security measures in place.

6. For a list of these cases of nuclear smuggling, see Government Accountability Office (2002).

References

Abe, Amii. 2009. "North Korea: Entering a New Phase." *Policy Forum Online* [of the Nautilus Institute], July 16. Available at: http://nautilus.org/napsnet/napsnet-policy-forum/north-korea-entering-a-new-phase-we-are-not-interested-in-the-u-s-anymore/.

Allison, Graham. 2008. "Securing the Nuclear Renaissance." Testimony to the House Subcommittee on Terrorism, Nonproliferation, and Trade, July 24.

Barnaby, Frank. 2009. "The Nuclear Renaissance: Nuclear Weapons Proliferation and Terrorism." Institute for Public Policy Research (March). Available at: http://www.ippr.org/publication/55/1679/the-nuclear-renaissance-nuclear-weapons-proliferation-and-terrorism.

Bluth, Christopher, Matthew Kroenig, Rensselaer Lee, William C. Sailor, and Matthew Fuhrmann. 2010. "Correspondence: Civilian Nuclear Cooperation and the Proliferation of Nuclear Weapons." *International Security* 35 (1): 184–200.

Borgder, Julian. 2009. "Burma Suspected of Forming Nuclear Link with North Korea." *Guardian*, July 21. Available at: http://www.guardian.co.uk/world/2009/jul/21/burma-north-korea-nuclear-clinton.

Braun, Chaim, and Christopher F. Chyba. 2004. "Proliferation Rings: New Challenges to the Nuclear Nonproliferation Regime." *International Security* 29 (2): 5–49.

Chestnut, Sheena. 2007. "Illicit Activity and Proliferation: North Korean Smuggling Networks." *International Security* 32 (1): 80–111.

ElBaradei, Mohamed. 2003. "Towards a Safer World." *The Economist*, October 16. Available at: http://www.economist.com/node/2137602.

Fuhrmann, Matthew. 2009. "Spreading Temptation: Proliferation and Peaceful Nuclear Cooperation Agreements." *International Security* 34 (1): 7–41.

Gartzke, Erik, and Matthew Kroenig. 2009. "A Strategic Approach to Nuclear Proliferation." *Journal of Conflict Resolution* 53 (2): 151–160.

Goldschmidt, Pierre. 2008. "Nuclear Renaissance and Non-Proliferation." Presentation delivered at the 24th Conference of the Nuclear Societies, February 19–21, Israel. Available at: http://www.carnegieendowment.org/2008/02/20/nuclear-renaissance-and-non-proliferation/3g0m.

Government Accountability Office. 2002. *Nuclear Nonproliferation: U.S. Efforts to Help Other Countries Combat Nuclear Smuggling Need Strengthened Coordination and Planning.* GAO-02-426. Washington, DC: GAO.

Jones, Rodney W. 1990. "Studying the Emerging Nuclear Suppliers." In *International Nuclear Trade and Nonproliferation: The Challenge of the Emerging Suppliers*, ed. William C. Potter. Lexington, MA: Lexington Books.

Karnad, Bharat. 2002. *Nuclear Weapons and Indian Security: The Realist Foundations of Strategy*. New York: Macmillan.

Kroenig, Matthew. 2009a. "Exporting the Bomb: Why States Provide Sensitive Nuclear Assistance." *American Political Science Review* 103 (1): 113–133.

———. 2009b. "Importing the Bomb: Sensitive Nuclear Assistance and Nuclear Proliferation." *Journal of Conflict Resolution* 53 (2): 161–180.

———. 2010. *Exporting the Bomb: Technology Transfer and the Spread of Nuclear Weapons*. Ithaca, NY: Cornell University Press.

Lauvergeon, Anne. 2009. "The Nuclear Renaissance: An Opportunity to Enhance the Culture of Nonproliferation." *Daedalus* 138 (4): 91–99.

Miller, Steven E., and Scott D. Sagan. 2009. "Nuclear Power Without Nuclear Proliferation?" *Daedalus* 138 (4): 7–18.

———. 2010. "Alternative Nuclear Futures." *Daedalus* 139 (1): 126–137.

Nutall, W. J. 2004. *Nuclear Renaissance: Technologies and Policies for the Future of Nuclear Power*. New York: Taylor & Francis.

Potter, William C. 1982. *Nuclear Power and Nonproliferation: An Interdisciplinary Perspective*. Cambridge, MA: Oelgeschlager, Gunn & Hain.

Sagan, Scott D. 2010. "Rethinking Nuclear Latency." In *Forecasting Nuclear Proliferation in the 21st Century: Volume 1, The Role of Theory*, ed. William Potter. Stanford, CA: Stanford University Press, pp. 80–101.

Schmid, Sonja D. 2006. "Nuclear Renaissance in the Age of Global Warming." *Bridges* 12. Available at: http://cisac.stanford.edu/publications/nuclear_renaissance_in_the_age_of_global_warming/.

Shea, Thomas E., and Michael D. Zentner. 2008. "Proliferation Resistance and the Nuclear Renaissance." *International Journal of Global Energy Issues* 30 (1): 376–392.

Tagarinski, Mario. 2009. *The Nuclear Renaissance. Committee Report.* NATO Parliamentary Assembly, Annual Session. Brussels, Belgium. Available at: http://www.nato-pa.int/default.asp?CAT2=1765&CAT1=16&CAT0=2&COM=1773&MOD=0&SMD=0&SSMD=0&STA=&ID=0&PAR=0&PRINT=1.

Troen, Selwyn Ilan, and Moshe Shemesh. 1990. *The Suez-Sinai Crisis 1956: Retrospective and Reappraisal*. New York: Columbia University Press.

9   Consequences of the Nuclear Renaissance
for Nonstate Nuclear Trafficking

Justin V. Hastings

THE POTENTIAL SPREAD OF CIVIL NUCLEAR TECHNOLOGY HAS
generally led to two concerns about an accompanying increased
threat from illicit nuclear trafficking. First, with the broadening of nuclear
power to more and more developing countries, nuclear technology and non-
trivial quantities of fissile material also could spread to countries with pro-
gressively weaker state capacity. Second, nuclear traffickers may be able to
take advantage of the corruption and poor administrative capacity in these
new nuclear states to obtain fissile materials and nuclear components, and
then use modern communications and transportation technology to move
those goods around the world. The globalization of illicit nuclear trafficking,
in other words, goes hand in hand with the globalization of nuclear power.

This chapter focuses on trafficking in stolen fissile material, including plutonium (Pu) and highly enriched uranium (HEU). Together with the gray-
market trade in the machine components needed to enrich uranium, nuclear
materials trafficking constitutes the bulk of the nonstate weapons of mass
destruction proliferation threat. In nonstate proliferation, at least one of the
actors involved in acquiring, moving, buying, or selling nuclear materials in
a given network is a nonstate entity acting without the knowledge (or at least
help) of the government(s) of one or more of the countries in which it is operating. As one of the means by which nuclear hopefuls, either state or nonstate
actors, acquire the physical ability (if not the technical knowledge) to build
nuclear weapons without needing the purposeful help of state actors, nuclear

trafficking falls in the middle of the proliferation process. The proliferator already has made the decision to acquire either a latent or an operational nuclear weapons capacity of some sort but needs the sensitive materials and components to build the weapons. The concern here, therefore, is not whether an actual weapon results from the process, but whether the proliferator is able to acquire and transport the goods it needs.

The nuclear renaissance, should it occur, will diversify the locations from which nuclear materials can be obtained, with the new sources being located in countries with lower average state capacity than is currently the case. However, the qualitative effects are likely to be limited. The quantitative increase in sites that need to be protected in weak states will be a concern that will require attention by nuclear powers and nuclear aspirants alike, but new power plants by and large will likely not be located in new nuclear states with low state capacity. Furthermore, the ways in which nuclear traffickers transport their materials will not change with the advent of a nuclear renaissance. They will remain dependent on commercial transportation infrastructure controlled at least in part by states, making them vulnerable to state crackdowns. The changes wrought by a nuclear renaissance (or, more likely, a nuclear resurgence) will not fundamentally change the nature of the illicit trafficking threat, but the threat nonetheless needs to be taken seriously. The chapter concludes with discussion of the implications and policy recommendations.

Approach

Analytically, nuclear smuggling networks can be disaggregated into the actors that participate in different stages of the smuggling process. First are the suppliers, the organizations that actually produce the nuclear material and components to be smuggled. "Nuclear material" in this context refers to fissile material used in nuclear reactors and weapons—HEU and Pu. "Nuclear components" means the components needed to make uranium enrichment centrifuges and to build centrifuge cascades, as well the machines that can be used to construct centrifuges. Steel and aluminum tubes, vacuum tubing, valves, gasification and solidification units, and precision machinery all fall into this category. This chapter focuses on trafficking in fissile material (HEU and Pu) and the machine components necessary for uranium enrichment. Since HEU and Pu are likely to be used for improvised nuclear devices, and enrichment components for helping states such as Iran and North Korea acquire regular nuclear devices, successful trafficking is likely to lead to weapons of mass destruction. Given the relatively poor tracking and wide geographic dispersion of nonfissile radioactive sources, even in developed countries, the threat from radiological dispersal devices (RDDs) is probably a more *likely* threat (regardless of the future of nuclear energy in developing countries); but RDDs would better be described as weapons of mass disruption rather than destruction. Emergency preparedness and educating the public are crucial aspects of minimizing the disruption from an RDD (Ferguson and Potter 2004). This is less true of nuclear devices, with fewer potential sources for their material but significantly greater potential for destruction should they be successfully developed and detonated.

Second are the coordinators—one or more people or organizations who either contract for goods from the (sometimes unwitting) suppliers or simply steal them, and then arrange to have them transported to the buyer, the third type of actors. Finally, the buyer is either a state, attempting to buy materials secretly, or a nonstate actor, such as a terrorist organization (Zaitseva and Hand 2003).

Some combinations of state and nonstate actors in a nuclear smuggling network are more or less plausible. It is difficult to think of a network in which a state is consciously using its state prerogatives to provide technology or facilitate the transfer of materials to another actor, either state or nonstate, as anything but an example of state proliferation. Likewise, a network where one state is providing technology to another state and covering its tracks by funneling technologies through private companies suffers some of the weaknesses of nonstate coordinators that will be discussed later in this chapter. But this is not what we generally mean when talking about nonstate proliferation. The focus here is on networks where either the suppliers or coordinators, or both, are nonstate actors.

At issue in this chapter is the effect that expansion in the number of civil nuclear facilities in new and current nuclear energy–producing countries would have on the problem of nonstate nuclear trafficking, as defined by the increased number (and number of locations) of potential sources for both nonstate actors and states operating illicitly to acquire nuclear-related material, and the possible routes for traffickers to transport them. To answer this question, the chapter takes a geographic approach to nonstate proliferation.

Traditional network analysis in international relations is primarily concerned with how a network affects its external environment or, more relevant here, how the internal structure of the network—the structure and relationships among the nodes—affects the actors within the network and leads to political outcomes (Hafner-Burton, Kahler, and Montgomery 2009). Although there is nothing stopping links between nodes from being the physical movement of goods, in practice most traditional network analysis in international relations takes nodes to be states or organizations (or, in the case of terrorist networks, individuals) (Krebs 2002; Sageman 2004) and the links between the nodes to be social or treaty relationships, or some other form of cooperation (Keck and Sikkink 1998; Hafner-Burton, Kahler, and Montgomery 2009).

In his work on proliferation networks, Montgomery treats entire countries as nodes, between which flow nuclear components and expertise, as do Braun and Chyba in their work on proliferation rings (Braun and Chyba 2004; Montgomery 2005). This approach works well if governments are the proliferators. In traditional proliferation rings, states are simultaneously the suppliers of technology and expertise, the coordinators (through government-to-government agreements) for the logistics networks that move goods between countries, and the buyers of that technology. There is little need to think about the logistics of cooperation, because the decision by one state to transfer physical technology and material to another state is essentially a done deal (as opposed to tacit knowledge, as Montgomery points out in Chapter 7 of this volume).

By contrast, the decision by nonstate traffickers is not straightforward, precisely because they must contend with the hostile states in which their sources, transportation infrastructure, or even buyers are located. This can be seen in other types of illicit nonstate actors, such as in terrorist organizations, where logistical challenges have sometimes been enough to scuttle operations (Hastings 2008). A geographic approach does not invalidate traditional approaches so much as takes them in a different direction; it applies conceptions of nodes and links based not only on the relationships of nodes to each other, but also on the relationships between nodes and links *and* territory. The nodes of geographers' illicit transnational networks are people or organizations that are anchored within a specific piece of territory—a city, region, or country with an "activity space," a specific set of political and economic characteristics that constrict, encourage, or otherwise shape their behavior (Murphy 2003). Of interest to geographers is not only where nodes are located, but also how (using different types of infrastructure) the people, goods, and information that flow between them move across (or above) territory (Kliot and

Newman 2000; Flint 2003). Although they do not necessarily take a specifically geographical approach, it is common for analysts who study illicit actors and state failure to see the activities of transnational illicit actors as embedded in specific characteristics of the territory in which they are operating. Al Qaeda's activities in Somalia in the early 1990s, for instance, were hindered by a lack of transportation and communications infrastructure and security concerns in Somalia's chaotic environment. Similarly, the difficult terrain and lack of state-provided infrastructure impedes operations of the insurgent groups in Mindanao in the southern Philippines (Rabasa et al. 2007; HARMONY 2007).

Applied to the suppliers and coordinators in nonstate proliferation networks, the geographic approach leads to two interrelated points for analysis: first, the governance environments in which potential suppliers for nuclear materials are embedded; and second, how the routes and infrastructure likely to be used by nuclear traffickers as they move goods from supplier countries to buyers are embedded in political and economic environments that constrain their behavior. In both cases, this chapter looks first at apparent patterns in past trafficking networks and determines the effect, if any, of an increase in the number and locations of suppliers of nuclear material on future patterns of nonstate proliferation.

Suppliers

The most obvious consequence of a successful nuclear renaissance for nonstate proliferation is the diversification of countries that have nuclear facilities and thus, theoretically, material available for trafficking. The political, economic, and social environments of the countries in which the sources are located will determine the extent to which they are proliferation risks.

The concern with the trafficking of nuclear materials, up to and including HEU and Pu, is that the nuclear facilities of weak and failed states are easy for smugglers to penetrate, whether by dint of lax security, safety standards, or simple corruption. It is indeed the case that the countries that have expressed interest in acquiring civil nuclear technology have, by any indicator, lower average state capacity than those that already possess nuclear reactors. Table 9.1 shows the mean percentile of the political stability, government effectiveness, regulatory quality, rule of law, and control of corruption (as measured by 2009 World Bank governance indicators) of the countries that (1) have civil nuclear power reactors (IAEA 2009), and (2) do not have civil nuclear power reactors but have expressed an interest in acquiring them, as claimed by the World Nuclear Association (WNA) (2012).[1] World Bank governance indicators are common measures of state capacity, particularly when the concern is the ability of governments to provide public security and economic goods, enforce regulations, and ensure consistent policy outcomes (Miller and Sagan 2009). For those studies that are more concerned with democratic accountability and the lack of institutional development associated with autocracy, Montgomery's use of Polity IV scores (Chapter 7 in this volume) may be more appropriate. Because this chapter is primarily concerned with the ability of new nuclear energy states to stop nuclear supply and trafficking, the World Bank governance indicators are preferable here.

As we move from Category 1 to Category 2, the level of corruption increases and governance indicators decrease. Few of the countries in Category 2 are actually failed states in the sense that state authority has broken down almost entirely across large parts of the country's territory (Rotberg 2002). Of the countries listed, Bangladesh, Sudan, North Korea, Yemen, Venezuela, and Nigeria are below the twentieth percentile in the World Bank's indicator for government effectiveness (and only Yemen and Sudan are below the twentieth percentile in all the listed indicators). It remains to be seen whether they will ever actually complete and operate a nuclear power plant (Gourley and Stulberg, Chapter 1 in this volume).

The specific conditions that encourage "loose" nuclear materials are more nuanced than simple state failure and can be gleaned from past instances of nuclear trafficking, many of which occurred in the former Soviet Union. Lyudmila Zaitseva has built an extensive database of nuclear material (and radioactive isotope) trafficking incidents from 1991 through 2002.[2] Of the 660 incidents in Zaitseva's database, 370 reportedly originated in the former Soviet Union (Zaitseva and Steinhausler 2003). Balatsky and Severe (2007) of Los Alamos National Laboratory determined that 41 percent of incidents between 1990 and 2006 originated in the former Soviet Union, lending some validity to Zaitseva's findings. While a combination of economic collapse, corruption, and nuclear facilities might seem to be the logical brew from which springs nuclear trafficking, the new wave of nuclear power plants and facilities constructed in weak states will not necessarily pose as large a risk as those in the former Soviet Union.

TABLE 9.1 Governance indicators for nuclear power countries and nuclear aspirants

Category		Political stability/no violence	Government effectiveness	Regulatory quality	Rule of law	Corruption
1[a]	Mean	60.0	74.0	74.0	68.0	68.0
	Std. dev.	24.3	20.7	21.3	25.3	24.6
2[b]	Mean	43.0	53.0	52.0	50.0	49.0
	Std. dev.	28.1	27.3	27.9	26.8	28.6

SOURCES: World Bank 2009; World Nuclear Association 2011; IAEA 2009a.

[a]*Category 1: Nuclear power countries*

Argentina	Hungary	Slovenia
Armenia	India	South Africa
Belgium	Japan	Spain
Brazil	Korea (South)	Sweden
Bulgaria	Lithuania	Switzerland
Canada	Mexico	Taiwan
China	Netherlands	Ukraine
Czech Republic	Pakistan	United Kingdom
Finland	Romania	United States
France	Russia	
Germany	Slovakia	

[b]*Category 2: Nuclear aspirants*

Albania	Italy	Portugal
Algeria	Jordan	Qatar
Australia	Kazakhstan	Saudi Arabia
Azerbaijan	Kenya	Senegal
Bangladesh	Korea (North)	Serbia
Belarus	Kuwait	Singapore
Chile	Latvia	Sri Lanka
Croatia	Libya	Sudan
Ecuador	Malaysia	Syria
Egypt	Mongolia	Thailand
Estonia	Morocco	Tunisia
Georgia	Namibia	Turkey
Ghana	New Zealand	Uganda
Indonesia	Nigeria	United Arab Emirates
Iran	Norway	Venezuela
Ireland	Philippines	Vietnam
Israel	Poland	Yemen

The Soviet Union is a rare example of a strong, technologically advanced state that collapsed rather suddenly, leaving a large, unguarded infrastructure (and thousands of employees who need income), as compared to a chronically weak state. According to Zaitseva and Hand (2003), the people who actually provided the radioactive isotopes and nuclear materials appear to have been, by and large, employees—scientists, soldiers, and guards—at nuclear facilities who were bucking safety and security regulations, and seeking monetary compensation, both of which had collapsed with the Soviet Union.

Moreover, these employees had access to a large amount of nuclear material. Because it had produced tens of thousands of warheads, the Soviet Union's indigenous nuclear complex was massive. Given the size of the USSR's civil and military nuclear complexes, there were many opportunities for traffickers to divert nuclear material. In May 1997, for instance, in the civil sector alone there were twenty-nine operating nuclear power plants in Russia, fourteen in the Ukraine, two in Lithuania, and one in Armenia (Nuclear Energy Institute 1998: 84); plus, in the military sector, a large number of research stations, nuclear material storage facilities, and weapons installations. Although there was apparently a decrease in smuggling incidents after 1995, by 2007 the main exporters of nuclear material remained countries such as Kazakhstan, Belarus, Russia, and Ukraine (Zaitseva 2007: 6). Most of the cases recorded by the IAEA of actual smuggling of HEU and Pu have come from the former Soviet Union or Eastern Europe: Of thirteen incidents reported between 1993 and 2006 involving HEU or Pu found outside of legal containers or facilities, ten involved illegal possession or trafficking and took place in Russia (2), Germany (1), France (1), Bulgaria (1), Georgia (2), and the Czech Republic (3) (IAEA 2007). Additional incidents of HEU or Pu smuggling have been reported as occurring since 2007. Between July 2009 and June 2010, for instance, there were five reported incidents involving HEU or Pu, of which one involved illegal possession (IAEA 2011), although it is unclear if these incidents took place in the former Soviet Union.

The former Soviet Union is attractive to nuclear smugglers because successful smuggling is, at its heart, a matter of volume—the assumption of both smugglers and the authorities is that a certain percentage of goods will be confiscated. The goods that are not intercepted must be sufficiently profitable to compensate for the probability of the loss of the rest of the goods, the cost in obtaining all the goods, the chances of being caught, and penalties for being caught. Many illicit goods are profitable enough that even being caught is not enough to discourage smugglers. For example, smugglers moving contraband liquor and cigarettes into Singapore in 2005 estimated that they could afford to lose one in three shipments (plus the boat) to confiscation and still make a profit (Hastings 2005a).

Drug traffickers, notably heroin and cocaine smugglers, perhaps the closest conventional analogue to nuclear traffickers, also produce and attempt to smuggle large quantities of their products. Opium poppies are grown almost entirely in three regions of the world: in Central Asia (Afghanistan and Pakistan); in Southeast Asia, in the so-called Golden Triangle (the point where Thailand, Myanmar, and Laos meet); and more recently in Mexico and Colombia (Chin 2009). Likewise, coca plant cultivation is confined to a band running the length of the northern Andes from Bolivia to Venezuela. While coca production is legal in nearly all Andean countries (with the exception of Colombia), for the most part mass production and refinement of cocaine itself takes place in "failed" areas of the countries that lack the continuing presence of the state, either its coercive abilities or its administrative apparatus (Rabasa and Chalk 2001). Some of the drug-producing areas, such as northeastern Myanmar, have never had any meaningful central state control (Chin 2009). High-volume production of drugs, then, seems to require a fairly large swath of territory where producers can operate without outside interference. In this they are similar to the political and economic environment provided to nuclear smugglers in the wake of the fall of the Soviet Union, when large numbers of corrupt officials and facilities enabled a high volume of smuggled goods.

Weak states that acquire new nuclear power plants, however, will not necessarily provide the same environment. The rumors of U.S. plans to secure Pakistan's nuclear weapons and facilities in case of a collapse of the government (or, more likely, the territorial proximity of those facilities to insurgent advances) may or not may have any truth to them, but the more interesting point is that such rumors are only credible because of the small number of facilities possessed by Pakistan (Hersh 2009; Reuters 2009). By contrast, the Cooperative Threat Reduction Program, begun in 1992 and intended to decommission weapons of mass destruction; improve the physical security and materials, protection, control, and accounting features of Russian and other former Soviet states' nuclear facilities; and turn underemployed Russian nuclear scientists toward productive ends, has consumed more than US$10 billion and to date has only partially achieved its ends (by 2006 only 50 percent of Russia's nonweapons fissile material had received security upgrades), partly due to disagreements between the United States and Russia, but also partly because of the number of facilities and material to be secured and scientists to be employed (Luongo and Hoehn 2005; Bunn 2010).

If we survey the states that have expressed interest in nuclear energy, we see that nuclear facilities in new nuclear energy states will present a small number of point targets for smugglers rather than, as in the Soviet Union, a

TABLE 9.2 Nuclear power and nuclear aspirations in weak states

Countries with civil nuclear power reactors and low state capacity	Number of operating units	Units under construction
Argentina	2	1
Ukraine	15	2
Pakistan	2	1
Russia	31	8
Iran	1	0

Countries without civil nuclear power reactors and low state capacity	Largest number of power plants considered
Azerbaijan	1 plant discussed
Syria	1 secret reactor destroyed by Israel
Ecuador	0 plants; agreement signed on nuclear cooperation
Indonesia	4 plants discussed
Algeria	1 plant discussed
Venezuela	0 plants; agreement signed on nuclear cooperation
Bangladesh	1 plant discussed; nuclear cooperation agreement signed
Yemen	0 plants; nuclear energy under discussion, but on hold
Nigeria	1 plant discussed; nuclear cooperation agreement signed
Kenya	1 plant discussed
North Korea	1 plant partially constructed, never operated
Senegal	1 plant discussed
Uganda	0 plants; framework for nuclear energy created
Sudan	1 plant discussed

SOURCES: World Nuclear Association 2011; IAEA 2009a.

virtual sea of targets. Table 9.2 shows the number of new nuclear reactors be-ing constructed (or considered) for each country below the fiftieth percentile in all the World Bank governance indicators listed above. Countries with low state capacity already have 51 nuclear power units (if we include Iran's Bushehr plant) and are building 12 more, while countries with stronger state capacity have 388 units and are building 31 more (IAEA 2009). According to descrip-tions by the WNA (2012), aspiring new nuclear states with low state capacity have discussed building 13 nuclear plants,[3] with agreements or discussion in several more countries, but so far no plans for a specific number of reactors. While these numbers do not include other future facilities, such as spent fuel storage or enrichment facilities, they do give the general contours of the scope and locations of potential future targets for illicit trafficking.

Most of the growth in reactors will likely come in countries such as China and Russia, which already have a long tradition of indigenous civil and mil-itary nuclear complexes (Gourley and Stulberg, Chapter 1 in this volume). Given Russia's history of illicit nuclear trafficking, it is possible that an in-crease in the number of reactors in Russia will increase the potential sources for nuclear materials and thus result in a greater actual supply of illicit nuclear goods. As discussed in the Introduction, this scenario could be characterized more accurately as a resurgence of nuclear power rather than a renaissance—most of the new point targets for smugglers are embedded in the same po-litical and economic conditions as the old targets. For smugglers used to operating in Russia, this presents more opportunities. Unlike a renaissance—where we would see a number of countries, possibly with lower state capac-ity than Russia, acquire nuclear facilities, and thus more points of origin for trafficked nuclear material and more potential routes used by traffickers—a resurgence of nuclear power does not present a greater potential for "state capacity arbitrage" than is currently the case. Smugglers will not have the ability to choose from many different countries that have the right combina-tion of technological strength, and regulatory and enforcement weakness. A resurgence of nuclear power, thus, will not fundamentally change the face of illicit nuclear trafficking, although smugglers will have more targets from which to choose, potentially stretching the regulatory resources of countries that already have experience with civil nuclear power.

A count of the number of new reactors does not correspond exactly to the vulnerability nuclear aspirants will have to illicit trafficking. Some of the states that are building reactors or signing nuclear power agreements do not

seem interested in acquiring command of the full nuclear fuel cycle. They
have either contracted with foreign companies to provide the fuel (and then
take it back once used) or have hired foreign contractors to run the plants entirely. Other countries, such as Jordan, have not ruled out mining and enriching their own uranium (WNA 2012). For instance, the United Arab Emirates
passed a law in October 2009 and set up a nuclear regulator but also banned
spent fuel reprocessing and uranium enrichment in the country (USGPO
2009), whereas Bangladesh has signed an agreement with Russia whereby the
latter would build a civil power plant as well as provide fuel and remove the
spent fuel rods (Stulberg, Chapter 4 in this volume; WNA 2012). In addition,
it would be difficult to categorize some of the weak states that do want control
of the entire fuel cycle as clear examples of a nuclear renaissance—almost
all of Pakistan's initial nuclear efforts were devoted to nuclear weapons production, and it is questionable whether Iran is even interested in civil power
generation. Iran and Pakistan aside, the manner in which some weak states
acquire nuclear power has the effect of minimizing the area that is theoretically open to exploitation by nuclear smugglers. The nuclear facilities are thus
point targets for would-be smugglers; points where even weak states should be
able to marshal resources to protect the nuclear plants and the fissile materials
they contain, as well as to pay employees wages sufficient to stymie corruption. Indonesia, for instance, long of concern to analysts due to a confluence
of interest in nuclear power and extremely high levels of corruption, has run
three research reactors and laboratory-level fuel preparation facilities without
reported problems (Department of Nuclear Energy 2004).[4] Given a likely resurgence scenario, nuclear materials smuggling will continue to be a problem
due to the large number of improperly secured sites around the world, but few
of those sites will be in new nuclear states.

   This is not to minimize the supply-side problems that will exist in fighting
illicit trafficking in a nuclear renaissance (or resurgence). The small number
of new point sources for nuclear material in low-state-capacity countries does
not warrant complacency. The strange case of the armed attack on the Pe-
lindaba nuclear facility in South Africa in 2007, for example, highlights that
even single points have security weaknesses and can be subject to concerted
attacks.

   The politics of fighting nuclear trafficking on the supply side also cannot
be ignored. The developing countries that may operate civil nuclear reactors
in the future may not have as strong a focus on illicit trafficking as developed

countries—illicit trafficking is not necessarily the first, or even tenth, security concern in a developing country with a raft of security problems. Moreover, concerns with sovereignty and national pride may take precedence over safeguarding materials and preventing smuggling, as arguably happened with Russia's lack of enthusiasm for cooperating with the United States to safeguard the USSR's leftover weapons and materials in the early 1990s (Allison et al. 1996). Developing countries may be especially sensitive to doubts about their ability to run nuclear power plants securely if the answer is measures that would impede their economic development.

There also is the problem of the lack of clear-cut evidence, at least up to this point, of nonstate actors obtaining improvised nuclear devices. Gartzke (Chapter 10 in this volume) discusses "the dog that did not bark" when wondering about the absence of nuclear weapons transfers, the reluctance of many countries to share nuclear technology, and the small number of nuclear weapons states. Although radioactive trafficking incidents in general are fairly common, HEU and Pu smuggling is not, leading to a high noise-to-signal ratio in illicit trafficking. Of the 1,773 incidents reported to the IAEA between 1993 and 2009, 15 involved HEU or Pu, with the majority of incidents involving radioactive sources commonly used in hospitals and industry, or contaminated scrap metal (IAEA 2011). While all these incidents have some level of danger associated with them, the relative rarity of incidents that can lead directly to improvised nuclear devices may make it difficult to convince developing countries with other pressing security concerns to prioritize illicit trafficking. Given that many developing countries are struggling to deal with insurgency, conventional terrorism, and the like—dogs that are barking right now—it may take an actual attack using nuclear material to focus countries' attention on illicit trafficking, similar to what happened when Malaysia was embarrassed by revelations of its role in the A. Q. Khan network in 2004.

Coordinators and Smuggling Routes

The second main aspect of a nonstate proliferation network possibly affected by a nuclear resurgence or renaissance relates to the coordinators and routes used by nonstate proliferators to move the illicit goods from the suppliers to the buyers. Just as with suppliers, both the coordinators and the routes they use are shaped by the political environments of the countries in which they operate and through which they move. Here a major question is the extent to which coordinators have access to their own transportation infrastructure (or have state-provided alternatives) or are forced to use commercial transportation infrastructure, and how they deal with the state hostility they face as they use that infrastructure (or avoid it). In this regard, traffickers of nuclear materials are no different than conventional smugglers, not only in their strengths, but also in their weaknesses. There is, of course, the possibility that terrorists who have acquired nuclear materials will not bother to transport their materials out of the country from which they stole it, and instead use it against targets near the source. In that scenario, concerns about the security of sources of nuclear materials, as outlined in the first section, are more relevant. Where traffickers are attempting to move across international boundaries, coordinators and routes become critical. Accordingly, this chapter compares the probable routes and transportation tools of nonstate nuclear material trafficking networks to, first, those of drug traffickers, who are nonstate actors with access to substantial nonstate coordinating and transportation resources, and then to those of the A. Q. Khan nuclear component smuggling networks, whose access to state resources varied over time.

Returning to drug smuggling: The ability of traffickers to move heroin and cocaine around the world despite strenuous international efforts to stop them is well documented. At first glance, drug trafficking would seem a poor analogy for the possibility of limiting the spread of nuclear materials. Yet one similarity between drug trafficking and probable transnational nuclear trafficking networks is that the actors are both trying to move goods from a limited number of weak or failed states to other, sometimes distant, countries. This has direct consequences pertaining to the routes they take.

The main markets for cocaine and heroin are concentrated geographically in North America and Western Europe. As a result, on a global scale drug traffickers must move the contraband from a relatively small number of production points to a relatively small number of markets. In practice, this means that there are a limited number of major smuggling routes. It is possible, with enough enforcement, to raise the costs of moving drugs along any particular route to a sufficient level that smugglers are forced to look for other options. In the 1980s, for instance, the Colombian cartels smuggled cocaine into the United States via planes that landed in Florida. The success of ensuing Drug Enforcement Agency interdiction efforts drove the cartels to begin dropping batches of drugs in the ocean off the coast of Florida, and then ferrying them to land. Eventually, the cartels stopped using that route and switched to contracting with Mexican organized crime as middlemen (Kenney 2007: 49–51).

The lack of a state presence introduces not only opportunities for the drug traffickers, but also liabilities, especially inasmuch as "failed" areas also lack good transportation and economic infrastructure. This led the Revolutionary Armed Forces of Colombia, for instance, to build its own jungle runways for drug flights. Likewise, the United Wa State Army, which controls much of the failed territory in Myanmar used for the production and refinement of heroin, built factories, roads, plantations, and even entire cities to support its business (Rabasa and Chalk 2001; Zhang and Chin 2007; Chin 2009). The routes and methods that the traffickers then use to move the drugs out of the failed areas depend a great deal on the resources available to the traffickers, as well as the state capacity and infrastructure of the countries that line the path from the source areas to the buyer countries.

Most drug traffickers seem content to resort to slow and inefficient methods that nonetheless bypass state power. This is evidenced most vividly by smuggling tunnels under the Mexico-United States border dug by Mexican smuggling syndicates, or routes that take advantage of the transportation infrastructure provided by states but then rely on evading that same state power, such as the use of "mules" to move heroin from Myanmar to China and countries in Southeast Asia on regularly scheduled passenger flights (Dupont 1999; Hastings 2005b). To date, Colombian traffickers are the only drug traffickers that have successfully operated their own transportation infrastructure outside the areas they control. They have built submarines to move drugs off the coast of Colombia (Meserve 2008), have run planes and boats into Florida, and have used oceangoing vessels to transport drugs to the coastal islands of Equatorial Guinea, from which they fly planes bearing the drugs into southern Europe. They are able to do this largely because of the vast sums of money that can be derived from smuggling cocaine into North America and Western Europe. These funds allow them to buy aircraft and boats, and buy off a large percentage of the officials in poor, corrupt countries (Walt 2007).

Nuclear traffickers can use some of the same routes and methods as drug traffickers, but to do so they need access to the same resources enjoyed by drug traffickers. Drug traffickers depend on volume for their profits. This is not available to nuclear traffickers, who typically move bits of material at a time. It appears that the profits that can be derived from smuggling nuclear materials are but a fraction of the drug trade, especially cocaine trafficking. Libya's deal with A. Q. Khan for nuclear components and some nuclear material was apparently worth approximately US$100 million (Powell and McGirk 2005). By contrast, *each* drug smuggling submarine captured by the United States in a 2008 investigation held drugs worth US$196 million (Meserve 2008). To date, nuclear materials smuggling networks have thus been at the mercy of transportation infrastructure created and policed by states. It is not even clear what motivates buyers of nuclear material (unlike with drug users). Although the reporting is piecemeal, incidents where smugglers in Western Europe attempted to sell such materials seem to have been sporadic, disorganized (in the sense that organized crime syndicates were involved in only about 10 percent of them), and low-stakes (Zaitseva 2007). Studies of nuclear trafficking in Georgia likewise find that the smugglers are not experts in nuclear trafficking, but rather are experienced conventional smugglers who perceived a market for nuclear material and used legitimate transportation infrastructure, whereas organized crime syndicates have tended to stay away from the enterprise (Sockova and Potter 2007; Kupatadze 2010). In general, the extent to which there is a large-scale market for nuclear material is unclear, although smugglers simply believing there is one could encourage attempts to steal nuclear material (Hoskins 2007).

When smuggling goods, illicit nonstate actors face a trade-off between the security and efficiency of the route (Hastings 2008). While nuclear traffickers could in theory use tunnels underneath borders or move over water, through the mountains and jungle, in practice they often try to smuggle their goods through minor border checkpoints, as when in 1995 customs officials caught a man trying to smuggle HEU through a land checkpoint in Bulgaria (IAEA 2007). That is, smugglers use the roads (and therefore border checkpoints) that are built by governments to facilitate travel and therefore have to deal with the state directly, but they try to minimize the chance of being caught by crossing the border at points where state security measures might be lackadaisical or officials might be more easily bribed. According to Lyudmila Zaitseva's research, the early 1990s saw many nuclear smugglers apparently moving directly from the former Soviet Union to Western Europe by road or rail. In the wake of European government crackdowns, it appears that since the later 1990s Georgia, which is adjacent to both Russia and Turkey, has seen a number of nuclear material transshipment cases as smugglers have shifted to more indirect routes that pass through the Caucasus and the Middle East. Turkey itself also may be a transshipment hub, especially for material smuggled by ship through the Black Sea (Nabakhtiani et al. 2007; Zaitseva 2007).

To get to the point where smugglers have the resources to begin buying and running their own transportation infrastructure (and thus avoid dealing with hostile states), there would have to be a substantially larger and more consistent market for illicit nuclear material than presently exists. A larger supply of nuclear material would perhaps increase the chances that a given buyer might be successful at locating a seller. Without sufficient resources to do without infrastructure controlled by hostile states, however, the routes the smugglers use would continue to be at the mercy of state-controlled infrastructure and chokepoints.

If the conclusion in the first section is accurate and there will be a limited number of nuclear facilities in countries with low state capacity and/or political instability that could conceivably supply nuclear materials traffickers, then the routes they can take also will be somewhat limited, particularly if the traffickers do not have access to state resources allowing them to bypass established infrastructure and chokepoints. The effect of not having access to these resources can be seen in the smuggling networks set up by a different type of nuclear trafficker—A. Q. Khan—who largely traded in nuclear components (and several shipments of starter materials for enriching uranium) with states. At times they had access to states resources—diplomatic prerogatives and state-owned transportation infrastructure—for smuggling and at times they did not. As one of the few nuclear smuggling networks about which fairly detailed operational information is known, the A. Q. Khan networks are useful exemplars of how state prerogatives change the rules of the nuclear trafficking game.

The first network Khan created, on behalf of the Pakistani government in 1970s, used that government's state prerogatives to the fullest extent. Many of the acquisitions agents were based at or near Pakistani diplomatic outposts and were accredited diplomats (with the resulting diplomatic immunity). The routes taken by the nuclear components purchased by Pakistan's agents were direct. In the first year of Pakistan's quest for centrifuge components, nearly all of the components were shipped by the supplier companies directly to organizations in Pakistan. When a given component presented logistical difficulties, the Pakistani state intervened. When a Swiss company built the massive piping and feed system for Pakistan's centrifuge facility, for example, the Pakistan Air Force sent three C-130s to pick up the components and fly them directly to Pakistan (Weissman and Krosney 1981; Armstrong and Trento 2007; Frantz and Collins 2007). In short, Pakistan's brazenness and initial use of resources typically only available to states allowed it to avoid being subject to the constraints placed on nonstate actors by commercial transportation infrastructure.

As European and North American states cracked down on the direct export of nuclear components to Pakistan, Khan resorted to greater levels of subterfuge. This allowed him to continue his work but denied him the convenience of state prerogatives. As noted above, Pakistan began setting up front companies and employing middlemen. Components began to be ordered by British and German businessmen and shipped to front companies in Dubai by commercial transport; from there they were shipped to Pakistan (Weissman and Krosney 1981; Armstrong and Trento 2007).

This shift in the structure and nature of the transport network used to traffic components became even more pronounced as Khan turned his contacts and experience to acquiring components for Libya. Many of the suppliers (and middlemen) remained the same as during Khan's time working on the Pakistani nuclear program; but Khan was now without access to state prerogatives or state transportation infrastructure.[5] As a result, nearly the entire Libyan supply network was routed through front companies owned by Khan's associates in Dubai (Dahlkamp, Mascolo, and Stark 2006; Armstrong and Trento 2007). Khan twice shipped uranium hexafluoride canisters (totaling approximately two tons) as cargo on Pakistani airliners from Pakistan to Tripoli through Dubai. Most of the components, however, were sent from their suppliers to Dubai via regular commercial shipping, and then on to Libya, often through other ports to mask their origins (Frantz and Collins 2007).

That Dubai emerged as the hub of the nuclear component trafficking network was no accident. The emirate's political and economic environment and its place in global commercial transportation networks made it a logical choice for Khan and his associates. After Dubai's oil revenues declined in the 1970s, the government began encouraging foreign direct investment through low taxes and lax regulations in designated free-trade zones. Expatriates flocked to the country, leading to the one of the highest percentage of foreign-born residents in the world (Corera 2006; Central Intelligence Agency 2008). Such an environment was less likely to attract attention to foreign companies interested in keeping a low profile. Moreover, the nature of the hub-and-spoke structure of the global shipping system, and Dubai's position as the busiest transshipment port for cargo containers in the Middle East, meant that if any company had wanted to ship large quantities of goods on commercial cargo ships from Southeast Asia (notably Malaysia) to the Mediterranean, in all likelihood it would have gone through Dubai (American Association of Port Authorities 2006).[6] For Khan, setting up a logistical network to transport thousands of components around the world required finding countries with the right combination of political and economic conditions friendly to foreign front companies and centrality in the global supply chain.

What is striking, then, about A. Q. Khan's Libya supply network is how ordinary it was. Khan used various tricks to hide his tracks—multiple destinations, false shipping forms, and front companies—but once he was denied use of the Pakistani government's resources, he fell back on the same locations, infrastructure and methods used by regular commercial shippers. This allowed him to move nuclear components from the suppliers to Libya quickly and cheaply, but also resulted in a geographic centralization of his operation in Dubai, placing him at the mercy of infrastructure controlled by other actors.

Khan was mostly not trafficking in stolen nuclear materials, but his experience, and that of drug traffickers, suggests that the routes of nonstate nuclear materials traffickers, and the methods they can use for transporting those materials, are influenced by their access to resources. Without state support or a guarantee of a continuing, significant market for their product, nonstate nuclear materials traffickers will remain dependent on commercial transportation infrastructure, or will follow traditional smuggling routes that will not change as a result of either the deepening or broadening of the global nuclear landscape.

Implications and Policy Recommendations

The implications of this chapter depend on what happens in the future. If we continue along the current trajectory, we will likely see a few more potential sources of nuclear material in Russia and continued instability in Pakistan, both of which are serious, but neither of which present fundamentally new problems. If we witness a resurgence of nuclear power generation predominantly in existing nuclear energy countries, the result will be continued problems in countries such as Russia but little increase in the ability of nuclear traffickers to engage in state capacity arbitrage—choosing the weakest country from which to extract stolen materials—and little increase in the number or diversity of routes available to traffickers. Alternatively, if we experience a renaissance, with more potential nuclear material sources popping up in developing countries, this will likely enhance the ability of traffickers to prey on countries that have the optimal combination of corruption, low state capacity, high technological capacity, and transportation options.

In his commentary, Gartzke (Chapter 10 in this volume) wonders whether the structure of the market for nuclear technology might change if the nuclear renaissance takes hold, weakening the taboo on advanced countries sharing nuclear technology and increasing economic incentives to sell even sensitive technology. While Gartzke is primarily concerned about states purposefully transferring technology (or finished weapons), the spread of nuclear and dual-use technology production to middle-income states (such as Malaysia and Turkey, in the case of the A. Q. Khan network) could in the long run change the structure of the supply side for illicit trafficking of nuclear components. States eager to give their private companies a competitive advantage in the global market are prone to being less careful about policing nuclear and dual-use transfers.

As Gartzke notes, we should not assume that what happened in the past will necessarily occur in the future. With that said, this analysis of illicit trafficking networks suggests that even if there is a weakening of the taboo on sharing technology as the nuclear renaissance encourages the diffusion of nuclear technology and sources of nuclear materials, there are still constraints on the illicit trafficking market that are unlikely to change. Irrespective of whether we experience a nuclear energy resurgence or renaissance, the routes used by future nonstate proliferators to move nuclear materials will likely be little affected. Where Montgomery notes the difficulty neopatrimonial states have in absorbing a well-run nuclear weapons program (Chapter 7 in this volume), this chapter highlights the logistical challenges that both states and nonstate actors have in acquiring and then moving nuclear materials illicitly without resorting to state resources. In the case of nuclear materials smugglers, in particular, the lack of a large-scale market in such materials means that future smugglers will likely remain dependent on commercial transportation infrastructure. While would-be nonstate smugglers may be able to take advantage of new sources of nuclear goods in the event of a nuclear renaissance, it would be no easier to transport them without state resources unless the market, and thus the profit, associated with illicit nuclear goods expands significantly. If that happens, the framework used in this chapter suggests that nonstate proliferators may be able to acquire their own logistical infrastructure, much as the drug trafficking syndicates have, allowing them to avoid transportation chokepoints controlled by states. This would render the fight against nonstate proliferation considerably more complicated and increase the importance of supplier oversight.

Given the importance of the physical security of nuclear materials, and recognizing that successfully implementing full-scale regulations designed for developed countries in societies with high corruption and low state capacity is unrealistic, it would behoove developing countries to identify the nuclear facilities that, being near smuggling routes to likely targets, are most *logistically* vulnerable to sabotage or theft, and focus training and resources on their employees. Likewise, developing countries should concentrate their stockpiles of HEU and Pu in as few locations as possible. New facilities, to the extent possible, should be logistically inconvenient to smugglers (although this conflicts with the need for legitimate ease of access for the facility operators). Improving physical protection and strengthening materials control and accounting procedures in and around nuclear facilities are especially important. This would include pouring resources into strategically important border checkpoints, integrating border guards and national police into nuclear power development plans from the outset, paying the workers and guards at the plants adequately (perhaps even at developed world standards), and generally treating nuclear plants as the vanguards of countries' modernization drives.

Theft or purchase of nuclear material or components to make functioning nuclear devices is the primary concern of this chapter. It is not, however, the only way that nonstate actors can take advantage of the existence of civilian nuclear power to further their own goals. Terrorists could sabotage or otherwise attack nuclear facilities in order to release radiation (or even just instill a general mistrust of nuclear power in a population). Spent fuel ponds and nuclear reactors themselves, for instance, could, if sabotaged, be used as dirty bombs, with radioactive explosions emanating directly from the nuclear facility site (Alvarez et al. 2003). The resources and procedures needed to harden a nuclear facility against sabotage or forcible entry are not exactly the same as those designed to protect nuclear material from theft, although both require an attention to physical protection and materials control and accounting procedures, and rigorous implementation. Limiting the number of nuclear facilities in a developing country would decrease the resources that would have to be expended to protect them.

States involved in uranium enrichment and fuel fabrication present sources for nuclear material other than just reactors, and as such could increase the opportunities for nuclear material acquisition and trafficking. In general, the absolute amount of nuclear material in the world could increase, and it certainly would increase in countries that, on average, had more governance problems than current nuclear energy countries. Stulberg's chapter (Chapter 4 in this volume) on multilateral nuclear approaches thus raises the possibility of states (or nonstate allies of states) acquiring fuel out in the open. While this could in theory make nuclear materials easier to obtain, successful multilateral nuclear approaches also would decrease the number of countries with nonreactor nuclear facilities, as well as the number of countries with nuclear-specific technology (decreasing the number of potential suppliers for nuclear components), thus minimizing the number of nodes that can be compromised. This would, however, necessitate more transport of nuclear reactor fuel assemblies across international boundaries. In theory, this could provide more opportunities for terrorists and criminals to divert nuclear materials. Something similar occurred in 1997 when the Liberation Tigers of Tamil Eelam, one of the most resourceful terrorist groups in recent history, managed to win the contract to transport weapons ordered by the Sri Lankan government from Tanzania to Sri Lanka and instead diverted the weapons to territory held by the Liberation Tigers (Thompson and Turlej 2003: 46). One solution is to move nuclear materials using means and along routes that are less susceptible to diversion by nonstate actors—nuclear materials should be transported using state-owned vehicles outside of typical commercial routes and hubs. This would probably cost more than using commercial infrastructure and its associated transportation efficiencies.

There are already programs focused on improving nuclear facilities' physical protection and securing transportation hubs against nuclear proliferators. United Nations Security Council Resolution 1540 requires all countries to take action against nuclear proliferation and at least notionally encourages developed countries with expertise to help developing countries with their nonproliferation regulations and enforcement. The U.S. National Nuclear Security Administration's Megaports Initiative also places radiation detection equipment in ports around the world in a bid to scan United States–bound container traffic. Both programs would benefit from a targeted approach to implementation informed by analysis of the intersection with commercial trafficking routes, given the limited resources at the disposal of most developing countries.

Furthermore, to the extent that nuclear materials traffickers are genuinely nonstate actors who are moving across international boundaries, they will likely have to move according to the dictates of global transportation networks. Bringing countries that are transit hubs into the Nuclear Suppliers Group and the Proliferation Security Initiative, and developing methods of checking for dual-use shipments without undue pressure on cargo shipping networks, is also necessary. Of the countries hosting the top ten transshipment ports, four—Singapore, the United Arab Emirates, Taiwan, and Malaysia—are not members of the Nuclear Suppliers Group (Deutsche Bank Research 2006). This would focus the attention of countries that are instrumental in the logistics of nonstate nuclear trafficking networks on nuclear trafficking issues and encourage collaboration in synchronizing regulations dealing not only with the exportation of nuclear material but also their transshipment. While the future expansion of nuclear power may increase the number of locations of potential suppliers of illicit nuclear material, effectively stretching the regulatory resources of some of the developing countries seeking civil nuclear energy, an examination of the environments in which suppliers would operate and the routes traffickers would take suggests that there are measures that both developed and developing countries can take that will at least make traffickers' lives difficult.

Notes

1. As an industry group, clearly the WNA has an interest in maximizing the number of countries interested in nuclear power, but its estimates are useful in providing an upper limit on the number of emerging nuclear energy countries.

2. The database, like all incident reports of illicit activities, is subject to reporting bias (not only because certain states do not regularly report incidents, but also because often only smuggling operations that failed actually show up in databases) but gives the rough outlines of the sources, coordinators, and buyers in nuclear smuggling networks before the nuclear renaissance.

3. This table includes the partially dismantled Yongbyon reactor in North Korea.

4. Care should be taken with such reports (or lack thereof), given the incentives that states, particularly developing countries, have to not report security breaches at nuclear facilities or missing materials.

5. There is considerable controversy about whether high-level officials within the Pakistani government knew or approved of Khan's nonstate activities. For the purposes of this chapter, the more important point is that if they did, they did not help Khan very much with transportation.

6. The next largest transshipment port in the Middle East, far below Dubai, is Salalah in Oman.

References

Allison, Graham T., Owen R. Coté, Richard A. Falkenrath, and Steven R. Miller. 1996. *Avoiding Nuclear Anarchy: Containing the Threat of Loose Russian Nuclear Weapons and Fissile Material.* Cambridge, MA: MIT Press.

Alvarez, R., J. Beyea, K. Janberg, J. Kang, E. Lyman, A. Macfarlane, G. Thompson, and F. N. von Hippel. 2003. "Reducing the Hazards from Stored Spent Power-Reactor Fuel in the United States." *Science and Global Security* 11 (1): 1–51.

American Association of Port Authorities. 2006. *World Port Rankings—2006.* Alexandria, VA: American Association of Port Authorities.

Armstrong, David, and Joseph Trento. 2007. *America and the Islamic Bomb: The Deadly Compromise.* Hanover, NH: Steerforth Press.

Balatsky, G. I., and W. Severe. 2007. "Assessing the Phenomenon of Nuclear Trafficking." *IAEA International Conference on Illicit Nuclear Trafficking: Collective Experience and the Way Forward.* Edinburgh, UK, November 19.

Braun, Chaim, and Christopher F. Chyba. 2004. "Proliferation Rings: New Challenges to the Nuclear Nonproliferation Regime." *International Security* 29 (2): 5–49.

Bunn, Matthew. 2010. *Securing the Bomb 2010.* Cambridge, MA: Belfer Center for Science and International Affairs at Harvard University.

Central Intelligence Agency. 2008. *CIA World Factbook.* Langley, VA: Central Intelligence Agency.

Chin, Ko-Lin. 2009. *The Golden Triangle: Inside Southeast Asia's Drug Trade.* Ithaca, NY: Cornell University Press.

Corera, Gordon. 2006. *Shopping for Bombs: Nuclear Proliferation, Global Insecurity and the Rise and Fall of the A. Q. Khan Network.* Oxford, UK: Oxford University Press.

Dahlkamp, Juerge, Georg Mascolo, and Holger Stark. 2006. "Network of Death on Trial." *Der Spiegel*, March 13. Available at: http://www.spiegel.de/international/spiegel/a-q-khan-s-nuclear-mafia-network-of-death-on-trial-a-405847.html.

Department of Nuclear Energy. 2004. "Country Nuclear Power Profiles: Indonesia." Vienna: International Atomic Energy Agency.

Deutsche Bank Research. 2006. *Container Shipping: Overcapacity Inevitable Despite Increasing Demand.* Frankfurt, Germany: Deutsche Bank.

Dupont, Alan. 1999. "Transnational Crime, Drugs, and Security in East Asia." *Asian Survey* 39 (3): 433–455.

Ferguson, Charles, and William Potter. 2004. *The Four Faces of Nuclear Terrorism.* Monterey, CA: Monterey Institute for International Studies.

Flint, Colin. 2003. "Terrorism and Counterterrorism: Geographic Research Questions and Agendas." *The Professional Geographer* 55 (2): 161–169.

Frantz, Douglas, and Catherine Collins. 2007. *The Nuclear Jihadist.* New York: Twelve.

Hafner-Burton, Emilie M., Miles Kahler, and Alexander H. Montgomery. 2009. "Network Analysis in International Relations." *International Organization* 63 (3): 559–592.

HARMONY. 2007. *Al-Qaida's (Mis)Adventures in the Horn of Africa.* West Point, NY: Combating Terrorism Center, United States Military Academy.

Hastings, Justin. 2005a. Author Interview, Buddhist Pandita and Chinese-Indonesian Businessmen. Cipayung, Bogor, Indonesia. July.

———. 2005b. Author Interview, Customs Intelligence Officer. Hong Kong. November.

———. 2008. "Geography, Globalization, and Terrorism: The Plots of Jemaah Islamiyah." *Security Studies* 17 (3): 505–530.

Hersh, Seymour M. 2009. "Defending the Arsenal: In an Unstable Pakistan, Can Nuclear Warheads Be Kept Safe?" *The New Yorker*, November 16. Available at: http://www.newyorker.com/reporting/2009/11/16/091116fa_fact_hersh.

Hoskins, R. A. G. 2007. "Illicit Nuclear Trafficking: Collective Experience and the Way Forward." In *IAEA International Conference on Illicit Nuclear Trafficking: Collective Experience and the Way Forward.* Edinburgh, UK, November 19.

IAEA. 2007. *Combating Illicit Trafficking in Nuclear and Other Radioactive Material Reference Manual.* Vienna: IAEA.

———. 2009. *Energy, Electricity and Nuclear Power Estimates for the Period up to 2030.* Vienna: IAEA.

———. 2011. *ITDB Factsheet.* Vienna: IAEA.

Keck, Margaret E., and Kathryn Sikkink. 1998. *Activists Beyond Borders: Transnational Advocacy Networks in International Politics.* Ithaca, NY: Cornell University Press.

Kenney, Michael. 2007. *From Pablo to Osama: Trafficking and Terrorist Networks, Government Bureaucracies, and Competitive Adaptation.* State College: Pennsylvania State University Press.

Kliot, Nurit, and David Newman. Eds. 2000. *Geopolitics at the End of the Twentieth Century: The Changing World Political Map.* London: Frank Cass.

Krebs, Valdis. 2002. "Uncloaking Terrorist Networks." *First Monday* 7 (4). Available at: http://firstmonday.org/htbin/cgiwrap/bin/ojs/index.php/fm/article/view/941/863/.

Kupatadze, Alexander. 2010. "Organized Crime and the Trafficking of Radiological Materials: The Case of Georgia." *Nonproliferation Review* 17 (2): 219–234.

Luongo, Kenneth, and William Hoehn. 2005. "An Ounce of Prevention." *Bulletin of the Atomic Scientists* 61 (2): 29–35.

Meserve, Jeanne. 2008. "Cocaine Smugglers Turn to Submarines, Feds Say." *CNN*, September 19. Available at: http://articles.cnn.com/2008-09-19/justice/drug.subs_1_cocaine-smugglers-coast-guard-cocaine-laden?_s=PM:CRIME.

Miller, Steven E., and Scott D. Sagan. 2009. "Nuclear Power Without Nuclear Proliferation?" *Daedalus* 138 (4): 7–18.

Montgomery, Alexander H. 2005. "Ringing in Proliferation: How to Dismantle an Atomic Bomb Network." *International Security* 30 (2): 153–187.

Murphy, Alexander. 2003. "The Spaces of Terror." In *The Geographical Dimensions of Terrorism*, eds. Susan L. Cutter, Douglas B. Richardson, and Thomas J. Wilbanks. New York: Routledge.

Nabakhtiani, G., S. Kakushadze, Z. Rostomashvili, G. Kiknadze, and E. Andronikashvili. 2007. "The Problem of Illicit Nuclear Trafficking in Georgia." In *IAEA International Conference on Illicit Nuclear Trafficking: Collective Experience and the Way Forward*. Edinburgh, UK, November 19.

Nuclear Energy Institute. 1998. *The Source Book on Soviet-Designed Nuclear Power Plants*, 5th ed. Washington, DC: Nuclear Energy Institute.

Powell, Bill, and Tim McGirk. 2005. "The Man Who Sold the Bomb." *Time*, February 6. Available at: http://www.time.com/time/magazine/article/0,9171,1025193,00.html.

Rabasa, Angel, and Peter Chalk. 2001. *Colombian Labyrinth: The Synergy of Drugs and Insurgency and Its Implications for Regional Stability*. Santa Monica, CA: RAND.

Rabasa, Angel, Steven Boraz, Peter Chalk, Kim Cragin, Theodore W. Karasik, Jennifer D. P. Moroney, Kevin A. O'Brien, and John E. Peters. 2007. *Ungoverned Territories: Understanding and Reducing Terrorism Risks*. Santa Monica, CA: RAND.

Reuters. 2009. "U.S. Believes Pakistan Nuclear Arms Are Secure: Gates," December 6. Available at: http://www.reuters.com/article/2009/12/06/us-pakistan-usa-nuclear-idUSTRE5B50R820091206.

Rotberg, Robert. 2002. "The New Nature of Nation-State Failure." *The Washington Quarterly* 25 (3): 85–96.

Sageman, Marc. 2004. *Understanding Terror Networks*. Philadelphia: University of Pennsylvania Press.

Sokova, E. K., and W. C. Potter. 2007. "The 2003 and 2006 High Enriched Uranium Seizures in Georgia: New Questions, Some Answers and Possible Lessons." *IAEA International Conference on Illicit Nuclear Trafficking: Collective Experience and the Way Forward*. Edinburgh, UK, November 19.

Thompson, John C., and Joe Turlej. 2003. *Other People's Wars: A Review of Overseas Terrorism in Canada*. Toronto, ON: The MacKenzie Institute.

USGPO (United States Government Printing Office). 2009. "Proposed Agreement for Cooperation Between the Government of the United States of America and the Government of the United Arab Emirates Concerning Peaceful Uses of Nuclear Energy." Available at: http://www.fas.org/man/eprint/uae-nuclear.pdf.

Walt, Vivienne. 2007. "Cocaine Country." *Time*, 27 June. Available at: http://www.time.com/time/magazine/article/0,9171,1637719,00.html.

Weissman, Steve, and Herbert Krosney. 1981. *The Islamic Bomb: The Nuclear Threat to Israel and the Middle East*. New York: New York Times Books.

WNA (World Nuclear Association). 2012. *World Nuclear Power Reactors & Uranium Requirements*. Available at: http://www.world-nuclear.org/info/reactors.html.

Zaitseva, Lyudmila. 2007. "Organized Crime, Terrorism and Nuclear Trafficking." *Strategic Insights* 6 (5). Available at: http://www.nps.edu/Academics/centers/ccc/publications/OnlineJournal/2007/Aug/zaitsevaAug07.pdf.

Zaitseva, Lyudmila, and Kevin Hand. 2003. "Nuclear Smuggling Chains: Suppliers, Intermediaries, and End-Users." *American Behavioral Scientist* 46 (6): 822–844.

Zaitseva, Lyudmila, and Friedrich Steinhausler. 2003. *International Dimension of Illicit Trafficking in Nuclear and Other Radioactive Material*. Stanford, CA: Center for International Security and Cooperation, Stanford University.

Zhang, Sheldon X., and Ko-lin Chin. 2007. *The Chinese Connection: Cross-border Drug Trafficking between Myanmar and China*. Washington, DC: United States Department of Justice.

10 The Logic of Nuclear Patronage

A Comment

Erik Gartzke

NUCLEAR PROLIFERATION OFFERS SOMETHING OF A PLEASANT surprise for students of international security. Early projections suggested the near inevitability of numerous nuclear nations by this point in history (c.f., Kahn 1960; Beaton and Maddox 1962). Most countries have not attempted to produce or acquire nuclear capabilities, and of the few dozen that have, the majority abandoned their efforts prior to achieving any meaningful milestone. Some may argue that the lack of nuclear proliferation is evidence of the success of international efforts to limit the spread of nuclear capabilities (c.f., Müller, Fischer, and Kötter 1994; Sagan 1996/97, 2011). Nations with nuclear know-how have succeeded in denying others access to critical technology and materials, even as organizations like the International Atomic Energy Agency (IAEA) monitor and control the peaceful use of nuclear power. The nuclear genie has been kept in its jealously guarded bottle, thanks to the constraining effects of intergovernmental organizations (IGOs) and the reticence of most potential suppliers.

Unfortunately, this explanation is inconsistent with several salient facts. As the chapters in this section make clear, nuclear-capable nations have not been all that assiduous in keeping nuclear secrets to themselves. Countries with nuclear weapons, or with important nuclear technologies and skills, have sold or donated parts, equipment, training, and plans to states intent on proliferating. For several nations, "sensitive nuclear assistance" has made critical contributions to their quest to enter the nuclear club (Kroenig, Chapter 8 in this volume; Kroenig 2009a,b).

An even broader group of countries has sold the tools, techniques, materials, and fuel for peaceful nuclear power. Multinationals can build entire nuclear power infrastructures. These efforts are enthusiastically marketed by parent governments as a means of generating revenue, providing employment, and redressing an unfavorable balance of payments. As research makes clear, assistance with construction of nuclear power infrastructure increases the chances that a nation will "go nuclear," developing both electrical power and nuclear weapons (Fuhrmann 2009).

Agreements like the nuclear Non-Proliferation Treaty (NPT) or organizations like the IAEA and the United Nations were designed or developed to bar expansion of the nuclear franchise. Partisans point to the slow pace of proliferation as evidence that formal (institutional) or informal (normative) mechanisms have been a success (Sagan 1996/97; Rublee 2009; Sasikumar and Way 2010). While it may be tempting to credit the modest and incremental level of proliferation to these mechanisms, especially as they are tasked with resisting the spread of nuclear munitions, assertions about the impact of such efforts remain controversial.

We still do not know whether there is a mighty tide of potential proliferators that has been thwarted by international and national efforts, or whether the lack of proliferation is due to internal (national) factors, including the limited fungibility of such weapons, their cost, and other factors. Without criticizing the motives or the potential contribution of such efforts, it may be reasonable to note limitations in the evidence crediting IGOs and other international and national entities with having prevented proliferation. The IAEA, for example, has often failed to identify proliferators, even late in the process. North Korea and Iran simply did not disclose the existence of sensitive nuclear facilities, and thus these sites were not subject to inspections. Though the inspection criteria have since been strengthened, lapses such as these indicate that safeguards were inadequate and that these organizations by themselves are not likely to be the major reason for the absence of nuclear proliferation. Of those states that were eventually cited by the IAEA, many have continued their efforts to acquire nuclear weapons, being thwarted (or not) only by the additional intervention of prominent states or coalitions. In any case, nations intent on proliferation could simply have avoided voluntary organizations like the IAEA, as India, Israel and Pakistan have done, or withdrawn their membership, as North Korea has done and as Iran has threatened to do, if the IAEA intends to impose punitive sanctions.

Other factors must account for the scarcity of nuclear-equipped nations today, as well as the persistence of proliferation by other nations in the face of efforts by states and institutions to prevent the spread of nuclear weapons, especially as those seeking to proliferate are often helped by the very governments that purportedly seek to combat the spread of nuclear weapons. The duality of incentives confronting nuclear producers that I discuss below may precipitate an internal conflict about the efficaciousness of counterproliferation efforts, possibly even undermining the norms and institutions that these nations purport to champion.

A strong case for the impact of international institutions or norms can be made for states that never intended to proliferate. These mechanisms might matter most when helping to stiffen the resolve of nations that are not inclined to proliferate, or by addressing prisoners' dilemmas produced by proliferation. A country could be willing to refrain from proliferating if it can be ascertained that other states are behaving likewise (Brown 2008). Monitoring and sanctions can have an effect by working to signal participants of defections, giving other states the opportunity to react in kind if counterproliferation is necessary.

Yet this argument again implies that most countries are not that inclined to proliferate. It seems that most states either cannot or do not want to own the bomb. Explaining the behavior of the few states that have actually proliferated, then, or that might be expected to in the future, may be as much about accounting for why most states have no desire to possess or do not know how to produce nuclear weapons as it is about explaining the behavior of those that can and do. Indeed, as research in the preceding section makes clear, nations may even be hindered in their efforts to proliferate by the impact of external assistance (Montgomery, Chapter 7 in this volume). Building nuclear weapons is hard work, and most nations simply cannot "try this at home."

We thus face a conundrum whose explication is at once critical and informative in trying to understand proliferation in the twenty-first century. The research offered by the authors in this section provides important insights into how proliferation works and where it fails. The studies fill key conceptual and empirical gaps in showing that many proliferators seek out, and obtain, various kinds of assistance from nuclear-capable nations or networks. The riddle of the nonproliferating state is made even more acute, then, when we relax the assumption that nations must build their own nuclear weapons (as they have to date) and allow that not all proliferation need be conducted under autarchic economic conditions. If nations get help in their efforts to build nuclear infrastructure (as the notion of a nuclear renaissance suggests) and even to make the bomb, then why do we not see more proliferation, and in particular more nuclear assistance, than we in fact observe? The effects of the market in civilian nuclear power and the transfer, sale, or smuggling of sensitive nuclear technologies exacerbate the difficulties in explaining why nations have refrained, at least to date, in supplying or selling completed nuclear weapons.

Buying the Bomb

Nuclear nations do not give or sell nuclear weapons to other countries, let alone nonstate actors. No instance has been documented of the transfer of a nuclear device from one state to another, let alone the transfer of a nuclear device to an individual or group, such as a terrorist organization.[1] If nuclear-capable nations already disseminate nuclear know-how, then why should they exhibit this apparent reluctance to sell or share the finished product? There are large, active markets in the sale or transfer of diverse and often technologically sophisticated conventional weapons. Governments, or firms under the supervision of governments, sell parts, technology, and knowledge; but to a considerable extent, conventional arms are transferred or sold as finished products. Whether the reader prefers a logic of profit or influence, the behavior of nuclear-capable nations is inconsistent with the expectations of the broader logic of weapons sales or influence peddling. At the same time, nuclear assistance does not appear to fit the stated objective of nuclear nations and IGOs of limiting the spread of nuclear capabilities. If nuclear-capable states are cheating by selling nuclear knowledge and equipment that assist nations in proliferating, then why not just sell finished weapons systems, as many of these same states regularly do with conventional arms? Conversely, if nuclear-capable countries are reluctant to see the spread of nuclear weapons, then why are these same states in the (often tacit) business of helping other countries acquire the components and skills to build nuclear devices?

Resolving the apparent contradiction of neither going all the way as a nuclear supplier, nor exercising more substantial restraint in the sale or transfer of nuclear power and sensitive nuclear technologies and training involves the contradictory objectives of potential nuclear suppliers. As with many choices, nations with nuclear power or weapons capabilities have dual interests that cannot simultaneously be satisfied. On one hand, nuclear nations constitute a small club. Members or supporters prefer to maintain the exclusivity of their membership. At least some of the advantages of being a nuclear power stem from the fact that other nations are not nuclear powers. Disseminating nuclear capabilities weakens the franchise while damaging the appeal of the logroll among nuclear nations to limit the diffusion of these capabilities. If the United States had supplied nuclear weapons to West Germany, Japan, or even Turkey, what would keep the Soviet Union from providing East Germany, China, or Cuba with similar capabilities? Cold War adversaries instead decided to keep a close hold on the nuclear franchise, arranging to deploy their weapons in sensitive regions but maintaining operational control. Supplying nuclear weapons to other nations is costly because of the tremendous strategic impact of nuclear capabilities, because of the problem of principal agency (how does one nation know or control what another will do with these capabilities?), and because it invites an ever broader and more general degradation of the nonproliferation logroll.

On the other hand, the very scarcity of nuclear capabilities adds to their appeal. Money can be made, jobs provided, and influence peddled. Nuclear weaponry could be shared or sold for power and profit. In this sense, the nuclear proliferation business is much like any other industry, as producers compete to capture markets and cement relationships. The incentives to participate in the nuclear trade may be those of the profiteer, or the mobster—if our nation does not accommodate demand, others will, and after all our participation cannot make or break the global effort to counter proliferation—but these incentives are also part of a familiar social conundrum. Nuclear nations, and those with nuclear technologies, belong to a cartel, raising prices and limiting supply in a way that also eats at the very logic of the process. Limiting access to the bomb serves to provide smugglers and other expedients a tidy profit, even as collective action undermines the social good of limiting proliferation (Hastings, Chapter 9 in this volume).

The result is, or should be, a curvilinear relationship between proliferation, nuclear sales or assistance, and national interests. On one dimension is what might be called the categorical impact of the transfer of nuclear technology or capabilities. Nations that appear likely to proliferate eventually regardless of whether they receive nuclear assistance pose a low cost to nuclear-capable states to profit from this eventuality. In these cases, such as perhaps Israel, the transfer of nuclear technologies is helpful and therefore valuable to the recipient in expediting the fruition of the proliferation effort, but it does not ultimately change history in the sense of making a state a nuclear power when it would not otherwise be. Since nuclear assistance does not alter the eventual status of the recipient state, only the timing of the change in status, the provision or sale of assistance can be seen by the provider as less pernicious. Indeed, because the actions of a firm or nation in violating norms and legal requirements not to proliferate are unlikely to actually produce proliferation where none would occur otherwise, there may be competition to act as the provider of nuclear technologies and equipment. The leverage of a recipient of nuclear assistance is also greatly enhanced if the recipient does not need assistance in order to eventually succeed in obtaining the bomb.

In contrast, supplying finished weapons is problematic precisely because complete devices are most valuable to states that would not be able to proliferate in the absence of a market for nuclear weapons. Selling bits and pieces, but not finished products, ensures providers that they are affecting at most the timing of nuclear proliferation but not serving directly as enablers. Nations that are unlikely to proliferate without substantial assistance (those that require the sale or transfer of finished nuclear devices in order to obtain any nuclear weapons capabilities) pose too great a cost to nuclear-capable nations, because proliferators diffuse the franchise and encourage further diffusion by other, competing nuclear powers. Despite considerable effort and wealth, Libya was unable to procure complete nuclear weapons. Libya's effort to develop its own nuclear weapons was also unsuccessful. Limited nuclear assistance, along with the refusal to sell or provide completed nuclear devices, has ensured that no new nuclear power has been created that would not otherwise have become a nuclear power. This is in the interest of established nuclear states, though the incentives to refrain from providing any form of assistance are insufficient, in part because the number of states that can render partial assistance is much greater than the number of states that can offer a partner completed nuclear weapons. The norm of not providing whole nuclear weapons is self-enforcing as long as the loss of welfare from diffusion of nuclear capabilities remains high and the likelihood of reciprocation by other powers is sufficiently potent to deter. This balance will likely decline over time, however, as more states proliferate, simultaneously increasing potential suppliers of nuclear capabilities and reducing the marginal cost of allowing yet more states to join the nuclear club.

The second dimension of the curvilinear relationship between providers and recipients of nuclear know-how and equipment involves interests. As should be obvious, nations with incompatible interests do not help one another proliferate. The United States did not assist China with its nuclear program, but it did help the United Kingdom. The Soviet Union assisted China, but withdrew its support as the interests of the two powers began to diverge. Even with similar interests, it does not follow that a nuclear-capable country will assist a nuclear aspirant. Distributing completed nuclear weapons dilutes the franchise, as noted above. Indeed, if two nations have very similar interests, the temptation for the nuclear-capable country may be to offer nuclear protection rather than to provide aid or trade in developing indigenous nuclear weapons. The United States preferred to cover NATO and its Asian allies with a "nuclear umbrella" rather than encourage preliminary efforts at nuclear proliferation among its protégés (although the United States did support a buildup in conventional weapons, particularly those that complemented the United States' conventional and nuclear capabilities). Having similar interests means that the protégé need have less fear of being abandoned, while both patron and protégé benefit from scale economies and comparative advantage in the provision of nuclear security. During the Cold War, Japan and most of NATO found it advantageous for the United States to build a larger nuclear arsenal and then to "trade" protection for access to bases and other forms of accommodation. Tensions with North Korea caused Japan to reconsider its nuclear status, though reassurances that the United States remains a committed protector led Japan to again defer proliferation.

One can infer from this argument that nations with compatible, but not necessarily similar, interests are the most likely to trade nuclear technologies. France, for example, assisted the Israeli nuclear program. Israel was going to acquire nuclear weapons eventually in any case. France could not prevent Israeli proliferation by credibly promising to protect Israel against other states in the Middle East. Nor could France credibly threaten to take actions that would deter or prevent Israel from proliferating. While not a direct benefit to French national security, Israeli nuclear ambitions were also not a substantial threat. Since France was neither intent on protecting Israel nor on protecting Israeli's enemies, and since the two nations had some common or complementary objectives, providing sensitive nuclear assistance was a pragmatic choice. Similarly, the Soviet Union aided China's nuclear program while failing to assist other allies with more, or significantly less, sophisticated industrial infrastructures. The closeness of ties to Warsaw Pact nations meant that a Soviet nuclear umbrella was more efficient in both economic and geostrategic terms. The Soviet deterrent was credible and practical. In other cases, clients like Vietnam and Egypt lacked the capability of producing nuclear weapons. Assistance would not have proven effective, while providing nuclear weapons violated the objective of limiting proliferation to those nations where proliferation could not be prevented. China alone received significant Soviet nuclear assistance because it was in the unique position of being able to capitalize on help while requiring its own autonomous nuclear capabilities due to critical differences of interest between the two major communist powers. In contrast, Cuba was given Soviet nuclear protection, even including the famous abortive deployment of Soviet-controlled long- and intermediate-range ballistic missiles at San Cristobal, but the request from Cuba for control of these or other Soviet-built nuclear weapons was refused.

Another indicator resides in the strange phenomenon that countries that cannot provide nuclear protection, but which have sophisticated nuclear industries, appear paradoxically to be even more likely to assist other states in proliferating. Both Iraqi and Iranian nuclear aspirations have received considerable assistance from European sources but less so from key European nuclear powers than from non-nuclear weapons states. Countries that have advanced nuclear technologies but no nuclear weapons capabilities are not in a position to guarantee a foreign state's national security. Nor are non-proliferating but technologically advanced countries likely to view a slight broadening of the nuclear franchise as fundamentally problematic in terms of their own national security interests. Where nuclear powers have considerable interest in limiting the acquisition of nuclear capabilities (proliferation degrades the ability of existing states to deter or compel), countries with nuclear knowledge but no nuclear weapons pay a more diffuse *social cost* for aiding proliferation in the form of ecological risks of nuclear war, and so forth. However, while another nuclear-capable country may certainly be a bad thing for the international community, it only harms the interests of a non-nuclear state if the recipient of weapons, assistance, or aid is itself an adversary of the recipient nation. Iraq and Iran are unlikely to target Belgium with newly acquired nuclear capabilities, while assistance provided by Germany, say, by itself again does not fundamentally alter the likelihood that Iraq or Iran will be successful in their attempts to proliferate. Iran will soon possess nuclear weapons, while Iraq will not, regardless of the actions of any nation in providing technology to either nuclear aspirant.

Enemies are unlikely to receive nuclear assistance because conflict discounts the future. Not only the status of nuclear states is salient, but also the timing. Russia can supply Iran with a nuclear reactor and other assistance because Russian officials reason that Iranian nuclear weapons are an eventuality, and because Iran is unlikely to turn its nuclear weapons on Russia. The timing of the Iranian (or Syrian) ascension to nuclear status is much more salient to Israel. On occasion, Israel has used military power to delay the nuclear aspirations of its enemies. The bombing of the Iraqi Osirak reactor in 1981 was widely viewed to be a stopgap measure, delaying but not preventing Iraqi nuclear aspirations. While the Israelis no doubt would have been delighted to see Iraq permanently denied nuclear capabilities, even a delay for an enemy is of considerable strategic value. This implies that adversaries should be extremely reluctant to assist each other in developing nuclear weapons. Enemies should be sensitive about the timing of nuclear ascension, attempting to thwart assistance from other sources even when nuclear assistance is not pivotal for successful proliferation.

The Dog That Did Not Bark

Nuclear weapons are not yet ubiquitous. In more than six decades, no nation has donated or sold a complete nuclear weapon to another state, let alone a nonstate actor. During this same period, countless billions of dollars worth of conventional armaments have changed hands, traded or transferred between states, organizations, and groups. The absence of a market in nuclear weapons is all the more remarkable because of the sale or exchange of dual-use technologies and even nuclear weapons plans and parts. Researchers have made strides in understanding the nature of the trade in nuclear equipment and know-how. Studies in this volume help explain how parts and materials find their way from producers to the end users through either authorized or informal networks. The work suggests that states are not primarily interested in the economic rewards of sharing nuclear secrets. Indeed, the assistance of nuclear-capable states may be counterproductive, as Montgomery suggests. The lack of narrow economic interest by major nuclear states may help explain both the absence of a developed nuclear weapons market and the rise of informal networks of covert agents involved in marketing nuclear materials.

Still, this does not mean that nuclear proliferation will continue to be modest in the future, or that the fears of early nuclear pioneers were unjustified. The studies in this section paint a relatively benign picture of the security implications of a renaissance in nuclear power generation. Each contributor draws heavily on existing conditions in concluding that the nuclear energy renaissance will generally be benign in terms of nuclear weapons proliferation. As I have suggested, however, the incentives for states to assist other states in nuclear weapons programs is roughly inversely proportional to what should be their valuation for the exclusivity of the nuclear franchise. Nuclear weapons states are paradoxically less eager to provide assistance than states with nuclear knowledge but no nuclear weapons. As nuclear skills and technology diffuse further, more nations will become able to provide at least nonsensitive assistance, and the taboo for provisioning such aid will decline further as it is more readily available. Even nuclear weapons states may find that private incentives for limiting the nuclear franchise will be less intense as the nuclear genie continues to seep out of the bottle. Incentives for nuclear-capable nations to refrain from helping friends will also decline as the logroll among existing nuclear states weakens with the introduction of new, more marginal nuclear powers. The United States, in particular, will find its role as leader of the counterproliferation movement strained as the once uniform incentive to keep the nuclear club exclusive gives way to parochial interests. U.S. attempts to counter proliferation are already in tension with the interests of other states. It may increasingly find itself in an isolated position, attempting to stem a tide that all agree should not occur but which individual providers find expedient to accommodate, particularly if it appears that a nation will cross the nuclear threshold one way or the other.

While much can be learned by looking at what is, there are circumstances where more insight can be gleaned by asking why something is absent. Researchers can gain an understanding of the nature of nuclear proliferation by asking why nations that sell nuclear technology to other countries also fail to do more. Most countries with nuclear know-how do not sell or provide knowledge, tools, or materials to most other states. The selectivity of the nuclear market has been lauded for normative reasons, without thorough assessment of what can restrain states from treating nuclear weapons like more conventional military equipment. The temptation to assign this effect to informal (norms/taboos) or formal (international institutions/hegemony) barriers is not without substance, but it is no less a temptation; we should not treat coincidence as evidence of cause, especially when other factors, such as the structural context, have yet to be factored in as possible determinants.

Nuclear suppliers are not primarily driven by economic motives—at least not yet. The risk that the nuclear renaissance will put nuclear technology in the hands of more actors, some of whom might be willing to market proliferation, has already been contemplated, and to a degree discounted, here. My concern is that this assumes agency without structure. If part of the reason that nations with nuclear know-how today only provide skills and equipment selectively, it may be because the social embargo is seen as relatively effective. In the same way that the NPT is thought to logroll nonproliferation on the demand side, informal and formal instruments discourage suppliers from providing nuclear assistance on the supply side *as long as these efforts are seen as effectual and mutually supporting.* No nuclear nation supplies nuclear weapons because no other nation does. The supply-side logroll is effective when and where each potential supplier nation sees that no other supplier will offer or sell assistance. Where nations appear likely to proliferate anyway, the logroll is not effective. Similarly, where nations have private incentives to assist states in proliferating, the impact of the logroll is marginal, preventing assistance where extended strategic deterrence is credible, or where a state probably will not be able to build its own nuclear weapons. The logroll fails where a state can credibly claim that it will succeed in an autonomous proliferation attempt and where a supplier has no direct interest in preventing proliferation. As the number of actors that can provide nuclear assistance (supply) or have the basic infrastructure to build the bomb (demand) grows, the supply-side logroll may weaken and fracture. Even if the nuclear renaissance does not alter the distribution of preferences among nuclear-capable countries, it could very well affect the structure of the tacit nuclear market, opening the floodgates for more states to proliferate, as supply and demand meet.

The sale or transfer of nuclear technology thus poses trade-offs between benefits and costs, which must be balanced in discussing the strategic implications of the nuclear renaissance. Evidence provided here seems to make clear that suppliers' primary interest is influence, at least at present. States with nuclear technology seem to walk a fine line between providing uniquely valuable insights and equipment, and openly abetting nuclear weapons proliferation. At times, security concerns would be maximized by the provision of actual nuclear weapons. Economic motives imply far more general efforts to supply marketable goods and services to any recipient with funding. Moral concerns might mitigate against any assistance; if a nation is really serious about preventing proliferation, then the most effective method appears to be nuclear abstinence. Thus, giving recipients some but not all of the tools and techniques for proliferation seems to be an optimal compromise for many supplier states.

There remain other questions raised by the three studies. It will be useful to learn about how assistance is actually converted into influence and how complementary aspects of assistance (sensitive and nonsensitive) interact. Are these complements (countries tend to receive both sensitive and nonsensitive aid from the same suppliers) or substitutes? If there are differences in the patterns of sensitive and nonsensitive, formal versus informal assistance, what explains them? Have these differences evolved or changed over time? Of course, these questions must await future inquiry by scholars.

I have attempted here a sketch of a study of a non-event, the causes of nuclear weapons arms sales. It seems an enormous blessing that no such market exists, yet we do not know why. As I hope I have suggested, while we can learn a great deal from studies in this section that address existing nuclear markets, it seems that we can learn even more by extending the scale of behaviors to what suppliers should arguably practice but do not do. Just as the evidence provided in this section suggests that economic incentives alone are not sufficient to account for the transfer or sale of nuclear skills and equipment, an absence of nuclear arms sales implies that security is also not the main reason for suppliers to share nuclear technology. Making a friend safer would best be accomplished by handing them the bomb. The presence of sensitive sales suggests that there are also problems with the strength at least of normative arguments against supplying nuclear technology. Instead, it appears that some complex combination of these motives best explains existing practices. Future research will help to further unravel these relationships and may explain what we do not see in the realm of nuclear proliferation as well as what we actually observe.

Notes

1. The emphasis here is on the transfer of a complete nuclear weapon system. This is not to suggest that significant weapons-related material has not been changed

international hands. For example, the 1958 US-UK Mutual Defence Agreement did permit exchange of classified information relevant to improving the nuclear weapons of the parties, as well as the transfer of sensitive nuclear material, components, and non-nuclear parts of atomic weapons. Although not a formal transfer of a nuclear weapons device, the United States did sell Polaris and Trident missiles, as well as allowed the United Kingdom to base development of an indigenous warhead on transferred technology that was related to the W28 warhead in the 1960s.

References

Beaton, Leonard, and John Maddox. 1966. *The Spread of Nuclear Weapons*. London: Chatto and Windus for the International Institute for Strategic Studies.

Brown, Robert. 2008. "Nonproliferation through Delegation." Ph.D. Dissertation, University of California, San Diego.

Fuhrmann, Matthew. 2009. "Spreading Temptation: Proliferation and Peaceful Nuclear Cooperation Agreements." *International Security* 34 (1): 7–41.

Kahn, Herman. 1960. *On Thermonuclear War*. Princeton, NJ: Princeton University Press.

Kroenig, Matthew. 2009a. "Exporting the Bomb: Why States Provide Sensitive Nuclear Assistance." *American Political Science Review* 103 (1): 113–133.

———. 2009b. "Importing the Bomb: Sensitive Nuclear Assistance and Nuclear Proliferation." *Journal of Conflict Resolution* 53 (2): 161–180.

Müller, Harald, David Fischer, and Wolfgang Kötter. 1994. *Nuclear Non-Proliferation and Global Order*. New York: Oxford University Press.

Rublee, Maria Rost. 2009. *Nonproliferation Norms: Why States Choose Nuclear Restraint*. Athens: University of Georgia Press.

Sagan, Scott D. 1996/97. "Why Do States Build Nuclear Weapons? Three Models in Search of a Bomb." *International Security* 21 (3): 54–86.

———. 2011. "The Causes of Nuclear Weapons Proliferation." *Annual Review of Political Science* 14: 225–244.

Sasikumar, Karthika, and Christopher Way. 2010. "Paper Tigers or Barrier to Proliferation? What Accessions Reveal about NPT Effectiveness." Ithaca, NY: Cornell University.

III THE NUCLEAR RENAISSANCE, INTERNATIONAL CRISES, AND VIOLENT CONFLICT

11 Nuclear Weapons Programs and the Security Dilemma

Kyle Beardsley and Victor Asal

WHILE THE FUKUSHIMA NUCLEAR DISASTER OF 2011 CAST a pall on calls for a nuclear energy renaissance in parts of the developed world, the increasing demand for energy in the developing world means that many countries are still considering the prospects for new or enhanced nuclear power capability. This ongoing move toward civilian nuclear power may potentially lead to an increase in the spread of nuclear weapons programs (NWPs).[1] While debate exists about whether and to what extent civilian programs and sensitive nuclear assistance will lead to the spread of such weapons programs, as seen in the chapters in this volume by Fuhrmann (Chapter 3), Montgomery (Chapter 7), and Kroenig (Chapter 8), it is worth considering how NWPs affect the strategic behavior of states.[2] We build on the basic logic of the security dilemma to form testable expectations of how NWPs might threaten stability in the international system.

This chapter examines whether the basic logic of the security dilemma applies to nuclear proliferation and takes up the question of whether proliferation attempts are causes for concern to international stability. There is anecdotal evidence that proliferation, or the threat thereof, destabilizes the international system in a way that fits into a security dilemma perspective. A cursory glance at the history of those states that developed nuclear weapons might suggest that proliferation begets proliferation as states threaten the security of others while trying to maximize their own. One common story is that Nazi Germany's nuclear program created the impetus for the American and Soviet programs; then Britain, France, and eventually Israel and South Africa proliferated in response to the Soviet threat; China proliferated in response to the American and Soviet threats; India proliferated in response to the Chinese nuclear capability; Pakistan proliferated in response to India's program; North Korea proliferated in response to fear of American weapons; and Iran is likely to attain nuclear weapons in response to the Israeli and American nuclear threats (Sagan 1996/97; Meyer 1984; Williams and Cantelon 1984).[3] Indeed, it was the fear of such a chain reaction that compelled most states to back the Nuclear Non-Proliferation Treaty (NPT) before the number of nuclear states multiplied (Müller, Fischer, and Kötter 1994).

That nuclear proliferation has an important relationship with security concerns has been extensively studied. However, the bulk of this scholarship has either focused on how security concerns lead to the development of nuclear weapons (Sagan 1996/97; Singh and Way 2004; Jo and Gartzke 2007; Fuhrmann 2009; Kroenig 2009) or how the possession of nuclear weapons influences the behavior of potential opponents (Intrilligator and Brito 1984; Betts 1987; Powell 1987, 1988, 1990; Jervis 1989; Geller 1990; Asal and Beardsley 2007; Beardsley and Asal 2009a,b; Gartzke and Jo 2009; Horowitz 2009; Rauchhaus 2009). Much less is understood regarding the impact of NWPs on the security concerns of other states in the international system. Since many states have sought but never attained nuclear weapons, and since the United States and its allies are at crisis with Iran over its almost-certain NWP, it is worth considering the consequences of such programs.

This chapter argues that the mere pursuit of nuclear weapons provides a security threat to potential opponents. The security threat, however, is not the existential one typically assumed in accounts of the security dilemma but rather a general fear that successful proliferation will confer substantial bargaining leverage, especially through enhanced deterrence capabilities. In this way, NWPs are more destabilizing than nuclear weapons themselves. A state that has an NWP challenges the status quo establishment of nuclear powers, while a state that already has nuclear weapons is simply part of that status quo establishment. Weapons programs do not in themselves give states additional bargaining power, but they carry a strong potential for greater bargaining power in the future. This is what threatens the interests of other states in the system. We find empirically that NWP states prove threatening to their potential opponents, who become more likely to enter into a militarized crisis with a proliferating state. The results confirm our basic theoretical framework informed by an understanding of the security dilemma.

Athens and Sparta in the Nuclear Age

The security dilemma—defined as the inability of states to increase their own security without threatening the security of others—has been understood to be a fundamental driver of international politics since ancient times. In explaining the Peloponnesian War, Thucydides describes a security dilemma, even if that terminology had not been invented yet, when arguing, "The real cause I consider to be the one which was formally most kept out of sight. The growth of the power of Athens, and the alarm which this inspired in Lacedaemon, made war inevitable" (Thucydides 431 BCE). Does the nuclear age change the logic and importance of the security dilemma? Waltz (1979) argues in *The Theory of International Politics* that, fundamentally, nuclear weapons do not change the basic logic laid down by Thucydides.[4]

The security dilemma plays an important role in understanding NWPs, which create windows of vulnerability and opportunities for aggression from other states in the system. By this we mean that states will feel threatened by proliferating states that pursue nuclear weapons status because, once achieved, the weapons will alter the distribution of bargaining power between the proliferators and their potential opponents. So, as states attempt to acquire nuclear weapons capabilities to increase their own security, they threaten the security of others. One important feature of this argument is that we are not, as is typically the case in discussions of the security dilemma, talking about an existential threat but rather a more political threat of leverage over international affairs.

The primary means by which nuclear weapons enhance an actor's ability to secure better bargains is through their deterrence potential. Classical deterrence theorists such as Schelling (1966), Snyder and Diesing (1977), Intrilligator and Brito (1984), Gaddis (1986), Powell (1987, 1988, 1990), Jervis (1989), and Waltz (1990; see also Sagan and Waltz 2002), while disagreeing on other matters, tend to argue that the potential costs of nuclear attack are so great that restraint from opponents of nuclear states follows. Even Zagare and Kilgour (2000), using perfect deterrence theory to demonstrate that nuclear weapons are probably not as stabilizing as the classical deterrence scholars expect, contend that nuclear weapons have the potential to increase the costs of conflict of their opponents and enhance their success in coercive diplomacy. Consistent with these expectations, previous work has shown empirically that nuclear weapons restrain opponents of nuclear states (Asal and Beardsley 2007; Beardsley and Asal 2009a; Rauchhaus 2009).

In another study, we found that nuclear weapons can increase the ability of states to prevail in their crises (Beardsley and Asal 2009b).[5] Related to the argument that nuclear weapons can deter potentially hostile states, the logic is that the possession of nuclear weapons increases the expected costs of aggressive bargaining by an opponent, which then encourages opponents of nuclear states to back down more often. Even though the use of nuclear weapons is rarely credible, having some probability, however small, that they might be used can be enough to affect the decision calculus of an opponent because the costs of potential use are so prodigious.

The ability of nuclear weapons possession to allow states to push harder and act more aggressively also has been highlighted in a number of historical cases. For example, Stalin repeatedly refused Kim Il-Sung's request to invade South Korea until after the Soviet Union tested its own nuclear weapons (Ochmanek and Schwartz 2008). Ochmanek and Schwartz also point to China's attack on the Soviet Union border in 1969—after China attained nuclear weapons. Nuclear weapons can embolden states in their crisis behavior.

This chapter maintains that the impact of nuclear weapons on the bargaining environment is primarily via deterrence rather than compulsion. A nuclear strike will be difficult to rationalize when the nuclear state is the sole aggressor as opposed to when a nuclear state is defending a basic value (Betts 1987; Zagare and Kilgour 2000). Even without much potential for use as a compellent, other states will still feel threatened by the extent to which nuclear weapons improve a state's bargaining position via deterrence. When a state acquires nuclear weapons, other states will be less able and less willing to use aggressive coercive diplomacy to attain desired outcomes. In the long run, this can decrease the influence and security of non-nuclear weapons states.

Potential opponents of NWP states, thus, become disadvantaged upon the successful acquisition of the nuclear weapons, as those opponents will be less able to extract concessions through challenges to the status quo. Following this logic of NWPs offering the promise of better deterrence capability once weapons are developed, we expect nuclear programs to prove destabilizing to the international system for two reasons. First, other states might try to prevent that shift in bargaining power from occurring through preventive action

(Fuhrmann and Kreps 2010).[6] Even if states are seeking weapons benignly as a deterrent, they cannot credibly threaten to not use any acquired weapons to improve the bargains they get in the future. This then gives the other actors in the system an incentive to try to prevent a program state from achieving weapons development. Similarly, Powell (2006) argues that the anticipation of future power shifts, a type of commitment problem, serves as a crucial mechanism behind preventive war. Aside from shifts in deterrent capability, states might want to prevent an NWP state from successfully developing weapons because the weapons can become a means of extortion. As observed with North Korea, states that have developed weapons might hint at being willing to disarm, or at least cease production, to extract concessions from other states.

A second reason why the potential for greater deterrence capability can make NWPs destabilizing is that other states may want to extract whatever concessions they can before the status quo becomes locked in. Again, if nuclear weapons are only useful for deterrence, then states will primarily only be able to benefit from their possession by defending the status quo. Accordingly, competitors may perceive an NWP as a diminishing opportunity to challenge the status quo before it becomes infeasible to threaten war. As one example of this effect, Pakistan engaged India in six crises and three wars from 1949 to 1974 before India demonstrated a nuclear weapons capability. For thirteen years following India's detonation of a nuclear device, when Pakistan lacked its own capability, there were no crises, as coded by the International Crisis Behavior (ICB) dataset. This suggests that India's capability constrained Pakistan's willingness to challenge the status quo. As this case helps demonstrate, we do not expect states that have successfully attained nuclear weapons to be similarly destabilizing. Once states successfully proliferate, their weapons have already shaped the distribution of bargaining, and the window of opportunity for other states to protect their relative bargaining power has closed.

In sum, when states begin seeking nuclear weapons, even if they are solely motivated by the need to deter security threats, they will become sources of threats to other states in the system. Here is where the security dilemma logic comes into play, although with a slight twist. The twist is that the threat is not an existential threat, such as that faced by the hunter in Jervis's (1978) stag hunt. The security threats that actors face from NWP states can be much more general. They can be simple shifts in bargaining power—specifically, deterrence capability—that cause actors to fear being disadvantaged in the future. This is not to say that existential threats are meaningless—indeed, the dilemma is maximized when there is an existential threat—just that other sources of threats are relevant.

The threat from NWPs is enhanced by the fact that once states acquire nuclear weapons, there is little that other states in the system can do to force a state to abdicate its weapons. Indeed, the only state to abandon its weapons once acquired is South Africa, which was probably motivated more by domestic politics than international politics (Solingen 2007). So, states will view weapons programs with great angst because they represent potentially *permanent* shifts in bargaining power, even if the proliferator makes no immediate attempt to use that leverage widely.[7]

This chapter also makes a distinction between NWPs, in which states are actively pursuing nuclear weapons, and simple latency, in which states possess dual-use technology, such as uranium enrichment or plutonium reprocessing, but without any perceived intent to weaponize the fissile material. The key issue is how other actors, especially potential opponents, perceive the intentions of the state with latent technology. Since states such as Japan and Canada have demonstrated satisfaction with just possession of dual-use technology without actual weapons development, such technology need not be threatening to relative bargaining positions. Those positions will only become threatened once a state makes clear moves toward acquiring weapons. At the same time, and related to the discussions elsewhere in this volume (Fuhrmann, Chapter 3; Kroenig, Chapter 8; Horowitz, Chapter 12), we recognize that by definition latency makes the pursuit of nuclear weapons more feasible if not more likely, so there is potentially an indirect relationship between latency and the security dilemma.

Hypothesis: States will be more likely to enter into a crisis against a potential opponent that has a nuclear weapons program.

The potential importance of rivalry needs to be addressed. Some pairs of states are much more prone than others to engage in disputes, crises, conflicts, and wars because of high opportunity for conflicts of interest and structural barriers for efficient bargaining. As a result, there always exist a set of rivals within which most of the conflict in the international system occurs (Diehl and Goertz 2000; Thompson 2001). This chapter proposes that because future renegotiation and bargaining is more likely to take place between rivals, opponents of a rival program state might be especially threatened, because states will be most negatively affected if their chief rivals successfully develop nuclear weapons.

Note, however, that the importance of rivalry should be less than if existential threats were in play. If the nuclear programs are primarily threatening through shifts in bargaining power, then many states beyond current rivals could be negatively affected. If the nuclear programs are primarily threatening through the potential ability to carry out existential threats, then rivals will be almost exclusively threatened, because other states would have little reason to fear that they would be the target of a nuclear attack. Only rival states would suspect that nuclear weapons would be used to exterminate them. This insight can be used to postulate that the findings detailed below, in which opponents of rivals with nuclear programs are not especially prone to perceive a crisis, suggest that the relevant security dilemma logic is not much related to existential threats.

Application to the Middle East

We can see the basic logic of the security dilemma in the context of nuclear proliferation across the Middle East. While the exact date of Israel's entrance into the nuclear weapons club is unclear (Hersh 1991; Burrows and Windrem 1994; Cohen 1998), there is some evidence that its nuclear program proved to be the impetus for the Six-Day War in 1967, as its Arab neighbors and the Soviet Union attempted to obliterate Israel's military capabilities before it consolidated its weapons program (Evron 1994; Karl 1996). Ginor and Remez (2006) find evidence that the Arab states and the Soviet Union had coordinated an attack on Israel that was primarily motivated by the progress toward atomic weapons at the Dimona facility. The preventive attempt failed because Israel's own preemptive strike succeeded too fast. If this account is accurate, it demonstrates the security dilemma logic well, in that Israel's nuclear program threatened other states which then took action to try and prevent Israel from succeeding.

The security dilemma has also shaped Israel's perceived insecurity from proliferation attempts by other states in the region. In June 1981, the Israeli Air Force launched an attack against the Iraqi Osirak nuclear power plant. The attack totally destroyed the plant. Flying over 1,000 miles (including over Jordanian and Saudi airspace) with over a dozen planes, the Israeli Air Force was able to plant each of its bombs on target and escape without incident.

International condemnation was swift. Characterized as "'vigilante' proliferation" (Smith 1987) by some, the attacks were condemned in the United Nations with a Security Council resolution chastising Israel for the attack. Israel's reasoning for launching the attack seems to fit directly within the window of opportunity argument from the security dilemma. Written by three Israelis, the book *Two Minutes over Baghdad* states the case clearly: "Nuclear weapons in the hands of fanatic dictators and unscrupulous terrorists committed to the annihilation of Israel was a *casus belli.* . . . There was no way Israel . . . would allow itself to be at the mercy of ultimate weapons owned by the most degenerate regime in the Middle East" (Perlmutter, Handel, and Bar-Joseph 2003: 152).[8]

Israel appeared to have achieved what it set out to do in terms of preventing the Iraqis from proliferating (Feldman 1982: 130). There is evidence as well that the Osirak attack has not been the only one by the Israelis. On September 6, 2007, the Israeli Air Force launched an attack against a facility in Syria that the Syrians have refused to identify. The target, almost certainly a nuclear reactor, was obliterated. One of the key differences between this attack and the previous one was that after this attack, unlike the one at Osirak some twenty six years before, there was almost no international outcry (Spector and Cohen 2008).

Given Israel's track record, it should be no surprise that the issue of a possible Israeli strike against Iranian nuclear facilities is a hotly discussed topic amongst both policy makers and academics. The Iranians are certainly aware of the threat and have made threats of their own (Kaye and Wehrey 2007; Raas and Long 2007). While the nuclear threat from the Iranians is seen as an existential threat by many Israelis, this is not their only concern, and it does not appear to be the primary concern of many of the other players in the region and in the West (Kaye and Wehrey 2007: 112). If Iran attains nuclear weapons, the United States, the European Union, and Israel will be less able to pressure Iran to modify its behavior (Pollack 2003; Russell 2004; Takeyh 2007; Bahgat 2008). Policy makers particularly fear that Iran may use future nuclear empowerment to keep at bay foreign pressure to stop collaborating with Hezbollah, Shia insurgents in Iraq, and the Taliban in Afghanistan, or to improve its human rights record (Kaye and Wehrey 2007: 111). A nuclear-weaponized Iran would not only limit Israel's ability to leverage Iran itself, but also would restrain Israeli activity against future aggression from Hezbollah and Syria (Kaye and Wehrey 2007).

Moreover, Iranian nuclear weapons can act as a type of equalizer against American power (Wehrey et al. 2009) and could increase Iran's bargaining position with the other states in the region (Yaphe and Lutes 2005; Guldimann 2007; Ochmanek and Schwartz 2008; Chubin 2009). Related, regional competitors such as Saudi Arabia might enter into a nuclear arms race to counter an Iranian bomb (Zuhur 2006; Mansour 2007). Fear of these regional side effects is one of the major reasons that Israel and Arab states have lobbied the United States to confront Iran before it proliferates (Nasr and Takeyh 2008).

The use of aggressive military action to confront Iran—though not likely for various political and economic reasons—has been on the table while Iran has not had nuclear weapons, but it would be nearly unthinkable once it develops nuclear weapons and achieves rudimentary second-strike capability. By ruling out a major potential stick, Iran will have even greater confidence that it can pursue its agendas without fear of military reprisals—hence, it will gain greater bargaining power on a number of issues.

Research Methods

While the above narrative of proliferation concerns in the Middle East is consistent with the logic that NWP states can be threatening, we also use quantitative methods to test systematically the central hypothesis. The base data comprises directed country dyads, from 1945 to 2000. The analyses treat each AB dyad as different from BA, where the dependent variable is specific to Actor A in the former case and Actor B in the latter. The ICB data, which are used to define crisis incidence, are structured such that it is possible for Actor A to perceive a crisis but for Actor B to not perceive a crisis. For the sake of clarity in presenting the results, Actor A will be referred to as the "actor" in question and Actor B will be referred to as the "opponent."

To balance between including irrelevant dyads in the analysis and excluding relevant ones, Quackenbush (2006) has identified a set of dyads in the international system that has the opportunity for being in conflict. These are *politically active dyads* and are defined by criteria related to contiguity, power status, and alliance ties. The politically active dyads, in comparison to *politically relevant dyads* (Lemke and Reed 2001), encompass a greater percentage of the ICB crisis dyads. Using a version of Hewitt's (2003) dyadic ICB data, of the 947 directed dyad crises between 1945 and 2000, 903 (95 percent) are included in a dataset with politically active dyads while only 792 (84 percent) are included in a dataset of politically relevant dyads. In addition, the politically active dyads are not so heavily weighted toward nuclear actors. Of the 295,892 politically active dyads from 1945 to 2000, 21.4 percent have at least one member as a nuclear weapons state. This contrasts to the 106,166 politically relevant dyads during the same period, in which 63.9 percent contain a nuclear actor. Using politically active dyads provides greater heterogeneity in the types of actors in a non-nuclear dyad, because the great-power criterion for political relevance overlaps so closely with nuclear status—virtually leaving contiguous dyads as the only possible candidates for non-nuclear politically relevant dyads.

To examine the relationship between nuclear programs and general crisis involvement, the dependent variable is whether an actor perceived a crisis or not. The ICB data employ Brecher and Wilkenfeld's (2000) definition of an international crisis. A crisis, as perceived by a state, has three necessary conditions that are jointly sufficient: a threat to one or more basic values, a finite time for response, and a heightened probability of escalation in military hostilities. Hewitt's (2003) dyadic ICB data are used to determine which directed dyads are in crisis. Note that an actor is coded as being involved in a crisis only if the actor perceives a crisis, and not necessarily when it triggers a crisis for another actor that may or may not reciprocate. To get a sense of the destabilizing effect of nuclear weapons pursuit, we are most interested in how the NWP status of an actor's *opponent* affects the actor's likelihood of perceiving a crisis.

Proliferation status is used to form independent variables. We thus need to be transparent in how we define NWP states and weapon states. Table 11.1 presents the dates that we use, consistent with our previous work. Data from Singh and Way (2004) are used to code program status, such that the existence of an NWP is coded as true if Singh and Way find that the state is actively pursuing nuclear weapons, evidenced by such actions as "a political decision by cabinet-level officials, movement toward weaponization, or development of single-use, dedicated technology." The NWP variables are set to zero when the relevant actors actually possess nuclear weapons. The dates for nuclear weapons acquisition are consistent with Beardsley and Asal (2009b) and the consensus coding in that special issue of *Journal of Conflict Resolution*.

As discussed above, rivalries might condition the effect of proliferation status. Since we use the ICB data to define crisis, we use Hewitt's (2003) list of

TABLE 11.1 Dates of NWPs and weapons acquisition

Country	Nuclear weapons		NWP	
	Start	End	Start	End
United States	1945	> 2000	< 1945	1945
Soviet Union/Russia	1949	> 2000	1945	1949
United Kingdom	1952	> 2000	1947	1952
France	1960	> 2000	1954	1960
China	1964	> 2000	1955	1964
Israel	1967	> 2000	1958	1967
India	1988	> 2000	1964	1988
South Africa	1982	1993	1974	1982
Pakistan	1990	> 2000	1972	1990
North Korea	> 2000	> 2000	1980	> 2000
Brazil	Never		1978	1990
Argentina	Never		1978	1990
Libya	Never		1970	> 2000
Iran	Never		1985	> 2000
Iraq	Never		1982	> 2000
South Korea	Never		1970	1979

SOURCES: Beardsley and Asal (2009b); Singh and Way (2004).
NOTE: NWPs = nuclear weapons programs.

rivalries. From this variable, a number of interaction terms and variations are generated, as detailed in the results section.

The models implement a combination of control variables. We control for nuclear weapon latent capability, so that we can distinguish between the pursuit of nuclear weapons and possession of the sensitive technology (including uranium enrichment and uranium reprocessing) needed to build them. We use Erik Gartzke's updated seven-point measure of latency (Jo and Gartzke 2007). Actors with nuclear weapons and programs generally have relatively large amounts of conventional capabilities that could make it difficult to separate whether conventional power balance or proliferation status is doing the heavy lifting. We thus also include the latent conventional capability of each actor, using the CINC indices from the Correlates of War National Military

Capabilities 3.01 index to control for power dynamics (Singer, Bremer, and Stuckey 1972; Singer 1987).

We also control for history of security threats, since NWPs might be responses to such threats, and prior threats could indicate a predisposition toward crisis. The measure of security threat counts the number of crises that each state has experienced in the previous ten years. The logic here is that a recent history of crisis should predict fairly well the propensity for conflict in the immediate future. In addition, we control for the time that has elapsed since 1945, when the nuclear age began. Finally, to account for possible duration dependence among the observations of the same directed dyads, we follow Carter and Signorino (2010) and include peace years, its square and its cube as covariates.

Because the dependent variable is dichotomous, probit models are appropriate. Nuclear weapons and NWPs are not distributed randomly in the international system (Sagan 1996/97; Singh and Way 2004; Jo and Gartzke 2007), which presents a serious problem to causal inference, because we must be concerned about the potential for any correlations between proliferation status and crisis behavior to be a product of underlying characteristics of the types of states that attempt to proliferate instead of the programs or weapons themselves. Aside from the use of control variables, we adopt a simultaneous equation–multivariate probit approach, with estimation conducted as seemingly unrelated regression. We specify three equations: the onset of crisis, the proliferation status of the actor, and the proliferation status of the opponent. To simplify slightly, an actor is defined as a proliferator in the latter two equations when it has either an NWP or nuclear weapons. The multivariate probit approach adjusts for correlations in the disturbances of each equation, which in essence controls for unobserved underlying factors that might be driving variation in both the proliferation choices and the crisis behavior. To increase the ease of estimation across the three equations, we are more restrictive of the number of variables in this model, as we include only those control variables listed above that a single-equation model demonstrates to have an impact on the onset of an NWP. These variables are consistent with the variables that Singh and Way (2004) and Jo and Gartzke (2007) use to measure technological capability and security threats. Note that the rivalry variables in the proliferation-status equations are sums of the number of rivalries that the respective actors have. As additional instruments for proliferation status, we also add measures of sensitive nuclear assistance from Kroenig (2009) and the cumulative number of nuclear cooperation agreements for which a state is a recipient from Fuhrmann (2009). We finally include the time since 1945 to account for duration dependence in the two equations of proliferation status.

Results and Discussion

Table 11.2 presents the findings of the probit model, while Table 11.3 presents the findings from the multivariate probit. For substantive interpretations, Figure 11.1 presents the relative risks of crisis onset for when the directed dyad is a rivalry and when it is not. The relative risks are calculated by taking the difference between the predicted probability of crisis onset with the treatment present and the predicted probability with the treatment absent, then dividing by the predicted probability of when the treatment is absent. All other variables are set at their minimums for categorical variables and at their means (rounded to the nearest integer when appropriate) for the interval-type variables. CLARIFY is used to generate the predicted probabilities (Tomz, Wittenberg, and King 2003).

In support of the main hypothesis, states that face potential opponents with NWPs are much more likely to experience a crisis, and this effect is statistically significant in both the probit and multivariate probit models. It appears that states feel more threatened by potential opponents that are attempting to achieve nuclear weapons. Substantively, we see in Figure 11.1 that opponents of nuclear program states are over 200 percent more likely to perceive a crisis. At the same time, and also consistent with the logic of the hypothesis, NWP states themselves are more likely to perceive a crisis. As other states feel threatened by and react to an actor's nuclear program, the proliferator becomes the target of aggression and is more likely to perceive a crisis.

Note that nuclear latency does not have the same effect as having an actual NWP. This means that potential opponents do distinguish between states that are actively seeking weapons and those that might have the requisite technology (including uranium enrichment and plutonium reprocessing) but are not perceived as pursuing atomic weapons. These findings speak to an underlying issue of the nuclear renaissance, providing a note of optimism associated with the broadening of nuclear energy possessor states, even with only weak "internationalization" of the fuel cycle. The mere spread of civilian or dual-use nuclear technology does not, in itself, appear to make the world a more dangerous place by exacerbating security dilemmas.

TABLE 11.2 Probit model of crisis onset

Actor's nuclear program	0.281* (0.170)
Opponent's nuclear program	0.322** (0.0624)
Actor's nuclear program × rivalry	−0.247 (0.271)
Opponent's nuclear program × rivalry	−0.245* (0.141)
Actor's nuclear status	−0.289 (0.226)
Opponent's nuclear status	−0.00784 (0.0817)
Actor's nuclear status × rivalry	−0.0560 (0.188)
Opponent's nuclear status × rivalry	−0.304** (0.118)
Rivalry	1.892** (0.0674)
Actor's nuclear program latency	−0.00458 (0.0103)
Opponent's nuclear program latency	0.0102 (0.00983)
Actor's latent military capability	2.349* (1.425)
Opponent's latent military capability	1.244** (0.512)
Actor's number of crises in past ten years	0.0725** (0.0202)
Opponent's number of crises in past ten years	0.0474** (0.0137)
Number of years since 1945	−0.00215 (0.00155)
Years of peace	−0.0777** (0.0127)
Years of peace squared	0.00272** (6.04e−04)
Years of peace cubed	−2.71e−05** (8.00e−06)
Constant	−2.635** (0.0840)
Observations	295,684

NOTE: $*p < .05$; $**p < .01$, one-tailed test.

TABLE 11.3 Multivariate probit model of crisis onset

CRISIS ONSET EQUATION	
Actor's nuclear program	0.391** (0.155)
Opponent's nuclear program	0.336** (0.0628)
Rivalry	1.756** (0.0812)
Actor's nuclear program × rivalry	−0.246 (0.267)
Opponent's nuclear program × rivalry	−0.150 (0.148)
Actor's latent military capability	1.272 (0.859)
Opponent's latent military capability	1.392** (0.437)
Actor's number of crises in past ten years	0.0502* (0.0242)
Opponent's number of crises in past ten years	0.0444** (0.0126)
Years of peace	−0.0775** (0.0128)
Years of peace squared	0.00265** (5.86e−04)
Years of peace cubed	−2.65e−05** (7.83e−06)
Constant	−2.649** (0.0781)

PROLIFERATION OF ACTOR EQUATION	
Number of actor rivalries	0.567** (0.124)
Actor's latent military capability	34.84** (7.910)
Actor's number of crises in past ten years	0.448** (0.102)
Actor's nuclear assistance	0.579 (0.463)
Actor's nuclear cooperation agreements	0.0612** (0.0227)
Number of years since 1945	0.00500 (0.0174)
Constant	−3.390** (0.453)

(*continued*)

TABLE 11.3 *(Continued)*

PROLIFERATION OF OPPONENT EQUATION

Number of opponent rivalries	0.605**
	(0.0158)
Opponent's latent military capability	37.88**
	(0.655)
Opponent's number of crises in past ten years	0.461**
	(0.0113)
Opponent's nuclear assistance	−0.0265
	(0.0756)
Opponent's nuclear cooperation agreements	0.0592**
	(0.00136)
Number of years since 1945	0.0115**
	(0.00118)
Constant	−3.609**
	(0.0432)
Rho12	−0.0266
Rho13	0.00400
Rho23	−0.0237
Observations	295,684

NOTE: $*p < .05$; $**p < 0.01$, one-tailed test; the rho coefficients are jointly significant at $p < 0.006$.

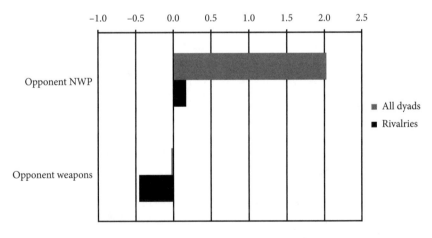

FIGURE 11.1 Relative risks of crisis onset

We do not see a positive conditioning effect of rivalry. The interaction term of an opponent's nuclear status and rivalry is actually negative. As evident in Figure 11.1, opponents with nuclear programs are not substantially more threatening than other opponents when looking at the set of rival dyads. Since it does not appear that states are particularly threatened by rival NWP states, we interpret this to mean that existential threats are not the key driver of the behavior here. Weapons programs are threatening, but apparently not because they hold the potential for states to obliterate their rivals. In looking at the set of nonrival dyads in which an opponent of an NWP state perceived a crisis, we see a number of instances of pairs that later become rivals, as for example between India and China before China acquired its weapons. So the potential for competition is still an important source of insecurity but not necessarily the potential for rival annihilation.

Our logic highlights the importance of potential bargaining power changes as the source of insecurity, which can affect all types of potential competitors. This argument receives even greater support when considering that nuclear states are not nearly as threatening as NWP states. In fact, among the set of rival dyads, potential opponents of nuclear states are significantly less likely to experience a crisis. The actors do not appear threatened by weapons per se, just the potential for actors to acquire weapons and gain substantial deterrence capability.

We get an additional sense of how the security dilemma plays out in the context of nuclear weapons by interpreting the equations of proliferation status in Table 11.3. We see that having many rivals and a lengthy crisis history leads to either the pursuit or possession of nuclear weapons. The security dilemma logic is thus solidified: One means for states to address substantial security threats is to pursue nuclear weapons, but by doing so they pose a threat to others in the international system.

Conclusion

The security dilemma, which has been used to explain both ancient and modern conflicts, serves a critical role in shaping the impact of NWPs. States seek nuclear weapons in part to address security threats, and, once states begin seeking weapons, that pursuit then becomes a source of threat for others in the international system which fear losing relative bargaining power once the weapons are realized. Thus NWP states are more likely to trigger crises for potential opponents.

In conjunction with the above, that we find nuclear weapons themselves to not be a source of crisis suggests two implications. First, the source of concern as actors proliferate is not as much a fear of mass destruction as it is a fear of shifting bargaining power via deterrence capability. While Waltz (Sagan and Waltz 2002) might be right about the relative stability that nuclear deterrence creates, we must be careful not to become overly optimistic about what that means, for it entails a transfer of deterrence capability to the proliferators that are increasingly the types of states that most threaten human security. The loss of the ability to use a credible stick against the Democratic People's Republic of Korea and potentially against Iran is no trivial consequence.

Second, and related, nuclear programs are much more destabilizing than nuclear weapons. Since states will rarely give up their nuclear weapons once they are achieved, and since the marginal increase in bargaining power from building one more weapon is insignificant compared to the increase when going from zero weapons to some weapons, it is during the program phase that a window of vulnerability and opportunity exists. Both nuclear and non-nuclear states have an incentive to prevent further proliferation, and they will take aggressive action to contain the number of nuclear powers if necessary or otherwise aggressively engage proliferating states before the status quo becomes entrenched.

It is worth comparing our results to those of Michael C. Horowitz in this volume (Chapter 12). Horowitz uses a different metric of conflict—instead of looking at ICB crises, he looks at militarized interstate disputes that are defined by different criteria. While there is considerable overlap between these two indicators of conflict, there are also a number of cases that are unique to each dataset. In both studies, and consistent with the main argument here, we see that states that are pursuing nuclear weapons are at greater risk of inciting conflict. One difference between this chapter's findings and those of Horowitz that is worth highlighting, however, is that he finds that the actual possession of nuclear weapons still has some destabilizing effects. This difference between militarized disputes and international crises is worthy of future investigation.

Nuclear latency is distinct from the NWPs in this study. The empirical evidence shows that possession of sensitive nuclear technology does not affect crisis behavior. Directly relating to the nuclear energy renaissance, this chapter's results indicate that the broadening and deepening of civilian nuclear programs will only prove destabilizing to the extent that such programs lead to greater pursuit of weapons. The civilian programs should not exacerbate security dilemmas. In this regard, any retreat from civilian nuclear power in the wake of the Fukushima crisis, which to this point appears to be confined to developed states without nuclear weapons ambitions, will not have much of an impact, for good or ill, on the proclivity of conflict across the international system.

Notes

1. NWPs are defined following Singh and Way (2004) as a state's active pursuit of the technology to manufacture nuclear weapons.

2. Also see Jo and Gartzke (2007) and Kroenig (2009) for accounts related to how the nuclear renaissance may affect the pursuit of nuclear weapons.

3. Many other factors are also key drivers of the opportunity and willingness for states to seek nuclear weapons, including conventional military threats (Jo and Gartzke 2007; Singh and Way 2004), nuclear assistance (Kroenig 2009; Fuhrmann 2009), prestige (Sagan 1996/97), identity (Montgomery 2005; Hymans 2006), domestic politics (Solingen 2007), and bargaining leverage (Beardsley and Asal 2009b).

4. See also Gilpin (1983).

5. See also Kroenig (2010).

6. The question of whether such attempts are effective is a different question. See Reiter (2006) for a critique of the efficacy of preventive airstrikes.

7. There is an assumption here that rudimentary second-strike capability, which locks in the deterrence potential, does not require more than a few warheads. This is a debated assumption in the literature (Montgomery and Sagan 2009). If second-strike capability is truly more difficult to achieve than assumed here, then we should expect that states with only a few nuclear weapons can continue to be threatening, as the window of vulnerability has not yet closed at the development of basic nuclear capability. We leave the testing of this to further analysis.

8. Despite the international outcry, the Israeli Prime Minister underlined the Israeli perspective when, after discussing the Holocaust, said, "This attack will be a precedent for every future government in Israel. . . . every future Israeli prime minister will act, in similar circumstances, in the same way" (Spector and Cohen 2008). See Reiter (2005) for an argument that finds preemptive strikes counterproductive, though this does not question that Israel was motivated in its strike by a perceived threat of Iraqi proliferation.

References

Asal, Victor, and Kyle Beardsley. 2007. "Proliferation and International Crisis Behavior." *Journal of Peace Research* 44 (2): 139–155.

Bahgat, Gawdat. 2008. "Security in the Persian Gulf: Two Conflicting Models." *Defense & Security Analysis* 24 (3): 237–245.

Beardsley, Kyle, and Victor Asal. 2009a. "Nuclear Weapons as Shields." *Conflict Management and Peace Science* 26 (3): 235–255.

———. 2009b. "Winning with the Bomb." *Journal of Conflict Resolution* 53 (2): 278–301.

Betts, Richard K. 1987. *Nuclear Blackmail and Nuclear Balance.* Washington, DC: Brookings Institution

Brecher, Michael, and Jonathan Wilkenfeld. 2000. *A Study of Crisis.* Ann Arbor: University of Michigan.

Burrows, William E., and Robert Windrem. 1994. *Critical Mass: The Dangerous Race for Superweapons in a Fragmenting World.* New York: Simon & Schuster.

Carter, David B., and Curtis S. Signorino. 2010. "Back to the Future: Modeling Time Dependency in Binary Data." *Political Analysis* 18 (3): 271–292.

Chubin, Shahram. 2009. "Iran's Power in Context." *Survival* 51 (1): 165–190.

Cohen, Avner. 1998. *Israel and the Bomb.* New York: Columbia University Press.

Diehl, Paul, and Gary Goertz. 2000. *War and Peace in International Rivalry.* Ann Arbor: University of Michigan Press.

Evron, Yair. 1994. *Israel's Nuclear Dilemma.* New York: Routledge.

Feldman, Shai. 1982. *Israeli Nuclear Deterrence: A Strategy for the 1980s.* New York: Columbia University Press.

Fuhrmann, Matthew. 2009. "Spreading Temptation: Proliferation and Peaceful Nuclear Cooperation Agreements." *International Security* 34 (1): 7–41.

Fuhrmann, Matthew, and Sarah E. Kreps. 2010. "Targeting Nuclear Programs in War and Peace: A Quantitative Empirical Analysis, 1941–2000." *Journal of Conflict Resolution* 54 (5): 831–859.

Gaddis, John Lewis. 1986. "The Long Peace: Elements of Stability in the Postwar International System." *International Security* 10: 99–142.

Gartzke, Erik, and Dong-Joon Jo. 2009. "Bargaining, Nuclear Proliferation, and Interstate Disputes." *Journal of Conflict Resolution* 53 (2): 209–233.

Geller, Daniel S. 1990. "Nuclear Weapons, Deterrence, and Crisis Escalation." *Journal of Conflict Resolution* 34 (2): 291–310.

Gilpin, Robert. 1983. *War and Change in World Politics,* New York: Cambridge University Press.

Ginor, Isabella. and Gideon Remez. 2006. "The Spymaster, the Communist, and Foxbats over Dimona." *Israel Studies* 11 (2): 88–130.

Guldimann, Tim. 2007. "The Iranian Nuclear Impasse." *Survival* 49 (3): 169–178.

Hersh, Seymour M. 1991. *The Samson Option: Israel's Nuclear Arsenal and American Foreign Policy.* New York: Random House.

Hewitt, Joseph. 2003. "Dyadic Processes and International Crises." *Journal of Conflict Resolution* 47 (5): 669–692.

Horowitz, Michael. 2009. "The Spread of Nuclear Weapons and International Conflict: Does Experience Matter?" *Journal of Conflict Resolution* 53 (2): 234–257.

Hymans, Jacques E. C. 2006. *The Psychology of Nuclear Proliferation: Identity, Emotions, and Foreign Policy.* New York: Cambridge University Press.

Intrilligator, Michael D., and Dagobert L. Brito. 1984. "Nuclear Proliferation and the Probability of Nuclear War." *Public Choice* 37 (2): 247–260.

Jervis, Robert. 1978. "Cooperation Under the Security Dilemma." *World Politics* 30 (2): 167–214.

———. 1989. *The Meaning of the Nuclear Revolution: Statecraft and the Prospect of Armageddon.* Ithaca, NY: Cornell University Press.

Jo, Dong-Joon, and Erik Gartzke. 2007. "Determinants of Nuclear Weapons Proliferation." *Journal of Conflict Resolution* 51 (1): 1–28.

Karl, David J. 1996. "Proliferation Pessimism and Emerging Nuclear Powers." *International Security* 21 (3): 87–119.

Kaye, Dalia Dassa, and Frederic M. Wehrey. 2007. "A Nuclear Iran: The Reactions of Neighbours." *Survival* 49 (2): 111–128.

Kroenig, Matthew. 2009. "Importing the Bomb: Sensitive Nuclear Assistance and Nuclear Proliferation." *Journal of Conflict Resolution* 53 (2): 161–180.

———. 2010. "Nuclear Superiority or the Balance of Resolve? Explaining Nuclear Crisis Outcomes." Working paper.

Lemke, Douglas, and William Reed. 2001. "The Relevance of Politically Relevant Dyads." *Journal of Conflict Resolution* 45 (1): 126–145.

Mansour, Imad. 2007. "Iran and Instability in the Middle East: How Preferences Influence the Regional Order." *International Journal* 63 (4): 941–964.

Meyer, Stephen M. 1984. *The Dynamics of Nuclear Proliferation.* Chicago: University of Chicago Press.

Montgomery, Alexander H. 2005. "Ringing in Proliferation: How to Dismantle an Atomic Bomb Network." *International Security* 30 (2): 153–187.

Montgomery, Alexander H., and Scott D. Sagan. 2009. "The Perils of Predicting Proliferation." *Journal of Conflict Resolution* 53 (2): 302–328.

Müller, Harald, David Fischer and Wolfgang Kötter. 1994. *Nuclear Non-Proliferation and Global Order.* New York: Oxford University Press.

Nasr, Vali, and Ray Takeyh. 2008. "The Costs of Containing Iran." *Foreign Affairs* 87 (1): 90–94.

Ochmanek, David, and Lowell H. Schwartz. 2008. *The Challenge of Nuclear-Armed Regional Adversaries*: Santa Monica, CA: Rand Corporation.

Perlmutter, Amos, Michael I. Handel, and Uri Bar-Joseph. 2003. *Two Minutes over Baghdad.* New York: Routledge.

Pollack, Kenneth M. 2003. "Securing the Gulf." *Foreign Affairs* 82 (4): 2–16.

Powell, Robert. 1987. "Crisis Bargaining, Escalation, and MAD." *American Political Science Review* 81 (3): 717–735.

———. 1988. "Nuclear Brinkmanship with Two-Sided Incomplete Information." *American Political Science Review* 82 (1): 155–178.

———. 1990. *Nuclear Deterrence Theory: The Search for Credibility.* New York: Cambridge University Press.

———. 2006. "War as a Commitment Problem." *International Organization* 60 (1): 169–203.

Quackenbush, Stephen L. 2006. "Identifying Opportunity for Conflict: Politically Active Dyads." *Conflict Management and Peace Science* 23 (1): 37–51.

Raas, Whitney, and Austin Long. 2007. "Osirak Redux? Assessing Israeli Capabilities to Destroy Iranian Nuclear Facilities." *International Security* 31 (4): 7–33.

Rauchhaus, Robert. 2009. "Evaluating the Nuclear Peace Hypothesis: A Quantitative Approach." *Journal of Conflict Resolution* 53 (2): 258–277.

Reiter, Dan. 2005. "Preventive Attacks Against Nuclear Programs and the 'Success' at Osiraq." *Nonproliferation Review* 12 (2): 355–371.

———. 2006. "Preventive Attacks against Nuclear, Biological, and Chemical Weapons Programs: The Track Record." In *Hitting First: Preventive Force in U.S. Security Strategy*, eds. William Walton Keller and Gordon R. Mitchell. Pittsburgh, PA: University of Pittsburgh Press.

Russell, Richard L. 2004. "Iran in Iraq's Shadow: Dealing with Tehran's Nuclear Weapons Bid." *Parameters* 34 (3): 31–45.

Sagan, Scott D. 1996/97. "Why Do States Build Nuclear Weapons?: Three Models in Search of a Bomb." *International Security* 21 (3): 54–86.

Sagan, Scott D., and Kenneth N. Waltz. 2002. *The Spread of Nuclear Weapons: A Debate Renewed.* New York: W. W. Norton & Company.

Schelling, Thomas C. 1966. *Arms and Influence.* New Haven, CT: Yale University Press.

Singer, J. David. 1987. "Reconstructing the Correlates of War Dataset on Material Capabilities of States, 1816–1985." *International Interactions* 14 (2): 115–132.

Singer, J. David, Stuart Bremer, and John Stuckey. 1972. "Capability Distribution, Uncertainty, and Major Power War, 1820–1965." In *Peace, War, and Numbers*, ed. Bruce Russett. Beverly Hills, CA: Sage.

Singh, Sonali, and Christopher Way. 2004. "The Correlates of Nuclear Proliferation: A Quantitative Test." *Journal of Conflict Resolution* 48 (6): 859–885.

Smith, Roger K. 1987. "Explaining the Non-proliferation Regime: Anomalies for Contemporary International Relations Theory." *International Organization* 41 (2): 253–281.

Snyder, Glenn H., and Paul Diesing. 1977. *Conflict among Nations.* Princeton, NJ: Princeton University Press.

Solingen, Etel. 2007. *Nuclear Logics: Contrasting Paths in East Asia and the Middle East.* Princeton, NJ: Princeton University Press.

Spector, Leonard S., and Avner Cohen. 2008. "Israel's Airstrike on Syria's Reactor: Implications for the Nonproliferation Regime." *Arms Control Today* 38 (6).

Takeyh, Ray. 2007. "Time for Détente with Iran." *Foreign Affairs* 86 (2): 17–32.

Thompson, William R. 2001. "Identifying Rivals and Rivalries in World Politics." *International Studies Quarterly* 45 (4): 557–586.

Thucydides. 431 BCE. *The History of the Peloponnesian War*, trans. Richard Crawley. In *The MIT Internet Classics Archive*. Available at: http://classics.mit.edu/Thucydides/pelopwar.1.first.html.

Tomz, Michael, Jason Wittenberg, and Gary King. 2003. "CLARIFY: Software for Interpreting and Presenting Statistical Results, Version 2.1." Stanford University, University of Wisconsin, and Harvard University. January 5. Available at: http://gking.harvard.edu/clarify.

Waltz, Kenneth N. 1979. *Theory of International Politics.* Boston: McGraw-Hill.

———. 1990. "Nuclear Myths and Political Realities." *American Political Science Review.* 84 (3): 731–745.

Wehrey, Frederic, David E. Thaler, Nora Bensahel, Kim Cragin, Jerrold D. Green, Dalia Dassa Kaye, Nadia Oweidat, and Jennifer Li. 2009. *Dangerous but Not Omnipotent: Exploring the Reach and Limitations of Iranian Power in the Middle East.* Santa Monica, CA: Rand Corporation.

Williams, Robert C., and Philip L. Cantelon. 1984. *The American Atom: A Documentary History of Nuclear Policies from the Discovery of Fission to the Present, 1939–1984.* Philadelphia: University of Pennsylvania Press.

Yaphe, Judith S., and Charles D. Lutes. 2005. *Reassessing the Implications of a Nuclear-Armed Iran.* Washington, DC: Institute for National Strategic Studies.

Zagare, Frank C., and D. Marc Kilgour. 2000. *Perfect Deterrence.* New York: Cambridge University Press.

Zuhur, Sherifa D. 2006. *Iran, Iraq, and the United States: The New Triangle's Impact on Sectarianism and the Nuclear Threat.* Carlisle, PA: Strategic Studies Institute.

12 Nuclear Power and Militarized Conflict

Is There a Link?

Michael C. Horowitz

W HY IS IT THAT THE WEST IS CONCERNED WITH THE implications of Iran gaining control over the nuclear fuel cycle but does not worry (much) about Japan's extensive nuclear power facilities? After all, Japan's complete control of the nuclear fuel cycle means it could quickly build a small nuclear arsenal if it ever decided that such a move was in its best interest.[1] From a strict capabilities perspective, why is Japan not considered more of a threat than Iran on the nuclear front?

The answer has to do with intentions—while most countries do not worry about Japanese proliferation at present, it appears to most commentators that nuclear power and uranium enrichment are simply way stations for Iran en route to building a small nuclear arsenal. The answer, therefore, also has to do with politics—who each country is friends with, its regime type, and the way others perceive its desire to change the international system. As more countries begin seriously considering using nuclear power as a future fuel source, these sorts of questions will become more important.

This chapter looks at the burgeoning renaissance in nuclear energy and nuclear power through the lens of the international security environment. The catastrophe at Fukushima represents a challenge for nuclear energy that some argue could end the "renaissance" in nuclear energy (Harrell 2011), but growing demand for energy around the world is likely to keep nuclear power in dialogues about future energy sources.[2] While new research is attempting to answer the question of how the possession of nuclear weapons by different types of states influences their propensity to initiate and escalate disputes and how others treat them, very little work examines the implications of capabilities lower down on the nuclear spectrum. Moreover, most research tends to assume that the impact of nuclear capabilities is static over time. This chapter attempts to address these issues by looking at how the pursuit of nuclear weapons and the possession of nuclear power each influence the propensity of states to initiate militarized disputes and to have those dispute actions reciprocated. It also looks at the impact of possessing these capabilities over time. The results show that, indeed, possessing commercial nuclear power is associated with different behavior than actively working to develop nuclear weapons. While states with active nuclear weapons development programs are significantly more likely to initiate militarized disputes, those with nuclear power are much less likely to do so. However, while the impact of possessing commercial nuclear power over time seems to matter, having a nuclear weapons development program for a short or long period does not appear to influence behavior.

In the rest of the chapter, the first section describes some of the relevant literature. This is followed by discussion of the research design. The third section describes several models depicting the relative impact of commercial nuclear power and nuclear weapons development programs. The conclusion follows.

Literature Review

Nuclear Power and Proliferation

The relationship between nuclear power—a key potential precursor to nuclear weapons capabilities—and the international security environment has not received a great deal of scrutiny from international relations scholars, though several in the policy community have written about the possibilities and potential downsides of a nuclear renaissance. Sharon Squassoni, for example, argues that the potential for new nuclear power plants to become a gateway to nuclear proliferation represents an important issue (Squassoni 2008). Some countries view nuclear power as a source of prestige, just like how several countries view nuclear weapons. Given current global instability, many people worry that a move to expand nuclear power could become the means by which potential proliferators get in the proliferation door, so to speak, which makes any nuclear renaissance potentially risky (Socolow and Glaser 2009). Even if many of those weapons were acquired for prestige reasons, they could still increase insecurity. Feiveson et al. (2008) conclude that a significant expansion of nuclear power might have to wait for more progress on the disarmament front, though institutional barriers to proliferation could help prevent new nuclear power plants from becoming loci for proliferation. Traditional opponents of nuclear power, such as Helen Caldicott (2006), have also weighed in on the political and security risks of a nuclear renaissance.

Scott Sagan has argued in multiple forums that whether or not the nuclear renaissance leads to risky nuclear proliferation depends a great deal on the character of the states that end up controlling the nuclear fuel cycle (specifically, whether or not they are democratic) and the ability of the international community to build strong supply-side controls and bolster the Non-Proliferation Treaty (NPT) (Miller and Sagan 2009; Sagan 2010). Diyakov (2009: 121), providing a Russian perspective, similarly argues that linking new states interested in nuclear power to established commercial nuclear power operators is one of the best ways to prevent the nuclear renaissance from harming the international security environment. Many, including Anne Lauvergeon, seem to believe that, despite some challenges, "The renewed interest in nuclear energy and the international growth of nuclear electricity generation do not equate—and should not be equated—with increasing proliferation risks" (Lauvergeon 2009: 93). Fitzpatrick (2008: 384) concludes that even a region like the Middle East could experience a nuclear power renaissance without a large risk of proliferation if countries transparently acquire nuclear power and utilize external commercial fuel cycle services.

As part of recent quantitative work on nuclear power, Matthew Fuhrmann focuses on nuclear cooperation agreements (NCAs) and the way they lower the barriers to proliferation for interested states. He argues that NCAs in most cases increase the risk of proliferation even if the specifics of those agreements seem innocuous at the time (Fuhrmann 2009a,b). Matthew Kroenig, in contrast, focuses on direct sensitive nuclear assistance, finding a strong link between those cases of sensitive nuclear assistance and proliferation (Kroenig 2009a,b). For Kroenig (2009a: 114), strategic considerations motivate these sensitive transfers rather than the economic incentives that often motivate the NCAs that Fuhrmann studies.

Concurrently, a new set of research builds on prior qualitative research concerning the link between nuclear weapons and the international security environment (Betts 1987; Powell 1989; Sagan 1995; Waltz 1995; Mueller 1999). Gartzke and Jo (2009) find that nuclear weapons possession only has a limited impact on militarized behavior, while Rauchhaus (2009) shows that nuclear weapons contribute to stability at higher levels of conflict while encouraging risk taking at lower levels. Beardsley and Asal (2009) provide evidence demonstrating that countries want nuclear weapons because they become more likely to succeed in international crises. Horowitz (2009) shows that the length of time countries have nuclear weapons influences their behavior.

How Could Nuclear Power Influence the International Security Environment?

This chapter also draws from research on bargaining and how expectations of changes in relative power influence behavior. As Fuhrmann (2009b) argues, all forms of nuclear power and the transfer of nuclear materials, whether explicitly sensitive or not, increase the risk of nuclear proliferation to some degree. Therefore, we should expect that as countries advance further along the road toward nuclear power and achieve mastery of the nuclear fuel cycle, they will gain some degree of power and confidence. This level of confidence should be lower than if they actually have nuclear weapons, but as Gartzke (2009) demonstrates, there is often uncertainty about whether or not countries have nuclear weapons, and that uncertainty can influence how other countries behave in militarized situations.

Thus, NCAs, sensitive nuclear transfers, and mastery of the nuclear fuel cycle may not simply be precursors of the acquisition of nuclear weapons.[3] These agreements and transfers may signal something about a state's capabilities that influences how it behaves in relation to other states and how other states respond. There are three different ways that the move to acquire nuclear materials related to nuclear power might influence how a state views its own relative power and how it behaves in the international security environment. First, a state may acquire nuclear power simply because it wants nuclear power as an electricity source—with no intention of converting those capabilities into nuclear weapons, even though such a conversion might be possible. Gourley and Stulberg (Chapter 1 in this volume) find that certain baseline levels of economic capability and energy insecurity systematically correlate with such development. Fuhrmann (2012) also shows that states with high levels of energy dependence on other countries are more likely to build nuclear power plants than other countries. Second, a state may acquire nuclear power because it wants the option of acquiring nuclear weapons in the future. While a state may lack an active nuclear weapons program, it may view control of the nuclear fuel cycle as a desirable way station, giving it the option to go nuclear if its security situation changes. Third, a state may acquire nuclear power as a deliberate step toward acquiring nuclear weapons. Beliefs about the incentives driving the acquisition of nuclear power can shape the way the international community responds. Iran, for example, claims that it simply wants nuclear power for the purposes of electricity generation. But many analysts in the West put Iran into the third category, believing its move toward developing nuclear power is part of a concerted effort to acquire nuclear weapons. In general, the possession of nuclear power may demonstrate the difference between capabilities and intentions when it comes to the production of nuclear weapons. Nuclear power, as explained above, significantly increases the ability of a state to build a nuclear weapon (which is not to say it would be easy or quick, just that it is theoretically possible). However, operating a nuclear power plant does not say anything, necessarily, about the desire of a state to acquire nuclear weapons (though there may be a link between the two, see Fuhrmann 2009b).[4]

From this simple way of conceptualizing the acquisition of nuclear power we can derive several different hypotheses, drawn from different theoretical logics that explain the possible relationship between a nuclear power program and the international security environment. There are signals and shifts in potential relative power that are associated with the possession of subcomponents or precursors to having nuclear weapons, rather than nuclear weapons themselves. First and most simply, the acquisition of commercial nuclear power, given the technological complexity, could signal something about the economic and overall power of a country. We know that countries with greater levels of power, all other things equal, are often more belligerent or more likely to achieve their goals in an international conflict scenario, though it depends on the gap between two countries in a given scenario (Bennett and Stam 2000). Countries that have just acquired nuclear power, since it gives them a larger capacity to build nuclear weapons, may seek to exert more power in the international security environment. Nuclear power becomes a potential proxy for nuclear weapons as countries leverage their nuclear power plants to show the international community that it had best cooperate with the demands of a country or else it might go nuclear. This is especially true for those states that have complete uranium enrichment or plutonium reprocessing capabilities—the latent capability to build a nuclear weapon. Possessing uranium enrichment or plutonium reprocessing means a country could, if it wanted to, divert the fuel necessary to build nuclear weapons, even if it does not have an active nuclear weapons program at present. Possessing that capability could be a key signal of the proliferation "potential" of a country, even more so than nuclear power itself.

Hypothesis 1: The further a country moves toward acquiring nuclear power, especially including uranium enrichment and plutonium reprocessing, the more likely it is to initiate militarized disputes.

This argument might also work the other way. It is possible that countries acquiring nuclear power may be especially sensitive to the opinions of the international community. A country in the first or second category described above may want to do whatever is necessary to assuage concerns about its potential acquisition of nuclear weapons. Therefore, the state may be less aggressive than it otherwise would be.

A country in the third category—using its nuclear power program specifically to build nuclear weapons—might also have strategic incentives to cooperate in the international security environment. Whether they fear an Osirak-style attack on their nuclear reactors or just excessive scrutiny, even a determined proliferator might become more conservative as it gets closer to mastering the nuclear fuel cycle and the period immediately following its completion of a nuclear power plant. The country might not want to provoke the international community so it can divert nuclear fuel in small quantities and build toward acquiring a nuclear weapon.

Hypothesis 2: The further a country moves toward acquiring nuclear power, especially including uranium enrichment and/or plutonium reprocessing, the less likely it is to initiate militarized disputes.

The possession of nuclear power may also be completely unrelated to the initiation of militarized disputes. Given that commercial nuclear power is not necessarily related to the possession of nuclear weapons, and at best may just signal levels of economic sophistication and energy insecurity, it is possible that no relationship exists. In fact, this is the most likely outcome. For example, compare how the international community views Canada's nuclear power program with how it evaluates Iran's nuclear power program. Countries do not fear Canadian revisionist policies resulting from Canada's possession of commercial nuclear power, but they do worry about the security implications of an Iranian nuclear bomb.

Hypothesis 3: There is no relationship between civilian nuclear power, especially including uranium enrichment and/or plutonium reprocessing, and militarized disputes.

These hypotheses are only applicable to those states that acquire nuclear power before they potentially acquire nuclear weapons. Since nuclear weapons predate nuclear power in international politics, several of the states that have acquired nuclear weapons did so before they created commercially viable nuclear power plants. Table 12.1 shows a list of when each of the first five states that acquired nuclear weapons first exploded a nuclear device, along with when they first completed a commercial nuclear power plant.[5]

Beginning with France, many of the states that have acquired nuclear weapons, besides China, mastered the nuclear fuel cycle prior to its acquisition of nuclear weapons. All except Israel have constructed working nuclear power plants that generated some sort of commercial electricity prior to their acquisition of nuclear weapons. Israel has two nuclear reactors that are theoretically utilized for research purposes only. The first went on line in 1960 and the second in 1962, meaning that both were producing nuclear energy prior to Israel's acquisition of nuclear weapons—whether that is coded as 1966, 1967, or 1973 (depending on the source).

Given that nuclear power preceded proliferation for many of the states that have acquired nuclear weapons since Great Britain did, it is possible to use nuclear power as a potentially useful data point to understand how movement along the nuclear fuel cycle may influence the behavior of potential

TABLE 12.1 Nuclear weapons acquisition versus nuclear power acquisition for first five nuclear weapons states

Country	Nuclear weapons acquisition	Nuclear power acquisition
United States	1945	1957
Soviet Union	1949	1954
United Kingdom	1952	1956
France	1960	1959
China	1964	1991

proliferators. This also means introducing the notion of time. Just as Horowitz (2009) finds that the length of time countries have nuclear weapons influences their behavior, with more experienced nuclear states more likely to succeed in their militarized challenges but also more likely to back down in nonvital issue areas, it is possible that the length of time countries have particular aspects of nuclear power also influences their behavior.

Possession of nuclear power for some length of time may influence how a nation views its potential to acquire nuclear weapons and its leverage in the international security environment. This sort of behavioral change could occur because of the reduction in uncertainty that accompanies how a state will behave once it gets a new capability—or a precursor capability like civilian nuclear power—as a state possesses that capability over time. For example, a country that has possessed nuclear power for a long period and reprocesses the spent fuel has clearly mastered the nuclear fuel cycle and likely has the ability to build nuclear weapons if it chooses, though the time between such a decision and actual proliferation could vary from country to country.

Therefore, states with established nuclear power programs that have not acquired nuclear weapons are probably feared as potential long-term proliferators but trusted as unlikely to proliferate in the short term; they have had nuclear power and sometimes even mastery of the fuel cycle for years but have not acquired nuclear weapons. This perception could, however, go both ways when it comes to how its militarized behavior gets "treated" in the international system. States with more experience with civilian nuclear power could experience greater success in militarized disputes because they are perceived as responsible, meaning when they decide to initiate a dispute it must be a serious issue. Conversely, a state that is "responsible" with nuclear power—that has had civilian nuclear power for a long period without proliferating—may not be considered a serious threat. Other states are unlikely to fear them, and their disputes are more likely to be reciprocated.

Hypothesis 4a: The longer a state has nuclear power, especially including uranium enrichment and/or plutonium reprocessing, without proliferating, the lower the chances that its disputes will be reciprocated.

Hypothesis 4b: The longer a state has nuclear power, especially including uranium enrichment and/or plutonium reprocessing, without proliferating, the higher the chances that its disputes will be reciprocated.

Research Design

Universe of Cases and Key Variables of Interest

To test the monadic relationship between different levels of nuclear capability and militarized behavior, this chapter utilizes a dataset of country-years from 1945 to 2000 drawn from universe of nation-states according to the Correlates of War project. This universe of country-years is identical to that used in previous published work on nuclear weapons, such as Singh and Way (2004) and Fuhrmann (2009b). The dependent variable for the first set of tests is whether a country initiated a militarized dispute in a given year. The militarized dispute data comes from the MIDS 3.02 dataset (Ghosn, Palmer, and Bremer 2003). Other dependent variables are described as appropriate in the results section.

There are several key independent variables of interest designed to help test the relationship between nuclear capabilities short of nuclear weapons and the international security environment. *Nuclear Power* (1 = yes, 0 = no) measures whether or not a country has an operational nuclear power plant in a given year. The data comes from a 2006 International Atomic Energy Agency (IAEA) report on nuclear reactors around the world that lists both operational and inactive reactors (IAEA 2006). Building on Horowitz (2009) and Gartzke (2009), the number of years a country has had nuclear power may also influence its behavior. Therefore, a count variable, *Nuclear Power Years*, is included to measure the number of years a country has had nuclear power. The variable is coded "0" the first year a country has nuclear power, "1" the second year, and so on.

The second key independent variable is whether a state has uranium enrichment and plutonium reprocessing capabilities. Data gathered by Zetner, Coles, and Talbert (2005) and Fuhrmann (2012) describe which countries possess full control of the nuclear fuel cycle in a given year. *Enrichment & Reprocessing* (1 = yes, 0 = no) measures whether or not a state has operational enrichment and/or reprocessing facilities in a given year.[6] *Enrichment & Reprocessing Years*, like *Nuclear Power Years*, measures the number of years a country has had enrichment and reprocessing capabilities.

Finally, based on prior work on nuclear transfers by Fuhrmann and Kroenig, additional variables are included measuring whether or not a state has signed an NCA in a given year—*NCA*, based on Fuhrmann (2009b)—and whether a state has received sensitive nuclear assistance in a given year—*Sensitive Nuclear Assistance* (Kroenig 2009a). Each is coded 1 if an agreement or transfer (depending on the variable) occurs in a given year, and 0 otherwise.

While the primary variables of interest in this chapter involve nuclear capabilities below that of having a nuclear arsenal, it is also important to control for whether or not states in question have nuclear weapons or intend to acquire nuclear weapons. This is especially true for the states with active nuclear power plants, since some of them, such as the United States, also have nuclear weapons. Therefore, two additional variables are created. First, *Nuclear Weapons Program* tests the difference between the capability of building nuclear weapons and the intention of using them. It measures whether or not a state has an active nuclear weapons program (once a state gets nuclear weapons, the variable becomes 0). Drawn from Singh and Way (2004), this variable combines those states that Singh and Way code as exploring nuclear weapons with those states coded as pursuing nuclear weapons.[7] A nuclear weapons program count variable, *Nuclear Weapons Program Years*, is also generated, which measures the number of years a country has had an active nuclear weapons program. Then, using the common set of proliferation dates used in this volume, a *Nuclear Weapons* variable is created and coded 0 if a state does not have nuclear weapons and 1 if it does.[8]

Control Variables

All results below are presented with and without control variables to demonstrate their consistency under a variety of specifications (Achen 2005). However, to help control for other factors that might be correlated with the pursuit of nuclear weapons or nuclear power and might also influence militarized dispute participation, several other control variables are added. It is possible that the possession of nuclear power is really just a proxy for the economic development level of a country, meaning, it is important to have an economic control. *GDP per capita* measures the per capita gross domestic product of each state in a given year (Singh and Way 2004).

The conventional power of countries may also influence their general propensity to be involved in militarized disputes—and prior research also demonstrates the way strategic considerations play an important role in the spread of nuclear weapons (Jo and Gartzke 2007; Kroenig 2009a). *Conventional Power* has the composite index of national capabilities (CINC) score of each country—the index is based on military size, military spending, population indicators, and economic development indicators. The index runs from 0 to 1, with higher scores representing a higher level of overall power. The data comes from the National Material Capabilities 3.02 dataset (Singer 1987; Correlates of War 2 Project 2006). Similarly, the models control for whether a state is involved in an enduring rivalry. *Rivalry*, taken from the Singh and Way dataset (2004), is coded 1 if a country is part of an enduring rivalry, meaning, it likely has a stronger security incentive to pursue nuclear weapons—and potentially a higher propensity to get involved in militarized disputes—and 0 otherwise. *Polity*, drawn from the Polity IV dataset (Jaggers and Gurr 1995), assesses a state's relative level of autocracy or democracy. It is coded from −10 to 10, with −10 signifying the most autocratic states and 10 signifying the most democratic states. Finally, given the importance of the nuclear Non-Proliferation Treaty since 1968 in serving as the coordinating basis for international discussions concerning nuclear weapons and IAEA inspection activities, an *NPT* variable is utilized, coded 1 if the country has ratified the NPT and 0 otherwise (drawn from Fuhrmann 2009a).

Results

Simple Statistics

As a first step in evaluating the relationship between nuclear power, nuclear weapons programs, and the international security environment, it makes sense to look at the correlation between nuclear weapons program and nuclear power. Table 12.2 displays the list of states the IAEA considers as nuclear power "operators" between 1945 and 2005 and compares it to the Singh and Way lists of states exploring nuclear weapons and with an active nuclear weapons program. The exploration and program variables are the deconstructed version of the *Nuclear Weapons Program Years* variable described above and discussed below.[9]

Displaying the IAEA list of nuclear power operators reveals an important potential limitation to the IAEA data: They only include states with nuclear reactors that connect to commercial grids. They exclude research reactors. For example, Greece operates a 10 megawatt (MW) research reactor that the IAEA data does not include. Australia also operates a small reactor designed for engineering and medical research. In most cases, this exclusion should not matter, since it is the operation of larger nuclear reactors that will definitively give states the expertise to build nuclear weapons. The IAEA data also does not include data on North Korea, since North Korea operates outside of IAEA constraints. Therefore, the North Korean reactor at Yongbyon, which was operational, according to most estimates, from 1987 to 1994, was added to the table.

TABLE 12.2 Relationship between nuclear power acquisition and nuclear weapons development programs

Country	Nuclear power acquisition	Nuclear weapons exploration	Nuclear weapons program
Soviet Union/Russia	1954		1945–1948
United Kingdom	1956	1945–1946	1947–1951
United States	1957		Already a nuclear power
France	1959	1946–1953	1954–1959
Canada	1962		
Belgium	1962		
Sweden	1964	1954–1969	
German Federal Rep.	1966		
Spain	1968		
Netherlands	1969		
Switzerland	1969	1946–1969	
Japan	1970		
Argentina	1974	1968–1977	1978–1990
Bulgaria	1974		
Finland	1977		
Yugoslavia	1981	1954–1965; 1974–1988	
Brazil	1982	1953–1977	1978–1990
South Africa	1984	1969–1973	1974–1978
North Korea[a]	1987	1965–1979	1980–2002
Mexico	1989		
Germany	1990		
Lithuania	1991		
Ukraine	1991		
Armenia	1991		
China	1991		1955–1963
Slovenia	1992		
Czech Republic	1993		
Slovakia	1993		
Romania	1996	1985–1993	

(continued)

TABLE 12.2 (*Continued*)

Country	Nuclear power acquisition	Nuclear weapons exploration	Nuclear weapons program
Italy	1963–1989		
Czechoslovakia	1985–1992		
Kazakhstan	1991–1998		
Hungary			
Libya			1970–2000
Algeria		1983–2000	
Iran		1984	1985–2000
Iraq		1976–1981	1982–2000
Israel		1949–1957	1958–1966
Taiwan		1967–1977	

[a]North Korea years drawn from Global Security Project at http://www.globalsecurity.org/wmd/world/dprk/yongbyon-5.htm. Other data drawn from IAEA 2006b, Zetner et al. 2005, and Fuhrmann 2010.

Table 12.2 is striking because it demonstrates significant variation between those states that acquire nuclear power and those states that have demonstrated at least some interest in getting nuclear weapons. The overall correlation between nuclear power and a nuclear weapons program is only 7.4 percent, though the correlation rises to 11.0 percent if those states with nuclear weapons are excluded from the list of states with nuclear power. While all the states that have acquired nuclear weapons have operational commercial nuclear power plants except for Israel (which has had research reactors since the early 1960s), many states with operational nuclear power either have defunct nuclear weapons programs—such as Argentina and Brazil—or have never had an active nuclear weapons program, such as Japan and Canada. By showing the variation between those states with nuclear power and those with nuclear weapons programs, Table 12.2 suggests that there are likely to be differences in the behavior of those with nuclear power and those with aspirations to acquire nuclear weapons.

Militarized Dispute Initiation

The hypotheses above are tested through regression analysis. The initial tests of Hypotheses 1 and 2 are conducted on a country-year dataset where there is one observation per country per year. Since the dependent variable is dichotomous, a probit regression with robust standard errors and cluster on specific countries is utilized to account for the disproportionate impact that individual countries might have on the results. Table 12.3 shows the results.

The results provide initial confirmation of a relationship between nuclear power and militarized behavior. In the simple model, the *Nuclear Power* coefficient is –0.530, though it is only significant to the 0.1 level. While only mildly significant by conventional standards, the result still demonstrates that possessing nuclear power predicts the opposite result of having a nuclear weapons program—a decline in the probability that a state initiates a militarized dispute. Conventional wisdom makes these results seem plausible. Many countries that rarely get involved in militarized disputes, such as Canada and Finland, possess nuclear power but do not have active nuclear weapons programs. The age variable for nuclear power is significant, however, though in a positive direction, meaning that the longer states have commercial nuclear power, the higher the probability that they initiate a militarized dispute. This is somewhat surprising since, as explained above, the theoretical warrant for why nuclear power should matter over time is limited.

Interestingly, the *Enrichment & Reprocessing* variable is not significant. This holds whether or not the value of the variable is set to 0 for countries that have acquired nuclear weapons. This is surprising because the strongest signal of the capacity to build nuclear weapons is not necessarily just having a nuclear power plant, but controlling the nuclear fuel cycle. Additionally, confirming some of the results in Beardsley and Asal (Chapter 11 in this volume), the control variable measuring whether or not states have a nuclear weapons program produced strong results. In the simple model, the *Nuclear Weapons Program* coefficient is 1.583 and significant to the .01 level, signifying a strong positive relationship between having a nuclear weapons program and Militarized Interstate Dispute (MID) initiation. While this initial test does not allow us to distinguish between whether or not states that are *already* at risk pursue nuclear weapons, making them more prone to initiating disputes, or whether there is something about the pursuit of nuclear weapons that leads a country to change its behavioral calculations, the significant result is encouraging.

Similarly, the coefficient for *Nuclear Weapons Program Years* is not statistically significant, suggesting that, whatever the causal pathway through which nuclear weapons programs are associated with a greater probability of dispute initiations, the length of time a country has an active program is not

TABLE 12.3 Relationship between nuclear power, nuclear weapons programs, and militarized dispute initiation

	Model 1: Simple model	Model 2: Additional assistance variables	Model 3: Full model	Model 4: MID count (negative binomial model)
	coefficent (standard error)	coefficent (standard error)	coefficent (standard error)	coefficent (standard error)
Nuclear weapons	1.667*** (0.376)	2.485** (1.019)	2.040 (1.467)	1.104*** (0.413)
Nuclear weapons program	1.583*** (0.366)	1.566*** (0.376)	1.061** (0.421)	0.801*** (0.275)
Nuclear weapons program years	−0.018 (0.0233)	−0.016 (0.0269)	0.010 (0.0222)	−0.004 (0.0142)
Nuclear power	−0.530* (0.318)	−0.848* (0.446)	−1.005* (0.552)	−0.633** (0.260)
Nuclear power years	0.017 (0.021)	0.043 (0.028)	0.053 (0.034)	0.025* (0.014)
Enrichment and reprocessing	0.408 (0.325)	0.207 (0.473)	−0.159 (0.464)	−0.287 (0.225)
Enrichment and reprocessing years	0.022 (0.020)	0.029 (0.022)	0.039 (0.026)	0.020 (0.013)
Sensitive nuclear assistance recipient		0.132 (0.450)	−0.656 (0.518)	0.217 (0.244)
Nuclear cooperation agreements count		−0.002 (0.007)	0.012 (0.009)	0.007 (0.005)
Gross domestic product per capita			−4.66e−05** (2.25e−05)	−1.40e−05 (1.43e−05)
Conventional power			14.46* (7.876)	8.222*** (2.979)
Polity			−0.019 (0.013)	−0.001 (0.009)
Enduring rivalry			1.599*** (0.195)	1.448*** (0.124)
Nuclear Non-Proliferation Treaty			0.269* (0.154)	0.175 (0.115)
Constant	−1.755*** (0.113)	−1.703*** (0.116)	−2.360*** (0.182)	−1.523*** (0.123)

NOTE: $*p < .1$, $**p < .05$, $***p < .01$; robust standard error in parentheses.

Model 1: N = 7,432, Wald X^2 (7): 93.78, Pseudo R^2: 0.084, Log pseudolikelihood: −3,277. 189 clusters.

Model 2: N = 5,895, Wald X^2 (9): 61.56, Pseudo R^2: 0.042, Log pseudolikelihood: −2,626. 156 clusters.

Model 3: N = 5,500, Wald X^2 (14): 200.3, Pseudo R^2: 0.148, Log pseudolikelihood: −2,209. 153 clusters.

Model 4: N = 5,500, Wald X^2 (14): 515.9, Log pseudolikelihood: −4,801, /lnalpha: −0.47 (0.183)***, alpha: 0.627 (.115). 153 clusters.

as relevant. In some ways, this is surprising. Countries such as Libya that had very active nuclear weapons programs for a long period are considered "risky" states in the West; if they are able to continue their program over time, presumably they would grow more powerful and then become more likely to initiate a MID. However, perhaps a greater length of time at pursuing nuclear weapons demonstrates that a country is not capable of succeeding at an acceptable cost. After all, if they had the ability to get nuclear weapons, presumably they would have "dropped out" of the nuclear weapons program category and acquired nuclear weapons.[10]

Model 2 adds the NCA and sensitive nuclear assistance recipient variables to try to get a further nuance on how different levels of nuclear capabilities might influence national behavior. The sensitive assistance variable is not significant in any of the models, and neither is the NCA variable. Model 3 shows why, in this case, it is important to control for some of the other factors that influence why states initiate militarized disputes. All of the variables are in the predicted directions, though many are not significant. Adding in the controls, however, shows the strength of the *Nuclear Power* variable and the *Nuclear Weapons Program* control variable. The coefficient and significance levels are nearly identical across all the models. Adding in the controls slightly increases the significance of the *Nuclear Power* variable and makes the *Nuclear Power Years* variable significant at the 0.1 level. This suggests that, in the mostly completely specified model, the longer countries have nuclear power, the less likely they become to initiate militarized disputes.[11]

As an additional test, Model 4 utilizes a different dependent variable. Instead of just testing for the probability of MID initiation, the dependent variation for Model 4 is a count of the number of MIDs a country is involved in during a given year. This is a way to understand the more general propensity of a country to get involved in disputes as opposed to the probability that a country will initiate disputes. Given the different form of the dependent variable, the appropriate model is a negative binomial (King 1989). The results confirm the findings in Models 1–3, increasing our confidence in the overall results.

Figure 12.1 shows the substantive effect on MID initiation of varying whether or not states have an active nuclear weapons program by whether or not they have commercial nuclear power and whether they have nuclear weapons.[12] High risk are those with a nuclear weapons program but which lack nuclear power—this makes sense, since those are the states, such as Iraq,

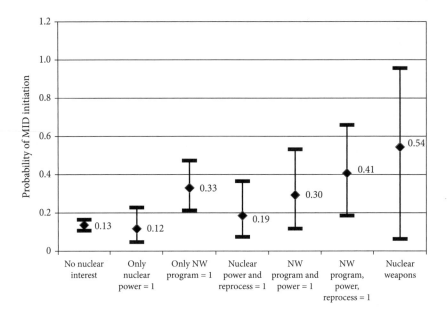

FIGURE 12.1 Substantive relationship between nuclear power, nuclear weapons development, and militarized dispute (MID) initiation for non-nuclear states

Iran, and North Korea (prior to the activation of the Yongbyon reactor), that are considered most risky by status quo states like the United States. Also, the cumulative effect of having a nuclear weapons program, nuclear power, and reprocessing shows the combined impact of capabilities and intentions on state behavior.

Militarized Dispute Reciprocation

Testing Hypotheses 3 and 4 involves changing the dependent variable to focus on dispute reciprocation. Here, the universe of cases changes to the directed dispute dyad, and the dependent variable, based on Schultz (1999) and Horowitz (2009), is whether a MID initiation is reciprocated. Several new control variables are included to ensure replicability with previous research, along with the Signorino/Ritter dyadic S score, the basis of the disputes (territory, regime change, or policy), the conventional balance between the two states, and regime type. For more on these variables, see Horowitz (2009).

A directed dispute dyads setup is the best way to test these hypotheses, which ask whether possessing nuclear power for an extended period of time makes a state seem nonthreatening—meaning, its MIDs are more likely to be reciprocated—or makes the challenges of such a state especially credible—meaning, its disputes are less likely to be reciprocated. Model 1 in Table 12.4 shows a conditional logit fixed-effects model with robust standard errors. As is obvious from the output, nonvarying outcomes within dyads, meaning, the high number of dyads without variation within observations, leads many observations and variables to be dropped. Model 2 turns to a simpler logit model. Even this model has some issues. There are only 525 observations, and the standard errors are adjusted for clustering on 247 observations—more than half.

The number of observations is sufficiently low that it is hard to make much out of these results, especially in Model 1. However, one interesting finding from Model 1 is that the *Enrichment & Reprocessing* variable, which was not significant in the monadic setup, becomes significant. For dispute initiators, the possession of a reprocessing or enrichment program makes other states much more likely to reciprocate those disputes. This suggests that countries do not want to allow potential proliferating states—those with control of the nuclear fuel cycle—to boss them around, especially when those states lack nuclear weapons. Additionally, the coefficient for states with enrichment or reprocessing that are responding to militarized challenges is −21.33 and significant to the 0.01 level. Countries with reprocessing programs, as the logic of Hypothesis 2 suggests, may seek to avoid confrontations by backing down in the face of militarized disputes. Similarly, for states with nuclear weapons programs that are responding to militarized challenges, the coefficient is also highly negative and significant. Those states that have the most to lose from escalating a dispute, because they do not have the nuclear weapons necessary to provide an existential deterrent but they do have some nuclear capabilities—either a weapons program or functioning enrichment and/or reprocessing—appear the most risk-averse. Almost none of the variables of interest in Model 2 are significant. One variable that is significant in both Model 1 and Model 2 is the coefficient for the *Side A Nuclear Power Years* variable. This means that the longer a state has an active nuclear power program, controlling for whether a state has nuclear weapons or a nuclear weapons program, the higher the chances that its disputes will be reciprocated. The result

TABLE 12.4 Relationship between nuclear power, nuclear weapons programs, and militarized dispute reciprocation

	Model 1: Conditional fixed effects logit	Model 2: Logit
	coefficient (standard error)	coefficient (standard error)
Side A nuclear weapons	Forcibly dropped	0.952 (1.382)
Side B nuclear weapons	Forcibly dropped	0.132 (1.158)
Side A nuclear power	0.503 (1.412)	−1.108 (0.870)
Side B nuclear power	3.803* (1.993)	0.147 (1.120)
Side A nuclear power years	1.440** (0.717)	0.165** (0.072)
Side B nuclear power years	−0.118 (0.205)	0.0255 (0.076)
Side A enrichment and reprocessing	4.271*** (1.293)	0.728 (0.562)
Side B enrichment and reprocessing	−21.33*** (5.778)	−0.530 (0.939)
Side A enrichment and reprocessing years	−0.318 (0.366)	−0.054 (0.050)
Side B enrichment and reprocessing years	1.717*** (0.374)	0.0349 (0.080)
Side A Nuclear Weapons Program	0.629 (0.888)	0.840 (0.664)
Side B nuclear weapons program	−20.01*** (2.485)	0.460 (0.572)
Side A nuclear weapons program years	0.001 (0.077)	0.006 (0.048)
Side B nuclear weapons program years	0.0233 (0.237)	0.0609 (0.065)
Side A nuclear cooperation agreements	−0.135* (0.078)	−0.0625** (0.025)
Side B nuclear cooperation agreements	−0.268** (0.127)	−0.028 (0.022)
Side A sensitive nuclear assistance recipient	1.854 (1.442)	−0.654 (0.599)
Side B sensitive nuclear assistance recipient	0.129 (0.918)	−0.437 (0.611)

(continued)

TABLE 12.4 *(Continued)*

	Model 1: Conditional fixed effects logit	Model 2: Logit
	coefficient (standard error)	coefficient (standard error)
Dyadic S score	1.208 (2.597)	0.546 (0.476)
Balance of forces	6.626 (5.691)	0.407 (0.504)
Side A democracy	0.840 (0.794)	−0.218 (0.326)
Side B democracy	1.474 (1.589)	−0.371 (0.407)
Territory	2.111* (1.172)	2.185*** (0.613)
Policy	0.931 (0.883)	0.587 (0.571)
Regime/government	3.002 (2.302)	1.375* (0.808)
Constant		−1.850** (0.790)

NOTE: $*p < .1$, $**p < .05$, $***p < .01$; robust standard error in parentheses.
Model 1: N, 224, Wald X^2 (26): 8.670e+10, Pseudo R^2: 0.199, Log pseudolikelihood: −70.89.
Model 2: N, 525, Wald X^2 (28): 118.3, Pseudo R^2: 0.204, Log pseudolikelihood: −275.7. Adjusted for 247 clusters.

confirms some of the logic behind Hypothesis 3—states that possess nuclear power but not nuclear weapons for a long period may be perceived as especially responsible rule followers, meaning, they are less likely to be feared by others.

It is possible that these variables are just not that important compared to the many factors that influence how a state responds to a militarized challenge. While the status of a country's nuclear power program may play some role in influencing how a state views its relative power and how other states perceive its relative power, other variables simply matter more.

Conclusion

As a look at the relationship between indicators of potential future nuclear capabilities—primarily civilian nuclear power and nuclear weapons development programs—this chapter reveals important differences in the way those two types of capabilities manifest themselves in the international security realm. States with nuclear weapons development programs are significantly more likely than similar states to initiate militarized disputes. Nuclear weapons development programs signal something about the intentions of a state and its dissatisfaction (in some way) with the status quo. Also, the amount of time that countries have nuclear weapons development programs does not appear to change significantly how those states behave (their probability of initiating MIDs) or how others view them (the probability that their MIDs are reciprocated). This suggests that the signal sent by a nuclear weapons development program is a weak one.

These results are only suggestive, because they do not resolve the fundamental question of whether correlations between nuclear weapons development programs and various MID-based dependent variables are due to actual substantive relationships. The results could mask conflictual behavior on the part of the involved states, meaning that nuclear weapons programs, especially, indicate conflict patterns rather than drive conflict patterns. Additionally, the impact of nuclear weapons is inconsistent throughout the statistical results, though the balance of the findings suggest a positive relationship between nuclear weapons possession and international disputes. Overall, the results show that nuclear power is not a panacea—if countries use it to acquire nuclear weapons, there are potentially negative consequences for international security.

This chapter also presents new data on civilian nuclear power—a dataset of active countries with civilian nuclear power from 1945 to 2000. Possessing civilian nuclear power, while a crucial stepping stone for many states on the way to acquiring nuclear weapons, is either negatively related to conflictual behavior or has no relationship at all. Given that many of the states with commercial nuclear power are not among the most risky in international politics in general—such as Canada—these results provide quantitative verification of the conventional wisdom. However, in light of research by Fuhrmann and others about the potential tacit links between NCAs, nuclear power, and proliferation, this negative or insignificant relationship might reverse itself in the future. In particular, in a world where progress toward nuclear reductions reverses, some states with civilian nuclear power might begin to prepare quietly for a world where they need to build their own small nuclear arsenal. Such an outcome might become likely if the ongoing economic struggles in the

United States lead the country to pull back significantly from its international obligations, including its extended deterrence umbrella. Therefore, while this chapter identifies important links between civilian nuclear power, nuclear weapons programs, and the international security environment, it is likely to be the first word on this subject rather than the last.

Notes

1. Some estimate that Japan could build a nuclear weapon within six months, though others think the real time would be closer to eighteen months or longer. For a discussion of this issue, see Lewis 2006. Also see Erikson 2003.

2. Alternatively, Hewitt (2011) suggests that public opinion has definitively turned against nuclear power.

3. Essentially, nuclear power and especially mastery of the fuel cycle would represent latent nuclear weapons potential.

4. In contrast, a state with a nuclear weapons program almost certainly wants to acquire nuclear weapons—unless the program is just meant as a signal of some sort and the state has no intention to acquire—but does not necessarily mean that a state has the capability to get nuclear weapons. For more on this, see the Beardsley and Asal chapter in this volume (Chapter 11).

5. The nuclear power data is taken from a 2006 IAEA report on nuclear energy (IAEA 2006).

6. Setting this variable and the enrichment and reprocessing age variable to 0 for countries that have actually acquired nuclear weapons does not change the results.

7. Future drafts could incorporate additional robustness tests evaluating different codings for nuclear weapons programs.

8. Since the dates do not entirely match up with the Singh and Way nuclear program data, the *Nuclear Weapons Program* variable was recoded to 0 for any instances where *Nuclear Weapons* was 1 but *Nuclear Weapons Program* was also 1. This influenced very few of the cases but was a necessary correction (the *Nuclear Weapons Program Years* variable was also changed ccordingly). The nuclear weapons data comes from the special issue of the *Journal of Conflict Resolution* on nuclear proliferation published in 2009. See Horowitz 2009.

9. The exploration and program codings are combined due to uncertainty about the extent to which some countries pursued nuclear weapons. Research published since 2000 suggests that Australia, for example, had a more extensive nuclear weapons development program than many scholars suspected (Hymans 2006; Reynolds 2000).

10. Alternatively, the mean nuclear weapons program time for states that have acquired nuclear weapons is 11.5 years while the mean for all states with nuclear weapons programs is 10.9 years.

11. Initial tests show that these results are consistent even when the universe of cases is expanded to the directed dyad. While advantageous in many ways because it

lets us see the interactive nature of behavior and how various levels of nuclear capabilities may matter for the defending side, the results are excluded because they are similar to those presented in Table 12.3. However, they are available upon request from the author at horom@sas.upenn.edu.

12. Generated using postgr3 in Stata 11. All variables are kept at their means except for the relevant *Nuclear Power, Nuclear Weapons Program*, and *Nuclear Weapon* variables.

References

Achen, Christopher H. 2005. "Let's Put Garbage-Can Regressions and Garbage-Can Probits Where They Belong." *Conflict Management and Peace Science* 22 (4): 327–339.

Beardsley, Kyle, and Victor Asal. 2009. "Winning with the Bomb." *Journal of Conflict Resolution* 53 (2): 278–301.

Bennett, D. Scott, and Allan C. Stam. 2000. "EUGene: A Conceptual Manual." *International Interactions* 26 (2): 179–204.

Betts, Richard K. 1987. *Nuclear Blackmail and Nuclear Balance.* Washington, DC: Brookings Institution.

Caldicott, Helen. 2006. *Nuclear Power Is Not the Answer to Global Warming or Anything Else.* New York: The New Press.

Correlates of War 2 Project. 2006. *National Material Capabilities Data Documentation, Updated for Version 3.2.* State College: Pennsylvania State University.

Diyakov, Anatoly S. 2009. "The Nuclear Renaissance and Preventing the Spread of Enrichment and Reprocessing Technologies: A Russian View." *Daedalus* 139 (1): 117–125.

Erikson, Marc. 2003. "Japan Could 'Go Nuclear' in Months." *Asia Times*, January 14. Available at: http://www.atimes.com/atimes/Japan/EA14Dh01.html.

Feiveson, Harold, Alexander Glaser, Marvin Miller, and Lawrence Scheinman. 2008. *Can Future Nuclear Power Be Made Proliferation Resistant?* Center for International and Security Studies at Maryland, July. Available at: http://www.cissm.umd.edu/papers/files/future_nuclear_power.pdf.

Fitzpatrick, Mark. 2008. "Will Nuclear Energy Plans in the Middle East Become Nuclear Weapons Strategies?" *International Relations* 22 (3): 381–385.

Fuhrmann, Matthew. 2009a. "Taking a Walk on the Supply Side: The Determinants of Civilian Nuclear Cooperation." *Journal of Conflict Resolution* 53 (2): 181–208.

———. 2009b. "Spreading Temptation: Proliferation and Peaceful Nuclear Cooperation Agreements." *International Security* 34 (1): 7–41.

———. 2012. "Splitting Atoms: Why Do Countries Build Nuclear Power Plants?" *International Interactions* 38 (1): 29–57.

Gartzke, Erik. 2009. "Proliferation Dynamics and Conventional Dispute Behavior." Presented at the Annual Meeting of the International Studies Association, New York.

Gartzke, Erik, and Dong-Joon Jo. 2009. "Bargaining, Nuclear Proliferation, and Inter-state Disputes." *Journal of Conflict Resolution* 53 (2): 209–233.

Ghosn, Faten, Glenn Palmer, and Stuart Bremer. 2004. "The MID3 Data Set, 1993–2001: Procedures, Coding Rules, and Description." *Conflict Management and Peace Science* 21: 133–154.

Harrell, Eben. 2011. "Fukushima: The End of the Nuclear Renaissance?" *Time*, March 14. Available at: http://science.time.com/2011/03/14/fukushima-the-end-of-the-nuclear-renaissance/.

Hewitt, Bill. 2011. "Nuclear Renaissance (Not)." *Foreign Policy Association*. June 17. Available at: http://foreignpolicyblogs.com/2011/06/17/nuclear-renaissance-not/.

Horowitz, Michael. 2009. "The Spread of Nuclear Weapons and International Conflict: Does Experience Matter?" *Journal of Conflict Resolution* 53 (2): 234–257.

Hymans, Jacques E. C. 2006. *The Psychology of Nuclear Proliferation: Identity, Emotions, and Foreign Policy.* New York: Cambridge University Press.

IAEA. 2006. "Nuclear Power Reactors in the World." *Reference Data Series #2.* Vienna: IAEA.

Jaggers, Keith, and Ted Robert Gurr. 1995. "Tracking Democracy's Third Wave with the Polity III Data." *Journal of Peace Research* 32 (4): 469–482.

Jo, Dong-Joon, and Erik Gartzke. 2007. "Determinants of Nuclear Weapons Proliferation." *Journal of Conflict Resolution* 51 (1): 1–28.

King, Gary. 1989. *Unifying Political Methodology: The Likelihood Theory of Statistical Inference.* Ann Arbor: University of Michigan Press.

Kroenig, Matthew. 2009a. "Exporting the Bomb: Why States Provide Sensitive Nuclear Assistance." *American Political Science Review* 103 (1): 113–133.

———. 2009b. "Importing the Bomb: Sensitive Nuclear Assistance and Nuclear Proliferation." *Journal of Conflict Resolution* 53 (2): 161–180.

Lauvergeon, Anne. 2009. "The Nuclear Renaissance: An Opportunity to Enhance the Culture of Nonproliferation." *Daedalus* 138 (4): 91–99.

Lewis, Jeffrey. 2006. "How Long for Japan to Build a Deterrent?" *Arms Control Wonk.* December 28. Available at: http://lewis.armscontrolwonk.com/archive/1339/japans-nuclear-status.

Miller, Steven E., and Scott D. Sagan. 2009. "Nuclear Power Without Nuclear Proliferation?" *Daedalus* 138 (4): 7–18.

Mueller, John. 1999. "The Escalating Irrelevance of Nuclear Weapons." In *The Absolute Weapon Revisited: Nuclear Arms and the Emerging International Order*, eds. T. V. Paul, R. J. Harknett, and J. Wirtz. Ann Arbor: University of Michigan Press.

Powell, Robert. 1989. "Crisis Stability in the Nuclear Age." *The American Political Science Review* 83 (1): 61–76.

Rauchhaus, Robert. 2009. "Evaluating the Nuclear Peace Hypothesis: A Quantitative Approach." *Journal of Conflict Resolution* 53 (2): 258–277.

Reynolds, Wayne. 2000. *Australia's Bid for the Atomic Bomb.* Carlton, Victoria, Australia: Melbourne University Press.

Sagan, Scott D. 1995. "More Will Be Worse." In *The Spread of Nuclear Weapons: A Debate*, eds. S. D. Sagan and K. N. Waltz. New York: W. W. Norton.

———. 2010. *Nuclear Power, Nuclear Proliferation, and the NPT.* Paper presented at the Annual Meeting of the American Political Science Association, Washington, DC, September 2–5.

Schultz, Kenneth A. 1999. "Do Democratic Institutions Constrain or Inform? Contrasting Two Institutional Perspectives on Democracy and War." *International Organization* 53 (2): 233–266.

Singer, J. David. 1987. "Reconstructing the Correlates of War Dataset on Material Capabilities of States, 1816–1985." *International Interactions* 14 (2): 115–132.

Singh, Sonali, and Christopher Way. 2004. "The Correlates of Nuclear Proliferation: A Quantitative Test." *Journal of Conflict Resolution* 48 (6): 859–885.

Socolow, Robert, and Alexander Glaser. 2009. "Balancing Risks: Nuclear Energy & Climate Change." *Daedalus.* 138 (4): 31–44.

Squassoni, Sharon. 2008. "Nuclear Renaissance: Is It Coming? Should It?" *Carnegie Endowment for International Peace Report on Foreign Policy for the Next President.* October. Available at: http://www.carnegieendowment.org/files/nuclear_renaissance1.pdf.

Waltz, Kenneth N. 1995. "More May Be Better." In *The Spread of Nuclear Weapons: A Debate*, eds. S. D. Sagan and K. N. Waltz. New York: W. W. Norton.

Zetner, M. D., G. L. Coles, and R. J. Talbert. 2005. *Nuclear Proliferation Technology Trends Analysis.* Richland, WA: Pacific Northwest National Laboratory.

13   The Global Nuclear Renaissance and the Spread of Violent Conflict

A Comment

Dan Reiter

S UPPOSE YOU APPROACHED SOMEONE AND ASKED HER, "Would you support an energy source that is relatively cheap, based on existing technology, draws on fuel that will not run out for centuries, can produce energy anywhere on the planet, does not contribute to global warming, does not flood vast areas, does not risk oil spills at sea, does not cause air pollution, does not require strip mining, and does not increase dependence on foreign imports?" Framed that way, she would likely say, yes, she would support such an energy source. Now suppose you instead asked, "Would you support that energy source if it increased the chances of violent clashes or even war between states?" Now, she might not be so sure.

This is exactly the dilemma that the world faces in thinking about the global energy crisis in general, and a possible global nuclear renaissance (GNR) in particular. No energy source is perfect: Coal and natural gas worsen global warming; solar is too expensive; wind and geothermal have sharply limited potential; oil is running out, fuels authoritarian regimes, and risks environmental catastrophes; hydroelectric has limited applications and often requires massive flooding.

The question we must ask is: When we choose our sources of energy, what mix of costs and benefits do we want? Answering that question, of course, requires that we fully understand the advantages and disadvantages of all energy sources. The two chapters authored by Kyle Beardsley and Victor Asal (Chapter 11) and Michael C. Horowitz (Chapter 12) give us a more complete sense of some of the potential risks of nuclear energy, better informing us about some of the dangers that a GNR poses, specifically how it might affect the likelihood of interstate violence. The chapters do so by applying quantitative analysis. This approach offers several benefits, including mathematical rigor, estimates of statistical as well as substantive significance, the ability to simultaneously analyze a number of possible explanations of a particular phenomenon, and the promise of greater ability to generalize.

The Findings

Past consideration of the possible connection between nuclear power and violent conflict has focused on nuclear terrorism. Scholars have speculated that fissile material might be stolen from nuclear energy facilities and converted into nuclear weapons or dirty bombs, or that terrorists might attack a nuclear facility intending to cause a release of radioactivity into the environment. Thankfully, nuclear terrorist events thus far have been few in number and minor in significance (see Allison 2004). The Horowitz and Beardsley/Asal chapters nicely broaden the discussion of the nuclear energy–conflict relationship, exploring the question of whether the spread of nuclear power will make conflict between states more likely. They describe both direct and indirect connections between nuclear power and violent conflict. States may attack nuclear power facilities to prevent the target state from developing nuclear weapons, such as Iraq and Iran attacking each other's nuclear reactors during the Iran–Iraq War. In other cases, it may be that a state possessing nuclear power might engage in aggressive foreign policy initiatives, emboldened by its atomic ace of spades. Finally, nuclear power might be pacifying. If nuclear power provides the foundation for nuclear weapons, and such weapons bolster deterrence, then peace may be strengthened, as foreseen in Winston Churchill's insight that nuclear weapons mean that "safety will be the sturdy child of terror, and survival the twin brother of annihilation."[1]

These are a tangle of ideas, and perhaps not surprisingly the two chapters present a nuanced set of empirical findings. Beardsley and Asal are somewhat pessimistic, finding that within a pair of states, if one state is pursuing nuclear weapons (but does not yet actually have a nuclear arsenal), it is more likely to participate in an international crisis; and a state facing a potential adversary that is pursuing nuclear weapons is itself also more likely to participate in an international crisis. Therefore, the pursuit of nuclear weapons can be an inspiration to aggression as well as a source of fear. Perhaps more encouraging, the physical capacity to acquire nuclear weapons uncoupled from a desire to acquire nuclear weapons (think of Japan's nuclear energy infrastructure blooming in a pacifist context) does not have these destabilizing effects.

Horowitz presents essentially similar findings. He also distinguishes between having a nuclear infrastructure, a civilian nuclear energy program, and pursuing nuclear weapons. Like Beardsley and Asal, he finds that a state pursuing nuclear weapons is more likely to initiate militarized international disputes, whereas a state possessing civilian nuclear energy but no nuclear weapons program is significantly less likely to initiate such disputes. He also explores whether nuclear power programs make the reciprocation of violent moves more likely, but here the inconsistency of the statistical results keeps the picture cloudy.

Israel's conflicts with its neighbors demonstrate these dynamics. It has launched airstrikes against the nuclear facilities of neighbors with nuclear power programs who appear to be pursuing but have not yet attained nuclear weapons, including Iraq in 1981 and Syria in 2007. As of March 2012, it appears that Iran may be next on Israel's list. Conversely, Israel has avoided launching attacks against the nuclear power facilities of Arab neighbors who do not appear to be pursuing nuclear weapons, such as Egypt.

The Big Picture

The central conclusions of these chapters are helpfully suggestive. The threat of more frequent interstate conflict does not emerge essentially and ineluctably from a GNR, as civilian nuclear energy does not by itself make interstate conflict more likely. Nuclear power only destabilizes international relations when it is coupled with the deliberate pursuit of nuclear weapons. One is tempted to say that the pursuit of nuclear weapons is destabilizing but the possession of nuclear weapons is not, as according to Beardsley/Asal the destabilizing effects of a nuclear weapons program fall away once a state actually attains nuclear weapons. But we cannot be too confident in this inverted Goldilocks effect of civilian energy being safe and civilian energy plus nuclear weapons being safe, but the pursuit (and nonpossession) of nuclear weapons with nuclear energy being dangerous, because most of Horowitz's analysis finds that the possession of nuclear weapons makes international disputes more likely, as well.

These chapters search for statistical correlations between nuclear power and interstate conflict. What about a closer look? The indirect effects of nuclear power on conflict, with nuclear power making a state generally more aggressive or making the neighbor of a state with nuclear power generally more insecure, may be, as Horowitz notes, difficult to assess, because nuclear power programs may reflect other factors that also drive conflict. We can get a better sense of the possible direct effects of nuclear power on conflict by examining cases where conflict centered on a state's nuclear power program. Indeed, at least occasionally a nuclear power plant seems to have been a necessary and sufficient cause for violent interstate conflict. We can be fairly certain, for instance, that if Iraq did not have a nuclear power program in 1981, Israel would not have launched an airstrike. Further, Israel would not have attacked Syria in 2007 if Syria had not been secretly building a North Korea–designed nuclear power plant. There have also been minor state-to-state operations omitted by the quantitative datasets used in these two chapters, such as Israeli commando operations against Iraqi scientists and French-built reactor cores destined for Iraq in the 1970s, Israeli cyberattacks on Iranian nuclear facilities in 2010, and others (Hamza 2000). We also know that sometimes nuclear power facilities are attacked in the context of an ongoing war, meaning that attacks on reactors are not always evidence that reactors are necessary or sufficient to cause conflicts. Think of Allied bombing raids on German heavy water production facilities in World War II, Iranian air strikes on Osirak, and Iraqi air strikes on the Iranian reactor at Bushehr during the Iran–Iraq War of the 1980s, and U.N. Coalition airstrikes against Iraqi nuclear facilities in the weeks before the liberation of Kuwait (Reiter 2006).

These instances provide additional insight into the interstate conflict ramifications of the anticipated GNR. When attacks on nuclear reactors have occurred during war, they have not substantially escalated the scope of violence. Allied air raids on Norwegian heavy water facilities in World War II were a minor component of the overall bombing campaign, as were the Coalition air strikes against Iraqi nuclear facilities during Operation Desert Storm. The air strikes in the Iraq–Iran War were small operations in a bloody conflict that killed hundreds of thousands. Further, the occasional violent, interstate conflicts directly caused by a nuclear power program have not been particularly deadly. The 1981 Israeli raid on the Iraqi reactor killed one French technician; several Iraqi soldiers were also killed, but they may have been mostly friendly-fire deaths from Iraqi antiaircraft fire (Hamza 2000: 129). The 2007

Israeli raid on the Syrian reactor may have killed ten or so North Koreans (Kumakura 2008). While any deaths are regrettable, the international community might be better off focusing on other, much more deadly patterns of violence, such as civil war and genocide. Put differently, the death of perhaps five or ten people per decade from interstate conflict caused by nuclear power plants might pale in comparison to the lives saved if nuclear power can ameliorate climate change, a phenomenon which according to one estimate already claims 150,000 lives per year (Patz et al. 2005). A caveat to this point about the relative bloodlessness of such attacks is the possibility that a military attack on a nuclear reactor might lead to the widespread release of radiation. Though none of the military attacks to date have triggered radiation releases (neither the Iraqi, Iranian, or Syrian reactors were operational when they were attacked), such an eventuality could potentially cause tens of thousands of deaths (Ramberg 1986).

One arguable case of a deadly conflict caused by nuclear power is the 2003 Iraq War. The American decision to invade was driven by fears about Iraq's nuclear weapons program and its ties to terrorist groups. Absent fears about Iraq's nuclear weapons ambitions, the war might not have occurred. However, after the 1981 Israeli attack, Iraq's nuclear weapons program became decoupled from its nuclear energy infrastructure. Iraq no longer planned to harvest plutonium from a nuclear reactor, and instead built secret facilities with a primary focus on uranium separation (Reiter 2005). That is, though fears about Iraq's nuclear weapons program were a major factor causing the 2003 war, those fears were not connected to Iraq's nuclear energy infrastructure.

Policy Recommendations

Based on the nuclear power conflict findings from these chapters, should we change our policies? Should we try to slow down or halt a GNR? As with all policy choices, we must carefully analyze the comparative risks of nuclear power. Policy makers have long weighed the risks and benefits of nuclear power, for example assessing the long-term dangers that earthquakes pose to nuclear power reactors and nuclear waste disposal sites (Reiter 1990). The public is familiar with the principal dangers of nuclear power, including nuclear terrorism and the potentially serious environmental problems created by nuclear waste disposal. Recently, concern over reactor accidents escalated following the calamitous 2011 Fukushima episode in Japan.

What about the risks of interstate conflict? We know that there is the potential for an attack motivated by a neighbor's nuclear power program to escalate into something much worse than a limited airstrike, perhaps a full-blown invasion. An attack could also release radiation into the environment, triggering an environmental catastrophe.

The nuclear power–violent conflict question generates an uncontroversial policy recommendation, as well as a more controversial one. The uncontroversial policy recommendation is that the international community should continue to make efforts to prevent nuclear energy programs from supporting nuclear weapons programs. The international community's best tool for severing the nuclear energy–nuclear weapons connection is the nuclear Non-Proliferation Treaty (NPT). The NPT has considerable resources at its disposal: strong global support; extensive and specific rules about what constitutes acceptable and unacceptable nuclear-related activities; a well-funded human infrastructure for inspecting nuclear power facilities; and a connection to the United Nations, which allows for violators to be subjected to economic sanctions. The results from these chapters suggest that if the NPT can successfully and transparently sever the tie between civilian nuclear energy programs and nuclear weapons programs, then a GNR will be less likely to spark international conflicts.

That said, we need to continue to find ways to make the NPT, and the global nonproliferation regime in general, more effective. Additional protocols adopted since the NPT was signed in 1968 have provided International Atomic Energy Agency inspectors with greater authority to examine the civilian nuclear infrastructures of signatory states. However, the ability of such protocols to slow proliferation will be limited as long as countries such as NPT signatories Iran, Syria, and Myanmar refuse to ratify them (none of those three states have yet ratified the 1997 Model Additional Protocol, for example). In particular, Iran's apparent pursuit of a nuclear weapons program while it remains an NPT signatory is a substantial challenge to the NPT. The international community's ongoing interaction with Iran is providing lessons about crafting effective inspection regimes and economic sanctions. Such lessons might help the international community bring future accused violators back into the nonproliferation fold. Beyond the NPT, we can encourage states to adopt proliferation-resistant light water reactor designs, and we can support efforts like the Proliferation Security Initiative, which aims to prevent the illicit transfer of nuclear technologies between nations.

Peaceful nonproliferation efforts aside, a more controversial policy issue is whether attacks on nuclear facilities should be opposed by the international community. Some people may recommend opposing any such attacks, for the sake of supporting international peace and avoiding possible environmental risks connected to such attacks. Observers in this camp might support, for example, international laws banning military attacks on nuclear power facilities, perhaps strengthening the vague language in a 1977 protocol to the Geneva Convention that provides some limits on attacks against such facilities (Ramberg 1986).

Other people may take a more measured view, arguing that attacks on nuclear power facilities might, in some circumstances, be a necessary and useful nonproliferation tool. Certainly, Israel views its attacks on Iraq and Syria as successful, and it is open to launching a future attack against Iranian nuclear facilities. The United States launched attacks against Iraqi facilities, considered launching attacks against Chinese and North Korean nuclear targets, and may yet launch attacks against Iranian nuclear assets. India and Pakistan have each considered launching attacks against each other's nuclear facilities. People who more highly prioritize nonproliferation in relation to maintaining peace are more likely to support at least occasional antinuclear attacks. Notably, some scholars have argued that the use of force as a nonproliferation tool can be costly, ineffective, and even counterproductive (Reiter 2005, 2006; Braut-Hegghammer 2011; see also Kreps and Fuhrmann 2011).

In sum, though factors such as accidents and waste storage pose serious risks and dangers for nuclear energy, the onset of international conflict is likely not a worrisome enough factor to justify trying to slow substantially or halt a GNR. Experience gives us confidence (though not certainty) that any interstate conflict caused by nuclear energy facilities will likely be rare and will produce very few casualties. And we know of effective, relatively cheap steps we can take to minimize the conflict risks that might emerge from a GNR by severing the nuclear energy–nuclear weapons connection. Lastly, energy sources alternative to nuclear would not be free of costs. Instead of mild increases in the risks of low-level conflict, we might see a substantial rise in global warming resulting from increased consumption of fossil fuels, along with associated disasters, such as oil spills, flooding from hydroelectric projects, and environmental destruction wrought by strip mining for coal and hydraulic fracturing techniques.

Notes

1. Churchill made this remark in a speech to the House of Commons, March 1, 1955. Available at http://www.winstonchurchill.org/learn/speeches/speeches-of-winston-churchill/102-never-despair.

References

Allison, Graham. 2004. *Nuclear Terrorism: The Ultimate Preventable Catastrophe.* New York: Henry Holt & Company.

Braut-Hegghammer, Målfrid. 2011. "Revisiting Osirak: Preventive Attacks and Nuclear Proliferation Risks." *International Security* 36 (1): 101–132.

Hamza, Khidhir, with Jeff Stein. 2000. *Saddam's Bombmaker: The Terrifying Inside Story of the Iraqi Nuclear and Biological Weapons Agenda.* New York: Touchstone.

Kreps, Sarah E., and Matthew Fuhrmann. 2011. "Attacking the Atom: Does Bombing Nuclear Facilities Affect Proliferation?" *Journal of Strategic Studies* 34 (2): 161–187.

Kumakura, Tak. 2008. "North Koreans May Have Died in Israel Attack on Syria, NHK Says." *Bloomberg,* April 27. Available at: http://www.bloomberg.com/apps/news?p id=newsarchive&sid=aErPTWRFZpJI&refer=japan.

Patz, Jonathan A., Diarmid Campbell-Lendrum, Tracey Holloway, and Jonathan A. Foley. 2005. "Impact of Regional Climate Change on Human Health." *Nature* 438 (November): 310–317.

Ramberg, Bennett. 1986. "Nuclear Plants—Military Hostages?" *Bulletin of the Atomic Scientists* 42: 17–21.

Reiter, Leon. 1990. *Earthquake Hazard Analysis: Issues and Insights.* New York: Columbia University Press.

Reiter, Dan. 2005. "Preventive Attacks Against Nuclear Programs and the 'Success' at Osiraq." *Nonproliferation Review* 12 (2): 355–371.

———. 2006. "Preventive Attacks against Nuclear, Biological, and Chemical Weapons Programs: The Track Record." In *Hitting First: Preventive Force in U.S. Security Strategy,* eds. William Walton Keller and Gordon R. Mitchell. Pittsburgh, PA: University of Pittsburgh Press.

Conclusion

What Future for Nuclear Energy?

Matthew Fuhrmann and Adam N. Stulberg

THIS BOOK ADDRESSES CENTRAL QUESTIONS RELATING TO the global diffusion of nuclear energy programs. Part I analyzes the causes of nuclear power development, and the chapters in that section probe three general questions: Why do countries rely on nuclear power to meet their energy needs? Why do states provide peaceful nuclear assistance to other countries? How effective are multilateral nuclear approaches (MNAs), such as the widely discussed proposals to "internationalize" the nuclear fuel cycle? Parts II and III look at the consequences of nuclear energy development, with Part II addressing the relationship between nuclear power and nuclear proliferation, and exploring the proliferation significance of a nuclear energy renaissance for countries and nonstate actors; and Part III examining the connection between civilian nuclear programs and international conflict.

This concluding chapter consists of four main parts. First, it comments on the future of nuclear power in light of the insights that emerged from the preceding chapters. Second, it discusses whether the nuclear future that we are predicting might be dangerous for international security. Third, it highlights the implications of the book for international relations theory. Fourth, it articulates policy recommendations for the United States and for countries that are considering building their first nuclear power plants.

Stagnation, Resurgence, or Renaissance?

In the Introduction, we develop three alternative futures for nuclear energy. The first, which we call stagnation, is characterized by negligible rates of global nuclear power plant construction. This scenario is analogous to what the nuclear industry experienced in the 1980s after it became clear that nuclear power was not "too cheap to meter." Resurgence is a second alternative future for nuclear energy. This scenario is marked by nuclear builds at a steady clip in countries such as China, Russia, and South Korea that already rely on nuclear power to meet their energy needs. Yet only a small number of non-nuclear power states that have expressed an interest in nuclear energy will actually build reactors. A final scenario is a global nuclear renaissance involving successful nuclear power programs in a sizable portion of the more than fifty aspirant countries. This alternative future, which is the most ambitious of the three, is characterized by a broadening and deepening of nuclear power generation and fuel cycle development.

What scenario is likely to emerge in the coming years? The book suggests that a nuclear resurgence is more likely than either a stagnation or a renaissance, in part because of the 2011 accident at Japan's Fukushima Daiichi nuclear power station. An earthquake and tsunami on March 11 led to mechanical failures that caused fuel rods to melt down, leading to the release of radioactive materials. The Japanese accident sent shockwaves throughout the nuclear industry and led some to argue that many countries would be deterred from building nuclear power plants. This perspective is at least partially understandable. Fukushima is only one of two accidents—the other being the 1986 Chernobyl disaster in the Soviet Union—to receive the highest rating on the International Nuclear and Radiological Event Scale (INES).[1] And because Fukushima occurred in a industrialized democratic country with decades of experience in operating nuclear plants, it is more difficult for nuclear energy advocates to argue that what happened in Japan could not happen elsewhere, as many suggested in the aftermath of Chernobyl (Fuhrmann 2012a). As a result of these circumstances, some countries that were "on the fence" when it came to nuclear energy development will probably opt against building power plants. Germany, for instance, pledged to phase out nuclear power in the aftermath of the Fukushima accident, and other countries may follow suit.

The historical record supports the notion that major nuclear accidents curtail global nuclear power plant construction. Bernard Gourley and

Adam N. Stulberg show in Chapter 1, for example, that the rate of reactor builds declined in the periods following the 1979 Three Mile Island accident and the Chernobyl disaster. Other research implies that Fukushima may have differential effects on nuclear energy development based on certain country characteristics. Matthew Fuhrmann (2012a) shows that past nuclear accidents have affected democracies more than nondemocracies, because the former are more susceptible to the negative public reactions that often ensue from nuclear disasters. He also shows that prior accidents have had a larger effect in countries that did not operate nuclear power plants at the time of a given disaster. Because nuclear power plants are characterized by sunk costs and path dependence, states that have previously built reactors are better able to absorb the costs that arise from major nuclear accidents. For example, countries that operated plants prior to the Three Mile Island incident, such as Czechoslovakia, France, and South Korea, continued to build reactors afterward, albeit at a slower rate than they did prior to 1979. In light of this evidence, it is likely that the Fukushima accident will have some degree of negative influence on global nuclear development.

It is important not to overstate the effect that Fukushima will have on the trajectory of global nuclear energy development, however. Our central conclusion—that a nuclear energy resurgence is the most likely scenario—would most likely hold even if the Japanese accident had not occurred. This is partly because of the economics of nuclear power. Nuclear power plants are expensive to build, and they are not cost-competitive with coal- or gas-fired power plants in the short term, as Allison Macfarlane emphasizes in Chapter 2. Countries such as Mexico and Pakistan operate nuclear plants, indicating that the highest levels of industrialization are not necessary to rely on nuclear energy. At the same time, the statistical analysis conducted by Gourley and Stulberg in Chapter 1 shows that a state's gross domestic product is positively correlated with nuclear plant construction, indicating that the likelihood that countries will build reactors rises as their economic capacity increases. Joshua William Busby reaffirms this conclusion in Chapter 5, as he shows that many of the nuclear energy aspirants have small power grids, making them poor candidates for nuclear power. Busby also documents that nuclear reactors are notorious for cost overruns and delays. This could lead countries to calculate that the economic hurdles associated with nuclear power are not worth the trouble, even if building reactors is within their industrial capacity. Ultimately, while many states may talk about building nuclear power plants, economic disincentives may deter them from following through on their rhet-oric (Davis 2012).

Nuclear energy is often touted as a possible solution to global climate change, because it produces relatively few greenhouse gases. Concerns about climate change could motivate states to subsidize nuclear power, potentially alleviating some of the aforementioned economic problems. But, for better or worse, this book suggests that climate change is unlikely to drive a nuclear re-naissance. Busby finds that public resistance to nuclear power in many West-ern countries is likely to trump the potential benefits of nuclear energy for climate change. A desire to reduce greenhouse gas emissions may motivate some states to build nuclear power plants, but we are unlikely to see the sus-tained construction (at least twenty plants a year every year for forty years) necessary to meaningfully address this problem.

The book highlights other factors that could stymie global nuclear de-velopment.[2] Busby's analysis reveals that concerns about the management of nuclear waste, a reduction in oil prices relative to the historic highs of the late 2000s, and limits in the number of trained personnel could make it difficult for some states to increase their reliance on nuclear energy. Concerns about nuclear proliferation also could dampen global interest in nuclear power, as Matthew Fuhrmann discusses in Chapter 3. One way to alleviate prolifera-tion concerns is to devise MNAs that limit the need for national control over uranium enrichment centers or plutonium reprocessing facilities. Stulberg demonstrates in Chapter 4, however, that MNAs are not a panacea to this problem, because they create credible commitment problems. Countries that are heavily dependent on nuclear power may be reluctant to submit to these arrangements because they are vulnerable to energy blackmail.

The discussion up to this point is fairly pessimistic about the prospects for global nuclear energy development. Yet many of the costs articulated above—especially safety concerns stemming from the Fukushima accident and the economic and financial hurdles associated with reactor construction—indeed may be mitigated for states that have already invested in nuclear power and robust regulatory systems, as underscored by a preliminary post-accident as-sessment by the British nuclear inspectorate (UKONR 2011). This will make it easier for existing nuclear countries to build plants in the coming years, as compared to the aspirant states.

Countries that already operate nuclear power plants also may have in-centives to ramp up their reliance on nuclear energy. Several of the chapters in Part I discuss the connection between energy security and nuclear power. Gourley and Stulberg (Chapter 1) find that dependence on energy imports is one of the most important correlates of nuclear power development. Macfarlane, likewise, emphasizes in Chapter 2 the importance of energy security in discourses about nuclear power. Countries that built reactors, in part, to lower their dependence on foreign energy imports may construct new plants in the future for the same reason. Argentina, for example, is planning to increase its nuclear power production capacity with civilian nuclear assistance from Canada to "guarantee nationwide energy security" (UPI 2011).

What about the more than fifty nuclear energy aspirants? The International Atomic Energy Agency (IAEA) projected before the Fukushima incident that twenty-five countries would connect their first nuclear power plants to electric grids by 2030. After the accident, IAEA Director General Yukiya Amano, a former Japanese diplomat, said, "The slowdown [in nuclear power plant construction] would not be that big" and there would not be a "huge" change in the prior projection (Dahl 2011). This spirit was reflected in the Turkish Prime Minister's seeming dismissal of any unique risks associated with nuclear power and his bullish defense of the decision to proceed with cooperation with Russia and planning for the country's first nuclear power plant in the wake of Fukushima.[3] However, this book indicates that this sentiment is overly sanguine. The costs identified above are likely to make many aspirant states think twice before moving forward with the nuclear power proposals. Additionally, some of them (such as Algeria, Saudi Arabia, and the United Arab Emirates [UAE]) are energy-rich nations, meaning that perhaps the most powerful historical motivation for reliance on nuclear power is not present in these cases.

It would not be surprising if a handful of countries built their first power plants over the next twenty years. Certain incentives might motivate non-nuclear energy states to build reactors in the post-Fukushima world, even if they do not rely on foreign energy imports. Prestige, for instance, can be a powerful motive for relying on nuclear energy, as Macfarlane highlights in Chapter 2. For example, the UAE perceives that nuclear power will bring prestige that might help offset Iran's rising influence in the region (Early 2010). This is part of the reason the UAE appears to be moving forward with its plans for civilian nuclear development. Other aspirants that covet the prestige associated with nuclear energy—particularly Indonesia, Jordan, Turkey, and

Vietnam—have likewise reaffirmed their support for nuclear power in the aftermath of the Japanese accident (Macfarlane, Chapter 2).

All of this points toward a nuclear resurgence. The most likely states to increase their reliance on nuclear energy are those that already operate nuclear power plants *and* have strong politico-economic incentives to build more reactors. Existing nuclear powers that lack these incentives may end their programs or refrain from ramping up their nuclear energy capabilities. Among the nuclear energy aspirants, the most likely candidates for expansion are states that need to enhance their energy security or believe that building power plants will enhance their standing in international politics. States that do not operate reactors and lack these important motives are the least likely contenders when it comes to civilian nuclear energy development.

The Strategic Effects of Nuclear Energy Development: Cause for Concern?

What does our forecast mean for international security? Should policy makers be worried about a nuclear energy resurgence? These questions do not have simple answers. The purpose of the book is not to claim that the diffusion of peaceful programs will definitely—or definitely not—affect nuclear proliferation and armed conflict. Rather, its objective is to augment existing debates about the strategic effects of nuclear programs and highlight factors and critical inflection points to which scholars and policy makers should devote greater attention. The book shows that the relationship between nuclear power and international security is interestingly nuanced, a point underscored in the critical commentaries by Christopher Way (Chapter 6), Erik Gartzke (Chapter 10), and Dan Reiter (Chapter 13).

On one hand, the book suggests that future nuclear power development will have fewer strategic effects than some scholars believe. This is partly because the pace of atomic energy development is likely to be slower than proponents of the global nuclear industry have claimed. The strategic effects of nuclear energy programs, to the extent that they exist, are proportional to the size of global nuclear expansion. In other words, the greater the diffusion of civilian nuclear programs, the more likely it is that they will have deleterious consequences for international security. The nuclear future we predict represents the middle-of-the-road scenario. A nuclear renaissance would probably affect international security to a greater degree but the effects of a resurgence are not necessarily inconsequential—especially relative to the stagnation scenario.

When it comes to nuclear proliferation, our colleagues are fairly optimistic about the dangers of a nuclear energy resurgence. They join other scholars who have posited that the relationship between nuclear power and nuclear proliferation is tenuous (e.g., Meyer 1984).[4] Previous studies have argued that the spread of nuclear weapons is mostly a political problem, and international institutions such as the nuclear Non-Proliferation Treaty (NPT) and the IAEA are able to separate the peaceful and military uses of the atom (e.g., Dai 2007). Other studies emphasize the complexity of the relationship between nuclear energy and nuclear proliferation. This perspective is exemplified by a recent volume on the nuclear renaissance edited by Steven Miller and Scott Sagan. Addressing whether the spread of nuclear energy programs will lead to nuclear proliferation, Miller and Sagan (2009: 8) conclude that the answer is simple: "It depends." The chapters in Part II of the book support that conclusion by highlighting nuances concerning the relationship between peaceful nuclear assistance and nuclear proliferation.

Fuhrmann (Chapter 3) argues that civilian nuclear aid is critical for most countries that are considering nuclear power buildups. However, the proliferation potential of this assistance may depend on certain country-level characteristics. Alexander Montgomery (Chapter 7) theorizes that some countries may not have the capacity to convert nuclear assistance into nuclear weapons. In particular, states with neopatrimonial ruling structures—which he states are "incompetent rather than poor"—may struggle to absorb assistance partly because they take shortcuts and fail to develop the requisite scientific knowledge base. Since states that may covet nuclear weapons in the future tend to have neopatrimonial regimes (for example, Myanmar), Montgomery concludes that the nuclear renaissance might not lead to further proliferation, at least for the foreseeable future, without transcending these internal structural obstacles to acquiring tacit knowledge. Matthew Kroenig (Chapter 8) reaches a similar conclusion but for a different reason. He suggests that whether the renaissance will fuel the spread of nuclear weapons depends on states' willingness to transfer enrichment and reprocessing activities to external facilities. Suppliers tend to transfer to these facilities under relatively rare circumstances. As a result, many states that want to build domestic enrichment and reprocessing plants will struggle to secure the requisite aid, thereby hindering their ability to build the bomb.

Another reason that the proliferation effects of the nuclear resurgence may be lessened is that some of the states that are likely to build additional nuclear power plants already possess the bomb. China and India—two states that are likely to be key players in any nuclear energy expansion that occurs—conducted their first nuclear tests in 1964 and 1974, respectively.[5] This does not mean that nuclear power buildups in these two countries will have no effect on nuclear proliferation. Depending on the degree of separation between the civilian and military programs, additional nuclear power plants could provide a source of plutonium for bombs, enabling China and India to expand the size of their arsenals.[6] Additionally, if constructing more reactors improves their ability to secure nuclear fuel from foreign sources, indigenous nuclear materials might be freed up for military uses (Sokolski 2005). The point here is that the increased reliance on nuclear energy in China and India (and other states that possess the bomb) will not result in new nuclear weapons states.

Other nuclear power states that are likely to ramp up their reliance on nuclear energy do not possess nuclear weapons. South Korea, for example, had a nuclear weapons program but abandoned it during the 1970s. A large-scale nuclear energy buildup in that country, however, could increase the odds that officials in South Korea opt for an independent nuclear deterrent, partially by making it more difficult for the United States to oppose the domestic development of fuel production facilities.

Our nuclear energy projection also has implications for the proliferation of nuclear or radiological weapons to nonstate actors. Many scholars have argued that the best way to prevent terrorists from acquiring nuclear weapons or so-called dirty bombs is to deny them access to nuclear materials (e.g., Allison 2004; Bunn 2010). Yet Justin Hastings (Chapter 9) posits that future nuclear energy development will have a relatively modest effect on global trafficking in nuclear materials, such as highly enriched uranium and plutonium. He reaches this conclusion because most nuclear energy development will not occur in countries with low state capacity, meaning that nonstate actors will not necessarily be able to exploit managerial weaknesses to steal or otherwise acquire nuclear materials. Moreover, trafficking transportation routes, which rely on state-controlled infrastructure, are unlikely to change as a result of a nuclear resurgence.

The book adds to our understanding of the relationship between nuclear energy programs and armed conflict. Kyle Beardsley and Victor Asal (Chapter 11) and Michael C. Horowitz (Chapter 12) are some of the first scholars to systematically evaluate whether national reliance on nuclear energy affects international conflict behavior. Their findings, which were summarized by Reiter in Chapter 13, indicate that nuclear power programs are unlikely to increase the odds of conflict. Should nuclear power lead to nuclear proliferation, however, the risk of conflict may rise.

Taken together, the chapters in Parts II and III suggest that there may be fewer reasons to worry about a nuclear energy resurgence than some people have suggested. This does not imply that there is no relationship between nuclear energy and international security. Rather, there are reasons to believe that the diffusion of civilian nuclear programs could raise the risk of nuclear weapons proliferation (e.g., Wohlstetter et al. 1979; Holdren 1983; Fuhrmann 2009, 2012b; Sokolski 2010). Because nuclear technology has both civilian and military purposes, it is possible for states to draw on nuclear energy programs to build the bomb. Several countries with large nuclear energy programs have not pursued nuclear weapons (e.g., post-WWII Germany) and others began pursuing the bomb in the absence of an interest in nuclear power (e.g., the United States). On average, the probability of proliferation increases as civilian nuclear programs expand—especially if states experience international crises after building up their nuclear infrastructure (Fuhrmann 2009, 2012b).

This last point is important because many of the countries that are likely to build nuclear power plants as part of the nuclear energy resurgence live in dangerous neighborhoods. History shows that nuclear programs often begin peacefully, but then states are tempted to draw on civilian technology for military purpose if they suffer a defeat in a war or experience other strategic failures. India, for example, began pursuing the atom during the 1940s and 1950s with peaceful intentions, but civilian nuclear assistance helped make it possible to chase the military applications of nuclear energy after China successfully tested the bomb in 1964.[7] Looking into the future, the risk that a nuclear renaissance will contribute to proliferation in countries such as Egypt, Jordan, or Saudi Arabia is greater than in places such as Mongolia, Poland, or Uruguay.

A nuclear resurgence also could increase the likelihood of international conflict. Beardsley/Asal, and Horowitz show that, on average, nuclear energy programs are not associated with international conflict. Yet we also know that there are isolated cases where the dual-use dilemma provides incentive for countries to launch preventive attacks on civilian nuclear facilities (Reiter 2005, 2006; Goldstein 2006; Fuhrmann and Kreps 2010). For instance, Iraq bombed Iranian nuclear power plants that were under construction during the 1980s. One question that emerges from such cases is whether there are certain country characteristics that make some states more likely to have their nuclear facilities attacked than others. Fuhrmann and Kreps (2010) show that authoritarian regimes are far more likely than democracies to be the targets of preventive strikes. This is because potential attackers have less confidence that civilian nuclear programs in these states will remain peaceful, and because they fear that autocrats will behave unpredictably if they acquire the bomb. The list of nuclear aspirants identified in this book and by other scholars (e.g., Miller and Sagan 2009) includes both democracies and autocracies; and many of the non-nuclear power states that appear to be moving forward most aggressively—such as the UAE and Venezuela—are authoritarian. This does not imply that they will have their nuclear facilities bombed by other states. But history indicates that the likelihood of this happening is higher for these states compared to developed democracies. This also could prove to be doubly destabilizing, as not only would dual-use programs in such states be more likely to incite a preemptive attack, but also the preemptive attack itself may trigger the pursuit of a covert (albeit technically cumbersome) weapons-related program, thus raising the long-term proliferation risks posed by these targeted states (Braut-Hegghammer 2011).

It is important to point out that, beyond Hastings' chapter (Chapter 9), the book does not devote much attention to the ways in which a nuclear resurgence will affect violent conflict orchestrated by nonstate actors. As we indicated above (and as Reiter points out in Chapter 13), many scholars and policy makers have suggested that nuclear programs could raise the risk of terrorism by providing materials that could be used in attacks or by serving as tempting targets of opportunity. Indeed, terrorists might try to sabotage a nuclear plant and trigger a Fukushima-like disaster. So even if nuclear power programs do not raise the probability of international conflict, they could enable violent extremism from nonstate actors. Future research might examine this issue in greater detail, especially since many policy makers and scholars indicate that nuclear terrorism represents the most pressing threat to international security (Allison 2004).[8]

Nuclear Energy and International Relations Theory

Many scholars have examined the causes of nuclear proliferation (e.g., Sagan 1996/97) and the strategic effects of possessing the bomb (e.g., Schelling 1966;

Sagan and Waltz 2002). Others have addressed the siting of nuclear power plants (e.g., Aldrich 2008), national decisions to expand reliance on nuclear energy (e.g., Jasper 1990; Price 1990; Jewell 2011; Fuhrmann 2012a), and the factors that determine public support for atomic power (e.g., Kuklinski, Metlay, and Kay 1982). Fewer studies have addressed the intersection of nuclear energy development and international security as their core theme. To be sure, it has been widely known since the dawn of the nuclear age that there is a connection between nuclear power and nuclear proliferation. For example, President Dwight D. Eisenhower said in his "Atoms for Peace" address that the United States must help "solve the fearful atomic dilemma" by devoting "its entire heart and mind to finding the way by which the miraculous inventiveness of man shall not be dedicated to his death, but consecrated to his life."[9] It is not surprising, therefore, that numerous scholars have addressed the nuclear energy–nuclear weapons connection (e.g., Potter 1982; Meyer 1984; Malley and Ogilvie-White 2009; Findlay 2011; Fuhrmann 2012b).

Our book builds on this literature in three main respects. First, it considers a broad set of strategic effects that could stem from nuclear energy development. Scholars who have studied the relationship between nuclear power and international security have focused largely on nuclear proliferation. Our colleagues address the issue by moving a few steps back from dedicated weapons programs to explore the proliferation effects of nuclear weapons latency and the impact of possession of other stages of the fuel cycle. They evaluate the potential proliferation effects of a nuclear resurgence but also look at non-state actors' ability to secure nuclear materials and the connection between nuclear energy and international conflict behavior.[10] Second, the book considers the drivers of nuclear energy development at the same time as it addresses the strategic effects of a nuclear resurgence. The extant security-oriented literature may consider whether peaceful nuclear programs lead to nuclear proliferation, but it rarely addresses the causes of national reliance on atomic energy. Third, the chapters in this volume combine qualitative and quantitative research methods to identify broad patterns and highlight evidence from specific cases.[11] Gourley and Stulberg, for example (Chapter 1), show that a state's reliance on energy imports is an important correlate of nuclear power plant construction, and Macfarlane adds to this finding (Chapter 2) by showing that energy security concerns have motivated countries such as Jordan and the UAE. In the end, we hope that the book helps build bridges between two disparate research communities—scholars primarily in political economy and comparative politics, and area experts who have studied the motivations for nuclear power development; and students of international security who are interested in systematically explaining nuclear proliferation and other potential strategic effects of nuclear power programs.

Although this book is principally about the causes and strategic consequences of nuclear energy development, it also speaks to central themes in international relations. To begin, some of the chapters touch on the role of trust in international politics.[12] The volume highlights two main ways in which trust relates to nuclear energy policy. The first has to do with the nuclear marketplace. As Fuhrmann underscores (Chapter 3), when countries provide assistance they are giving the recipient state a foundation on which a nuclear weapons program could draw. While one might imagine that trust would play an important role in nuclear exports under these circumstances, he shows that this is generally not the case.[13] Perhaps countries would have better luck reducing the proliferation potential of peaceful nuclear assistance (see Fuhrmann 2012b) if they provided aid according to a recipient's level of trustworthiness rather than on the basis of short-term political calculations.[14] Trust also plays a central role in Stulberg's chapter (4) on MNAs, in which he argues that rational states often struggle to devise effective MNAs, in part, because nuclear energy aspirants lack confidence that suppliers will provide nuclear fuel without disruptions. This conundrum is analogous to the classic commitment problem in international bargaining (e.g., Fearon 1995). Stulberg shows that whether states can overcome this problem depends on the power asymmetry and vulnerability of the prospective parties to an MNA. These arrangements are likely to emerge when a specific supplier does not control an overwhelming portion of the market and the customer does not expect to be overly reliant on nuclear power. These are two conditions under which both the risks of mistrust and reneging on commitments are not too great for customers, and deceitful and noncommercial motivations for acquiring nuclear energy can be most readily exposed. However, should trust be built up from other normative or material conditions, the prospects for increasing internationalization of the fuel cycle and the attendant implications for a nuclear energy expansion should be enhanced. Taken together, the chapters by Stulberg and Fuhrmann indicate that the nuclear marketplace is a ripe area for future research about the sources and role of trust in interstate relations.

Trust also appears as a theme in Part III. Beardsley and Asal (Chapter 11) discuss the security dilemma—a situation wherein one state cannot increase its own security without threatening the security of others. A variant of this dilemma applies to nuclear energy development. Gourley, Stulberg, Macfarlane, and others emphasize that states begin nuclear power programs largely for peaceful reasons. But because the technology involved is dual-use in nature, states may be threatened by their adversaries' possession of civil nuclear power plants. This perceived threat may motivate states to consider using military force to destroy civilian facilities, as Horowitz, Beardsley, and Asal emphasize in their chapters (Chapters 12 and 11, respectively). Although the authors do not find a robust relationship between having a nuclear power program and being targeted with militarized disputes, it is not hard to imagine a situation where civilian nuclear development could create an energy security dilemma. The United States, for instance, would probably remain ill at ease if Syria built nuclear power plants, even if there was no concrete evidence that Damascus harbored nuclear weapons ambitions.

Additionally, the book addresses important debates about the efficacy of international institutions. Many scholars have shown that institutions can promote and sustain cooperation by reducing uncertainty, identifying states that do not comply with commitments, and punishing violators (e.g., Keohane 1984; Fortna 2004; Simmons 2009). Other scholars suggest that institutions have a limited effect on state behavior (e.g., Mearsheimer 1994/95; von Stein 2005) and that they can even exacerbate the problems that they were designed to solve (Bueno de Mesquita 1981; Fuhrmann 2012b). This book discusses the virtues of the nonproliferation regime while underscoring some of its limitations. For example, Fuhrmann finds that NPT members are no more likely than nonmembers to provide peaceful nuclear assistance, which could suggest that suppliers are not living up to their end of the Article IV bargain.[15] Nevertheless, as Macfarlane and Way argue in Chapters 2 and 6, potential buyers of nuclear technology routinely cite the NPT as the basis for their "right" to build nuclear power plants. Montgomery (Chapter 7) presents some findings that could be interpreted as good news for the nonproliferation regime. He finds that membership in the NPT decreases the likelihood that countries will explore nuclear weapons and, further, the longer that states go without exploring the bomb, the less likely it is that they will ever attempt to proliferate. Claims made by Montgomery (Chapter 7) and Kroenig (Chapter 8) that the diffusion of nuclear energy programs will not lead directly to proliferation also suggest that the nonproliferation regime may be achieving one of its intended objectives.

The chapters by Beardsley/Asal and Horowitz (Chapters 11 and 12, respectively) also give us reason to be optimistic about the viability of the nonproliferation regime. When countries attack civilian nuclear facilities, it is often seen as an indictment of the IAEA—especially if the destroyed facilities were under safeguards and subject to international inspections. For example, when the Israelis destroyed an Iraqi research reactor during a "bolt from the blue" raid in 1981, Sigvard Eklund, the Director General of the IAEA, said that the raid "was also an attack on the Agency's safeguards."[16] That these types of attacks do not occur more often could suggest that, on average, states may have confidence that the nonproliferation regime will deter countries from drawing on civilian facilities to build nuclear weapons.

The book only scratches the surface when it comes to understanding the role of the NPT and the IAEA in international politics. As Gartzke notes (Chapter 10), claims about the efficacy of the nonproliferation regime—whether they are positive or negative—remain controversial. We need to know much more about how the NPT actually works, a point recently underscored by Scott Sagan (2011). This is especially true because limiting the strategic consequences of the nuclear resurgence depends, at least in part, on the stability of the nonproliferation regime (see Reiter, Chapter 13). One important area about which we know relatively little is international cooperation on nuclear safety. While the accident at Fukushima made clear that nuclear safety is critical for the functioning of a civilian nuclear program, very little research (e.g., Barkenbus 1987) has explored the ways that the IAEA and other institutions have affected cooperation in this domain. In addition, as discussed by Stulberg (Chapter 4), risk and vulnerability are critical elements that inform international nuclear energy transactions but are concepts only partially addressed by literature on the formation and maintenance of international institutions.

Finally, the book contributes to efforts under way in comparative politics and international relations to unpack domestic political institutions. A state's regime type is thought to be important for explaining a variety of international outcomes, such as militarized conflict, the effectiveness of coercive threats, and compliance with treaties. Typical indicators of regime-type capture whether a state is a democracy or an autocracy using datasets such as Polity IV (Marshall and Jaggers 2009), which measures the relative openness of a country's political institutions using a twenty-one-point scale. Scholars are increasingly realizing, however, that not all democracies and autocracies are created equal (e.g., Weeks 2008). As Way argues in Chapter 6, the chapters in this book likewise suggest that rethinking traditional conceptions of regime type and further refining exploration of domestic institutions can help us better understand the causes and effects of nuclear power development. Gourley and Stulberg's statistical analysis (Chapter 1) indicates that there is not a relationship between democracy and nuclear plant construction. At the same time, developed democracies often behave quite differently, as illustrated by Japan (which increased its reliance on nuclear energy over the last several decades preceding the Fukushima accident) and the United States (which has not been enthusiastic about building nuclear power plants since the late 1970s). Rather than linking democracy with nuclear energy development, Gourley and Stulberg suggest that it might be fruitful to explore the degree to which private firms play a role in the decision-making process. States with mostly publicly owned utilities (e.g., France) might have an easier time embracing nuclear power than countries that have a private utility market (e.g., Germany). Montgomery's analysis (Chapter 7) also brings to light the value of moving beyond traditional indicators of regime type. As previously noted, he places an emphasis on neopatrimonial regimes, which may be similar to autocracies but are distinct in some important respects (see also Hymans 2008). The focus on this concept turns out to be productive, because states characterized by neopatrimonial ruling structures seem to be less of a proliferation risk when it comes to receiving nuclear assistance. Such regimes, however, also represent a large number of nuclear energy aspirants.

As underscored by the Fukushima accident, even highly developed and democratic states can be haunted by lax oversight, "captured" regulatory systems, failed infrastructure, and deficient emergency response. Moreover, as again highlighted by the politics in Japan and other nuclear energy states, public attitudes toward nuclear energy vary both across and within regime types. Gaps between public opinion on nuclear energy and state policies—as well as the intensity of local co-optation by the nuclear industry—cut across democratic and authoritarian regimes, suggesting that domestic factors aside from civic attitudes may be crucial for determining nuclear futures. Accordingly, future research might devote more attention to the ways that certain types of domestic institutions can be distinguished in terms of transparency, regulatory effectiveness, allocation of property rights, safety and security cultures, distribution of side payments, and political economic fault lines, and the related influence on nuclear energy development, nuclear proliferation, and other events in the international sphere.

Policy Implications

We began this project, in part, because we wanted to offer lessons to policy makers around the world who were considering expanding their civilian nuclear programs. For better or worse, at the end of our endeavor, we are left without crystal-clear advice for governments. If nothing else, the book has shown that the causes and strategic effects of nuclear energy development are complex. Accordingly, it is difficult to present practitioners with a to-do list for safely and securely emerging as a nuclear energy state. There are some practical recommendations we can make on the basis of the analysis conducted in the book, but they should be viewed cautiously in light of the uncertainty surrounding future events. It is perhaps best to view this discussion as spotlighting critical issues to which policy makers should devote greater attention rather than providing them with foolproof guidance.

One natural question that emerges from the book is whether countries would be wise to expand their reliance on nuclear energy. The answer depends on the specific conditions in a given state. If a country does not have strong political and economic incentives to build nuclear power plants, it may not be able to tolerate the downsides of nuclear energy—especially after the Fukushima disaster. Conversely, ramping up nuclear energy production might make sense for a country seeking to diversify its sources of electricity production or meet growing energy demands that would be difficult to address with coal, natural gas, or alternative sources of baseload power. Nuclear aspirants would do well to remember that nuclear power plants are notorious for construction delays and cost overruns even in developed countries. Developing states, in particular, should think carefully about whether they have the economic capacity to absorb these plants before wholeheartedly embracing nuclear power. They should also not be under any illusions about the benefits they will reap from building reactors. The chapters in Part I highlight some important upsides of nuclear energy development, but making a meaningful contribution to global climate change does not appear to be one of them. States that are interested in nuclear energy primarily for this reason may not have the political will to withstand the economic and political challenges that can accompany nuclear power plant construction.

Aspirant states also should be aware that their civilian nuclear programs could be a source of armed conflict, although the book shows that this may be less of a concern than one might fear. The countries most likely to be the targets of militarized disputes are those that create ambiguities—either intentionally or unintentionally—about the purpose of their program. If states fear that a nuclear power program may become part of a campaign to build nuclear weapons, they are more likely to think about using preventive military force. To avoid this possibility, countries should consider confidence-building measures that might alleviate concerns about their peaceful programs taking on military purposes. One such concrete measure would be ratifying the Additional Protocol (AP), which provides the IAEA with an enhanced ability to monitor nuclear activities. About 70 percent of the states that are members of the IAEA have an AP agreement in force with the IAEA. Among the 30 percent of countries that do not are some nuclear energy aspirants such as Bolivia, Myanmar, Syria, and Venezuela. If these states do in fact have peaceful intentions, they are not doing themselves any favors by delaying their AP ratifications.

While the book devotes only a limited attention to the terrorism risks of nuclear power, this is a security concern with which countries must grapple. To echo a point previously made, we know too little about the relationship between nuclear energy and violent conflict orchestrated by nonstate actors, and more research in this area in government and academia would be welcome. It also would be fruitful to further explore the ways in which nuclear facilities could provide targets of opportunity for insurgents during civil wars. The so-called Arab Spring, which led to the toppling of Hosni Mubarak in Egypt and Muammar Gadhafi in Libya, has led some commentators (e.g., Pearl 2011) to argue that nuclear plants could become targets of sabotage during future revolutions. It would be useful to know the degree to which this concern is legitimate, given that some of the nuclear energy aspirants (e.g., Jordan) could be prone to domestic instability in the future.

Another important policy issue is what powerful countries such as the United States can do to minimize the strategic consequences of nuclear energy expansion. Should nuclear suppliers assist aspirants in building nuclear power plants? If so, under what conditions? Kroenig's chapter (8) indicates that *what* suppliers transfer determines the effects for nuclear proliferation. For Montgomery (Chapter 7), the more important issue is *who* is receiving assistance. He also draws attention to the need to monitor, if not restrict, the flow of human capital, especially scientists with experiential nuclear knowledge, who are critical to a state's capacity to absorb the flow of nuclear materials and convert a commercial program into a latent weapons concern. These chapters present nuclear suppliers with a bit of a conundrum. Sheer disparities in power—strategic, market, and otherwise—between existing suppliers and many aspirants complicate even purely commercial nuclear energy bargains. Similarly, withholding certain technologies and refusing to assist certain states runs counter to the spirit of the NPT. At the same time, if governments truly want to reduce proliferation, they should exercise discrimination in the nuclear marketplace both in terms of what they are willing to supply and to whom they are willing to supply it. This is a dilemma for which there is no easy answer.

Policy makers might be able to further reduce the risk that peaceful nuclear assistance contributes to nuclear proliferation by strengthening the nonproliferation regime.[17] The NPT-backed regime has achieved a number of successes, which are well documented (e.g., Reiss 1988; Rublee 2009). At the same time, it suffers from weaknesses that sometimes limit its viability. One thing policy makers could do to strengthen the NPT and reduce the proliferation risks of nuclear cooperation is to explicitly link assistance and the AP. This proposal has been raised by the United States in a number of international forums in recent years. It would send a clear message to nuclear energy aspirants: If you want help in building nuclear power plants, you must subject your program to the most stringent form of international inspections that is currently practiced. The cases of Iraq, North Korea, Syria, and others demonstrate that safeguards are by no means foolproof, but the IAEA is better off with the enhanced power that comes with the AP than it is without it. The United States and other suppliers might also consider adopting policies that have been called the "gold standard" for civilian nuclear cooperation (e.g., Early 2010). This requires recipient states to refrain from developing indigenous reprocessing or enrichment facilities. If governments violate pledges not to build these plants, according to this standard, they must return foreign-supplied technology and materials to the exporting country.[18] Countries seeking to promote nonproliferation should also pursue multinational fuel banks to limit the need for indigenous fuel cycle facilities, although Stulberg reminds us that not all countries are likely to embrace this idea with open arms. Moreover, not all forms of internationalization of the fuel cycle are appropriate for redressing either the market or energy security strategies of even benignly motivated customers; they must be tailored to alleviate specific risks and costs. It would be no doubt difficult to get aspirant states to agree to stringent nonproliferation policies such as those outlined above, but doing so might help keep the world safer as civilian nuclear programs diffuse around the globe.

Strengthening the broader nonproliferation regime also may rest with drawing more attention to the link between international safety and security concerns associated with a nuclear energy resurgence. The Fukushima disaster reminds us that low probability–high consequence crises—such as nuclear terrorism, nuclear accidents, and even nuclear weapons proliferation—not only can undermine global security and cannot afford to be ignored, but also require a changed attitude toward risk. As Charles Perrow (2011) warns, "probabilistic assumptions" based on precedent are simply not up to the task of planning for unexpected sources and catastrophic effects of a global nuclear crisis, precipitated either by human maliciousness, inadvertence, or natural disaster. Accordingly, because the steps needed to secure fissile materials at their source can directly mitigate all of these types of nuclear risk, it would behoove statesmen to be proactive in upgrading international standards for safety and security stress tests. By redoubling these diplomatic efforts and institutionalizing new standards, policy makers stand to make great strides toward inculcating safety and security as basic costs of doing business for the nuclear industry. In so doing, they can direct technological and political innovation, as well as commercial best practices, toward redressing fundamental international aversions that, in turn, can strengthen the global nuclear security regime (Luongo 2011).

Finally, the arguments presented in this book underscore that time cuts two ways in the nuclear realm for policy makers. On one hand, there may be built-in structural, political, economic, normative, and logistical impediments that stymie the global diffusion of nuclear energy and weapons latency. Similarly, the spread of commercial nuclear programs is unlikely to have a direct effect on international crisis behavior. As a result, policy makers have time to make critical adjustments to ensure a safe and secure future with nuclear energy. On the other hand, the future by definition is laden with unknowns. Past performance provides a thin reed of reassurance and only a starting point for assessing the sources, modalities, and consequences of future state and nonstate nuclear behavior. Thus, the message is clear: There is no room for complacency when it comes to contending with the challenges and risks presented under any alternative future for nuclear energy.

Notes

1. The economic and human costs of Chernobyl were far greater than Fukushima, but both accidents released substantial amounts of radiation into the environment.

2. Notably, an ability to secure peaceful nuclear assistance is not among the factors limiting the potential for growth in the nuclear sector. Matthew Fuhrmann argues in Chapter 3 that nuclear suppliers provide aid to enhance their political influence. While individual suppliers withhold assistance to some countries for politico-strategic reasons, the likelihood that a state will be unable to find a single exporter willing to provide aid is low.

3. In a pointed rebuke of the domestic anti-nuclear lobby, the Turkish Prime Minister asserted: "Any project can go wrong, you can't just drop it because of that. Otherwise, you shouldn't be using gas bottles in your houses, and we shouldn't have an oil pipeline passing through the country" (Gusten 2011). *New York Times*, 23 March 2011.

4. Scott Sagan (1996/97: 56) underscores this when he emphasizes "the policy importance of addressing the sources of the political *demand* nuclear weapons, rather than focusing primarily on efforts . . . to restrict the *supply* of specific weapons technology." Much of the recent literature on nuclear proliferation probes the demand side of the proliferation equation and downplays the supply side (e.g., Hymans 2006; Solingen 2007; Rublee 2009).

5. Note, however, that India did not deploy a nuclear arsenal until more than two decades later.

6. France, for example, does not maintain a strict separation between civilian and military nuclear facilities and has drawn on the former to produce nuclear materials for bombs.

7. For further details on this case, see Fuhrmann (2012b, Chapter 7).

8. For one recent empirical analysis on this subject, see Early, Fuhrmann, and Li (n.d.).

9. The text of Eisenhower's speech is available on the IAEA's website: http://www .iaea.org/About/history_speech.html.

10. This does not imply that the book examines *all* the potential strategic effects of nuclear energy development.

11. Most of the existing studies rely exclusively on qualitative analysis. This work adds to our understanding of nuclear power development by advancing novel theoretical arguments and by illuminating evidence from a particular subset of countries. It is less clear whether these explanations apply to a broad set of cases across space and time, a void that can be addressed by employing statistical analysis. For a discussion of the strengths and weaknesses of statistical analysis, see Mahoney and Goertz (2006).

12. For examples of research on trust in international relations and comparative politics, see, for example Kydd (2005) and Putnam (1993).

13. Trust may play a role, however, when it comes to the export of other dual-use commodities (Fuhrmann 2008).

14. On the other hand, any time countries overtly restrict nuclear exports to a state that is in good standing with the NPT they risk undermining the spirit of Article IV of the treaty, which requires states to freely share nuclear technology, materials, and know-how.

15. See Fuhrmann (2012b) for further analysis on the relationship between peaceful nuclear assistance and NPT membership.

16. Quoted in Feldman (1982: 114).

17. See Fuhrmann (2012b) for a more detailed discussion on how the international community can reduce the dangers of peaceful nuclear assistance.

18. The United States achieved this gold standard when it concluded a nuclear cooperation agreement with the UAE; but, unfortunately, it has not pushed for similar demands when negotiating deals with other aspirants, such as Jordan and Vietnam.

References

Aldrich, Daniel. 2008. *Site Fights: Divisive Facilities and Civil Society in Japan and the West.* Ithaca, NY: Cornell University Press.

Allison, Graham. 2004. *Nuclear Terrorism: The Ultimate Preventable Catastrophe.* New York: Henry Holt & Company.

Barkenbus, Jack. 1987. "Nuclear Power Safety and the Role of International Organization." *International Organization* 41 (3): 475–490.

Braut-Hegghammer, Målfrid. 2011. "Revisiting Osirak: Preventive Attacks and Nuclear Proliferation Risks." *International Security* 36 (1): 101–132.

Bueno de Mesquita, Bruce. 1981. *The War Trap.* New Haven, CT: Yale University Press.

Bunn, Matthew. 2010. *Securing the Bomb 2010.* Cambridge, MA: Belfer Center for Science and International Affairs at Harvard University.

Dahl, Fredrik. 2011. "UN Atom Chief Plays Down Safety Cost Concerns." *Reuters*, August 21.

Dai, Xinyuan. 2007. *International Institutions and National Policies.* New York: Cambridge University Press.

Davis, Lucas W. 2012. "Prospects for Nuclear Power." *Journal of Economic Perspectives* 26 (1): 49–66.

Early, Bryan R., Matthew Fuhrmann, and Quan Li. n.d. "Atoms for Terror? Nuclear Programs and Noncatastrophic Nuclear and Radiological Terrorism." *British Journal of Political Science*, forthcoming.

Early, Bryan. 2010. "Acquiring Foreign Nuclear Assistance in the Middle East." *The Nonproliferation Review* 17 (2): 259–280.

Fearon, James D. 1995. "Rationalist Explanations of War." *International Organization* 49 (3): 379–414.

Feldman, Shai. 1982. *Israeli Nuclear Deterrence: A Strategy for the 1980s.* New York: Columbia University Press.

Findlay, Trevor. 2011. *Nuclear Energy and Global Governance: Ensuring Safety, Security, and Non-Proliferation.* London: Routledge.

Fortna, Virginia Page. 2004. *Peace Time: Cease-Fire Agreements and the Durability of Peace*. Princeton, NJ: Princeton University Press.

Fuhrmann, Matthew. 2008. "Exporting Mass Destruction? The Determinants of Dual-Use Trade." *Journal of Peace Research* 45 (5): 633–652.

———. 2009. "Spreading Temptation: Proliferation and Peaceful Nuclear Cooperation Agreements." *International Security* 34 (1): 7–41.

———. 2012a. "Splitting Atoms: Why Do Countries Build Nuclear Power Plants?" *International Interactions* 38 (1): 29–57.

———. 2012b. *Atomic Assistance: How "Atoms for Peace" Programs Cause Nuclear Insecurity*. Ithaca, NY: Cornell University Press.

Fuhrmann, Matthew, and Sarah E. Kreps. 2010. "Targeting Nuclear Programs in War and Peace: A Quantitative Empirical Analysis, 1941–2000." *Journal of Conflict Resolution* 54 (5): 831–859.

Goldstein, Lyle. 2006. *Preventive Attack and Weapons of Mass Destruction: A Comparative Historical Analysis*. Stanford, CA: Stanford University Press.

Gusten, Susanne. 2011. "Forging Ahead on Nuclear Energy in Turkey." *New York Times*, March 23.

Holdren, John. 1983. "Nuclear Power and Nuclear Weapons: The Connection Is Dangerous." *Bulletin of the Atomic Scientists* 39 (1): 40–45.

Hymans, Jacques E. C. 2006. *The Psychology of Nuclear Proliferation: Identity, Emotions, and Foreign Policy*. New York: Cambridge University Press.

———. 2008. "Assessing North Korean Nuclear Intentions and Capacities: A New Approach." *Journal of East Asian Studies* 8 (2): 259–292.

Jasper, James M. 1990. *Nuclear Politics: Energy and the State in the United States, Sweden, and France*. Princeton, NJ: Princeton University Press.

Jewell, Jessica. 2011. "Ready for Nuclear Energy? An Assessment of Capacities and Motivation for Launching New National Nuclear Programs." *Energy Policy* 39 (3): 1041–1055.

Keohane, Robert. 1984. *After Hegemony: Cooperation and Discord in the World Political Economy*. Princeton, NJ: Princeton University Press.

Kuklinski, James H., Daniel S. Metlay, and W. D. Kay. 1982. "Citizen Knowledge and Choices on the Complex Issue of Nuclear Energy." *American Journal of Political Science* 26 (4): 615–642.

Luongo, Kenneth. 2011. "Preventing a Nuclear Terrorist Version of Fukushima." *Bulletin of the Atomic Scientists* (online version), April 8. Available at: http://www.thebulletin.org/web-edition/features/preventing-nuclear-terrorist-version-of-fukushima.

Kydd, Andrew H. 2005. *Trust and Mistrust in International Relations*. Princeton, NJ: Princeton University Press.

Mahoney, James, and Gary Goertz. 2006. "A Tale of Two Cultures: Contrasting Quantitative and Qualitative Research." *Political Analysis* 14 (3): 227–249.

Malley, Michael S., and Tanya Ogilvie-White. 2009. "Nuclear Capabilities in Southeast Asia." *The Nonproliferation Review* 16 (1): 25–45.

Marshall, Monty, and Keith Jaggers. 2009. "Polity IV Project: Political Regime Characteristics and Transitions, 1800–2007." Severn, MD: Center for Systematic Peace.

Mearsheimer, John. 1994/95. "The False Promise of International Institutions." *International Security* 19 (1): 5–49.

Meyer, Stephen M. 1984. *The Dynamics of Nuclear Proliferation.* Chicago: University of Chicago Press.

Miller, Steven E., and Scott D. Sagan. 2009. "Nuclear Power Without Nuclear Proliferation?" *Daedalus* 138 (4): 7–18.

Pearl, Jonathan. 2011. "Nuclear Concerns in Unstable Middle East." *Council on Foreign Relations Expert Brief*, May 23. Available at: http://www.cfr.org/middle-east/nuclear-concerns-unstable-mideast/p25038.

Perrow, Charles. 2011. "Fukushima, Risk, and Probability: Expect the Unexpected." *Bulletin of the Atomic Scientists* (online version), April 1. Available at: http://thebulletin.org/web-edition/features/fukushima-risk-and-probability-expect-the-unexpected.

Potter, William C. 1982. *Nuclear Power and Nonproliferation: An Interdisciplinary Perspective.* Cambridge, MA: Oelgeschlager, Gunn & Hain.

Price, Terrence. 1990. *Political Electricity: What Future for Nuclear Energy?* New York: Oxford University Press.

Putnam, Robert. 1993. *Making Democracy Work: Civic Traditions in Modern Italy.* Princeton, NJ: Princeton University Press.

Reiss, Mitchell. 1988. *Without the Bomb: The Politics of Nuclear Nonproliferation.* New York: Columbia University Press.

Reiter, Dan. 2005. "Preventive Attacks Against Nuclear Programs and the 'Success' at Osiraq." *Nonproliferation Review* 12 (2): 355–371.

———. 2006. "Preventive Attacks against Nuclear, Biological, and Chemical Weapons Programs: The Track Record." In *Hitting First: Preventive Force in U.S. Security Strategy*, eds. William Walton Keller and Gordon R. Mitchell. Pittsburgh, PA: University of Pittsburgh Press.

Rublee, Maria Rost. 2009. *Nonproliferation Norms: Why States Choose Nuclear Restraint.* Athens: University of Georgia Press.

Sagan, Scott D. 1996/97. "Why Do States Build Nuclear Weapons? Three Models in Search of a Bomb." *International Security* 21 (3): 54–86.

———. 2011. "The Causes of Nuclear Weapons Proliferation." *Annual Review of Political Science* 14: 225–244.

Sagan, Scott D., and Kenneth N. Waltz. 2002. *The Spread of Nuclear Weapons: A Debate Renewed.* New York: W. W. Norton & Company.

Schelling, Thomas C. 1966. *Arms and Influence.* New Haven, CT: Yale University Press.

Simmons, Beth. 2009. *Mobilizing for Human Rights: International Law in Domestic Politics.* New York: Cambridge University Press.

Sokolski, Henry. 2005. "Backing the U.S.-India Nuclear Deal and Nonproliferation: What's Required." Testimony Before a Hearing of the Senate Foreign Relations

Committee, *The Nonproliferation Implications of the July 18, 2005 U.S.-India Joint Statement*, Washington, DC, November 3.

———. 2010. "The High and Hidden Costs of Nuclear Power." *Policy Review* 162 (August 1). Available at: http://www.hoover.org/publications/policy-review/article/43316.

Solingen, Etel. 2007. *Nuclear Logics: Contrasting Paths in East Asia and the Middle East.* Princeton, NJ: Princeton University Press.

UKONR (UK Office for Nuclear Regulation). 2011. *Japanese Earthquake and Tsunami: Implications for the UK Nuclear Industry.* Interim Report, May.

UPI. 2011. "Argentina Keen for More Nuclear Power." August 25. Available at: http://www.upi.com/Business_News/Energy-Resources/2011/08/25/Argentina-keen-for-more-nuclear-power/UPI-42281314304135/.

von Stein, Jana. 2005. "Do Treaties Constrain or Screen? Selection Bias in Treaty Compliance." *American Political Science Review* 99 (4): 611–622.

Weeks, Jessica. 2008. "Autocratic Audience Costs: Regime Type and Signaling Resolve." *International Organization* 62 (1): 35–64.

Wohlstetter, Albert, Thomas Brown, Gregory Jones, David McGarvey, Henry Rowen, Vince Taylor, and Roberta Wohlstetter. 1979. *Swords from Ploughshares: The Military Potential of Civilian Nuclear Energy.* Chicago: University of Chicago Press.

Index

Italic page numbers indicate material in tables or figures.

"national identity conception," 155, 168

national income and nuclear energy, 23

natural gas: carbon dioxide emissions from, *130*; lower prices for, 65, 136; and reducing risk of MNAs, 111–112

NCAs (nuclear cooperation agreements), 296; bilateral civilian dataset, *75–76*, 79–82, 87; competition for, 158; and proliferation, 208, 290; as signals, 291

neoliberalism, 101

neomercantilism, 101

neopatrimonialism: as distinguished from underdevelopment, 179; and nuclear weapons acquisition, 185, *188–191*; and proliferation concerns, 327, 335; scoring, 182–185; and sensitive assistance, 193–195, 198

Netherlands: and A. Q. Khan, 220–221n5; as capable nuclear supplier, *215*; nuclear energy without weaponry, 23; nuclear power acquisition, 299; reactors planned/proposed, *135*; as supplier, 80; and uranium enrichment, 119

networks: vs. hierarchies, 177–178; proliferation, 224–227

Nigeria, 1, 228, 232

NIMBY, 143

nodes, network, 226

Non-Aligned Movement, 102, 110

nonaspiring states, 268

nonstate proliferation, 225; A. Q. Khan network, 207, 210, 213, 238–241, 246n5; coordinators and smuggling routes, 235–241; and resurgence scenario, 328, 330

North Atlantic high-income democracies, 23

North Korea. *See* Korea, North

Norway, *215*, 316

NPPs (nuclear power plants): basic requirements for building, 24–25;

as cause of interstate conflict, 14, 315–319; construction model, *28–29*; construction starts by decade, *27*; currently operating commercial, 23; economics of, 323; international law regarding attacks on, 319; and option to acquire weapons, 292; peak of construction of, 43n8; as sign of peaceful motivations, 29

NPT (Non-Proliferation Treaty): Article IV, 51, 81, 87, 157–158, 333; as demand-side influence, 260; effectiveness of, 91–92, *186–189*, 197, 251, 290; enhancing usefulness of, 318, 327, 333, 338; "grand bargains" of, 81, 90; India's refusal to ratify, 77; and peaceful nuclear assistance, *85*, 87, 90, 178; prompted by fear of chain reaction, 266; and right to enrich uranium, 53, 58

NSG (Nuclear Suppliers Group), 88

nuclear alarmists, 125, 132

"nuclear components," 224

nuclear energy states: common characteristics of, 22–26; "nuclear club," 61; prestige of, 51

nuclear fuel production. *See* fuel cycle

"nuclear material," 224

nuclear plant construction: costs of, 2; infrastructure, 2

nuclear power: as proxy for nuclear weapons, 292–293; strategic effects of development, 326–330; years in possession of, *295*, 296

nuclear power countries vs. nuclear-capable nonproliferating countries, *229*, 257–258, 291, 295

nuclear power plants (NPPs). *See* NPPs (nuclear power plants)

Nuclear Suppliers Group (NSG), 88

nuclear technological optimists, 125, 132

nuclear umbrella, 256–257

state-to-state transfers: no completed weapons, 253, 258; Proliferation Security Initiative, 318; state-sponsored transfer of nuclear technology, 209–214

strategic forecasting, 8–9

submarines, Colombian drug, 237–238

substate smuggling of nuclear materials and technology, 209–210, 213

Sudan, 228, 232

superpowers: allies of, 88, 211; nuclear aid to maintain status, 77; nuclear sales to achieve status of, 59; uranium export to achieve status of, 77

suppliers of nuclear technology, 64–65; and ability to project power, 215; as a cartel, 254; cases of state-sponsored transfer, 209–214; commitment/"hold-up" problem, 159–160; contradictory objectives of, 254–258; economic incentives for export, 203; focus of, 64–65; increase of, 157–158; mitigating uncertainty for customer, 112–114; motivations of, 58–60; nonstate proliferation networks, 225–227; and proliferation risks, 227–228; unlikely to be U.S. allies, 214–215

supply chain of nuclear fuel, 31

Sweden: MNA endorsement, 118; as non-aligned nuclear supplier, 93n13; and nuclear waste disposal, 65; nuclear weapons exploration, 299; parallel development of weapons and energy, 23; plans to keep current reactors, 144; proliferation transitions, 181; reputation of, 102; as supplier, 80

Switzerland, 1; and A. Q. Khan, 213, 239; as nonaligned country, 78, 93n13; and nuclear waste disposal, 65; nuclear weapons exploration, 299; post-Fukushima cancellation of new NPPs, 23, 63, 65, 143; proliferation transitions, 181; reactors planned/proposed, 135; as supplier, 80

Syria: Israeli attack on reactor, 3, 216, 272, 283n8, 315–317, 319; low state capacity of, 232; and North Korea, 216; not ratifying Model Additional Protocol, 318, 337–338; possibility of securing assistance, 91, 216, 219; and United States, 216, 219, 333; weaponized Iran as protection for, 272

Taiwan: neopatrimonial level of, 193; not Nuclear Suppliers Group member, 245; nuclear weapons exploration, 300; parallel development of weapons and energy, 23; proliferation transitions, 181; reactors planned/proposed, 135; reactors under construction, 132–133; rising energy demand, 33; sensitive nuclear assistance to, 186, 216–217

Taliban, 272

Tanzania, 90, 244

technological innovation, 7

technology, supply of, 156–159

technology transfers, 177–178, 209–214, 253, 258

TEPCo (Tokyo Electric Power Company), 19

terrorism, 3, 226, 236, 243–244, 314, 337

Thailand, 135, 136, 231

The Theory of International Politics (Waltz), 267

Three Mile Island accident, 7, 35, 39, 65, 138

Thucydides, 267

Tokyo Electric Power Company (TEPCo), 19

"too risky" as MNA assessment, 108–110, 109

Toshiba, 59

Toukan, Khaled, 55, 58

trade, emissions, 145